Engaging the Passion

Engaging the Passion

Perspectives on the Death of Jesus

Oliver Larry Yarbrough, editor

Fortress Press
Minneapolis

ENGAGING THE PASSION

Perspectives on the Death of Jesus

Cover image: English: *The Dead Christ with Angels*; Français: *Le Christ mort et les anges / Le Christ aux anges*. Édouard Manet. Courtesy of Wikimedia Commons.

Cover design: Joe Reinke

Library of Congress Cataloging-in-Publication Data

Print ISBN: 978-1-4514-7215-8

eBook ISBN: 978-1-5064-0047-1

The paper used in this publication meets the minimum requirements of American National Standard for Information Sciences — Permanence of Paper for Printed Library Materials, ANSI Z329.48-1984.

Manufactured in the U.S.A.

This book was produced using PressBooks.com, and PDF rendering was done by PrinceXML.

Contents

Acknowledgements

Some of the essays in this volume are based on lectures presented at a symposium held at Middlebury College under the auspices of the Charles P. Scott Endowment. Funds from the Pardon Tillinghast Professorship at Middlebury supported much of the subsequent work on it. I gratefully acknowledge this support, especially since both Charles and Pardon, members of the faculty when I first arrived at Middlebury, were friends as well as colleagues. I am confident they would be pleased that funds honoring their memory helped make the volume possible—and that they would have enjoyed reading it.

I am grateful to the colleagues and guests who participated in the symposium and for their patience in waiting to see their work in print. In editing the essays for publication, I came to the conclusion that there were two distinct volumes, rather than the one I had originally conceived. Consequently, some of the essays from the symposium have already appeared in *Passion: Contemporary Writers on the Story of Calvary* (Maryknoll, NY: Orbis Books, 2015). The others appear here, supplemented by new essays commissioned for this significantly expanded volume. To all the contributors, I express my thanks. Each contribution can stand alone, but together they make for a multifaceted exploration of a seminal story.

I also express my thanks to Matthew Weinert-Stein, Megan Battey, Greg Vitercik, and Christopher Ross, who helped with research, permissions, and editing.

And I gratefully acknowledge the role that Neil Elliott and his colleagues at Fortress Press played in bringing this volume to completion, and for their care in designing it.

As ever, I am grateful to (and for) Amy.

Contributors

Katherine Smith Abbott is the Vice-President for Student Affairs at Middlebury College, where she has been teaching in the Department of the History of Art and Architecture since 1996. Her research focuses on the production and reception of devotional painting in early-fifteenth-century Florence. Professor Smith Abbott received her M.A. and Ph.D. from Indiana University in Bloomington, where she wrote her dissertation on Titian and the development of portrait painting in Venice. She recently served as Guest Curator for the exhibition, The Art of Devotion: Panel Painting in Early Renaissance Italy, on view at the Middlebury College Museum of Art in Fall, 2009, and at the Mount Holyoke College Art Museum in Spring, 2010. **Elizabeth Oyler** is a student at Middlebury College double-majoring in English and American Literature and History of Art and Architecture.

Robert Atwell is the Bishop of Exeter in the United Kingdom. A former Benedictine monk, he maintains his Benedictine vocation as an oblate of the Abbey of Le Bec in Normandy. Bishop Atwell read theology at Durham University and studied for the priesthood at Westcott House, Cambridge University, where he later served as Chaplain of Trinity College and taught patristics. Subsequently, he served as a parish priest before his consecration as bishop of Stockport (Chester, England) in 2008. His publications have focused on liturgy and pastoral care, the most recent being *The Contented Life* (Canterbury, 2011). Bishop Atwell currently chairs the Church of England's liturgical commission.

Jouette Bassler is Professor Emerita of New Testament at Perkins School of Theology, Southern Methodist University. She is the author of numerous articles on a variety of New Testament topics and several books on Paul, including *Divine Impartiality: Paul and a Theological Axiom* (Scholars Press, 1982); *1 Timothy, 2 Timothy, Titus* (Abingdon Press, 1996); and *Navigating Paul: An Introduction to Key Theological Concepts* (Westminster John Knox Press, 2007).

Jeremy Cohen is the Spiegel Family Foundation Professor of European Jewish History at Tel Aviv University. A scholar of late antiquity and the Middle Ages, his research has focused on various aspects of Jewish-Christian relations, most notably Christian anti-Judaism, Jewish-Christian polemic, and the ambivalence and nuance that pervade Christian perceptions of the Jews. Professor Cohen has written or edited nine books, four of which have won the National Jewish Book Award or other recognition. They include *The Friars and the Jews: The Evolution of Medieval Anti-Judaism* (Cornell University Press, 1982), *Living Letters of the Law: Ideas of the Jews in Medieval Christianity* (University of California Press, 1999), and *Christ Killers: The Jews and the Passion from the Bible to the Big Screen* (Oxford University Press, 2007). He is currently working on sixteenth-century responses to the persecution of the Jews in Spain and Portugal in Solomon ibn Verga's *Shevet Yehuda (The Rod of Judah).*

Matt Dickerson, a professor of Computer Science at Middlebury College is an internationally recognized Tolkien scholar. His books on Tolkien and mythopoetic literature include: *Ents, Elves and Eriador: the Environmental Vision of J. R. R. Tolkien* (with Jonathan Evans, University Press of Kentucky, 2006), *Following Gandalf: Epic Battles and Moral Victory in the Lord of the Rings* (Brazos Press, 2004), and *Narnia and the Fields of Arbol: the Environmental Vision of C. S. Lewis* (with David O'Hara, University Press of Kentucky, 2009).

Emmie Donadio, Chief Curator at the Middlebury College Museum of Art, has organized exhibitions and published studies of the works of Richard Stankiewicz and Vito Acconci. Other projects include surveys of contemporary photography and street art from around the world.

Eliza Garrison is associate professor of History of Art and Architecture at Middlebury College. Her research focuses on the art of the Carolingian and Ottonian Empires and the historiography, production, and political use of art in the Early Middle Ages. Her work has appeared in the *Oxford Art Journal, Gesta*, *Peregrinations*, and *Postmedieval Forum*. She is the author of *Ottonian Imperial Art and Portraiture: The Artistic Patronage of Otto III and Henry II* (Ashgate, 2012).

John Hunisak is Professor of Art and Architecture Emeritus at Middlebury College. His scholarly interests focus on painting and sculpture, primarily from the Italian Renaissance through early modernism in Europe and America. He is a co-author of the highly regarded *The Art of Florence* (Abbeville Press, 1988) and the author of *The Sculptor Jules Dalou: Studies in His Style and Imagery* (Abbeville Press, 1977) and numerous scholarly essays and exhibit catalogues.

After extensive research in the archives of The Andy Warhol Museum in Pittsburgh, he is currently engaged in a book-length study, called *Andy Warhol: the Serious Side.*

Michael R. Katz is the C. V. Starr Professor Emeritus of Russian and East European Studies at Middlebury College. He is the author of two books, one on the literary ballad in early-nineteenth-century Russian poetry and the other on dreams and the unconscious in nineteenth-century Russian prose—and numerous essays. He has translated major Russian writers into English, including Herzen, Chernyshevsky, Dostoevsky, Turgenev, Tolstoy, Mikhail Artsybashev, Vladimir Jabotinsky, Ivan Shcheglov, and Boris Akunin. He is currently retranslating Dostoevsky's *Crime and Punishment* for a new Norton Critical Edition.

John McWilliams, who is College Professor of the Humanities Emeritus at Middlebury College, has written widely on American literature, especially in the early period. His books include: *Political Justice In A Republic: James Fenimore Cooper's America* (University of California Press, 1972); *Hawthorne, Melville and the American Character: A Looking-Glass Business* (Cambridge University Press, 1984); *The American Epic: Transforming A Genre,* (Cambridge University Press, 1989), *The Last of the Mohicans: Civil Savagery and Savage Civility* (Twayne-Macmillan, 1994); and *New England's Crises and Cultural Memory* (Cambridge University Press, 2004).

Suleiman Ali Mourad is Professor of Religion at Smith College. Professor Mourad's research and publications focus on medieval Islamic history and religious thought, including jihad ideology, the sacredness of Jerusalem, Qur'anic studies, and the presentation of Jesus and Mary in the Qur'an and Islamic tradition. He is the co-author of *The Intensification and Reorientation of Sunni Jihad Ideology in the Crusader Period* (Brill, 2013), co-editor of *Jerusalem: Idea and Reality* (Routledge, 2008), and author of *Early Islam between Myth and History* (Brill, 2005). His current projects include editing the forthcoming *Routledge Handbook on Jerusalem* (Routledge).

Kimberly Pinder is the Dean of the College of Fine Arts at the University of New Mexico. She is the editor of *Race-ing Art History: Critical Essays in Race and Art History* (Routledge, 2002); her essays and reviews have appeared in *The Art Bulletin, The Art Journal, Third Text*, and *African American Review*, among other periodicals. Her latest book is *Black Public Art and Religion in Chicago*, which is forthcoming from the University of Illinois Press. Dean Pinder graduated with a B.A. from Middlebury College and M.Phil, M.A. and Ph.D. from Yale University, all in Art History.

Adele Reinhartz is a professor in the Department of Classics and Religious Studies at the University of Ottawa, in Canada. Her main areas of research are the New Testament, early Jewish-Christian relations, the Bible and Film, and feminist biblical criticism. Her studies of the Bible and Film include: *The Bible and Cinema: An Introduction* (Routledge, 2013), *Jesus of Hollywood* (Oxford University Press, 2007), and *Scripture on the Silver Screen* (Westminster John Knox, 2003). Continuing her important studies in the Gospel of John, Dr. Reinhartz is currently completing *The Johannine Community: A Counter History* for Fortress Press. She was elected to the Royal Society of Canada in 2005.

David Rensberger is professor of New Testament emeritus at the Interdenominational Theological Center in Atlanta. He continues to research and write on the Bible and on Christian spirituality.

His work on the Johannine community includes *Johannine Faith and Liberating Community* (Westminster/John Knox, 1996) and *The Epistles of John* (Westminster/John Knox, 2001)

Andrew Shenton is Conductor and Director of the Boston Choral Ensemble and Associate Professor of Music and James R. Houghton Scholar of Sacred Music at Boston University, where he also serves as Director of the Master of Sacred Music program, Director of the Boston University Messiaen Project, and Director of the Religion and Arts Initiative. His books include *Olivier Messiaen's System of Signs* (Ashgate, 2008), which won the 2010 Miller Book Award, *Messiaen the Theologian* (Ashgate, 2010), and *The Cambridge Companion to Arvo Pärt* (Cambridge University Press, 2012). He is currently conducting research for a book on Arvo Pärt's choral and organ music.

Katherine Sonderegger holds the William Meade Chair in Systematic Theology at Virginia Theological Seminary in Alexandria, Virginia. She is the author of *That Jesus Christ was born a Jew* (Penn State Press, 1992), and *Systematic Theology: Volume 1, The Doctrine of God* (Fortress Press, 2015).

Margaret O'Brien Steinfels and her husband, Peter Steinfels, are the founding co-directors of the Fordham Center on Religion and Culture, an academic initiative devoted to the study of issues at the intersection of today's political and religious discourses. Ms. Steinfels contributes frequently to *Commonweal*, an independent biweekly journal of political, religious, and literary opinion, where she served as editor (1988-2002). She holds a bachelor's degree in history from Loyola University in Chicago, a master's degree in history from New York University, as well as seven honorary degrees.

William Werpehowski holds the Robert L. McDevitt and Catherine H. McDevitt Chair in Catholic Theology at Georgetown University. His areas of scholarly interest include Christian theological ethics, Catholic social thought, and the ethics of war and peace. He is the author of *Karl Barth and Christian Ethics: Living in Truth* (2014) and *American Protestant Ethics and the Legacy of H. Richard Niebuhr* (2002) and co-editor of *The Oxford Handbook of Theological Ethics* (Oxford University Press, 2005). He was previously professor of Theology and director of the Center for Peace and Justice Education at Villanova University.

Christopher Kent Wilson is College Professor of Humanities at Middlebury College, teaching a variety of interdisciplinary courses that include Art and the Bible, American Landscape, Art and the Civil War, Knickerbocker New York, and Winslow Homer. He received his Master of Arts in Religion from Yale Divinity School and his M.A., M.Phil, and Ph.D. from Yale University.

Oliver Larry Yarbrough is the Tillinghast Professor of Religion and Director of the Scott Center for Spiritual and Religious Life at Middlebury College; he is also an Episcopal priest in the Diocese of Vermont. A scholar of the New Testament, early Christianity and early Judaism, he is the author of *Not Like the Gentiles: Marriage Rules in the Letters of Paul* (Scholars Press, 1984), co-editor of *The Social world of the First Christians: Essays in Honor of Wayne A. Meeks* (Fortress Press, 1995), and editor of *Passion: Contemporary Writers on the Story of Calvary* (Orbis Books, 2015).

Illustrations

5.1. Unknown, Tu es deus, with litterae significativae, from the Cantatorium of St. Gallen, Codex Sangallensis 359. Public Domain. Courtesy of Wikimedia Commons.

5.2. J. S. Bach, *St. Matthew Passion*, Exordium, systems 1-2. Published in Richard Davy: *St. Matthew Passion: Reconstructed from the Eton Choirbook with Lyrics in Latin and English*, edited by Ross W. Duffin, Collegium Music: Yale University, Second Series. Vol. 17. Middleton, WI: A-R Editions, Inc., 2011. Used with permission. All Rights Reserved.

5.3. Heinrich Schütz, *Matthäus-Passion*, SWV 479. Editor: Philipp Spitta (1841-1894). Publisher Information: Heinrich Schütz: *Sämtliche Werke*, Band I. Leipzig: Breitkopf und Härtel, 1885. Plate H.S. I. Copyright: Public Domain. ISMLP Creative Commons.

5.4. Giulio Caccini, *Le nuove musiche*. Publisher Information: Firenze: Marescotti, 1601; Ii Here di Giorgio Marescotti, 1602. Copyright: Public Domain. ISMLP Creative Commons.

5.5. J. S. Bach, *St. Matthew Passion*, "Aus Liebe will mein Heiland sterben." Typeset and edited by Alexander E. Volkov

{https://facebook.com/avoff}, 2013–2015. CCBY-SA 4.0. https://creativecommons.org/licenses/by-sa/4.0/legalcode.

5.6. Krysztof Penderecki. *Passio et Mors Domini nostri Jesu Christi.* Copyright © 1966 by Schott Music GmbH & Co. KG, Mainz, Germany. Copyright © renewed. All Rights Reserved. Used by permission of European American Music Distributors Company, sole U.S. and Canadian agent for Schott Music GmbH & Co. KG, Mainz, Germany.

5.7. Arvo Pärt. *Passio Domino Nostri Jesu Christi Secundum Joannem.* Copyright © 1982 by Universal Edition A.G., Vienna. All Rights Reserved. Used by permission of European American Music Distributors Company, U.S. and Canadian agent for Universal Edition A.G., Vienna.

7.1. Unknown artist, *The Raising of Lazarus* (Icon). Fifteenth century. Novgorod © 2014 State Russian Museum, St. Petersburg. Used with permission.

7.2. Hans Holbein the Younger, *The Body of Christ in the Tomb.* 1521. Kunstmuseum, Basel. Photo Credit: Erich Lessing / Art Resource, NY. Used with permission.

9.1. The Alexamenos Graffito from the Domus Gelotiana, Palatine, Rome. Second-third century C.E. Photo Credit: Scala/Art Resource. Used with permission.

9.2. The Crucifixion of Christ, upper-left panel of the main entrance door to the Santa Sabina Basilica, Rome. Fifth century C.E. Photo Credit: ©DeA Picture Library/Art Resource. Used with permission.

10.1. Lothar Cross, jeweled side front. Photo Credit: © Domkapitel Aachen, Photo: Ann Münchow. Used with permission.

10.2. Lothar Cross, engraved side back. Photo Credit: © Domkapitel Aachen, Photo: Ann Münchow. Used with permission.

11.1. Albrecht Dürer, woodcut. *Betrayal of Christ (Small Passion)* 1509-11. Photograph © 2015 Museum of Fine Arts, Boston. Used with permission.

11.2. Albrecht Dürer, *The Kiss of Judas* from *The Great Passion*, 1510, woodcut on paper, 15 9/16 x 11 inches. Collection of Middlebury College Museum of Art, Vermont. Purchased with funds provided by the Electra Havemeyer Webb Memorial Fund, 1969.022. Used with permission.

12.1. Titian (Tiziano Veccellio). *Noli me Tangere.* © National Gallery, London / Art Resource, NY.

13.1. Édouard Manet, *The Dead Christ with the Angels,* 1864. Image provided by The Metropolitan Museum of Art. Used with permission.

13.2. Manet, *The Dead Christ and the Angels,* close-up.

14.1. Marc Chagall, *White Crucifixion.* Art Institute of Chicago. Gift of Alfred S. Altschuler, 1946.925. © 2015 Artists Rights Society (ARS), New York / ADAGP, Paris. Used with permission.

14.2. Marc Chagall, *The Exodus,* 1952/1966 © ARS, NY. Used with permission.

14.3. Marc Chagall, *The Yellow Crucifixion,* 1942 © ARS, NY. Used with permission.

15.1. Damon Lamar Reed, Mural on the Firehouse Community Center run by the House Covenant Church in the Lawndale neighborhood of Chicago, Illinois. Used with permission of the artist.

15.2. Damon Lamar Reed, "Listen Up." Image for embossed T-shirts. Used with permission of the artist.

15.3. Damon Lamar Reed, "He Gave." Image for embossed T-shirts. Used with permission of the artist.

16.1. Banksy, *Christ with Shopping Bags*, 2004, screenprint on paper. Collection of Middlebury College Museum of Art, Vermont. Purchase with funds provided by the Foster Family Art Acquisition Fund, 2012.037. Used with permission.

18.1. Unknown, *The Crucifixion of Jesus: Synagoga and Ecclesia*. Ivory. Cologne region, mid-eleventh century. Hessisches Landesmuseum Darmstadt. Photo: Wolfgang Fuhrmannek. Used with permission.

18.2. Unknown, *The Slaughter of the Innocents: Rachel Weeping Over Her Children*. Ivory. Lower Rhine Valley, eleventh century. Reproduced with permission of the Victoria and Albert Museum, London.

18.3. Uri Zvi Grinberg, "Uri Zvi in Front of the Cross." *Collected Yiddish Works of Uri Zvi Grinberg*, Jerusalem 1975, 2:432. © The Hebrew University Magnes Press, Jerusalem. Used with permission.

Preface

In presenting these essays, I invite readers to look again at a familiar story—or more precisely, several stories that tradition has woven into one. We know the story of Jesus' passion from many sources. The Gospels of the New Testament provide its core elements. But liturgy, music, and art influence the ways most of us read their stories. Cultural settings—both ancient and modern, religious and secular—also affect the way we read the story of the passion, whether we are consciously aware of them or not. Changing tastes in the music and art of the passion make this clear.

The essays in this volume "read" the story of Jesus' passion from many perspectives. The first essays examine the primary biblical texts. Those that follow look at the ways the story has influenced (and been influenced by) liturgies, music, literature, art, cinema, theology, and ethics. Within each section, the authors approach the passion from their own perspectives: Christian, Jewish, Muslim, and secular—or some combination of them all. Sometimes, they survey a broad sweep of history; other times, they focus on one writer or painter, or even a single painting or image, that captures a particular moment in the story or an era's response to the story as a whole.

Together these essays engage the depth and complexity of the story of the passion and of human response to it. They invite us not only to reread the passion but also to hear, see, and experience it. In short, they invite us to engage the passion.

PART I

The Texts

Paul's letters and the Gospel of Mark are the earliest written witnesses to stories of the passion—and to the ways they were used in early Christian communities. But neither Paul nor Mark was the first to tell the stories, or to interpret them. Paul explicitly refers to the traditions he received about the passion. The most obvious examples appear in 1 Cor. 15:3-4 where he writes that he handed on what he had received—"that Christ died for our sins in accordance with the scriptures, and that he was buried, and that he was raised on the third day in accordance with the scriptures"—and in 1 Cor. 11:17-26, where he reminds the Corinthians that he had handed on to them the tradition that

> the Lord Jesus on the night when he was betrayed took a loaf of bread, and when he had given thanks, he broke it and said, "This is my body that is for you. Do this in remembrance of me." In the same way he took the cup also, after supper, saying, "This cup is the new covenant in my blood. Do this, as often as you drink it, in remembrance of me."

The author of the Gospel of Mark does not mention sources. Though the earliest reference to the Gospel claimed that Peter was the source, modern studies suggest that Mark drew on a combination of oral and written sources—from the tradition that the events of the passion fulfilled the Scriptures to a story of the Last Supper that is similar to Paul's, and yet different. Studies of the canonical Gospels of Matthew, Luke, and John, the noncanonical Gospel of Peter, and other early Christian writings show that some later writers used Mark and that all drew on a wide variety of other passion traditions.

The results of these studies of the passion narratives vary widely, though there is broad consensus that Matthew and Luke used Mark by adding, removing, rearranging, and rewriting. The relation between Mark and the Gospel of John is less clear, at least with regard to the question of whether Mark (or any of the other Gospels) was a source for the author of John. One way or another, it is clear that the story of the passion in the Fourth Gospel represents a new direction in telling it. By the end of the second century, as Matthew, Mark, Luke, and John become more and more widely used in prominent Christian centers, writers begin to weave all four together into one document. Tatian's *Diatessaron*, a Syriac harmony of Matthew, Mark, Luke, and John (and perhaps some other sources), presents one such attempt to write a single life of Jesus. This kind of harmonizing was especially important in the development of the stories of the passion, for it fixed the notion of *one* passion story. It was not without problems, however, since the four passions are not easily harmonized. Tatian and Augustine, for example, order Jesus' last words in the four Gospels differently. The Acts of Pilate, an account of the passion and resurrection written in the fourth century (and revised frequently thereafter) in the name of the Roman governor who condemned Jesus to death, is another example of the interest in weaving the passion narratives into one. (It also shows how individual episodes within the passion grow over the course of time.) The development of early Christian liturgies for Holy Week gives yet another example of the way the stories in the four Gospels were woven together.

Though Paul's letters have very few explicit references to the story of the passion, they reflect the many ways Paul interpreted various aspects of it. Here, too, we can see traces of earlier traditions. First Corinthians 15:3-4 contains not only references to the story (Christ died and was buried), but also to the early tradition that he died "for our sins in accordance with the scriptures"—two claims that have more to do with interpretations of the story than with the story itself. Such interpretations continue to flourish after (and alongside) Paul. For example, Hebrews, 1 Peter, and Revelation within the canon, and the Epistle of Barnabas outside of it, develop the notion of Jesus' death as a sacrifice—either in broad terms or with specific reference to the Jerusalem (or heavenly) temple. The authors of Matthew, Mark, Luke, and John also refer to the sacrificial character of Jesus' death, sometimes in very specific terms and at other times in allusions that only those with deep knowledge of Jewish Scriptures will see—which may well indicate that the Gospels were primarily written for readers who already knew the story and its interpretations.

From the beginning, or as close to it as we can come using the writings we have, stories of the passion are linked to the interpretations of it. We see this most clearly in the letters of Paul, in Hebrews, in 1 Peter, in Revelation, and in writings like the Epistle of Barnabas—all of which have more interpretation than story. But we also see it in the Gospels, where the interpretation is part and parcel of the story.

This section begins with Jouette Bassler's essay "The Passion of Christ in the Letters of Paul." Bassler argues that although Paul's letters contain only echoes of the passion story he used in his preaching, the death of Jesus "was at the heart of the arguments Paul presented to his sometimes suffering, sometimes rebellious, sometimes puzzled churches." Masterfully, Bassler works her way through the major letters, showing how Paul draws on the passion to engage his readers regarding the issues they faced—sometimes using the same aspect of the story to quite different effect. Paul applies Jesus' suffering, for example, to himself as an apostle, to the church, and to the cosmos; he can speak of participation in the death of Christ in terms that range from the mystical to the ethical to the liturgical; he focuses at times on the christological aspects of the passion and at others on the theological; and when he writes of the "atoning" significance of Jesus death, he is remarkably inventive in the language and imagery he uses.

In the next essay, "Synoptic Passions," I examine the passion narratives in Matthew, Mark, and Luke—the "Synoptic" Gospels. While taking note of their many similarities, the essay focuses on the distinctive features of each Gospel, arguing that differences among the three Gospels provide rich material for assessing how the evangelists *interpret* the death of Jesus. By emphasizing Jesus' abandonment, suffering, and death, the Gospel of Mark forces its readers to recognize not only the horrors of crucifixion but also the cost of following Jesus. The Gospel of Matthew shifts the focus of Mark's story in many ways, by lessening the emphasis on the disciples' abandonment and dramatizing the trials, the moment of Jesus' death, and tensions with the Jews. The Gospel of Luke differs from Mark even more, showing Jesus calmly facing his trials and crucifixion, caring for the disciples and those around him, and thus providing a model for how to face persecution and death. Luke shifts the blame for Jesus' death from the Romans to the Jewish leaders in Jerusalem.

David Rensberger begins his essay "It Is Accomplished!: The Passion in the Gospel of John" by examining the differences that set the Gospel of John apart from Matthew, Mark, and Luke. He draws attention to the difference in John's language, for example, reminding us that early readers referred to John as the "spiritual"

Gospel. Exploring the language of John in more modern terms, Rensberger refers to it as "symbolic" and "ironic," and suggests that John is more concerned with *truth* than with *fact*. To make this clear, Rensberger looks at the ways the author of John interprets traditions, by making the passion a theme throughout the Gospel—not simply through predictions as Mark does but by demonstrating that Jesus' last words—"It is accomplished"—are to be understood in light of all that Jesus has said and done from the very beginning of the story.

By engaging Paul, the Synoptic Gospels, and John, these essays prepare the way for engaging the story of the passion and its interpretation in liturgy, music, literature, art, cinema, other traditions, theology, and ethics.

1

The Passion of Christ in the Letters of Paul

Jouette Bassler

The passion narrative—a recounting of events leading up to and culminating in Jesus' crucifixion—does not appear in any of Paul's letters. It is, of course, beyond question that Paul relayed some version of this story to the churches he founded, and indeed echoes of it, some faint and some clear, appear throughout his letters. More important, however, than teasing out the content and nuance of the passion narrative that Paul received and passed on to his churches, is the task of exploring how Paul used this material. His letters were instruments of persuasion, and the climax of the passion narrative, Jesus' death, was at the heart of the arguments Paul presented to his sometimes suffering, sometimes rebellious, sometimes puzzled churches. Indeed, the death of Jesus was the primary lens through which Paul interpreted the events that were roiling his congregations, and as

Paul used Jesus' death to illuminate these events, he developed very distinctive interpretations of the theological and ethical implications of the passion. In what follows I will explore the letters one by one, in the sequence in which Paul probably wrote them, in order to let the distinctive role of the death of Jesus in the argument of each letter emerge.[1]

1 Thessalonians

First Thessalonians is the earliest letter in the Pauline canon, written about the year 51 C.E. It is striking, especially in light of the pattern in subsequent letters, how little Jesus' death figures in Paul's rhetoric. This can be explained, however, by the nature of the problems Paul was addressing. After establishing a church in this city, Paul was apparently forced to leave rather abruptly because of intense persecution (1 Thess. 2:17–3:5). The believers, left on their own in a very hostile environment, were anxious over Paul's departure. They had also been persuaded (perhaps by Paul) that Jesus would quickly return from heaven to gather them up into the safety and glory of heaven and were unprepared when some members died before the Parousia (4:13-18).

In his message of comfort to this church, Paul draws on those aspects of the passion narrative that will address their concerns. He first emphasizes the persecution of Jesus, for that established the destiny of his followers, whose own current endurance under persecution was in turn a model and inspiration for others (1:6-7; 2:14; 3:3-4). In a vitriolic tirade (2:15-16), Paul identifies the Jews as Jesus' persecutors, a reference to the role of the chief priests and scribes (or elders) in the passion narrative (Matt. 26:3-4; Mark 14:1; Luke 22:2; John 11:47-53). Surprisingly, this is the only place in all of

1. I will only treat the letters that are indisputably by Paul. Philemon falls into that category, but Paul makes no reference to the passion in that short letter.

his letters that Paul shows any interest in the human agents of Jesus' death.

A second emphasis is established in the opening creedal summary, which focuses on Jesus' resurrection and Parousia as the events that guarantee believers' salvation "from the wrath that is coming" (1:10; see also 2:12; 2:19; 3:13; 5:23).[2] This theme is developed at length in 4:13–5:11, where Paul assures the anxious Thessalonians that they will indeed "meet the Lord in the air; and . . . be with the Lord forever" (4:17). Within this passage Paul makes a very brief allusion to the doctrine of atonement ("who died for us"). The very brevity of this comment indicates that Paul's earlier preaching on the subject had been extensive enough that the hearers of the letter could fill in the theological details. Here, though, Paul does not mention sin or atonement or grace, but moves immediately to the apocalyptic implications for believers: "[Christ] died for us, so that whether we are awake [alive] or asleep [dead] we may live with him [at the Parousia]" (5:10).

Philippians

Philippians is a remarkably upbeat letter, even though the church in Philippi was afflicted with opposition from outsiders (1:28), tension created by rival missionaries (3:2, 18-19), and discord within (2:1-4; 4:2); and Paul himself is in prison (1:12-14). Paul deals with these difficulties with themes drawn from the passion narrative. Two themes, suffering and the cross, get striking emphasis in a letter otherwise dominated by expressions of joy, confidence, and gratitude.

In 1 Thessalonians, Paul interpreted the church's difficult experiences as the persecution that was their destiny, and this led

2. Unless otherwise indicated, all Scripture quotations are from the NRSV.

to his verbal attacks on the persecutors of Christ and the church. In this letter, Paul speaks of suffering instead of persecution and describes it as a gift instead of a destiny—subtle verbal changes that lead to more profound theological ones. In the first development of this theme, Paul states, "[God] has graciously given you the gift not only of believing in Christ but also of suffering for him" (1:29).[3] The Philippians' suffering is as much a divine gift as their faith and is therefore proof of their salvation (1:28). Paul returns to this point later in the letter: "I want to know Christ and the power of his resurrection and the sharing of his sufferings by becoming like him in his death, if somehow I may attain the resurrection from the dead" (3:10-11). Here suffering is presented not as a gift in hand, but as a passionately desired goal, because through it Paul—and the faithful Philippians—will *know* Christ (vv. 8, 10), *gain* Christ (v. 8), be *found in* Christ (v. 9), becoming like him in his death (v. 10). Jesus' suffering and death here are not simply a template for the fate of his followers. The language points more toward suffering as the vehicle for a mystical participation in, or union with, Christ in this life. Such a mystical union is not an end in itself; it anticipates and facilitates the believer's ultimate reunion with Christ in resurrection.

The first mention of the cross appears in a remarkable hymn that Paul quotes in 2:6-11. The hymn speaks of Jesus emptying himself, renouncing all trappings of divine status and advantage. He became "obedient to the point of death—even death on a cross" and was subsequently rewarded by God with unsurpassed heavenly honors. Here the cross is viewed from a cosmic perspective as the absolute nadir of Jesus' obedient and humble act of self-emptying. It is a jarring reference (quite possibly added by Paul to the pre-Pauline hymn), for the cross in Roman times was a brutal instrument of

3. Author's translation.

corporal punishment reserved for the lowest classes and most heinous criminals. It inflicted not just intense and prolonged suffering but also—and intentionally—public humiliation and shame. This, then, is the ultimate level of humility; there is no lower status to sink to. It is therefore paradoxically the apex of Jesus' obedience and the basis for the supreme reward that followed.

There are several echoes here of the lengthier passion narratives of the Gospels. The degrading horrors of the crucifixion scene are clearly evoked with the reference to a cross, and there are echoes of the synoptic Gethsemane scene, with its emphasis on Jesus' obedience to God's will (Mark 14:32-42). Here the hymn is clearly intended to present a model for the Philippian church. Paul opens and closes the passage containing the hymn with exhortations to humility (2:3) and obedience (2:12), describes his own life as a reflection of Christ's model, and encourages imitation of himself and others who, like him, follow that model (3:4–17). Those who do not follow it (probably the rival Christian missionaries) are denounced as "enemies of the cross of Christ" (3:18), and with this phrase Paul elevates the cross from an instrument of torture to a symbol and metaphor for authentic Christian life: a life of humility, self-renunciation, and obedience to God's will.

1 Corinthians

The church in Corinth was rife with problems—factions, spiritual and social elitism, blatant sexual misconduct, lawsuits, abuses of marriage and divorce, idolatry. When Paul wrote this lengthy letter to address these issues, he invoked again and again the death of Jesus, in each case tweaking the way he presented that death so as to address the problem in view with the greatest theological and rhetorical force. Also in this letter—and only in this letter—he quotes traditional material concerning the Lord's Supper and a creedal summary of the passion narrative. This material, like the references to Jesus' death, is shaped in subtle ways to make it a more effective part of Paul's argument. Most striking, however, is the extraordinary emphasis Paul gives to the cross in the opening salvo of the letter.

The opening argument (1:10–4:21) deals with divisions within the church. Because these divisions were linked in some way with rival missionaries and other apostles, they were undermining Paul's authority: "Each of you says, 'I belong to Paul,' or 'I belong to Apollos,' or 'I belong to Cephas,' or 'I belong to Christ'" (1:12). Before he could give directions about how to deal with the myriad problems within the church, he had to reestablish his authority *over* the church. And central to *that* argument is his discourse on "the message of the cross" (1:18, REB).

As in Philippians, Paul describes the crucified Christ as a figure the world regards as weak, low, and despised (1:27-28), but he does not turn the cross into a metaphor and model of humility and obedience. Instead he describes it as a deliberate act of divine *foolishness*: "God chose what is foolish in the world to shame the wise" (1:27). With deep irony Paul declares that by choosing to save the faithful through a crucified Messiah, a concept that the world in its wisdom rejects as impossibly foolish, God reveals the tragic shortcomings of the world's wisdom. The full development of this theme (1:18–2:5) contains some of the most powerful rhetoric in Paul's letters. Beyond asserting that the cross upends human concepts of wisdom (how God can "reasonably" be expected to act) and reveals the true nature of God's wisdom (God acts through the weak, the lowly, and the despised), this passage makes two other striking claims. The first is that the crucifixion of Jesus was the result of *God's* choice and *God's* wisdom. This stands in some tension with the emphasis in Philippians on the cross as the climax of *Jesus'* act of self-emptying, and in strong contrast to numerous passages in the book of Acts that place full blame for Jesus' crucifixion on the Jews and locate God's action in the resurrection (Acts 3:14–15; 4:10; 7:52). The second striking claim is that God chose to save the faithful through the cross in order to *shame* the wise (1:27). There is no reference here to divine *love* as a motivating factor (compare Rom. 5:8); the focus is on exposing the folly of the world's norms.

The unusual emphases in this passage can be understood in terms of Paul's rhetorical goal: to regain the church's allegiance. The appeal of the rival missionaries seemed to lie in their rhetoric, which was shaped by human standards of eloquence ("eloquent wisdom," 1:17). Paul presents his own work as aligned instead with God's wisdom, for God has chosen the "foolish" cross as the means of salvation (1:21), and the cross is the sum and substance of Paul's message: "For I decided to know nothing among you except Jesus Christ, and him crucified. . . . My speech and my proclamation were not with plausible words of wisdom, but with a demonstration of the Spirit and of power, so that your faith might rest not on human wisdom but on the power of God" (2:2–5). Among those shamed by this are those who have preferred the "wise" and eloquent words of rival preachers, and so Paul concludes, ironically, "I am not writing this to make you ashamed [yes, he is!], but to admonish you as my beloved children" (4:14).

Paul does not return to the language of the cross and crucifixion after this opening argument, but references to Jesus' death punctuate exhortations in the rest of the letter. He grounds his instructions to "clean out the old yeast" (that is, to expel a member engaged in blatant sexual immorality) by drawing on the connection established in the passion narratives between Jesus' death and Passover. According to Exod. 12, the Festival of Unleavened Bread, which requires purging the home of old leaven (yeast), immediately follows Passover. Thus when Paul asserts, "our paschal lamb, Christ, has been sacrificed" (5:7), the point he is making is one of timing: the Passover lamb has been sacrificed; it's time to clean out the old leaven. He does not develop here any notion of the atoning or redemptive aspects of Christ's death.

In several other places, however, he does develop those notions. Twice he describes the Corinthians as having been "bought with a price" (6:20; 7:23). This language interprets Jesus' death as a payment that releases a servant from bondage to one master *in order to serve another*: "You are not your own" (6:20); you are "a slave of Christ" (7:22). The immediate point is behavior that pleases the new master. In another passage, Paul addresses those who ignore the religious scruples of less enlightened believers by eating food sacrificed to idols. Though idols have no real existence and thus believers are (theoretically) free to eat the food offered to them, "by your knowledge those weak believers for whom Christ died are destroyed" (8:11). Paul uses the theological language of atonement, but his primary intent is to increase the pathos of the situation: they are harming those for whom Christ died!

In two passages Paul directly and emphatically quotes liturgical material that is part of the synoptic passion narratives. Close comparison of the Pauline and synoptic versions reveals both the stability and the flexibility of the transmitted traditions. The situation Paul is addressing in 1 Cor. 11 is one of serious divisions within the church along social and economic lines. When church members gathered for their communal meal, those who were able to bring food were not sharing with those who had nothing (11:21-22). Paul brings the tradition of the Lord's Supper to bear on this intolerable situation (11:23-26). The tradition he cites is distinctive in several ways. In Matthew and Mark, the ritual acts with bread and cup follow the communal meal (Matt. 26:17-30; Mark 14:17-26), but in Paul's version (and in Luke's) the bread and cup bracket the meal, thus incorporating the meal itself tightly into the ritual. Thus abuses of the communal meal become abuses to the ritual, and Paul can assert, "Whoever, therefore, eats the bread or drinks the cup of the Lord in an unworthy manner will be answerable for the body and blood of the Lord" (11:27). This is a remarkable charge: those who abuse the Lord's Supper by refusing to share food in the communal meal are liable for Christ's death!

In a second variant, Paul's version (again like Luke's) links the bread, which is the body, with the atoning effect of Christ's death ("this is my body that is *for you,*" 11:24, emphasis added), whereas Matthew and Mark link this effect with the cup and the blood. Paul's version draws attention to the body and anticipates his subsequent and lengthy focus on abuses within and to the corporate body of Christ, that is, the church: "For all who eat and drink without discerning the body [that is, discerning Christ's body in the eucharistic bread and discerning the church as the body of Christ], eat and drink judgment against themselves" (11:29). Finally, Paul's comment on the tradition he has cited defines participation in this ritual not simply as an act of remembrance, but more significantly as a proclamation of the message of the cross: "As often as you eat this bread and drink the cup, you proclaim the Lord's death until he comes" (11:26).

The second tradition that Paul cites—again with great emphasis—is a summary of the gospel (15:1-11). It contains the familiar elements of Christ's death "for our sins," his burial, his resurrection on the third day, and appearances of the resurrected Christ. This is tersely presented until the last element, which receives astonishing expansion. Paul lists appearances to Cephas (Peter) and the twelve ("eleven" in Matt. 28:16 and Luke 24:28-36), then to more than five hundred believers (unrecorded elsewhere, but see Acts 1:15), then to James (Jesus' brother) and all the apostles (also unrecorded), and finally to Paul himself (Gal. 1:15-16). This list, for all its inclusiveness, does not record the resurrection appearances to women that are so striking a component of the Gospels. No other tradition, however, brings all the male resurrection witnesses together like this. It seems to be Paul's own expansion of the creedal material and it identifies his purpose, which is not to confirm the atoning power of Jesus' death, but to present overwhelming evidence for his resurrection *from the dead* (15:12). Some in Corinth were claiming that they *already had* resurrection status (4:8) and the spiritual gifts to prove it (ch. 12–14), and they disdained those who did not. Paul cites this amplified Gospel tradition—which they received and accepted (15:1-2)—to support his argument that resurrection follows death and cannot precede it. Thus the shift in Paul's message from the cross in the opening chapters to the resurrection in this closing chapter is only illusory. Paul's point is that, while their resurrection (like Christ's) is secure "if you hold firmly to the message that I proclaimed to you" (15:2), their resurrection is future. In the present age they are to live their social and liturgical lives as a proclamation of the cross.

2 Corinthians

This is a very disjointed letter. The tone and content vary from tender reconciliation to angry verbal attacks; from calm plans for an offering project to defensive posturing and outbursts of frustration. These tensions might indicate that 2 Corinthians is a composite document in which fragments of several letters have been rather awkwardly stitched together. On the other hand, the chaotic contents might reflect Paul's agitated state of mind as he confronted a church in full rebellion against him, his ministry, and his message. There is no consensus on this. At frequent points in the letter (or letters) Paul invokes the passion, sometimes with familiar nuances but other times with new theological content. Moreover, even where the passion is not explicitly mentioned, it hovers over Paul's words about the pain, suffering, and anguish this church has caused him.

Like the letter itself, Paul's discussions of Jesus' passion are sometimes disjointed, pulling in several directions at once. "We are convinced," he writes, "that one has died for all" (5:14). He does not continue the atonement metaphor with the expected statement about all being thereby reconciled to God or saved from wrath (see Rom. 5:6-11). Instead he surprises by asserting, "Therefore all have died." The catalogs of Paul's suffering that appear in several places in the Corinthian correspondence (1 Cor. 4:9-13; 2 Cor. 4:7-10; 6:4-10; 11:23-29) suggest an affinity with the passion of Christ, but Paul reaches further, as he did in Philippians, to the more profound claim of participation in that passion. This is not a mystical participation that transports the ecstatic believer out of the body and the world (but see 12:1-5). Rather, this participation occurs precisely in and through the trauma of the body in the world: "We are afflicted in every way, but not crushed; perplexed, but not driven to despair; persecuted, but not forsaken; struck down, but not destroyed; always carrying in the body the death of Jesus, so that the life of Jesus may also be made visible in our bodies" (4:8-10).

A few verses later Paul expands the theological significance of Christ's passion in yet another direction: "In Christ God was reconciling the world to himself" (5:19). In Romans and Galatians, Paul describes the result of Christ's death as justification, a forensic term for being set right with the righteous Judge. In this letter, to address the extreme alienation in Corinth, Paul prefers the language of reconciliation, a term that focuses on social rather than legal consequences. Paul continues by drawing attention to his own role in God's act of reconciliation: "All this is from God, who reconciled *us* to himself through Christ, and has given *us* the ministry of reconciliation . . . entrusting the message of reconciliation to *us* . . . since God is making his appeal through *us*" (5:18–20, emphasis added). God's reconciling act thus embraces both Christ and Paul, so when Paul concludes by urging the Corinthians to "be reconciled to God," the subtext is clear: and be reconciled to me.

The concluding chapters of the letter echo the rhetoric of 1 Corinthians, which ironically finds God's power and wisdom in the weakness and foolishness and humility of the cross. Here, though, for three chapters Paul presents *himself* as weak, foolish, and humble, and only at the conclusion grounds the argument in the crucifixion and in his own participation in Christ, whose very weakness confirms God's power: "For he was crucified in weakness, but lives by the power of God. For we are weak in him, but in dealing with you we will live with him by the power of God" (13:4). To an astonishing degree in this anguished letter, Paul describes himself not only as one chosen by God to proclaim the passion but also as one who embodies the passion. Thus his weakness, though derided and rejected by the Corinthians, validates his apostleship over that of his vigorous opponents.

Galatians

In 1 Corinthians, Paul insisted that the new age was future and would only be accomplished at the parousia: "Then comes the end, when he hands over the kingdom to God the Father, after he has destroyed every ruler and every authority and power" (1 Cor. 15:24). In Galatians, he insists that new creation is now. What caused this change in perspective? In brief, the opponents changed. His opponents in Corinth had suggested that resurrection life was already present, a view that affected the behavior of believers in unfortunate ways. In Galatia, different teachers were insisting that (male) gentile believers needed to complement their faith journey with circumcision as a mark of membership in the people of God. For Paul, this position was absolutely unacceptable: faith alone is necessary. Indeed, faith and circumcision are completely incompatible. They belong to two different worlds or ages, and the age of the law had come to an end on the cross. Paul thus presents a simple choice to the Galatian churches: either the old evil age or new creation; either the law and circumcision or faith. There is no place in Paul's apocalyptic scenario for compromise.

Paul opens the letter with a stunning claim about Christ's death. He first presents the familiar creedal message of atonement ("[Christ] gave himself for our sins") but then strikes a new, apocalyptic note: "[he did this] to set us free from the present evil age" (1:4). Paul hammers this theme home throughout the letter, asserting in various ways that there has been a cosmic change, the turning point of the ages. He develops this theme-setting verse by first exploring the phrase "he gave himself," which he restates in terms of Jesus' faithfulness (2:15-21).[4] This terse phrase evokes the Gethsemane scene in the Gospels, which portrays Jesus' faithful obedience to God. Here Paul sets that action over against another: works of the law. "We know that a person is reckoned as righteous [NRSV: justified] not by works of the law but through the faithfulness of Jesus Christ" (2:16).[5] Paul turns this contrast over and over, finally reaching the dramatic and nearly blasphemous conclusion: "If justification comes through the law, then Christ died for nothing" (2:21).

4. The Greek phrase here rendered "Jesus' faithfulness" (*pistis Iēsou*) is "faith in Jesus" in the NRSV and other major translations. Only the NRSV textual note and the KJB offer the alternative reading used here, but there is strong support for it among contemporary scholars. For a discussion of this issue, see Jouette M. Bassler, "Faith," in *Navigating Paul* (Louisville: Westminster John Knox, 2007), 23–33.

5. Author's translation.

In other letters Paul asserts that Jesus' death results in a change in servitude from one master to another. In Galatians he states the result more starkly. There is for believers, he says, a release from slavery and a new life of freedom—freedom from the present evil age (1:4), freedom from the demonic powers (NRSV: elemental spirits) that rule this age (4:3, 8–10), and most significantly, freedom from the law (4:5; 5:1). In developing this idea, Paul makes an astonishing assertion about the passion: "Christ redeemed us [set us free] from the curse of the law [the curse that the law pronounces on all who do not obey it] by becoming a curse for us" (3:13). Just as, according to Leviticus, the sins of the people of Israel were transferred to an animal (Lev. 16:20-22), so the curse that the law pronounces on all who do not obey has been transferred to Christ.

This is far more explicit and dramatic than earlier statements regarding the atonement, and Paul backs it up with a proof text from Deuteronomy, the only time he cites Scripture to interpret the passion: "Cursed is everyone who hangs on a tree" (3:13, citing Deut. 21:23). Paul deletes several words from the original text, the most significant being the phrase "by God" (that is, "cursed by God"). God is thus disassociated from the curse and linked instead to a blessing, specifically a blessing to gentiles (3:8–9, 14). This marks another new emphasis in this letter, though it has been implicit in Paul's ministry. In the cross, the law—which separated Jew from gentile; placed a curse on all, Jew or gentile, who did not obey it completely (3:11); and placed a special curse on the crucified one—this law is revealed as belonging to an age that is past, even as its power to curse is annulled on the cross (3:19–4:7).

Among the many allusions to the passion in this letter, one more stands out as distinctive. Paul has written in several places of participating in Christ's death: "I have been crucified with Christ" (2:19-20; see also 2 Cor. 4:10; Rom. 6:5–8). In his closing remarks in this letter, however, he speaks not only of his participation in Christ's crucifixion, but of the world's participation in it as well. "May I never boast of anything except the cross of our Lord Jesus Christ, by which the world has been crucified to me, and I to the world" (6:14). For the world, this participation means a terminus, a final end to the yoke of slavery it imposed through the law; for Paul it means new creation (6:15).

In no other letter are cross and crucifixion mentioned so frequently (seven times, compared with six times in the much longer 1 Corinthians and only once in Romans) and so forcefully. A likely explanation is that the concreteness of the crucifixion, with all the violence associated with it, made it a powerful symbol for Paul's apocalyptic message of the end of the age of the law (see also Rev. 5:6–14). Moreover, the stigmata of the crucifixion, metaphorically applied to the bruises received in proclaiming and living the gospel, effectively supplanted circumcision as the physical mark of God's people in the new age: "From now on, let no one cause trouble for me; for I bear the stigmata of Jesus on my body" (6:17).[6]

Romans

Romans is different. Paul had never been to Rome and played no role in establishing the churches there. He is not focused in this letter on correcting problems within the Roman churches, nor is he engaged in heated polemics with rival missionaries. In fact, *he* is the rival missionary and as such he shows great circumspection in presenting, via this letter, himself and his gospel to this group of unknown churches. In place of the often disjointed, passionate, polemical arguments of earlier letters, here Paul develops a careful analysis of his gospel from an entirely new perspective.

6. Author's translation.

In the opening salutation, Paul refers to "the gospel of God" (1:1), not, as elsewhere, "the gospel of Christ" (see 1 Cor. 9:12; 2 Cor. 9:13; Gal. 1:7). This signals that God, not Christ's passion, will be the focus of the letter. This is confirmed several verses later in the initial presentation of the letter's theme: "For I am not ashamed of the gospel; it is the power of God for salvation to everyone who has faith, to the Jew first and also to the Greek. For in it the righteousness of God is revealed through faith for faith; as it is written, 'The one who is righteous will live by faith'" (1:16-17). Strikingly, there is also no reference to Jesus in this thematic statement. It presents the gospel not in terms of its christological content but in terms of what it reveals about the righteousness of God.

The concept of God's righteousness is found in many Jewish writings. It conveys notions of God's rightness, fairness, and justice, as well as God's covenant faithfulness, steadfast love, and saving actions. All these aspects surface in this letter, but Paul's primary concern, anticipated in this statement, is to show how God's righteousness is consistent with, even demands, a ministry—his ministry—to gentiles.

In spite of Paul's initial silence regarding the passion, when he begins to develop the letter's theme, he invokes Christ's death several times using the familiar categories of redemption and atonement (3:21-31). Paul's focus, however, is not on what Jesus' death accomplished for humankind, but on what it reveals about God: "For there is no distinction, since all have sinned and fall short of the glory of God; they are now justified by his grace as a gift, through the redemption that is in Christ Jesus, whom God put forward as a sacrifice of atonement by his blood, effective through faith. He did this to show his righteousness, because in his divine forbearance he had passed over the sins previously committed" (3:22-25).

Paul has just documented at almost morbid length the pervasive sinfulness of all humankind (1:18–3:20). For God to freely pardon such people would amount to letting them get away with "every kind of wickedness, evil, covetousness, malice, . . . [and] murder" (1:29). Jesus' atoning death, however, pays the penalty for these sins and thus preserves the righteousness, that is, the righteous justice, of God's verdict of acquittal. To highlight his primary point here, Paul uses Israel's cultic imagery of sacrifice and blood. (The phrase "sacrifice of atonement" in the NRSV is more accurately translated "mercy seat," a direct allusion to Lev. 16:15.) Paul also strongly emphasizes God's initiative in orchestrating the passion, stating that "God put [him] forward" ("designed him," REB; "appointed him," NJB) as a sacrifice. Jesus' role, on the other hand, is presented more passively as faithfulness, the better translation of the Greek rendered "faith in Christ" by the NRSV.

The same emphasis on God's role in the passion surfaces in chapter 5. Paul initially uses traditional atonement language: "While we were still weak . . . Christ died for the ungodly" (5:6). When he repeats the point, though, he presents God as the primary actor: "God proves his love for us in that while we still were sinners Christ died for us" (5:8). Christ's passion reveals God's love, an aspect of righteousness that emphasizes faithfulness to God's people. Paul also mentions the consequences of Christ's death for humankind. Those who were formerly weak, ungodly, sinners, and enemies of God have been reconciled to God (mentioned three times) by the death of God's son. As a consequence, though, they now boast not in Christ, whose death effects the reconciliation, but in God, who has orchestrated it (5:11).

In the second half of chapter 5, Paul turns more emphatically to Christ, whose actions are compared with those of Adam. Here Christ's passion is summarized as an "act of righteousness" in contrast to Adam's trespass, and as an "act of obedience" in contrast to Adam's disobedience (5:18-19). Paul does not explicitly state it here, but it is clearly implied that Christ's act of righteousness—his faithful obedience unto death—enables God's righteousness to be revealed in the "free gift following many trespasses" (5:15-17).

The argument so far has centered on Jesus' atoning death as the vehicle by which the righteousness of the forgiving God is maintained. However, this message of radical grace opens another challenge to the concept of divine righteousness. If, through the cross, God's grace is always available to redeem sinful humanity, why not "continue in sin that grace may abound"? (6:1). This seems to be a charge that has trailed Paul and his gospel for some time (3:8), and it seriously challenges the notion of an upright God. To deal with it here, Paul appeals again to Jesus' passion, viewed now as a participatory, not sacrificial, event.

Participation in Christ's death, a familiar motif from earlier letters, is here for the first time linked with the rite of baptism, which imparts a measure of concreteness to the event (6:3, see 1 Cor. 12:13; Gal. 3:27). Paul asserts that by participating in Christ's death, baptized believers have themselves died to sin, construed as an enslaving power. He links this to assurances of future participation in Christ's resurrection, but this "resurrection" is described in both eschatological and ethical terms: "Therefore we have been buried with him by baptism into death, so that, just as Christ was raised from the dead . . . so we too might walk [that is, conduct ourselves] in newness of life" (6:4).

Participation in Christ's death also means dying to the law (7:4-6), probably primarily, but not exclusively, a reference to Jewish law. The law, Paul argues, is ineffective as a moral guide because those who try to obey it are "of the flesh" (7:14). This is Paul's shorthand for the physical self so controlled by sin that it is incapable of doing good even when it wishes to do so (7:15-25). In place of the law, God now provides the Spirit as a powerful internal guide for those who are in Christ, "so that the just requirement of the law might be fulfilled in us, who walk not according to the flesh but according to the Spirit" (8:4). Just as dying with Christ provides assurance of also sharing his resurrection, so too this indwelling Spirit bears witness "that we are children of God, and if children then heirs, heirs of God and joint heirs with Christ." Surprisingly, this guarantee ends with a proviso: "if, in fact, we suffer with him so that we may also be glorified with him" (8:17).

Participation in Christ's sufferings is a familiar theme in Paul's letters, but here participation is not identified with apostolic sufferings or the sufferings inflicted on the church by an unbelieving world. Rather, the suffering is cosmic in scope, the suffering of all creation as it groans under the burden of mortality (8:18-25). Moreover, the eschatological relief from this suffering is promised not solely to those who are "joint heirs with Christ," for "the creation itself will be set free from its bondage to decay and will obtain the freedom of the glory of the children of God" (8:21).

In chapters 9–11, Paul shows how God's righteousness, in the form of faithfulness to the covenant people, is not annulled when Israel rejects the gospel, but he makes this argument without reference to the passion of Christ. In the ethical section (ch. 12–15), Paul appeals rarely to the passion and then in very familiar ways. It is only in the first eight chapters that Paul invokes the passion of Christ with the theological innovation and rhetorical boldness that characterize this theme in the rest of his letters. There it has been, by turns, a lens, a mirror, an example, a sacrifice, a cosmic event, and an eternity of events repeated over and over in the lives of those who participate in Christ's death.

Bibliography

Bassler, Jouette M. *Navigating Paul: An Introduction to Key Theological Concepts.* Louisville: Westminster John Knox, 2007.

Cousar, Charles B. *A Theology of the Cross: The Death of Jesus in the Pauline Letters.* Overtures to Biblical Theology 24. Minneapolis: Fortress Press, 1990.

Grieb, A. Katherine. *The Story of Romans: A Narrative Defense of God's Righteousness.* Louisville: Westminster John Knox, 2002.

Tannehill, Robert. *Dying and Rising with Christ: A Study in Pauline Theology*. BZNW 32. Berlin: Töpelmann, 1966.

2

Synoptic Passions

Oliver Larry Yarbrough

The passion narrative—the story of Jesus' last days and death in Jerusalem—is the culminating moment for all the Gospels in the New Testament.[1] Each Gospel foreshadows the passion with early stories of conflict between Jesus and various religious authorities; and though all of them end with stories of resurrection, they treat the resurrection in direct relation to the passion. This essay focuses on the passion in Matthew, Mark, and Luke because they are very similar throughout, as the term "synoptic" suggests. They have a common outline for most of Jesus' life; they tell many of the same stories; and they share many common themes.[2] In all these areas the Synoptic

1. This may be the case with the noncanonical Gospel of Peter also, at least based on the surviving fragments.
2. For a good introduction to Matthew, Mark, and Luke, see Pheme Perkins, *Introduction to the Synoptic Gospels* (Grand Rapids, MI: Eerdmans, 2007).

Gospels differ significantly from the Gospel of John, which will be treated separately.[3] The Gospel of Mark contains the earliest story of the passion to have survived from antiquity, though its author almost certainly had access to written material that has not survived.[4] Matthew and Luke, who knew Mark's Gospel in an early version, show us how later writers revised the story—by adding material from other sources (both oral and written) or by rearranging and rewriting Mark's account.[5] Though it is not clear whether the author of the Gospel of John knew Mark, Matthew, or Luke, it provides further evidence of the ways the narratives of the passion developed as Christians continued to explore its meaning. The Gospel of Peter, the Acts of Pilate, and early harmonies of the Gospels show how differently it could be told with the passing of time.[6]

The synoptic passion narratives appear in Matt. 26–27, Mark 14–15, and Luke 22–23.[7] In all three Gospels, the story begins just before Passover and continues through a series of events that involve Jesus, his disciples, the religious leaders in Jerusalem, the people of the city, and the Roman officials who control it. The story concludes with Jesus' condemnation, crucifixion, and burial. There are only a few differences in the basic flow of events: Matthew has two scenes that the other Gospels do not have (The Death of Judas and The Guard at the Tomb); Luke omits one scene (The Anointing

3. See David Rensberger's essay in this volume for a discussion of the issues.

4. Identifying Mark's sources in the passion narrative is the topic of a number of specialized studies. For a survey of the issues and a proposed reconstruction of the passion narrative Mark used, see Adela Yarbro Collins, *Mark: A Commentary*, Hermeneia, ed. Harold W. Attridge (Minneapolis: Fortress Press, 2007), 620–27 and 819. This commentary contains a wealth of information on all questions related to the Gospel of Mark, with judicious and insightful analysis of them.

5. I use the traditional names Matthew, Mark, and Luke in reference to the authors of the Synoptic Gospels, but do not attempt to identify them further.

6. The Gospel of Thomas and other collections of Jesus' sayings (like the one containing the two hundred verses that Matthew and Luke used in addition to Mark) show that some early Christians had little interest in the story of Jesus' death, focusing instead on his teaching.

7. See the Appendix at the end of the present chapter for a list of the individual units (pericopes) in the synoptic passions.

at Bethany) and includes two others (The Need for Swords and The Trial before Herod). But if the basic structure of the narrative is the same, the individual episodes in it are different—sometimes significantly. These differences will occupy us here, since they are especially revealing of the evangelists' interests in telling the story.

We begin with the Gospel of Mark. It establishes the common story, making it one of the most important pieces of early Christian literature to have survived from antiquity. Fixing Mark's story allows us to see more clearly when and how Matthew and Luke diverge from it, and in the process become interpreters of the story they tell. At the same time, we must bear in mind that the way Mark crafts the story makes him an interpreter too, whatever sources he may have had.

Mark's Passion

Three times in the middle of the Gospel of Mark, Jesus predicts his death and resurrection.[8] The last—and longest—of these predictions provides an outline of Mark's passion narrative:

> See, we are going up to Jerusalem, and the Son of Man will be handed over to the chief priests and the scribes, and they will condemn him to death; then they will hand him over to the Gentiles; they will mock him, and spit upon him, and flog him, and kill him; and after three days he will rise again.

It is a somber story, in spite of the ending.

Even before the three passion predictions, Mark raises the specter of the conflict that leads to Jesus' death. In chapter 2, scribes question Jesus about forgiving sins and healing on the Sabbath. By chapter 3, the conflict is so severe that Jesus looks at the Pharisees in anger,

8. Mark 8:31, 9:31, and 10:33-34.

grieved at their hardness of heart; in response they begin to conspire with the Herodians in order to destroy him.[9]

When Jesus and the disciples finally arrive in Jerusalem (ch. 11), the conflict heats up again when Jesus drives the buyers and sellers out of the temple and engages in debates with leaders of various religious factions in Jerusalem that will carry through into chapter 12. Finally, in chapter 13, just before the passion begins, Jesus meets privately with four of his disciples and, in the longest discourse of this Gospel, tells them of the days to come—days of wars and rumors of wars, earthquakes and famines, trials and beatings, and days of suffering that have never been seen before and will never be seen again. Directly after this ominous warning, Mark turns to the passion. Little wonder that it is so somber.

Mark sets the tone of the passion in its first story, The Anointing in Bethany (14:3-9), which tells of a woman who breaks open a jar of ointment and pours it over Jesus' head. Her act provokes anger and a scolding comment from the guests at the table: "Why was the ointment wasted in this way? For this ointment could have been sold for more than three hundred denarii, and the money given to the poor." Saying that they can help the poor any time and calling what she has done "a good service for me," Jesus tells those who scolded her that the woman had anointed his body for burial. Significantly, the story ends with Jesus' saying that what she has done will be remembered wherever the good news is proclaimed—a hint of what is to come and why Mark writes.

The last story in Mark's passion, The Burial (15:42-47), circles back to its beginning:

9. Pharisees and Sadducees are the most commonly mentioned opponents of Jesus in the Synoptic Gospels, though their role in the passion narrative is not prominent. The identity of the Herodians is not clear. But they must have had some association with the dynasty founded by Herod the Great and supported by the Romans.

> When Pilate learned from the centurion that [Jesus] was dead, he granted the *corpse* to Joseph. Then Joseph bought a linen cloth, and taking *it* down, wrapped *it* in the linen cloth, and laid *it* in a tomb that had been hewn out of the rock. He then rolled a stone against the door of the tomb. Mary Magdalene and Mary the mother of Joses saw where *it* was laid.[10]

By beginning and ending with stories of death and burial, Mark establishes the mood of his passion. The stories in between are equally somber, even if they point to a time beyond the passion. They also raise many questions.

After a brief editorial note that Judas has put in motion a plan to betray Jesus to the religious authorities in Jerusalem (14:10-11),[11] Mark describes the preparation for Passover and introduces a theme that will appear throughout the passion: everything happens according to plan (14:12-16). Here it involves so small a thing as a man carrying a jar and Jesus' sending the disciples to an upstairs room that is already "furnished and ready." During the Passover meal itself (14:17-21), Jesus' prediction of what is to come is more ominous: one of the twelve will betray him. The news provokes distress among the disciples, leading each to ask, "Is it I?" Yet when Jesus identifies the betrayer as "one who is dipping bread into the dish with me" (a poignant phrase to suggest he is close by), there is no response—neither from Judas nor any of the others at the table.[12] For Mark it is enough to speak of the betrayal, and to note that it will take place "as it is written" (14:20-21). Time and again, both explicitly and

10. Joseph asks for the *body* (*sōma*) of Jesus (15:43); Pilate grants him the *corpse* (*ptōmas*). I modify the NRSV's translation of 15:45 to make this clear. The only other time Mark uses *ptōmas* is in 6:29, when he refers to the burial of John the Baptist. The NRSV translates it *body* there also.

11. The reference to the betrayal marks the first point in the outline of 10:33-34: "the Son of Man will be handed over to the chief priests and the scribes."

12. In Matthew, Jesus speaks directly to Judas (26:25). Luke places the prediction of the betrayal *after* Jesus gives the bread and wine to the disciples (22:21-23).

through allusions, Mark's story of the passion conforms not only to Jesus' prediction but also to Scripture.[13]

Mark strips the rest of the Passover meal to bare essentials: a loaf of bread and a cup of wine. But in a marked departure from the Passover service, Jesus refers to the bread and wine as his body and blood—"poured out for many."[14] His last words at the meal allude to his impending death, but point to a time beyond it:

> Truly I tell you, I will *never again* drink of the fruit of the vine
> *until that day* when I drink it new in the kingdom of God.

The Passover meal ends with the singing of a hymn.

After the meal, Jesus and his disciples go to the Mount of Olives, where the tension of the passion builds when Jesus reveals to the disciples more of what is to come: "You will all become deserters" (14:26-31). As it was when Jesus predicted Judas's betrayal, so it is here: the desertion will take place "as it is written." This time, however, Mark cites the Scriptures explicitly, as if to emphasize the importance of the moment.

> I will strike the shepherd,
> and the sheep will be scattered.[15]

Peter's protest that he will not desert Jesus, even if the rest of them do, leads to Jesus' prediction that Peter will desert him—and prolongs the tension in the story. His vehement denial of the prediction, which the

13. Belief that Jesus' death happens "as it is written" predates not only the Gospel of Mark but also the letters of Paul, as his comment in 1 Cor. 15:3-4 indicates. Over the course of time, more and more scriptural references appear in passion narratives. Mark's use of Scripture in the passion narrative has been studied extensively. See the survey and analysis by Kelli S. O'Brien in *The Use of Scripture in the Markan Passion Narrative* (Bloomsbury: T&T Clark, 2010). As with the other Synoptic Gospels, Ps. 22 (21 in the Greek version) and Isa. 52:13—53:12 appear most commonly, whether in quotations or allusions.
14. See Mark 10:45 for another allusion to the significance of Jesus' death. Mark does not explicitly develop either, suggesting that his readers already knew them.
15. The quotation comes from Zech. 13:7.

other disciples echo, makes the moment all the more poignant. But in the middle of this foreboding treatment of the disciples' desertion, Mark looks beyond it again: "After I am raised," Jesus says, "I will go before you to Galilee."

Two important scenes in Gethsemane follow. In the first (14:32-42), Mark focuses on Jesus' emotions, in a way that heightens the tension of the passion. He writes that Jesus "began to be distressed and agitated" and that he says to Peter, James, and John, "I am deeply grieved, even to death." Jesus then goes away from the disciples to pray, *falls* on the ground, and asks that the hour might pass from him, agitatedly moving back and forth between the place where he prays and the place where they sleep—not once but three times. "Keep awake and pray," he tells the disciples repeatedly, just as he had done when he warned them about the days leading up to the coming of the Son of Man, with their wars and rumors of wars, earthquakes and famines, betrayals and sufferings (ch. 13). It is as though Jesus' crisis in Gethsemane foreshadows the crisis that is to take place before the coming of God's kingdom.

The emotional intensity of the first Gethsemane scene continues in the second (14:33-52), though Mark now focuses on the agitation of those around Jesus. The action is frenetic: Judas and an armed crowd from the ruling elite in Jerusalem arrive; Judas kisses Jesus; members of the crowd lay hands on Jesus and arrest him; someone who was standing nearby draws a sword and strikes a slave of the high priest, cutting off his ear.[16] Though Jesus challenges the crowd for not arresting him while he was teaching in the temple, his command "let the scriptures be fulfilled" reveals the real purpose of this scene. For almost on cue, the disciples abandon Jesus, fulfilling both his earlier prediction and the Jewish Scriptures on which it is based. The

16. Mark says nothing of Jesus' healing the slave, one of many elements in the passion that Luke adds (22:51).

disciples are exposed as deserters—like the mysterious young follower who drops the linen cloth he had been wearing and runs away naked.

After Gethsemane come the "trials" before the Jewish council and Pilate.[17] Both have gaps, twists, and turns that make them difficult to accept as real judicial proceedings.[18] But as stories they are richly evocative—even if at times provokingly enigmatic. Indeed, from the trial before the council to Jesus' death (14:53—15:39) there are numerous puzzles in Mark's passion.

The story of Jesus' appearance before the council (14:53-65) unfolds in two parts.[19] The first focuses on testimony from outside witnesses, the second on an interrogation by the high priest. The witnesses accuse Jesus of saying he will destroy the temple "made with hands" and replace it with a temple "not made with hands"—in three days. But Mark calls them *false* witnesses, which raises the question of how seriously he takes the accusation. It is telling, however, that he says the high priest does not pursue this line of inquiry when Jesus does not respond to his opening question. So although Mark shows considerable concern with the temple, he does not make the accusation that Jesus planned to destroy it a factor in the council's decision.[20]

The high priest's interrogation of Jesus (14:60-64) is the turning point in the trial, because of Jesus' response to the question "Are you

17. Pilate is the Roman governor of Judea who served from 26–36 C.E. Interestingly, however, Mark never accords him a title, always referring to him simply as "Pilate." By contrast, Matthew emphasizes his official title, repeatedly referring to him as "governor."

18. There are problems with the interpretation of the trial scenes in all the Gospels. For a good introduction to the issues, see Gerard S. Sloyan, *Jesus on Trial: A Study of the Gospels*, 2nd ed. (Minneapolis: Fortress Press, 2006).

19. With the trial before the council, Mark turns to the second point in Jesus' prediction of the passion in 10:33-34: "they will condemn him to death."

20. Jesus' prediction that the temple will be destroyed is the occasion for his apocalyptic discourse in chapter 13, which factors prominently in Mark's Gospel. Jesus is in the temple daily, he tells those who come to arrest him (14:49). The charge about destroying the temple becomes one of the taunts during the crucifixion (15:29); and at Jesus' death the curtain in the temple is torn from top to bottom (15:38).

the Messiah, the Son of the Blessed One?"[21] Remarkably, Jesus breaks his silence and answers the high priest directly and clearly, "I am." And if that were not enough, he goes on to say,

> 'you will see the Son of Man seated at the right hand of the Power,'[22] and 'coming with the clouds of heaven.'[23]

Heretofore in the Gospel of Mark, Jesus has never made such a confession. In fact, he has avoided openly discussing his identity, repeatedly telling the disciples and those he heals to keep silent.[24] Thus, simply to admit to the high priest that he is the Messiah, the Son of God, *and* the Son of Man is a turning in the narrative. But to make the confession at such a dark moment—just after his disciples have abandoned him and he is on trial for his life—is bold. The way Mark interweaves the trial before the council and Peter's threefold denial of Jesus (14:54 and 66-72) adds to the significance of Jesus' confession even further, by inviting a comparison between Jesus and Peter: Jesus speaks boldly, Peter does not. Over the course of several hours and in the darkness of night, Peter first denies knowing Jesus and then twice denies being one of his followers. This goes back not only to Jesus' prediction of Peter's denial but also to what he tells the disciples after the first prediction of the passion: "If any want to become my followers," he says, "let them deny themselves and take up their cross and follow me" (8:34). Peter does neither.

In the "trial" before Pilate (15:1-20), Mark focuses on yet another title, "the King of the Jews."[25] Mark introduces it abruptly. Without

21. "The Blessed One" is a euphemism for "God," so that the high priest asks Jesus, "Are you the Son of God?"
22. "Power" is another euphemism for "God," one that also appears in the Gospel of Peter 5:19.
23. Jesus' reply draws on Ps. 110:1 and Dan. 7:13-14. Mark had used the psalm in 12:36, when Jesus challenges the scribes' interpretation of the title "the son of David." He refers to the passage from Daniel in the apocalyptic discourse that precedes the passion narrative (13:26).
24. See 1:26, 34, 43; 3:11; 5:43; 7:36; 8:26, 30; and 9:9.
25. With the trial before Pilate, Mark turns to the third point in Jesus' prediction of the passion in 10:33-34: "they will hand him over to the Gentiles."

any prompting from the (large!) delegation that handed him over, Pilate asks Jesus, "Are you the King of the Jews?"[26] And in spite of the ambiguity of Jesus' answer to Pilate's question—"You say so"—Pilate keeps using it, even after the chief priests bring other charges.[27] When the crowd asks him to release Barabbas, Pilate responds with a question of his own, "Do you want me to release for you the King of the Jews?" And when they persist in seeking the release of Barabbas, he pushes back, "Then what do you wish me to do with the man you call the King of the Jews?"[28] When they shout, "Crucify him!" Pilate poses the last of his five questions: "Why, what evil has he done?" No one answers. But simply by posing the question, Pilate makes Mark's point: the King of the Jews has done nothing wrong and does not deserve to be killed.

By the end of the trials, Mark has established Jesus as the Messiah, the Son of God, the Son of Man, and the King of the Jews. Three of the four titles also appear in his account of the crucifixion, each time with deepening irony.[29]

After flogging Jesus, Pilate turns him over to be crucified. Before setting out on their mission, however, the soldiers mock Jesus by dressing him in royal garb and hailing him as "King of the Jews" (15:16-20). Their actions and words continue Mark's ironic use of the title in the trial before Pilate. So, too, does the inscription identifying him as "The King of the Jews" (15:26) that the soldiers attach to the cross. Jesus the king is increasingly shamed and humiliated.[30]

26. This is the first of five questions Pilate poses during the trial.

27. Jesus says nothing in answer to these unspecified charges, which amazes Pilate. Such a response to Jesus is typical in the Gospel of Mark. See 1:27, 2:12, 5:20, 10:32, and 12:17. Some see Jesus' silence here and elsewhere in Mark's passion as allusions to the suffering servant in Isa. 52:13—53:12, especially to 53:7-9.

28. Other early manuscripts read, "What do you want me to do with the King of the Jews?"

29. The title "Son of Man" does not appear in the crucifixion stories.

30. With the flogging, mocking, spitting, and killing, Mark turns to the fourth point in Jesus' prediction of the passion in 10:33-34: "they will mock him, and spit upon him, and flog him,

The passers-by, chief priests, scribes, and bystanders who are present at the crucifixion take up the mocking, in language that echoes the trials and evokes passages from Scripture that Mark and his sources see as messianic prophecies (15:29-36). The passers-by *deride* Jesus, wag their heads at him, and taunt him with "Aha! You who would destroy the temple and build it in three days, save yourself and come down from the cross." The chief priests and scribes are even more pointed in their mockery, saying, "He saved others; he cannot save himself. Let the Messiah, the King of Israel, come down from the cross now, so that we may see and believe."[31] *Save/come down* are the key phrases in these taunts: The passers-by, chief priests, and scribes hold that Jesus could (and should) save himself, if he is the messiah and king of Israel. Saving himself and coming down from the cross, they say, would prove his claim and elicit their faith/belief—through a sign of his power and demonstration of his status.

A shift, subtle but noteworthy, occurs when just before he dies Jesus cries out, "Eloi, Eloi, lema sabachthani?" (15:33-39)—a shift from the taunt that Jesus should save himself and come down from the cross to the bystanders' belief that he was crying out for Elijah to come and take him down. But as Mark's translation makes clear, the bystanders, like the disciples, misunderstand Jesus. He does not call to Elijah, but to God. And is cry is not a call for help, but the opening words of a psalm of lament—*My God, my God, why have you forsaken me?* Thus, Mark's translation of the Aramaic hardly makes Jesus' last words any easier to understand. Indeed, they are among the most perplexing puzzles in Mark's passion. Is this Mark's

and kill him." None of the three passion predictions in Mark mentions "crucifixion," though 8:34 anticipates it.

31. Note that the order here is the same as in the trials: destruction of the temple and then the titles. This is the only time Mark links "Messiah" and "King of the Jews." (Romans use the title "King of the Jews" in Mark; "King of Israel," which appears in 15:32, is the title the chief priests and scribes use.)

way of signaling Jesus' complete abandonment—Judas's betrayal, the disciples' desertion, Peter's denials, and now God's forsaking? Or, does Mark anticipate that readers will know—and find comfort in knowing—that Ps. 22 contains prayers for deliverance and that it ends with a statement of confidence in God's deliverance of all who call upon him?[32]

Similar questions can be asked about many other aspects of Mark's account of Jesus' death. What is the meaning of the tearing of the curtain of the temple? Proposals include a foreshadowing of the destruction of the temple made with hands in preparation for the building of a temple not made with hands; a miraculous sign of Jesus' importance—like the darkness from noon until three; and an allusion to the opening of salvation to all.

And how is the tearing of the curtain related to what follows—the centurion's saying, "Truly this man was God's Son"? Does Mark suggest the centurion actually saw the tearing of the curtain, and took it as a sign of Jesus' divine status? Or does he simply put the two statements together and let the reader make connections? More importantly, what does the centurion's declaration mean? Is it a final taunt—"So *this* is God's Son?" Or does the centurion give voice to the confession Mark wants his readers to make? And if so, does Mark mean that the centurion recognized Jesus as God's son simply by seeing him die and that the resurrection is not necessary?

Indeed, what about Mark's resurrection story, which marks the fifth point in the prediction of the passion in 10:33-34: "and after three days he will rise again"? If the resurrection is the fulfillment of the final prediction, why do the earliest manuscripts of Mark end with the women going out of the tomb and fleeing in terror, amazement, and fear? Why do they not tell the disciples what they

32. For the prayers for deliverance, see verses 11 and 19-21; for the confidence in God's deliverance, see verses 21b-31.

have heard? Did Mark end the Gospel at 16:8, or was there another ending—a more "satisfying" ending—that was somehow separated from the rest of the manuscript and is now lost? Engaging Mark's passion requires wrestling with such puzzling questions.

In following Mark's story of the passion, we have noted how it tracks the outline of the last of the three passion predictions. Though there are some parts of Mark's passion that do not easily fit the outline, his story claims that what Jesus predicted came to pass. Mark also claims that what Jesus predicted was in keeping with God's plan as it was revealed in "what was written." So to some extent the Gospel of Mark is complete with the announcement of the resurrection.

But Jesus makes another prediction in Mark, one that looks beyond the resurrection. When he and his disciples get to Jerusalem, one of the disciples looks at the temple and marvels at the "large stones" and "large buildings" that comprise its precincts. In response, Jesus says

> Do you see these great buildings? Not one stone will be left here upon another; all will be thrown down. (13:1-2)

Peter, James, John, and Andrew later ask Jesus, "Tell us, when will this be, and what will be the sign that all these things are about to be accomplished" (13:3-4). His response to their questions is the apocalyptic discourse that takes up the rest of chapter 13. Jesus says it will be a time of great disquiet. There will be wars and rumors of wars, earthquakes and famines, darkening of the sun and moon, and suffering such as has never been or will ever be again. The disciples will be handed over to councils and beaten; brother will betray brother to death. Many will be led astray. "Truly I tell you," Jesus says, "this generation will not pass away until all these things have taken place" and finally the Son of Man will come in clouds with great power and glory—to gather the elect from the ends of the earth. But no one knows when it will happen. All Jesus can say to his disciples is "Beware, keep alert; for you do not know when the time will come."[33] At the end of the chapter, however, Mark extends the range of Jesus' warning: "And what I say to you, I say *to all*: Keep awake."[34] And with these words, he turns to the passion.

From Mark's point of view, Jesus' predictions of the passion and resurrection have come to pass. In his Gospel, Mark tells the story. Because Jesus' predictions of the coming of the Son of Man in power and great glory have not come to pass, however, he cannot tell that story. He can only point to signs that it is coming and warn his readers that they will experience suffering just as Jesus did. This leads to another alternative to understanding Jesus' last words. For Mark, they underscore not only the depth of Jesus' suffering but also the suffering his followers will experience in the last days. As he put it in 13:19,

> For in those days there will be suffering such as has not been from the beginning of the creation that God created until now, no, and never will be.

Just like him, Jesus' followers will be handed over to councils, beaten, and stand before governors and kings, betrayed, and put to death.[35] Thus, as Jesus puts it after the first passion prediction and Peter's rejection of it,

> If any want to become my followers, let them deny themselves and take up their cross and follow me. For those who want to save their life will lose it, and those who lose their life for my sake, and for the sake of the gospel, will save it. For what will it profit them to gain the whole world and forfeit their life? Indeed, what can they give in return for their life? Those who are ashamed of me and of my words in this adulterous and

33. 13:33
34. 13:37
35. See 13:9-13. These verses follow the outline of Mark's passion more closely than the passion prediction of 10:33-34.

> sinful generation, of them the Son of Man will also be ashamed when he comes in the glory of his Father with the holy angels. (8:34-38)

To follow Jesus is to follow one who suffers. But as the next two sayings in Mark's prediction-misunderstanding-teaching cycle show, this does not mean that following requires suffering. In the second cycle, Jesus says,

> Whoever wants to be first must be last of all and servant of all. (9:35)

And in the third cycle, he says,

> Whoever wishes to become great among you must be your servant, and whoever wishes to be first among you must be slave of all. For the Son of Man came not to be served but to serve, and to give his life a ransom for many. (10:43b-45)

In these two sayings, Mark changes the metaphor from suffering to serving. Thus, while the first saying equates taking up one's cross to following Jesus, the second and third give substance to it, indicating that being first among Jesus' followers requires being servant of them all. The third saying also establishes the measure of serving—willingness to give one's life as Jesus did. Dying itself, however, is not the measure; neither is suffering. Thus, the poor widow who gave "her whole life," in the form of two small copper coins, is one of Mark's most striking examples of how one attains the level of serving Jesus requires.[36] The rich man who "lacks one thing" and the scribe who is "not far from the kingdom of God" are examples of the ones who do not.[37]

Mark's carefully constructed sequence of the passion predictions points *to* Jesus' death and resurrection; the sayings about following

36. See 12:42-44. "Her whole life" is a more literal translation of the phrase the NRSV renders "all she had to live on." Mark may have some of his readers in mind when he contrasts the poor widow to the scribes and rich people in 12:38-44.
37. See Mark 10:17-22 (with the explication in vv. 23-31) and 12:28-34.

Jesus that are closely related to the predictions point to the time *beyond* the passion and resurrection—the time in which Mark and his readers live, in anticipation of the coming of the Son of Man.

Matthew's Passion

Though the Gospel of Matthew has 90 percent of the material that appears in Mark (mostly in the same order), its additions and changes make for a different story. The additions begin with Matthew's stories of Jesus' birth, extend through five collections of sayings and parables dispersed throughout the Gospel, and conclude with additional episodes in the passion and resurrection stories. Matthew also includes numerous additional references to events that fulfill prophecies in Scripture, especially at the beginning and ending of the Gospel.

In the passion narrative, Matthew makes numerous small changes. Sometimes, he simply adds minor details to the story, like the name of the high priest (Caiaphas)[38] or Pilate's title (governor).[39] At other times, he explains an incident, as when he writes that it is Peter's accent that betrays him as a Galilean when the bystanders identify him as a follower of Jesus.[40] Among Matthew's additions to the growing list of scriptural allusions in the passion tradition are the thirty pieces of silver that Judas received for betraying Jesus and the use of the money to buy a potter's field when he throws it on the floor of the temple at the feet of the chief priests and elders before hanging himself.[41] Matthew's additional references to Jesus as the Messiah (in the trials before the council and Pilate) and as the Son of God (during the crucifixion) may be more substantive, however, since they serve to emphasize his status.[42]

38. 26:3 and 57.
39. Frequently in chapter 27.
40. 26:73.
41. See 26:15 and 27:3-10. The references are to Zech. 11:12-13 and, imprecisely, to Jer. 18:1-3, 19:1-13, and 32:6-15.

Matthew also extends episodes in Mark's passion, by adding additional dialogue. During the arrest in the Garden of Gethsemane, for example, Matthew adds that Jesus turns on the disciple who pulls his sword and strikes the high priest's slave and rebukes him by saying:

> Put your sword back into its place; for all who take the sword will perish by the sword. Do you think that I cannot appeal to my Father, and he will at once send me more than twelve legions of angels?[43]

This comment, like the addition of the titles during the trials and crucifixion, clearly emphasizes Jesus' power and closeness to his *Father*, which Matthew had already done in the earlier scene in Gethsemane when Jesus addresses God as "*My* Father."[44] Jesus' rebuke of the disciple who strikes the slave also stresses his acceptance of God's plan to which he had surrendered himself when he prayed, "yet not what I want but what you want."[45]

Matthew's addition of five blocks of material that deal with the roles Jews play in his story of the passion are very difficult. They reflect the notable animus against the Pharisees Matthew demonstrates throughout the Gospel, but focuses it first by blaming the Jews for Jesus' death and then for spreading rumors to discredit the resurrection.

The first of these stories recounts Judas's hanging himself—in remorse for having betrayed "innocent blood" (27:3-10). The chief priests and elders dismiss him, with "What is that to us? See to it yourself"—words that Pilate will use later.[46] Judas's reference to "blood" is echoed when the chief priests pick up the thirty pieces of

42. For the additional references to Jesus as the Messiah, see 26:68 and 27:17 and 22; for the references to the title Son of God, see 27:40 and 43.
43. See 26:52-53.
44. See 26:39 and 42. Matthew makes other minor changes to the words of Jesus' prayer and to his response to Judas that soften the effects of Jesus' distress.
45. 26:39

silver and say they cannot put them in the temple treasury because they amount to "blood money." It is echoed twice more in the most difficult of Matthew's additions to Mark's passion:

> So when Pilate saw that he could do nothing, but rather that a riot was beginning, he took some water and washed his hands before the crowd, saying, "*I am innocent of this man's blood*; see to it yourselves." Then the people as a whole answered, "*His blood be on us and on our children*!"[47]

This kind of anti-Jewish polemic appears frequently in Matthew and was common in religious disputes between and within religious and ethnic factions in the Greco-Roman world.[48] But Matthew's repeated use of the term "blood," makes these two scenes especially inflammatory, echoing as they do the "blood of the covenant" in the traditions about Jesus' Passover meal with the disciples just before the crucifixion. The deep and abiding tragedy for Christians who make the meal a remembrance of the passion is the way Matthew's language has been used to justify anti-Jewish and anti-Semitic attitudes and the actions to which they lead, especially when held and perpetrated by those in power.[49]

Matthew adds to Mark's narrative two stories about the placement of guards at Jesus' tomb. In the first, he reports that the chief priests and Pharisees ask Pilate to put a guard at the "imposter's" tomb, lest

46. Pilate tells the chief priests, elders, and the crowd that he will not be responsible for Jesus' death, with the saying "See to it yourselves" (27:24). This, and the recurring references to "blood" in the scenes, suggests both are Matthew's creation. Note that in Acts 1:18-20 Luke cites a different tradition regarding Judas's death.
47. Matt. 27:25, emphasis added. In 27:19, Pilate's wife refers to Jesus as "that innocent man," though the Greek term for "innocent" here is different from the one used in 27:4 and 24. Pilate's wife says Jesus is *dikaiōs*, which is sometimes translated "just" or "righteous"; Judas and Pilate use *athoōs*, a more narrowly legal term.
48. Note especially the polemic against the "scribes and Pharisees" in Matt. 23. On the widespread used of polemically charged rhetoric in the Greco-Roman world, see Luke T. Johnson, "The New Testament's Anti-Jewish Slander and the Conventions of Ancient Polemic," *Journal of Biblical Literature* 108 (1989): 419–41.
49. See Jeremy Cohen's essay in this volume and, for a fuller treatment, his book *Christ Killers: The Jews and the Passion from the Bible to the Big Screen* (Oxford: Oxford University Press, 2007).

his disciples steal the body and claim he has been raised from the dead, so that "the last deception would be worse than the first" (27:62-66).[50] In the second, he writes that the guards report to the chief priests what they had seen and were paid to keep it quiet—a story, Matthew says, that "is still told among the Jews to this day" (28:11-15).[51]

The last major addition Matthew makes to Mark's passion is the report of what happens when Jesus "cried again with a loud voice and breathed his last":

> At that moment the curtain of the temple was torn in two, from top to bottom. The earth shook, and the rocks were split. The tombs also were opened, and many bodies of the saints who had fallen asleep were raised. After his resurrection they came out of the tombs and entered the holy city and appeared to many. Now when the centurion and those with him, who were keeping watch over Jesus, saw the earthquake and what took place, they were terrified and said, "Truly this man was God's Son!" (Matt. 27:51-54)

With his additions Matthew greatly heightens the drama of Mark's passion. Whatever symbolic meaning Mark may have attributed to the tearing of the curtain of the temple, Matthew sees it as the first of a series of cataclysmic events that demonstrate the significance of Jesus and his death.[52] The earthquake, mentioned only by Matthew, changes the whole scene. It splits rocks and opens tombs, allowing the bodies of saints to rise and (eventually!) walk through the streets of Jerusalem. Similarly, Matthew's decision to make the centurion only one of many to see the events as proof that something miraculous has happened and proclaim Jesus to be the Son of God

50. This is the only time in the passions of the Synoptic Gospels that Pharisees are explicitly mentioned, which suggests that this scene also derives from Matthew. The Gospel of John includes Pharisees in the crowd that comes to arrest Jesus (18:3).

51. The phrase "to this day," which also appears in 28:15, confirms the argument that Matthew's polemic against the Jews was sharpened by conflicts in his own time.

52. Matthew writes that there was "a great earthquake" when an angel came down from heaven to role away the stone (28:2-4). This frightens the guards at the tomb but without provoking belief.

also heightens the dramatic effect of Jesus' death. Historians of the period frequently include stories of cataclysmic events at the birth and death of important figures. Though many of Matthew's readers have responded favorably to his dramatic revisions of Mark's story of Jesus' death, one wonders what Mark would have thought.

Matthew includes all of Mark's passion predictions, though he changes each one and adds material that interrupts Mark's carefully constructed cycle of prediction—misunderstanding—following. More significantly, Matthew adds to Mark's Gospel a considerable amount of material devoted to Jesus' teaching. Together, these editorial changes have the effect of lessening Mark's emphasis on the passion. Still, because much of the material Matthew adds concerns the ethics by which his community is to live, he too emphasizes living between the resurrection and the coming of the Son of Man in power and great glory. The Sermon on the Mount is the best example of Matthew's focus on the ethics of the community, especially with its blessing on "those who are persecuted for righteousness sake" (5:10-11). But his use of Mark's apocalyptic teaching in Jesus' discourse on discipleship in chapter 10 and the parables of judgment in chapters 24–25 also reflect Matthew's interest in the ethics of the kingdom of God. So like Mark, Matthew looks beyond the passion and resurrection, with instructions from the Lord regarding how his community and his readers are to live.

Luke's Passion

Like Matthew, the author of the Gospel of Luke uses Mark's passion as a source, but omits more, adds less, repositions many of the stories, and rewrites almost everything.[53] The difference is most evident in

53. Though some of the differences in the passions of Mark and Luke derive from the additional sources Luke uses, his approach to Mark demonstrates a willingness to revise source material liberally.

the way Luke portrays Jesus, but also appears in his treatment of the Jewish leaders, the Romans, Judas, Peter, and the other disciples. Alone among the synoptic evangelists, Luke also includes a role for Satan, which adds a distinctive element to the story.

From the very beginning of the passion, Luke sets a different tone by omitting Mark's story of the woman who anoints Jesus—with its emphasis on death and burial—and going straight to Judas's conspiracy to betray Jesus.[54] With this repositioning of stories, Luke focuses the reader's attention on the conflict between Jesus and his adversaries. But to emphasize the significance of this conflict, Luke takes it to a higher level than Mark does, by making Satan the catalyst for Judas's betrayal.[55] Judas does not confer with the chief priests and officers of the temple police, that is, until *after* Satan has entered him (22:3).[56] Another sign of the heightened significance Luke gives to the conflict appears when Jesus tells Peter that Satan demanded to sift him and the other disciples like wheat (22:31), just the kind of sifting Jesus himself goes through when the devil tests him in the wilderness.[57]

Mostly, however, Luke deals with the conflict at a more mundane level, focusing on the role of Jewish leaders as Jesus' adversaries. We see this as early as 22:2, when Luke distinguishes between the

54. Luke includes an anointing scene in 7:36-50, though it is closer to the one in John 12:1-8 than to the one in Mark. Luke's differs from both of them, however, by omitting all references burial.

55. Luke makes use of several traditions about Satan, the devil, and Beelzebul. Weaving them together, Luke portrays Satan as a dark spiritual power opposed to God and controlling a kingdom of his own (Acts 26:18; Luke 4:6 and 11:18). Thus, Satan's presence is implied when Jesus says to the crowd that comes to arrest him on the Mount of Olives, "When I was with you day after day in the temple, you did not lay hands on me. *But this is your hour, and the power of darkness!*" (22:53). On the role of Satan in Luke-Acts, especially with regard to magic and healing, see Susan Garrett, *The Demise of the Devil* (Minneapolis: Fortress Press, 1989).

56. This is apparently the "opportune time" that Luke mentions in 4:13. Neither Mark nor Matthew refers to Satan (or the "devil") here or anywhere else in their passion narratives. But see John 13:2 and 27, which appears to echo a tradition similar to the one Luke knows.

57. See 4:1-13. Luke also refers to testing (or "the time of trial") in 8:13, 11:4 and 16, and 22:28, 40, and 46.

chief priests and scribes who sought Jesus' death and the people who showed interest in him. This distinction appears again in 22:4, when Judas agrees to betray Jesus to the chief priests and officers of the temple *away from the crowd.* Even more pointedly, Luke writes that the crowd that comes with Judas to arrest Jesus includes "the chief priests," "the officers of the temple police," and "the elders" (22:47-55).[58] Luke identifies them as the ones who seize Jesus (22:54), mock and beat him (22:63), and finally take him to the whole council (22:66).

Luke's description of the proceedings before the council is strikingly different from the account in Mark and Matthew, most notably because it omits all references to witnesses—whether false or otherwise—who speak of Jesus' claim that he will destroy the temple and rebuild it.[59] Thus, Luke's "trial" before the council has only one focus: the elders' demand that Jesus tell them if he is the Messiah. By the end of their interrogation, Luke writes, the elders have no need of witnesses, since they have heard *for themselves* what Jesus says (22:71). *They* are the ones who take Jesus to Pilate (23:1-5) and accompany him when he is sent to Herod, "vehemently" pressing their charges (23:6-10).[60]

Even when Pilate calls "the chief priests, the leaders, and the people" together after Herod sends Jesus back to him (23:13-25), it is not clear that *the people* have a role in the proceedings, for Luke focuses on the charge the *leaders* make in the first "trial" before Pilate—that Jesus was perverting *the people* (23:2)—and omits Mark's claim that the chief priests stirred up the crowd to call for the release of Barabbas.[61] So, at most, Luke includes the people in the indefinite

58. Luke 22:50 and 52. Luke is the only evangelist to mention such high officials at the arrest.
59. Mark 14:58 and Matt. 26:59-61.
60. Luke alone mentions this trial before Herod.
61. See Mark 15:11.

"they" who call for the release of Barabbas and the crucifixion of Jesus.[62]

In the rest of the passion, Luke again emphasizes the divisions between the leaders and the people, most notably during the crucifixion, when "the people stood by, watching," when "the leaders scoffed at him" (23:35). After Jesus dies, Luke reports, members of the crowd who witnessed the crucifixion "returned home, beating their breasts" (23:48), a sign of remorse that shows the continuing division between the leaders and the people.[63] Luke even suggests there was a division *within* the council, when he describes Joseph of Arimathea as "a good and righteous man" who, though a member of the council, had not agreed on the plan to kill Jesus (23:50–51).

Luke gives the last word on the responsibility for the crucifixion to one of the men who encounter the risen Jesus on the road to Emmaus (24:13–32). In response to Jesus' question about what they had been discussing when he met them on the way, the disciple replies,

> [We were discussing] the things about Jesus of Nazareth, who was a prophet mighty in deed and word before God and all the people, and how our chief priests and leaders handed him over to be condemned to death and crucified him. But we had hoped that he was the one to redeem Israel.

Here the division between the leaders and the people is starkly set, at least for the Jews who were drawn to Jesus: *They* condemned; *we* hoped. Though there are differences in emphasis, Luke's second volume, the Acts of the Apostles, explores the divisions further, claiming that many Jews found their hopes fulfilled in the proclamation of Jesus' death and resurrection.[64]

62. Luke 23:18, 21, 23, and 25.
63. See also "the great number of people" who followed Jesus on the road to the site of the crucifixion (23:27).
64. See especially Acts 2:1—6:7.

A prominent feature of Luke's treatment of the Jewish leaders who oppose Jesus is the inclusion of the charge they brought against him in the "trial" before Pilate (23:1-25):

> We found this man perverting our nation, forbidding us to pay taxes to the emperor, and saying that he himself is the Messiah, a king. (v. 2)[65]

When Pilate finds no basis for the accusation, the leaders push back, saying, "He stirs up the people by teaching throughout all Judea from Galilee where he began even to this place" (v. 5). Still, Pilate dismisses the charges related to insurrection—three times—and reports further that Herod did not find them convincing either (23:4, 14-15, and 22). Later, in a significant rewriting of the exchange between Jesus and the criminals hanged beside him, Luke returns to the charge of insurrection and offers another testimony to Jesus' innocence. While one of the criminals "derides" Jesus by saying, "Save yourself and us," the other replies, "we indeed have been condemned justly (*dikaiōs*), for we are getting what we deserve for our deeds, *but this man has done nothing wrong*" (23:40-41). A convicted insurrectionist refuses to include Jesus in their ranks.[66]

At the moment of Jesus' death, Luke provides one more witness to rebut the charge of insurrection—the centurion who sees what had taken place. In sharp contrast to his words in Mark, the centurion in Luke says, "Certainly this man was *dikaiōs*."[67] The NRSV translates the term as "innocent," which is perfectly appropriate in light of the argument Luke has been making.[68] The centurion confirms what Pilate, Herod, and the crucified criminal said repeatedly: Jesus was not an insurrectionist, and therefore is *innocent* of the charge. The point is important for Luke, because it allows him to show in Acts

65. Neither Mark nor Matthew is so explicit in the charge—or in the defense against it.
66. For Mark's version, see 15:32b.
67. In Mark, the centurion says, "Truly this man was God's Son" (15:39).
68. The NRSV also translates *dikaiōs* as "innocent' in Matt. 27:19. See n. 47 above.

that Roman officials have no reason to fear the apostles since they do not follow an insurrectionist. Nor do they disturb the peace any more than he did.[69] Still, because there is more to Luke's portrayal of Jesus (especially in the passion), the term "innocent" is too limited to express what he means to express with the centurion's words.

Like Mark, Luke shows that Jesus knows and accepts the task that God has set for him; but unlike Mark, Luke emphasizes that Jesus accomplishes the task calmly and with quiet confidence. The centurion's comment at the moment of Jesus' death speaks as much to this aspect of Luke's passion as it does to Jesus' innocence. For Luke, who uses language that resonates with Jewish Scriptures (in their Greek translations) and Greco-Roman moral philosophy, *dikaiōs* describes one who lives (and dies) in conformity to God's righteousness or to the notion of justice that characterizes the ideal human being. To capture this part of Luke's treatment of Jesus, the centurion's comment would be better translated "Truly this man was *righteous*" or "Truly this man was *just*."[70]

Luke's rewriting of two major scenes in Mark's passion narrative exemplifies his concern with portraying Jesus in this way.[71] The first is his account of the events on the Mount of Olives (22:39-55), which differs from Mark's considerably. Luke does not describe Jesus as "distressed," "agitated," and "grieved" when he enters the garden; nor does he portray Jesus falling on the ground when he prays—only

69. The topic appears repeatedly in Acts 16–28. Note also Luke's use of Isa. 53:12 to explain why one of the disciples had a sword and struck the high priest's slave with it (Luke 22:36-38). Jesus' healing the slave shows that he is not interested in violent resistance (22:49-51).

70. The issue here is not what a centurion might have meant by the term *dikaiōs*, but what Luke and his readers might have understood. In his Gospel, Luke uses *dikaiōs* in the sense of "righteous" in 1:6, 17; 2:25; 5:32; 14;14; and 15:7. In Acts 3:14; 7:52; and 22:14, *dikaiōs* has the sense of "the righteous one," perhaps echoing Isa. 53:11. In Greek moral/ethical discourse, *dikaiōs* has a wide range of meanings, but frequently appears in lists of virtues that describe the highest ideal for being human.

71. The stories of the Jewish martyrs in 4 Macc. 7–18 reflect a similar concern with courage, self-control, and righteousness in the face of torture and death. See also Wisd. of Sol. 3:1-9 and 5:1-2.

once!—that his Father might remove the cup.[72] Rather, as a righteous/just man, he is concerned with those around him, twice exhorting the disciples to pray that *they* may not fall into temptation.[73] As a result of these changes, there is no agony in the garden in Luke as there is in Mark.[74]

The second scene in which Luke emphasizes Jesus' quiet confidence is the moment of his death. Setting Mark and Luke side-by-side makes this clear:

Mark 15	Luke 23
33 When it was noon, darkness came over the whole land until three in the afternoon.	44 It was now about noon, and darkness came over the whole land until three in the afternoon, 45 while the sun's light failed; and the curtain of the temple was torn in two.
34 At three o'clock Jesus cried out with a loud voice, "Eloi, Eloi, lema sabachthani?" which means, "My God, my God, why have you forsaken me?"	46 Then Jesus, crying with a loud voice, said, "Father, into your hands I commend my spirit."

The differences between Jesus' last words in Mark and Luke are stark. Readers who know both Gospels commonly resolve the differences by imagining a progression from Mark to Luke, from despair to acceptance. Luke could have done this, too, by adding the quotation from Ps. 31:5 to Mark's quotation from Ps. 22:1. Instead, he changed it, just as he did with the prayer in Gethsemane. For Luke, there is no

72. Compare Mark 14:32-42 and Luke 22:39-46.
73. See 22:40 and 46. For further references, see n. 57. In 22:45, Luke transfers grief from Jesus to the disciples.
74. Some early manuscripts of Luke include two additional verses in this pericope: "Then an angel from heaven appeared to him and gave him strength. In his anguish he prayed more earnestly, and his sweat became like great drops of blood falling down on the ground." When included, they appear in printed editions as Luke 22:43-44. I agree with scholars who regard these verses as additions to Luke, though from a very early period. Most commentaries on the Gospel of Luke discuss the evidence.

agony in the garden and no despair on the cross. He portrays Jesus as calmly facing his death, with confidence in the Father to whom he commends his spirit.

Portraying Jesus' confidence in prayer before his arrest and in his death on the cross, Luke, more than any of the other evangelists, provides a model for the disciples and other followers. His account of Stephen's death in Acts 7 makes this clear. Stephen makes the most of his "opportunity to testify," speaking of Jesus as "the Righteous One" whom the prophets foretold, proclaiming that he sees Jesus as the Son of Man "standing at the right hand of God," and praying (as he is being stoned), "Lord Jesus, receive my spirit."[75]

Through Jesus' treatment of the disciples during the passion, Luke provides further support and encouragement for those who will be leaders in Acts. He shows this in numerous ways, both great and small, frequently linking them to the Passover meal. In initiating the preparation for Passover, for example, Jesus tells Peter and John, "Go and prepare the Passover Meal *for us* that *we* may eat it" (22:8) and when the meal begins he tells the disciples, "I have eagerly desired to eat this Passover with you before I suffer" (22:15). Later in the meal, Luke introduces a dispute that arose between the disciples regarding who was the greatest. Like Mark, who places the dispute earlier in the life of Jesus, Luke uses it as an opportunity for Jesus to teach the disciples about service—"I am among you as one who serves," he tells them.[76] But Luke adds the affirming statement,

> You are those who have stood by me in my trials; and I confer on you, *just as my Father has conferred on me*, a kingdom, so that you may eat and drink at my table in my kingdom, and you will sit on thrones judging the twelve tribes of Israel. (22:28-30)[77]

75. Stephen's words echo Luke 21:12-19; 23:44; 22:69; and 23:46.
76. See Mark 9:33-35 and 10:42-45. Luke omits Jesus' reference to the Son of Man giving his life as "a ransom for many."
77. Matthew has a similar saying in a different context. See 19:28.

This is remarkably different from Jesus' treatment of the disciples in Mark and points to a time beyond the passion when they will hold positions of authority, not simply at the end of the age but also in the time of the church narrated in Acts. Thus, significantly, Luke softens Jesus' prediction of Peter's denial—by prefacing it with Jesus' prayer for Peter and his assurance that all will be well, since Jesus knows he will prevail in his conflict with Satan.[78] In a similar way, Luke omits Mark's prediction that the disciples will desert Jesus and passes over his pointed comment that at the moment of Jesus' arrest they desert him and flee.[79] Consequently, readers of Luke's Gospel are not surprised to see the disciples featured so prominently in his second volume.

The second volume also provides Luke occasion to develop one of the themes he emphasizes in the Gospel—that the messiah must suffer. Each of the evangelists (like Paul before them) refers to Scripture in telling the story of the passion, sharing some passages and introducing others. Mark's passion predictions provide the basis for Luke's treatment, but Luke goes beyond them by speaking not only of the suffering of the Son of Man but also of the *messiah*. Luke introduces this theme when the risen Jesus appears to two disciples on the way to Emmaus. Still not knowing who he is, they tell him about their disappointment that Jesus, who they now believe dead, had not redeemed Israel as they expected. In response he tells them,

> "Oh, how foolish you are, and how slow of heart to believe all that the

78. See 22:32. In 10:18-20, Luke anticipates Satan's defeat when Jesus says to the disciples, "I watched Satan fall from heaven like a flash of lightening," and gives them authority "over all the power of the enemy."
79. Compare Mark 14:27-28 and Luke 22:24-34 and Mark 14:48-50 and Luke 22:52-53. Luke had already omitted Peter's rebuking Jesus after the first passion prediction. Compare Mark 8:27-33 and Luke 9:18-22. For other examples of Jesus' concern for those around him in Luke's passion, see 22:15, 23:28, and 23:43. There is another example of Jesus' concern—a very striking one—in a group of early manuscripts of the Gospel of Luke: "Father, forgive them; for they do not know what they are doing." See n. 74.

> prophets have declared! Was it not necessary that the Messiah should suffer these things and then enter into his glory?" Then beginning with Moses and all the prophets, he interpreted to them the things about himself in all the scriptures. (24:25–27)

Luke includes similar language in his account of Jesus' appearance to the eleven disciples and their companions:

> Then he said to them, "These are my words that I spoke to you while I was still with you—that everything written about me in the law of Moses, the prophets, and the psalms must be fulfilled." Then he opened their minds to understand the scriptures, and he said to them, "Thus it is written, that the Messiah is to suffer and to rise from the dead on the third day, and that repentance and forgiveness of sins is to be proclaimed in his name to all nations, beginning from Jerusalem. (24:44–47)

With these words, Jesus sums up his teaching with reference to the necessity of the messiah's suffering and rising. In the summation, however, Luke clearly points ahead, by adding another element to what Scripture predicts: the proclamation of repentance and forgiveness of sins, which is precisely the story Luke tells in Acts.[80] So, like Mark, Luke looks beyond the predictions of the passion and resurrection. His concern is with the disciples' mission "to be . . . witnesses in Jerusalem, in all Judea and Samaria, and to the ends of the earth."[81]

Themes of the passion narrative permeate all three of the Synoptic Gospels. Some are common; others are unique. Engaging their passions requires moving back and forth between the common story and the ways each evangelist tells it. All three were concerned with more than recounting what happened, however, so that reading them requires attention to the way they tell the story to make it gospel.

80. See especially the speeches in Acts 2–8.

81. Acts 1:8. The resurrected Jesus dismisses the disciples' concern with restoring the kingdom in 1:6–7.

For Further Reading

Brown, Raymond E. *The Death of the Messiah: From Gethsemane to the Grave.* 2 vols. New York: Doubleday, 1994. This is an encyclopedic commentary on the passion narratives of all four Gospels. Though much of Brown's attention concerns reconstructing a historical account of the death of Jesus, he is also attuned to the literary and theological concerns of the evangelists.

Crossan, John Dominic. *Who Killed Jesus?* New York: HarperCollins, 1995. Written in part as a response to *The Death of the Messiah,* this book offers a very different assessment of the historical interests of the evangelists. One of its major concerns is "the Roots of Anti-Semitism in the Gospel Story of the Death of Jesus." Crossan also rehearses his arguments for dating the Gospel of Peter *before* the canonical Gospels.

Matera, Frank J. *Passion Narratives and Gospel Theologies: Interpreting the Synoptics Through Their Passion Stories.* Eugene, OR: Wipf & Stock, 2001. A reprint of an edition published by Paulist Press in 1986, this book offers overviews of the passion in each of the Synoptic Gospels followed by detailed commentaries and studies of the theological themes Matera identifies in them. It reflects a traditional approach.

Williams, Rowan. *Christ on Trial: How the Gospels Unsettles Our Judgment.* 2nd ed. Grand Rapids, MI: Eerdmans, 2003. Williams, the former Archbishop of Canterbury, reflects on the passion narratives of each of the four canonical Gospels, bringing to bear his deep theological insights and ethical concerns.

Appendix

An Outline of the Passion in the Synoptic Gospels:

1. The Plan to Kill Jesus MMkL
2. The Anointing at Bethany MMk (L has a similar story earlier)
3. Judas's Betrayal MMkL
4. The Passover Meal
    a. Preparation for the Passover MMkL
    b. Jesus Predicts His Betrayal MMkL (L reorders the story)
    c. The Bread and Wine MMkL
    d. Precedence among the Disciples L (placed earlier in MMk)
    e. Peter's Denial Predicted MMkL
    f. The Need for Swords L
5. Gethsemane
    a. The Prayer MMkL (L differs from MM)
    b. The Arrest MMkL (M and L differ from Mark)
6. Jesus before the High Priest and Council MMkL
    a. Peter's Denial MMkL (L reorders the story)
7. Jesus Delivered to Pilate MMkL
8. The Death of Judas M
9. Trial before Pilate MMkL (L reorders the story)
10. Jesus before Herod L
11. Pilate and Herod Declare Jesus Innocent L
12. Jesus or Barabbas MMkL (L reorders the story)
13. Pilate Delivers Jesus to be Crucified MMkL
14. Jesus Mocked by the Soldiers MMk
15. Carrying the Cross MMkL

16. The Crucifixion MMkL
17. Jesus Derided on the Cross MMkL
18. The Two Thieves MMkL
19. Jesus' Last Words and Death MMkL
    a. My God, my God MMk
    b. Father, into your hands L
20. The Burial MMkL
21. The Guard at the Tomb M

3

It Is Accomplished!

The Passion in the Gospel of John

David Rensberger

Why John? That is, why a separate chapter on the passion in the Gospel of John? The answer lies not only in the fact that its passion narrative differs from the passions in the Synoptic Gospels (Matthew, Mark, and Luke), but also in the differences one finds throughout this Gospel. John, in fact, has relatively few of the stories and teachings found in the Synoptic Gospels—and much that they do not contain. Both John's content and its basic nature are unlike those of the other New Testament Gospels. We must begin with these broad differences before we can look at the Passion Narrative in John.[1]

1. Although, like many other modern scholars, I do not believe that the apostle John personally wrote this Gospel, I will continue, for simplicity's sake, to speak of "John" in reference to the book itself.

A Different Book

The differences in John's content are many. For instance, John narrates only seven miracles during Jesus' lifetime, but they tend to be of the most spectacular kind, such as changing water into wine, feeding the multitude, walking on water, and raising Lazarus from the dead. Of the most common type of miracle in the Synoptics, casting out a demon, there is not one in John. In addition, several significant people appear only in John: the disciple Nathanael, Nicodemus, the Samaritan woman. There are also differences in arrangement. Jesus "cleanses" the temple early in his public ministry in John (ch. 2), instead of shortly before his crucifixion as in the Synoptics. Geography is different, too: in John, most of Jesus' ministry takes place, not in Galilee, but in Jerusalem, which he visits several times.

Most importantly, however, how and what Jesus teaches is strikingly different in John's Gospel. In the Synoptics, Jesus speaks in parables and short sayings about the kingdom of God. There are no parables in John, and "kingdom of God" occurs in only one place (3:3-5). Instead, Jesus engages in long monologues and disputes that center on himself and his relation to God. The language used in these speeches is indistinguishable from the style of the Gospel's author, who uses expressions that are not common in the other Gospels—or anywhere else in the New Testament (apart from the closely related Letters of John). In chapter 3, for instance, it is difficult to tell where Jesus' words end and the narrator's comments begin.

A Different Kind of Book

From early days, Christian interpreters have recognized that John is also a different *kind* of book from the other Gospels. In the late-second century C.E., Clement of Alexandria, a leading Christian theologian and teacher, gave some account of the origins of the New Testament writings. This writing is lost, but was cited in the early-fourth century by Eusebius, who wrote the first known church history. Some of Clement's information is quite dubious, though it reflects conceptions about the earliest days of Christianity that were widely held in his day. Clement regarded John as the last of the New Testament Gospels to be written, and claimed that it came into being because John realized that the existing Gospels contained the "bodily" data, and so, being urged on by his friends and possessed by the Spirit, he created a "spiritual gospel."[2]

Thus careful readers of the Bible have always been aware that John is unlike the Synoptics. Elsewhere, Eusebius himself says only that John's Gospel differs from the Synoptics because it contains an account of Jesus' earlier activity, before John the Baptist was imprisoned;[3] but this does not square at all with the actual material in the Gospels. The differences between John and the others go deeper than just content and sequence. Jesus' language, resembling that of the Gospel's writer, is at variance in many ways with his language in the Synoptics. This difference goes hand in hand with the difference in theme, the focus on Jesus' relationship with God rather than on the kingdom and the way of life appropriate to it.

John's basic theme is stated at the end of chapter 20: "These things have been written so that you may believe that Jesus is the Messiah, the Son of God, and so that by believing you may have life in his name" (v. 31).[4] It is put more metaphorically at the book's beginning: "The true light that enlightens every human being was coming into the world. He was in the world, and the world came into existence through him, yet the world did not recognize him. . . . But to all who

2. Eusebius, *Church History*, 6.14.1-7.
3. Ibid., 3.24.7-13.
4. Scripture translations are my own.

did receive him—to those who believed in his name—he gave power to become children of God" (1:9-10, 12). John asserts that God sent into the world this Being, who was one with God and yet became entirely human, in order to represent God (in multiple senses) and to give divine life, the life of eternity, to those who accepted this mission. Ironically, however, when the one who made the world, the entire universe, entered it in this unique way, the world—the *human* world—did not recognize or accept him.

A Different Kind of Reading

Both Jesus' representation of God and the irony of his reception condition the narrative of John in fundamental ways, and therefore condition how it must be read.

Jesus, as representing God, is a *symbol* of God, that is, an entity that makes a transcendent reality present and available to people in a multifaceted subject-to-subject relationship.[5] Because this symbolism is at the core of its message, the Gospel of John offers a thoroughly symbolic narrative. Both the narrator and Jesus himself use common terms such as light, water, and bread as symbols for what he is and does (for example, 1:3-9; 3:19-21; 4:10-14; 6:32-35, 48-58; 8:12; 12:35-36). Jesus' actions are spoken of as "signs," meaning not what are ordinarily called "signs" today but precisely symbols.[6] The pervasive presence of this symbolism is intimately connected to what this gospel has to say.

The failure of many of the people with whom Jesus interacts to interpret the symbols correctly, to recognize his identity and the significance of his coming, produces irony, that is, a situation in which the reader of the story has information unknown to some of

5. Sandra M. Schneiders, *Written That You May Believe: Encountering Jesus in the Fourth Gospel*, 2nd ed. (New York: Crossroad, 2003), 65–69.
6. Ibid., 65–66.

its characters.[7] John 7 and 8, for instance, are full of rather frustrating dialogues in which Jesus and his hearers seem to be talking past one another with regard to who he is, where he is from, and where he will go. Often enough, the other speakers make statements that betray their ignorance, and yet ironically are, on a deeper level, truer than they know: "Will he kill himself—since he's saying, 'Where I am going you cannot come'?" (8:22; and yet Jesus does command his own death, as he says, "I have power to lay [my life] down, and I have power to take it again" [10:18]). Jesus comes into the world to bring it eternal life; he is not recognized and is widely rejected; as a result, he is crucified—and *as a result of his death* the world receives life. This is ironic, and thus irony is also fundamental to John's message.

John's symbolism may be connected to what Clement of Alexandria meant by its "spiritual" quality; and modern and postmodern readers may be intrigued by Johannine irony. Along with John's differences from the Synoptics in content, this Gospel's essentially symbolic and ironic nature shows us how to read the book. A simple quest for "the facts" is liable to be disappointed, and worse yet, is liable to keep us from receiving what John wants to offer us. John is about truth: "If you remain in my word, you are truly my disciples; and you will know the truth, and the truth will set you free" (8:31-32). Indeed, says Jesus, "I am the way, and truth, and life" (14:6). "Truth" here means reality, divine reality, the reality that is the basis for all real, authentic, and therefore free living. *Truth in this sense is not identical with facts.* John communicates truth by means of symbols (which are facts put to a purpose beyond their mere existence) and irony (in which facts are disputed or unknown). As distant as it often seems from Jesus as he appears in the Synoptic Gospels, the Gospel of John uses the same method to make its point

7. Paul D. Duke, *Irony in the Fourth Gospel* (Atlanta: John Knox, 1985); Gail R. O'Day, *Revelation in the Fourth Gospel: Narrative Mode and Theological Claim* (Philadelphia: Fortress Press, 1986).

as Jesus does in his parables: both tell stories that have a variety of connections to "the facts," but point insistently toward what their tellers consider to be true.

This kind of book requires a different sort of reading from what most of us are used to. A book that is intrinsically symbolic may be unfamiliar reading, both for people inside the Christian tradition and for those outside, if both have accepted the premise that truth can only be presented by a literal recounting of the facts. We are taught to read in search of those facts. When we read fiction—even grand, myth-making fiction like *The Lord of the Rings*—we do so for entertainment, seldom to seek larger truths (and we hardly read poetry at all anymore). John's presentation of Jesus is not at all like a modern biography or documentary, yet it is not really what we think of as "fiction" either. It is grounded in real traditions about Jesus, whether they reached the Gospel's author through contact with the Synoptics or through oral channels independent of them.[8] In either case, the traditions went through a process of interpretation in particular contexts for particular purposes (as is also true of the Synoptics). It is possible to root around in John for evidence of those original traditions, in search of information about Jesus not found in the other Gospels; but this is a much more precarious task than with the Synoptics, and its results will always be slender. It also misses John's point. It is precisely the *interpretation* that the author wants us to grasp, or at least to wrestle with. This Gospel's relation to Jesus is something like that of *Citizen Kane* to William Randolph Hearst, or better yet, like that of *A Beautiful Mind* to John Nash. You can learn

8. Barnabas Lindars, *The Gospel of John*, New Century Bible Commentary (Grand Rapids, MI: Eerdmans, 1972), 46–54; D. Moody Smith, *John*, Abingdon New Testament Commentaries (Nashville: Abingdon, 1999), 27–33; George R. Beasley-Murray, *John*, Word Biblical Commentary 36 (Waco, TX: Word Books, 1987), xxxv–liii.

something about those people from those films; but you can learn much, much else as well.

As we approach the treatment of the passion narrative in the Gospel of John, we have to keep all these factors in mind: the different content of John's story and the different arrangement of the content; the irony produced by Jesus' unique mission and the response to it; the symbolic nature of that mission and of John's story about it; and this Gospel's presentation of truth by means other than mere reporting of facts. Two points must be kept in mind, to avoid an overreaction to these factors. First, I do not mean that we can dispense with the "real," historical Jesus, but that *in the Johannine view*, knowing the obvious facts about him is only the beginning of understanding his reality. Second, by "symbolic" I do not mean "merely symbolic." Though symbols begin as facts (light, water, bread), their use as symbols elevates their reality rather than lessening it. A true symbol is never "mere."

Differences in John's Passion Narrative

To begin with the content, we may ask how John's passion narrative is differently arranged from that of the Synoptics, and what this narrative may add to or subtract from theirs. If we begin with Jesus' (final) entry into Jerusalem, and compare John 12–19 with Mark 11–14, we find most obviously that John places Jesus' action in the temple much earlier in the narrative than Mark (John 2:13-22; Mark 11:15-19). In John 12, the anointing in Bethany takes place *before* the entry into Jerusalem, whereas Mark puts it three chapters later. The anointing scene in John is followed by a public speech (12:23-36) that partly resembles the agony in Gethsemane in Mark 14. John thus seems to have a pattern of moving passion narrative material to earlier locations in the story, even within the passion narrative itself.

The events of John's passion narrative themselves also show some unique features, especially in the meal (ch. 13–17). John does actually call it a "supper" or "dinner," but it is not a "last supper," since, unlike the Synoptics, John has not portrayed Jesus eating meals with his followers and others. It is also not called a Passover meal. (In John, the preparations for Passover take place on Friday, and Jesus is condemned to death at the hour when the Passover lambs were being slaughtered [John 18:28; 19:14-16, 31].) Most remarkably, there is no inauguration of the Eucharist, no "Lord's Supper." Instead, Jesus washes his disciples' feet, an event not found anywhere in the Synoptics. After the foot washing and the identification and departure of Judas, Jesus begins a long series of dialogues and monologues with his disciples (13:31–16:33), unlike anything earlier in John, and unlike anything in the Synoptics, though a number of the sayings can be paralleled there. This teaching is followed in chapter 17 by a long prayer for unity among the believers.

There are fewer differences between John and the Synoptics in the trial and crucifixion scenes (ch. 18–19). The most notable change is that the Gospel writer cannot resist having Jesus give speeches—to those who arrest him, to the high priest, to Pilate, and even, on the cross, to his mother and "the disciple whom he loved." These are all brief (a sentence or two at a time), but unique to John—and quite in contrast to Mark, which emphasizes Jesus' silence (14:60-61; 15:1-4). In all the speeches, we have the distinct impression that it is Jesus who is in charge, practically directing his own arrest and its consequences. His last word, rather than the inarticulate cry of Mark and Matthew or Luke's "Father, into your hands I commend my spirit," seems a cry of triumph: *tetelestai*, "It is accomplished!"

The passion narrative in John thus resembles the rest of the Gospel in its relationship to the Synoptics. It shows connections with similar or identical traditions, but these are reshaped and refocused and often given ironic or symbolic coloring; and many scenes are simply unique to John. After considering one particular instance of it, we will look at what all this reshaping and supplementing of the traditions may tell us about John's interpretation of the passion narrative.

All of the New Testament passion narratives shift blame for the death of Jesus to some extent from the Roman governor Pontius Pilate, whose responsibility it truly was, to the Jewish leaders in Jerusalem (see, for instance, Matt. 27:24-25; Luke 23:1-25). The effect of this in helping to create and sustain violent anti-Judaism among Christians over the centuries has been very grievous.[9] John actually does less of this than Matthew and Luke, however. There are Roman soldiers present at Jesus' arrest, for instance, a realistic feature found only in John. As for Pilate, John does not let him off the hook. Unlike the good-hearted but easily manipulated figure of the Synoptics, here we find a hard-nosed colonial governor maneuvering the indigenous leadership into betraying their hopes for liberation (see further below).

In one important respect, however, John increases the potential for anti-Judaism. Unlike the Synoptics, John's passion narrative constantly refers to "the Jews" as the instigators of Jesus' arrest and trial, with whom Pilate cooperates for his own purposes. The significance of this can be seen if we start with John 18:36: "Jesus replied [to Pilate], 'My reign does not belong to this world. If my reign did belong to this world, my attendants[10] would fight so that I would not be handed over to the Jews.'" But—aren't Jesus and his "attendants" Jews? Careful study shows that when "the Jews" are

9. Craig A. Evans and Donald A. Hagner, ed., *Anti-Semitism and Early Christianity: Issues of Polemic and Faith* (Minneapolis: Fortress Press, 1993).

10. Here the author uses the same term for a servant or assistant that he has been applying to the temple police, the only place in the Gospels where this word is used for Jesus' followers. Jesus speaks as a true king with a retinue—ironically made up of fishermen rather courtiers.

spoken of in John as distinct from Jesus and his disciples and hostile to them, the reference is not to Jewish people as such but specifically to *religious authorities*. This likely reflects circumstances long after the time of Jesus, when the Christian community, still largely of Jewish origin, was undergoing a bitter and emotionally wrenching separation from still-developing synagogue Judaism, in the difficult years after the Jewish revolt against Rome came to a disastrous end in 70 C.E.

Thus one reason the Gospel of John can refrain from blaming "the Jews" for Jesus' crucifixion is that it has already shown the Jewish religious authorities condemning him—and Jesus condemning them—at many earlier points in the story (for instance, 8:31-59; 10:31-39). Such texts, read as Holy Scripture down through the centuries and applied to the Jewish people as a whole, have also contributed terribly to Christian prejudice against Jews and persecution of them.[11] They are one more reason John cannot be read simply as presenting "the facts" about Jesus and his mission.

The Passion Narrative within the Fourth Gospel

We have seen this writer's practice of taking material that belongs in the passion narrative and redistributing it to earlier points in the Gospel. This practice may include the peculiar discourse about "eating the flesh of the Son of Man and drinking his blood" in 6:52-58, which is reminiscent of the language used in the Synoptics when Jesus inaugurates the Eucharist at the Last Supper. John, then, seems to move this topic from the supper to this earlier location, and

11. David Rensberger, "Anti-Judaism and the Gospel of John," in *Anti-Judaism and the Gospels*, ed. William R. Farmer (Harrisburg, PA: Trinity Press International, 1999), 120–57; Robert Kysar, "Anti-Semitism and the Gospel of John," in *Anti-Semitism and Early Christianity*, 113–27; David Granskou, "Anti-Judaism in the Passion Accounts of the Fourth Gospel," in *Anti-Judaism in Early Christianity*, Studies in Christianity and Judaism 2, eds. Peter Richardson and David Granskou (Waterloo, Ontario: Wilfrid Laurier University Press, 1986), 1:201–16.

to highlight it by the mention of "abiding," which cross-references the same language during the last meal (to be discussed below).

Very likely the writer of John expected its first hearers (the gospels and other writings were read aloud in early Christian assemblies, not studied as books in private) to have some familiarity with the traditions about Jesus, especially those in the passion narrative, whether from hearing other gospels read or from oral tradition, which by no means died out when the gospels began to be written. They would recognize that the "cleansing" of the temple belonged to the events leading to Jesus' crucifixion. The narrator even helps them out, asserting that Jesus "was talking about the temple of his body" in the context of the temple action, and that his disciples remembered this when he was raised from the dead (2:19-22). Similarly they would realize that John 12:27-28 belonged to Jesus' desperate last hour before his arrest, not to the time before his entry into Jerusalem. The sayings there are surrounded by ones about death and life, and about Jesus being lifted up from the earth, where once again the helpful narrator pops in with, "Now, he said this by way of indicating what sort of death he was going to die." The writer wanted the hearers/readers to connect these passages to Jesus' passion; by redistributing passion narrative material in this way, he placed the passion before them from early on in the Gospel.

The whole series of passion-related sayings in John 12 begins with Jesus saying, "The hour has come that the Son of Man may be glorified" (12:23). These two concepts, the "hour" of Jesus and his glorification, are used frequently in this Gospel (and no other) to refer to Jesus' crucifixion, resurrection, and exaltation, considered together as one single moment of "glorification" (see, for instance, 2:4; 7:6-8, 30, 39; 12:16; and throughout the Last Supper narrative).

We can study the complex irony of this idea of Jesus' "glorification" in John 11:4 and its aftermath. Jesus says that Lazarus's illness "is not destined for death but for the glory of God, so that the Son of God may be glorified through it." Lazarus does die, but Jesus travels to his hometown and eventually calls him forth from his tomb (11:5-44). Thus God is glorified by the raising of Lazarus. After the miracle, however, the religious leaders meet to determine what to do about Jesus. The high priest declares that "it is better for you that one person die for the people and the whole nation not be destroyed." Once more the helpful narrator: "Now, he did not say this on his own"; rather, as high priest he was (unknowingly, ironically) prophesying Jesus' coming death, not only for the Jewish nation, "but to gather the scattered children of God into one" (11:47-52). Thus the Son of God is glorified first by giving life to Lazarus, but then also because this leads to his own crucifixion and life-giving death. The giving of life leads to death, and this death leads to life for all "the scattered children of God," which is also "for the glory of God."

It was the world's failure to see the glory of the incarnate Word (John 1:9-14) that led to his climactic glorification on the cross and in the resurrection. This is John's understanding of the meaning of Jesus' passion: God's purposes will not be thwarted, even if God has to use the very means of their thwarting to accomplish them. The Word *will* bring life to the world, even if it must be through death at the world's own hands. It is because of this central narrative thread that the Gospel writer distributes elements of the passion narrative throughout the story.

Jesus Prepares His Disciples for His Departure

The long series of dialogues and monologues in chapters 13–16, set during Jesus' last meal with his disciples, constitutes the one major instance of his teaching them in John. At first, individual disciples ask Jesus questions; but chapters 15–16 are practically one long speech, and chapter 17 consists entirely of Jesus praying for unity among believers. The purpose of these "farewell discourses" is to teach what life would be like for the believers after Jesus' departure, his "glorification," not only for his immediate disciples but also for the church of subsequent generations (17:20). In Johannine thinking, the death of Jesus left a gap in divine presence in the world. The farewell discourses suggest several ways in which this gap would be filled.

For one thing, Jesus' death leaves room for his disciples themselves to continue his work of making God known. "The one who believes in me will also do the works that I do, and will do even greater ones" (14:12). The revelatory "works" of Jesus are his compassionate and life-giving "signs": as believers continue to do such works, they too make God known. Note also the "new commandment" only a few verses earlier: "love one another" (13:34–35; also 15:12–17). Concrete acts of mutual love (which in the Bible is at least as much a matter of action as of feeling) will be how people recognize believers as Jesus' disciples. Continuing Jesus' work of love, they continue to make God known.

Secondly, the coming of the Holy Spirit fills the gap left by Jesus' death. John (uniquely in early Christian literature) uses the Greek term *paraklētos* and the title "Spirit of Truth" for the Holy Spirit (14:15–17, 26; 15:26; 16:7–15). *Paraklētos* (sometimes written "Paraclete" in English) means a sponsor or patron, an intercessor or mediator, an "advocate" or "counselor" in court or elsewhere. In chapter 16, the Spirit functions as a kind of defense attorney for the believing community endangered by the world. But there and in chapter 14, the Spirit also teaches them, recalling Jesus' words but leading them into further truth as well. (Perhaps the Gospel of John intends to present this further truth.) Much that is said of the Spirit in these passages is said of Jesus elsewhere in the Gospel, so that not only is the Spirit a successor to Jesus, but Jesus himself in a sense "returns" in the Paraclete.[12]

A third response to Jesus' absence is the appeal to "abide" in him in 15:1-17. This use of the verb *menō* is again unique to the Johannine writings, not only in the New Testament but in Greek religious literature in general. The verb implies inhabiting a place and remaining there over time, hence "abiding" or "dwelling" or "staying." Abiding, or simply *being*, in one another is the fundamental term used to describe the spiritual relationship among disciples, Jesus, and God in John, especially in chapters 14–17.[13] The connotation of *persistence* that *menō* has suggests that abiding means remaining in relationship with Jesus, remaining oriented toward him and toward belief in him, despite all inducements to the contrary. This language also has what might be called "mystical" implications, indicating a kind of deeply intimate being-present-to another, though there are no instructions for attaining this state. What is called for in Jesus' absence is persisting in intimate relationship with him, a ceaseless and resolute orientation toward him.

Thus the Gospel of John uses the early part of the passion narrative to deal with a major consequence of Jesus' passion. Believers, across multiple generations, continue to experience divine presence through the work of the Paraclete and through persevering in profound mutual relationship with Jesus himself, as they keep his commandment of love. In these ways, Jesus "returns" long before a second coming, and his followers become his continuing presence in the world. They are enabled to assume this role—ironically, paradoxically—by Jesus' departure on the cross.

12. Craig S. Keener, *The Gospel of John: A Commentary* (Peabody, MA: Hendrickson, 2003), 2:953–71.
13. David Rensberger, "Spirituality and Christology in Johannine Sectarianism," in *Word, Theology, and Community in John*, ed. John Painter, Alan Culpepper, and Fernando Segovia (St. Louis: Chalice, 2002), 178–79.

Jesus' Arrest, Trial, and Crucifixion

This part of John's passion narrative features events mostly similar to the Synoptics, but also employs the irony and symbolism typical of John and gives new shape and focus to the traditional material. There are careful restructurings, especially in the trial scene; many more words of Jesus; and a few additional characters and incidents. We can't analyze each scene in detail, of course, but only look at some highlights.

Even as he is taken into custody, interrogated, and crucified, Jesus remains remarkably in command. This is evident already at his arrest (John 18:1-9). When the Roman soldiers and Jewish officials appear, Jesus takes the initiative. "For whom are you looking?" "Jesus of Nazareth." "I am he." At this they all collapse to the ground, and Jesus has to repeat the exchange with them. The key to this bizarre scene is Jesus' words "I am he." Here and elsewhere in John (for example, 4:26; 8:24, 58; 13:19), they reflect the divine Name in the Hebrew Scriptures (Exod. 3:14; also passages in Isaiah such as 43:10-11; 51:12; 52:6). Jesus' declaration is a *theophany*, a divine revelation, and it overwhelms the dozens of armed men sent to arrest him. We see Jesus already manifesting his glory, his divine identity, as his passion begins. John's passion narrative will therefore be ironic; how else can the "I am," the one through whom life itself came into being (John 1:3-4), be put to death? The irony will appear in the frequent misunderstanding of Jesus' words. Because the one being crucified is the symbol of God, there will be symbolism throughout the passion narrative as well, starting with "I am he," the name that also symbolizes the deity.

In view of this, it is perhaps surprising that Jesus' trial before the Roman governor focuses on his kingship. "Are you the King of the Jews?" says Pilate. "My reign does not belong to this world." "You are a king, then?" "You call me a king." The Roman soldiers crown Jesus with thorns, robe him in purple, and mockingly hail him as "King of the Jews." Pilate brings him out before the Jewish leaders in that condition, and, seeing their national hopes parodied like this, they renounce them and call for his crucifixion. "Shall I crucify your king?" "We have no king but Caesar!" (John 18:33-37; 19:1-6, 13-15). This portrayal of Pilate is not a sympathetic one. He cares nothing about God's people, or about Jesus' life or death, and utterly fails to understand him. He responds to John's central concern by asking "What is truth?" but does not wait for the answer (18:38). The insistently political coloring of Jesus' trial (not unrealistic given what is known of Jesus' mission, Jewish life under Roman imperialism, and Pilate's character) makes it clear that divine revelation and politics are not mutually exclusive for this Gospel.[14] Jesus' reign may not belong to this world, but it is *in* this world, and it commands an allegiance that challenges both emperors and revolutionaries. To abide in the "I Am," therefore, is to persist in a community that is resistant to things as they are and yields allegiance to the sovereign who, without violence, accomplished his mission on an empire's cross. Christians in the early centuries were persecuted, not because of their beliefs, but because their beliefs led them to transfer their allegiance from the political-religious-economic structures of the western world's greatest empire to this crucified king.

Three details of the crucifixion scene in John seem symbolic, but are mysterious enough to defy exact interpretation. Jesus entrusts his mother to the care of "the disciple whom he loved" (19:25-27), generally taken to be the apostle John, though the text does not say so. But what does this signify? Perhaps estrangement from Jesus'

14. David Rensberger, *Johannine Faith and Liberating Community* (Philadelphia: Westminster, 1988), 87–106; Warren Carter, *John and Empire: Initial Explorations* (New York: T&T Clark, 2008), 289–314.

brothers, who would naturally have had this duty (John 7:1-8); or simply the importance of loving care within the believing community.[15]

When Jesus fulfills the Scripture by saying, "I am thirsty," a sponge full of sour wine is put on some hyssop and offered to him (19:28-29). But hyssop is a small shrub, much too small and flimsy to hold a wet sponge up to a crucified man. The image is more absurd than ironic, and the absurdity has caused scholars to seek a symbolic reference.[16] Passover is one possibility, since hyssop figures in the Passover ritual (Exod. 12:21-27) and John uses other Passover imagery in the passion narrative.[17] Hyssop is also used in purification rituals involving both blood and water (Lev. 14:1-7, 49-53; Num. 19:1-9, 17-19; Ps. 51:7).

The latter connection brings us to the subsequent scene in which a soldier pierces Jesus' side, releasing a flow of blood and water. Scholars have labored mightily over the physiological likelihood of this flow; but the unrealistic hyssop makes it unlikely that physiological realism is the point here either. There may be symbolic reference to the life-giving power of Jesus' death, and/or to the sacraments and the Spirit.[18] In any case, these elements are present, not for factual realism, but to complete the symbolic image of the death of Jesus bringing purification from sin and all that keeps human beings apart from God. The hyssop, blood, and water are not meant

15. Raymond E. Brown sees more symbolic interpretations, such as Jesus' mother representing Israel's legacy coming over to the church, or, by contrast, a new Eve or a new Zion as the mother of God's new people. See Brown, *The Gospel According to John*, Anchor Bible 29–29A (Garden City, NY: Doubleday, 1966–70), 2:922–27. Many scholars find such symbolic interpretations unconvincing here and regard the dispossession of the Jewish people from their traditions and heritage as inappropriate. See, for example, Smith, *John*, 359–60; Keener, *Gospel of John*, 2:1144–45.
16. Robert L. Brawley, "An Absent Complement and Intertextuality in John 19:28-29," *Journal of Biblical Literature* 112 (1993): 433.
17. Brown, *Gospel*, 2:930; Francis J. Moloney, *The Gospel of John*, Sacra Pagina (Collegeville, MN: Liturgical Press, 1998), 504.
18. Brown, *Gospel*, 2:946–52; Moloney, *Gospel of John*, 505–506, 509; Keener, *Gospel of John*, 2:1151–54.

to be realistic. Rather, their strange unreality is meant to puzzle the hearer/reader and to point beyond the physically immediate to symbolize—that is, to make concrete and present—another reality.

The Passion and Its Meaning

Jesus' final utterance on the cross is a single Greek word, *tetelestai* (John 19:30). The traditional translation "It is finished" barely touches what it means. Jesus is not saying, "Well, that's that. I'm done for." The verb *teleō* has to do with reaching a goal, completing a task or course. Jesus' cry is positive, not negative—something more like, "It's completed! It is accomplished! The goal is achieved!" *What Jesus came to do has been done.*

Not that he simply came to die. Jesus came to bring life, light, and salvation (1:9-13; 10:10; 12:44-50), to testify to the truth, to divine reality (18:37). He came from God to make God known (1:18; 17:1-8), to give sight to the blind, but to blind those who are confident that they see (9:39-41; compare 3:17-21). He also came as the "Lamb of God" to "take away the sin of the world" (1:29). In the rituals of the Hebrew Bible, lambs are not sacrificed for sin. They are used in the Passover rituals, however, and John presents Jesus on the cross as the Passover lamb whose bones are not broken (19:36; see Exod. 12:46). The blood of the first Passover lambs was a *sign* that marked off Israelite houses and saved them from judgment (Exod. 12:13). Jesus as the Lamb of God is still also the sign, the symbol, of God. Those who see this sign and believe cross over from death to life (5:24), marking their liberation from sin (8:31-36) as the Passover lamb marked the Israelites' freedom from slavery.[19]

19. Willard M. Swartley, *John*, Believers Church Bible Commentary (Harrisonburg, VA: Herald Press, 2013), 75.

Jesus declares that his mission of bearing the presence and reality of God into the world to give it life has been accomplished on the cross. Yet it is not easy to pin down the exact mechanism by which this accomplishment takes place. (Substitutionary atonement, for instance, is not part of John's theology.) Our difficulty is due to John's portrayal of Jesus' mission as symbolic, since symbols are open to multiple interpretations. The transcendent reality that a symbol makes present "is essentially many-faceted," and so the symbol "resists translation or explanation."[20] Thus the Gospel writer does not specify precisely how Jesus accomplishes his mission to reestablish a life-giving relationship with God. And this is typical of John. This Gospel happily offers us stark contradictions: the Word was *with* God and *was* God (1:1); Jesus is both the shepherd and the gate (10:7–18). The purpose is not that we solve the puzzles, but that we live with them and among them, abiding in him. The good shepherd lays down his life for the sheep—this is as close as John comes to explaining the content of "It is accomplished!" In a symbolic, paradoxical, ironic way, life comes to the world through the death of him who incarnates the world's Creator. Any further explanation must come from our own inventiveness, not from this story itself. All that the writer asks is that we see the sign and believe.

20. Schneiders, *Written That You May Believe*, 67.

PART II

Liturgy and Music

Liturgy and music are the ways many people engage the passion. This has been so from the very beginning. In a letter to the Corinthians, for example, Paul appeals to the tradition he had received about "the Lord's Supper" and passed on to them. It included references to the bread and cup Jesus shared with the disciples "on the night he was betrayed" (1 Cor. 11:20-26). The Synoptic Gospels, written 25–30 years later, have varying versions of this tradition and set it in the context of the Passover meal Jesus ate with his disciples just before he was arrested, tried, and crucified (Matt. 26:26-30; Mark 14:22-25; and Luke 22:14-20).

As Jouette Bassler notes, Paul is also the earliest witness to hymns that reference the passion. In his letter to the Philippians he quotes one that includes the lines

> And being found in human form,
> [Christ Jesus] humbled himself
> and became obedient to the point of death—
> even death on a cross. (2:7d-8)

In a letter addressed to the emperor seeking advice on how to deal with Christians (c. 110), Pliny, the governor of the Roman province Bithynia, provides evidence for how these hymns were used. He tells

Trajan that in his investigation of the Christian sect he discovered that they gather early on a fixed day and sing hymns "to Christ as if to a god" and after dispersing gather again to eat food "of an ordinary, common kind."

The essays in this section show how richly varied Christian liturgy and music became through the centuries. Robert Atwell traces the ways the passion has been used in liturgy, focusing especially on the many liturgies of Holy Week. He shows that from very early on, liturgies involved not only word and music, but also vigils, processions, and other dramatic reenactments. He notes that by the third century, pilgrims were traveling from Europe to what was becoming the "Holy Land" to take part in the liturgies that were developing at churches in Jerusalem built over sites mentioned in the passion narratives. Over time, these Jerusalem liturgies influenced the ways Christians remembered Holy Week around the world, adapting them for local use. Atwell also shows that music was a major part of the liturgies of Holy Week, tracing the development of texts based on Scripture—the last words of Jesus, for example—that would be set again and again as musical tastes changed. He also attends to some of the hymns that are commonly sung during Lent and Holy Week. Throughout he focuses on the passion in worship.

Andrew Shenton's essay addresses some of the same questions as Atwell's, but attends more to the music, showing how texts influence music and how music affects the way we read or, more precisely, *hear* the text. Shenton also approaches the music of the passion with a view to showing how it differs from place to place and develops over time. And while he also traces the relation between liturgy and music, he turns in the latter part of his survey to the emergence of musical settings for audiences outside the church—from concert halls to stages to cinemas. His last examples are twenty-first century musical settings of the passion written by composers from around the world—and from many religious perspectives. Among them is the Buddhist composer Tan Dun, whose *Water Passion after St. Matthew* (2002) pays homage to one of Bach's great settings of the passion. This complex contemporary setting for the concert hall is orchestrated for seventeen transparent water bowls (differently pitched), stringed instruments (of both western orchestras *and* Silk Road musicians), Tibetan bells, a variety of small instruments, and stones of varying sizes. Dun includes singing styles as diverse as Tuvan overtone singing from Mongolia, Chinese opera, and Bach-influenced chorales. Shenton provides a list of recommended recordings of most of the music he discusses and gives links to the websites of modern composers, allowing readers to hear (and see) performances of these works.

Beyond the essays in this section of the book, other writers also address music of the passion. John McWilliams, for example, examines the ways Marion Anderson, Harry Belafonte, and Johnny Cash adapt the lyrics of the African-American spiritual "Were You There?" and compares the lyrics of their recordings to Thomas Jefferson's treatment of Jesus in his rewriting of the Gospels and to Walt Whitman's poem "Song of Myself." Kymberly Pinder discusses the lyrics of Christian artist and rap-composer/performer Damon Lamar Reed, placing them in the context of the language and liturgy of other holy hip-hop Theolyricists.

Liturgy and music, whether together or separate, are evocative means of engaging the passion. As Shenton observes, "It is difficult to express in words the additional depth of emotion achieved by adding music to any text, let alone a story that concerns cruelty and death and is directly related to religious beliefs." The two essays offered here and the references to music and liturgy elsewhere in the volume show the variety of ways music adds to the story, especially when set in the context of liturgy. They also show, however, that the passion inspires musical expressions well beyond the walls of churches and cathedrals—and that the music of concert halls, theaters, cinemas, and the streets is making its way into those churches and cathedrals, as it always has.

4

The Passion in Christian Liturgy

Robert Atwell

We have become so familiar with crosses displayed in churches or hung around people's necks as jewelry that we forget that originally the cross was an object of horror. For early Christians it brought to mind the sight of a tortured man in his death throes. The apostle Paul knew just how much the preaching of a crucified Savior was scandalous to the Jews and stupidity to the Greeks. Today, familiarity has bred in us a measure of indifference and we no longer see the cross for what it is. We need to imagine a modern equivalent to recapture that original sense of shock in the ancient world, such as a criminal on death row dying in an electric chair or a prisoner of war being beaten to death, and then declare, *This* is my Savior.

Crucifixion was a terrible reality that confronted people on an almost daily basis in first-century Palestine because it was part of the machinery of repression of the Roman state. You could not have traveled around the country for very long without coming across pitiful processions of prisoners, dragging crossbars to the places of execution. It was a painful and ignominious form of punishment, reserved for rebellious slaves and criminals. Contrary to the majority of paintings depicting the crucifixion, the crosses to which the naked victims were nailed were in fact only about seven feet tall. At that height it was easy for passers-by to mock the helpless victims who were hanging just above their heads. The Romans thought of every form of degradation.

The consensus among biblical commentators is that the passion narratives—the accounts of Jesus' last supper with his disciples, his betrayal, arrest, trial, and subsequent crucifixion—were the first parts of the Gospels to be written down. Some scholars go further and suggest that these narratives existed independently from quite an early date before finding their way into their present form of the Gospels. They are called passion narratives because they record God's passionate love revealed in the crucifixion of Jesus, the Latin root of the word *passio* meaning "suffering."

It is difficult to overstate the importance of the passion narratives in Christian thinking, but no matter how early a date is assigned to their emergence as written texts, what is incontrovertible is that they appeared later than that other commemoration of the saving death of Christ: the Eucharist. "Do this in remembrance of me," said Jesus, and the first Christians were faithful to his command. They remembered their Savior in this way because they believed as St. Paul declared when writing to the church in Corinth, "As often as you eat this bread and drink the cup, you proclaim the Lord's death until he comes" (1 Cor. 11:26). In Christian worship the Eucharist (a Greek word meaning "thanksgiving"), or the "breaking of bread" as it is called in the New Testament, has always been poised between two worlds. It is seen as both a memorial of the death of Christ and an anticipation of his future return in glory. It is described as an *anamnesis*, meaning "memorial."[1] In all probability, Christians used and understood this term much in the way that first-century Jews spoke of the Passover as a "memorial" of God's saving action in rescuing them from slavery in Egypt. It was believed that an event in the past could be made effective here and now in the present. For Christians, therefore, the eucharistic memorial was not merely a calling to mind of the significance of a historical event, but the effectual proclamation of the totality of God's reconciling action in Jesus Christ.

The oldest celebration of the Eucharist (at least in some places and at least for a few decades) took the form of an actual meal, perhaps modeled on the Jewish Sabbath meal.[2] Gradually, however, the meal disappeared and the distinctive shape of the eucharistic celebration as we would recognize it today emerged, held not in the evening as part of the Jewish Sabbath but on a Sunday morning, "the first day of the week," in commemoration of Jesus' resurrection. Exactly when and how and why this transition happened is still a matter of conjecture, but in large part it reflects the movement of the primitive Christian church away from its Jewish roots in Palestine and its engagement with the wider Hellenistic world.

It is also uncertain when Christians first began to make an annual, as opposed to a weekly, memorial of the death and resurrection of Christ. The fact that the dating of Easter was fixed according to the Jewish (lunar) calendar whereas every other Christian feast depends on the solar calendar suggests that, like Sunday, it was custom observed from apostolic days. For the first three centuries

1. 1 Cor. 11:24; Luke 22:19.
2. See Paul Bradshaw, *The Search for the Origins of Christian Worship*, 2nd ed. (Notre Dame, IN: University of Notre Dame Press, 2002).

there was no uniformity in the observance of Easter, but increasingly in the West, and especially in Rome, it became the tradition that Easter should always be celebrated on a Sunday, and gradually the Roman custom prevailed.

The English word *paschal* comes from the Greek word for Easter, *pascha*, which in turn derives indirectly from *Pesach*, the Hebrew word for "Passover." From at least the second century, Pascha was observed with an all-night vigil, followed by a celebration of the Eucharist at cockcrow. It was a single great festival that celebrated both the passion and the resurrection of Christ all in one. By the time of Tertullian (c. 160–225) this annual liturgy also included the baptism of candidates, with baptism being understood as a mystical sharing in the death and resurrection of Christ (Rom. 6:4).[3] Initially all the great themes of redemption were included in this one great Easter liturgy, but with the development of the liturgical year, after the reign of Constantine (d. 337), the first Christian emperor, the celebration of the Pascha began to differentiate, admittedly in a rather haphazard sort of way, into a series of commemorations. Gradually the structure of Holy Week and Easter services that we know today emerged as a coherent liturgical presentation of the events of the last week of Jesus' life.

Over the centuries the pattern of Holy Week has remained remarkably constant, though individual customs and observances have varied. Those who participate in the whole sequence of services, beginning with the triumphal entry of Jesus into Jerusalem on Palm Sunday, then progressing through the commemoration of the Last Supper and foot-washing on Maundy Thursday, the crucifixion on Good Friday, and climaxing with the empty tomb and resurrection on Easter Day, find themselves sharing in a profound way in Christ's

3. Tertullian, *de Baptismo*, 19.

self-offering. From the outset the liturgy was designed to foster in the worshipper a spirituality of *imitatio Christi*, which is uniquely transformative. We turn now to see how this great liturgical drama is constructed.[4]

Palm Sunday

Many of the observances of Holy Week and Easter have their origin in Jerusalem. The procession of palms, for example, was already being observed in Jerusalem in the fourth century, as attested by Egeria. Egeria was an educated woman from Gaul who around 381 went on an extended pilgrimage to Jerusalem. Her travel diary survived and provides extraordinary insight into the pattern of early Christian devotion. It is from Egeria that we learn that a procession from the summit of the Mount of Olives into the city took place during the afternoon of Palm Sunday. All those sharing in the celebration, including children, carried branches of palm or olive.[5] This custom was imitated first in Spain in the fifth century; in 709, in England, St. Aldhelm (639–709) mentions the singing of Hosannas; and finally in the twelfth century the custom was adopted in Rome itself.[6] Traditionally, the procession began at some place outside the main church to permit a dramatic commemoration of Jesus' triumphal entry, with the clergy wearing vestments of passion red—a deep blood-red color—which were often embroidered with symbols of the passion.

It is a truism of church history that in the early centuries the secular buildings that Christians borrowed for their services shaped their

4. For further reading, see Kenneth Stephenson, *Jerusalem Revisited: The Liturgical Meaning of Holy Week* (Washington, DC: Pastoral Press, 1988), and Paul Bradshaw and Lawrence Hoffman, *Passover and Easter: Their Origin & History to Modern Times* (Notre Dame, IN: University of Notre Dame Press, 1999).
5. *Egeria's Travels 31*, trans. John Wilkinson (Warminster, England: Aris & Phillips, 1999).
6. Aldhelm, *de Laud. Virg.*, PL 89.103.

worship, but thereafter it was the liturgy of the church that shaped its sacred buildings. Nowhere is this clearer than in the architecture of the English cathedrals of the "old foundation" (that is, those that were not monastic foundations). During the medieval period, for example, the procession of palms became increasingly elaborate. In obedience to a rubric in the Sarum Rite, which stipulated that on Palm Sunday there should be "seven boys in an elevated position" to sing the entrance antiphon "Hosanna to the Son of David," galleries were constructed at the west end of cathedrals to accommodate the *pueri hebraeorum*. If permanent structures could not be afforded, temporary wooden ones were assembled instead. At Exeter Cathedral a handsome stone singing gallery was constructed high on the north side of the nave, and at the west front of Wells, with its gallery inside, holes were cut at different levels: lower for the boys, higher for the singing men, so they could more easily project their voices to the assembled ranks of worshippers gathered outside on the cathedral green. There were even secret holes behind the statues of the angels from which trumpeters could sound their instruments. The performance of the liturgy was energized by the conviction that the message of the passion had to be projected into the world for its salvation. Liturgy had a missionary task.

The ceremony of the palms is followed by the reading or singing of the passion narrative in which the whole story of the week is anticipated. Now, as then, this is often performed dramatically, with different voices for the various characters, including the crowd. In modern practice, however, where this custom is retained, the congregation invariably takes on the role of the crowd, shouting, "Crucify! Crucify!" The wisdom behind this ancient practice is to give expression to the belief that the rejection, abandonment, betrayal, and crucifixion of Jesus are not what "they" did (whether "they" be conceived as "the Jews" or "the Romans"). They indeed did reject and execute Jesus, but the whole truth of this terrible event is not acknowledged until we acknowledge "we" did it. This insight is something we shall return to later.

From at least the fourth century and before the invention of printing made possible a wider use of texts, the passion according to St. Matthew was always preferred, in part because it was believed to be the earliest of the Gospels. On Good Friday when the passion was also sung or read, St. John's Gospel was used. Modern liturgical usage continues the tradition of using St. John's Gospel on Good Friday, but on Palm Sunday the three Synoptic Gospels are now read in rotation. However, the dominant liturgical usage of Matthew and John's Gospels down the centuries has meant that these texts have exercised a unique influence on the mind and imagination of Christians, and beyond that on the evolution of church music.

Medieval plainsong settings of the passion required three singers: a tenor to sing the part of the evangelist; a bass to sing the part of Christ; and an alto, whose voice was deemed fickle, to sing the part of Judas. Motet choruses sung in polyphony were added in the fifteenth century, one of the earliest extant versions of which is by the English composer Richard Davy. Settings of the passion, pioneered largely by English choirs, were further developed during the sixteenth century in Germany, notably by Johann Walther (1496–1570), Martin Luther's musical adviser, whose German passion was the first to be written in a vernacular language. These compositions were ideally suited to the new Lutheran worship with its stress on the importance of Scripture. Heinrich Schütz (1585–1672) brought the singing of the passion to the fore of the German music scene. His work gave impetus to a compositional movement that encouraged writing music that reflected the dignity of the text as well as the emotional intensity of a generation recovering from the trauma of the Thirty Years' War. The passions of J. S. Bach (1685–1750), which represent the apotheosis of this musical genre, utilize orchestra and chorales to be sung by the congregation. Again the choice of texts, those of the St. John passion (1723) and the St. Matthew passion (1729), is traditional. Bach did write a setting for Luke's passion narrative but it survives only in fragmentary form and is not considered to be of the same quality.

Maundy Thursday

The day before Good Friday marks the beginning of the *triduum sacrum.* The Latin word *triduum* means "three-day period" and in this case designates the time from the Last Supper and betrayal of Jesus to his resurrection. The liturgy of Holy Thursday (known in the East as "Great Thursday") is a rich tapestry of themes: humble service expressed through Jesus' washing of his disciples' feet, the institution of the Eucharist, and Christ's obedience to the Father in the agony of Gethsemane. The traditional English name for the day, Maundy Thursday, derives via Middle English from the first Latin antiphon, *mandatum novum,* sung during the foot-washing ceremony: "A *new commandment* I give you that you love one another." The words come from Jesus' farewell discourse to his disciples as recorded by St. John (13:34).

Liturgically, Maundy Thursday is one of the most complex days of the ecclesiastical year, combining at least three elements: the commemoration of the Last Supper, the Blessing of the Holy Oils (originally in preparation for the baptisms that were to take place at Easter), and the public Reconciliation of Penitents, though the latter has long been obsolete. In Germany the day is also known as "Green Thursday" (*Gründonnerstag*), from the custom of providing penitents, who had made their confession on Ash Wednesday, with green branches as tokens of their reception back into full communion with the Church.

A special celebration in commemoration of the institution of the Eucharist on Maundy Thursday appears first in the time of St. Augustine (354–430) in North Africa, and is attested by the Council of Hippo in 393. In recent years this service has been celebrated in the evening. White vestments are worn, and in the East the severity of the Lenten fast is temporarily relaxed. In Milan in the fourth century it is apparent from the writings of Ambrose (339–397) that the ceremony of the foot-washing or *pedilavium* took place on Holy Saturday, and this may be its original position.[7] The ceremony is attested in Toledo in 694 and later in Rome, where it was celebrated on Maundy Thursday but as a separate service. Its observance was often confined to cathedral and abbey churches and presided over by the bishop or abbot who, representing Christ, ceremonially washed the feet of twelve people, typically men representing the apostles. In recent years the custom has become more widespread and usually has twelve people, both men and women, chosen as a cross-section of the local community.

Since at least medieval times the Maundy Thursday Eucharist in the Latin rite has been followed by a vigil in remembrance of Christ's agony in Gethsemane, focusing on the words, "Could you not watch with me one hour?" In Catholic devotion this watch occurs before the Altar of Repose where the consecrated host is reserved, usually surrounded by lights and flowers symbolizing the Garden of Gethsemane. In remembrance of the Roman soldiers' dividing his garments among them, the liturgy concludes with the symbolic stripping of the altar(s) of a church, often accompanied by the recitation of Ps. 22. In recent liturgical reforms, however, this custom

7. Ambrose, *de Sacramentis*. 3. 4, 5, 7.

has gone somewhat out of fashion and been shorn of ceremony. It was also formerly the custom to wash the altar with a bunch of hyssop dipped in wine and water. St. Isidore of Seville (c. 560–636) said that this ceremony was intended as a form of homage to Christ in return for the humility with which he had washed his disciples' feet.[8]

Good Friday

Good Friday stands at the heart of the Christian observance of Holy Week and its commemoration of the passion preserves some of the oldest liturgical texts still in current use. The custom of venerating the cross can be traced back to the fourth century and may have been inaugurated by St. Cyril of Jerusalem himself (c. 315–386). Egeria on her travels certainly provides us with a vivid description of the liturgy as she experienced it.[9] She tells us that before dawn on Good Friday a procession of clergy and pilgrims from Gethsemane would enter the city, and upon their arrival at the Church of the Holy Sepulchre the entire narrative of the trial before Pilate would be read. Still before sunrise, all would then go to pray at the column where Jesus was believed to have been scourged.

After a short rest, the people would reassemble in the church, where a box containing a section of wood, believed to be from the actual cross on which Jesus had been crucified, was placed on a linen-covered table in front of the bishop. By tradition, the discovery of the true cross was made by Helena (d. 330), the mother of Constantine.[10] The people then filed past in silence, bowing and touching or kissing the cross. Later, from noon until three o'clock, the period when Jesus hung on the cross, there were readings from Scripture and the recitation of psalms, culminating in the reading of St. John's passion.

8. Isidore of Seville, *de Eccles. Off.*, I, 28.
9. *Egeria's Travels*, 37.
10. Socrates Scholasticus, *Ecclesiastical History*, I, 17.

In the evening there was a commemoration of the burial of Christ, and for those who could cope, a further vigil throughout the night.

We can see the core of the Latin rite in this early Jerusalem liturgy. Three parts are clearly visible: the reading of Scripture, including the passion according to John, combined with prayer; the proclamation and veneration of the cross; and finally, the Mass of the Pre-sanctified (communion from elements reserved on Maundy Thursday on the Altar of Repose).

It is highly likely that the custom of venerating the cross spread with the dissemination of relics of the true cross, and certainly by the eighth century it was being observed in Rome. Churches in the West without a relic substituted a plain wooden cross, which in later centuries was exchanged for a crucifix. Ironically, the custom disappeared from the rite in Jerusalem at the beginning of the seventh century when the city was sacked by the first wave of Muslim invaders, but in 629, it was transferred to September 14, becoming known henceforth as the Feast of the Exaltation of the Cross or "Holy Cross Day." Alone among the Eastern rites, the Syrian Church has preserved the custom.

In Spain and Gaul, venerating the cross was dramatized; and a more solemn form of the ritual, which was to become normative in the West, appears for the first time in the Roman-German Pontifical of Mainz (c. 950). During Lent or at least Passiontide, it became customary for all crosses, statues, and icons in churches to be veiled in either purple or unbleached linen, the latter often having emblems of the passion stenciled in red, black, or blue on them. The significance of this custom becomes apparent when on Good Friday the priest brings into the church a large cross for all to see and ceremonially unveils it, saying three times to the congregation, "Behold, the wood of the cross, on which was hung the Savior of the world." The purpose of the liturgical drama is to confront the faithful with the reality of the cross and to invite them to meditate on the universal significance of Christ's saving death. The faithful look up at the cross and witness the very act of redemption. Christ's suffering is seen as the supreme gesture of love. Christ is proclaimed as both sacrifice and Savior.

In response, the congregation comes forward one by one to pray before the cross, sometimes holding it, maybe kissing it—hence the expressions "touch wood" and "knock on wood." The veneration is a long and moving ceremony, and over the centuries it accrued some of the most beautiful and evocative music ever written to accompany the Christian liturgy: the Byzantine *trisagion* (Holy God, Holy and Strong, Holy and Immortal); the anthem (We venerate your cross, O Lord, and praise and glorify your resurrection: for by virtue of the cross, joy has come to the whole world); the dialogue chant of the Reproaches; and finally, the magnificent hymn by Venantius Fortunatus (530–609), "Pange Lingua," "Sing, my tongue, the glorious battle," with its refrain *Crux fidelis*. Here is a sample of its verses with its powerful meditation on the cross as a tree of glory:

Faithful Cross! above all other,
one and only noble tree!
None in foliage, none in blossom,
none in fruit thy peer may be;
sweetest wood and sweetest iron,
sweetest weight is hung on thee.

Sing, my tongue, the glorious battle,
sing the ending of the fray,
o'er the cross, the victor's trophy,
sound the loud triumphant lay:
Tell how Christ, the world's Redeemer,
as a victim won the day.

Thirty years among us dwelling,

now at length his hour fulfilled,
born for this, he meets his Passion,
for that this he freely willed,
on the cross the lamb is lifted,
where his life-blood shall be spilled.

Bend thy boughs, O tree of glory,
thy too rigid sinews bend:
for a while the ancient rigor
that thy birth bestowed, suspend,
and the King of heavenly beauty
on thy bosom gently tend.

Thou alone wast counted worthy
this world's ransom to sustain,
that a shipwrecked race might ever
thus a port of refuge gain,
with the sacred blood anointed
from the lamb for sinners slain.

He endured the nails, the spitting,
vinegar and spear and reed:
from that holy body pierced
blood and water forth proceed:
earth and stars and sky and ocean
by that flood from stain are freed.[11]

Even more famous than this hymn are the Improperia or Reproaches, a poetic dialogue of uncertain date and authorship, but which began to develop from as early as the time of Melito of Sardis (d. c. 190) in the latter half of the second century. The text does not appear in its final form until the eleventh century, but verses are found in ninth- and tenth-century documents, and traces of it are evident in documents of the seventh century. The Reproaches represent a collage of texts from the Old Testament celebrating the divine

11. Venantius Fortunatus, "Sing, My Tongue, the Glorious Battle," trans. J. M. Neale, http://www.hymnary.org/text/sing_my_tongue_the_glorious_battle.

compassion for the people of Israel, juxtaposed with outrage at the appalling treatment of Christ in his passion. In the course of the meditation, the crucified Jesus "reproaches" the faithlessness and hardness of heart of his people with the disturbing refrain "O my people, what have I done to you? How have I wearied you? Answer me!"

This haunting and poignant meditation on the dying Christ is chanted by two choirs immediately before the singing of the veneration hymn, often to a setting by Tomás Luis de Victoria (1548–1611). Each of the first three verses is followed by the *trisagion*, sung alternately in Latin (or the vernacular) and Greek (a sure sign in a Western text of its ancient origin), and the other verses by the chorus, "O my people." As the faithful come forward to reverence the cross it creates the drama of a divine conversation in which we are invited to respond personally.

O my people, what have I done to you?
How have I wearied you?
Answer me!

Holy God,
Holy and Mighty,
Holy and Immortal,
have mercy upon us.

I led you out of the land of Egypt,
From slavery I set you free.
I brought you into a land of promise:
But you have prepared a cross for your Savior.

I led you as a shepherd for forty years through the desert,
I brought you dry-shod through the sea;
I fed you manna in the wilderness:
But you have prepared a cross for me.

I fought for you in battles,
I won you strength and victory;
I gave you a royal crown and scepter:
But you have plaited a crown of thorns for me.

I planted you, my choicest vine,
And cared for you most tenderly;
But when I was thirsty you gave me vinegar to drink
and pierced with a spear the side of your Savior.

Then listen to my pleading.
Do not turn away from me.
You are my people: will you reject me?
For you I suffer bitterly.

Sadly, this ancient text has helped spread negative, anti-Jewish stereotypes. Rather than hear the words of Christ directed to themselves and their own failures in discipleship, some Christians have chosen to interpret "my people" as God's condemnation of the people of Israel. Even the liturgical reading of the passion narrative has been used to stir up hatred toward the Jews. In past centuries when the passion according to John was recited or sung dramatically on Good Friday, reference to the *ioudaioi* (perhaps originally simply "the people of Judah," that is, the inhabitants of Jerusalem and the surrounding countryside) was often interpreted as a blanket condemnation of the Jews as a whole. There is no doubt that the combination of word, music, and drama in the liturgy of Good Friday creates a powerful cocktail and cumulatively, as Pope John Paul II observed, it helped to make Christians in the twentieth century less vigilant when the Nazi fury was unleashed against the Jews. It eased the way, he said, albeit indirectly, for the coming of the Holocaust.

Recent liturgical revision has highlighted the vital importance of handling these ancient texts with care and of being alert to anything that might foster anti-Semitism. The Second Vatican Council put it as follows: "It is true that the Jewish authorities and those who followed their lead pressed for the death of Christ; nevertheless, what happened in his Passion cannot be charged against all the Jews then alive, without distinction, nor against the Jews of today."[12] The Reproaches are still sung in the Roman liturgy but today are understood and taught as a reminder of God's faithfulness, not as an accusation of Israel's faithlessness. In a post-Holocaust era, however, some liturgists feel that this is not enough and argue that in their historic form these texts are unusable, and accordingly have either abandoned them or, as in the case of the Church of England, have substantially rewritten them.[13]

The Three Hours Devotion

In the sixteenth century, the Church of England, in company with other churches of the Reformation, rejected elaborate liturgical commemoration of the passion, and in particular the custom of "creeping to the cross," as its detractors called it. Anything that smacked of "superstition" was excluded in favor of devotion that was scriptural. As a result worship became by necessity both more cerebral and static. Anglicanism and some Lutheran churches did, however, retain the framework of the liturgical year with its rhythm of feasts and fasts, including the observance of Holy Week, and the nineteenth century saw a revival of primitive and medieval observance that began to reclothe these bare ecclesiastical bones.

One effect of the great choral revival in the Church of England in the wake of the Oxford Movement was to promote a new wave of

12. Pope Paul VI, *Nostra Aetate*, October 28, 1965, section 4, http://www.vatican.va/archive/hist_councils/ii_vatican_council/documents/vat-ii_decl_19651028_nostra-aetate_en.html.
13. See *Services and Prayers for the Church of England: Times and Seasons* (London: CHP, 2006), 310–11.

musical compositions to commemorate the passion, such as Stainer's *Crucifixion*, written for Marylebone Parish Church in London in 1887, and J. H. Maunder's *Olivet to Calvary*. These quasi-liturgical works were taken up with alacrity by the burgeoning parish choirs of Victorian England and subsequently exported to the English-speaking world. They provided a musical framework in which congregations could meditate on the passion without leaving their seats.

Another form of devotion that became popular in Anglican churches during the nineteenth century was "The Three Hours Devotion." Ironically, it began its life in Lima, Peru, where it was instituted by the Jesuit priest Alphonsus Messia (d. 1732) and known as "The Three Hours Agony." From Peru, it was exported to Spain and Rome by the Jesuits around 1780, and gradually this extra-liturgical devotion spread throughout Europe. Commemorating the time Jesus hung on the cross, it is held typically between noon and three o'clock and traditionally consists of a series of meditations or sermons based on the so-called Seven Last Words—the seven things that Jesus spoke from the cross. According to the evangelists these were:

"My God, my God, why have you forsaken me?" (Matt. 27:46)

"Father, forgive them; for they know not what they do." (Luke 23:34)

"Truly, I say to you, today you will be with me in paradise." (Luke 23:43)

"Woman, behold your son!" and "Behold, your mother!" (John 19:26-7)

"I thirst." (John 19:28)

"It is finished!" (John 19:30)

"Father, into your hands I commend my spirit." (Luke 23:46)

A new liturgical form requires new music, and around 1785 Joseph Haydn was commissioned by a canon of Cádiz to write a new passion for the city's cathedral. Haydn entitled the work *The Seven Words of the Savior on the Cross.* Describing the customary performances of the oratorio in Cádiz, he wrote in his preface to the score published in 1801,

> The walls, windows, and pillars of the church were hung with black cloth, and only one large lamp hanging from the center of the roof broke the solemn obscurity. At midday, the doors were closed and the ceremony began. After a short service the bishop ascended the pulpit, pronounced the first of the seven words (or sentences) and delivered a discourse thereon. This ended, he left the pulpit and prostrated himself before the altar. The pause was filled with music. The bishop then in like manner pronounced the second word, then the third, and so on, the orchestra following on the conclusion of each discourse.[14]

In its original form, the *Seven Words* consisted of seven slow movements (each of which is entitled with one of the "words" of Christ) and was scored for full orchestra, complete with trumpets and kettledrums.

Tenebrae

Since the twelfth century, the Latin word *tenebrae,* meaning "shadows," has been the title of a special form of Matins and Lauds provided for the last three days of Holy Week. To encourage greater participation of lay people, these offices were conflated and said in anticipation on the eve of the day in question (thus the Tenebrae of Maundy Thursday was sung on the evening of Wednesday). The term probably derived from the ceremony of extinguishing the lights

14. Quoted in Karl Geiringer, *Haydn: A Creative Life in Music* (Berkeley: University of California Press, 1982), 83.

(candles) in church one by one during the service, with the result that all departed in darkness (*tenebrae*) and silence.

Matins and Lauds on these days were originally simply the ordinary offices sung by monastic or collegiate communities. The office was pared down. There were no hymns, no invitatory, no introductory versicles and responses, and by custom the Gloria Patri at the end of each psalm was omitted. Before the liturgical revisions of the Second Vatican Council, Matins (also known as "Vigils") on these days consisted of nine psalms and nine readings from the Lamentations of Jeremiah, the Fathers, and the New Testament. The book of Lamentations describes the desolation of the prophet in the face of the destruction of Jerusalem, and it provides the perfect theological counterpoint to the story of the passion as it unfolds. The psalms were sung to a chant of singular poignancy and the readings were separated by responsories of great musical beauty, which almost certainly derive from the Roman schola cantorum of the seventh, eighth, and ninth centuries.

Tenebrae was an extended meditation on the passion of Christ, from the Last Supper to his burial. The note of betrayal is sounded in the Thursday office, the judgment, crucifixion, and death of Christ on Friday, and his burial and the expectation of his resurrection on Saturday. A unique feature of the offices on these days was the triangular candlestick, which was erected before the altar or in the midst of the monastic choir, and on which were placed fifteen candles. These were extinguished one by one after each psalm (nine for Matins and five for Lauds) until only one candle remained. This was then hidden behind the altar at the end of the Benedictus, signifying Christ's death. At the end of the service it was replaced on the top of the candlestick. Not surprisingly, this has been understood as an anticipated sign of the resurrection, but in reality it was probably no more than a way of providing light for people to leave the building safely.

The origin of the rites associated with Tenebrae is obscure, but they may have derived from customs connected with the Jewish fast of Tisha B'Av (the Ninth Day of Av, a day of commemoration for the destruction of the temple in 586 B.C.E. and 70 C.E.). On this day the book of Lamentations is read, the synagogue is darkened, and decorative elements are removed. Following the liturgical reforms of the Second Vatican Council, the service has fallen out of favor, though paradoxically forms of the service are still maintained by some Lutheran congregations, particularly in the United States.

Stations of the Cross

"If any want to become my followers, let them deny themselves and take up their cross and follow me. For those who want to save their life will lose it, and those who lose their life for my sake will find it" (Matt. 16:24). Stations of the Cross have formed a popular Christian devotion for centuries. They are a simple but profound way of responding to Jesus' challenge to follow in his footsteps, and like many observances they probably have their origin in Jerusalem. From the earliest days Christians have visited the sites associated with the passion, real and supposed. For our medieval forebears, a pilgrimage to Jerusalem was itself a *via crucis*. By identifying more closely with Christ, particularly in his last and painful journey to the cross, pilgrims hoped to be able to pray more fervently and more effectively. It is likely that the devotion of Stations of the Cross evolved as a conscious attempt to recreate (or perhaps provide a substitute for) this pilgrimage route in Jerusalem.

The word *station* (*statio*) implies either standing still or gathering at a place. From the fifteenth century onward, we find the term applied to the way pilgrims would pause for prayer at what were believed to be the sites of specific events and encounters along the Via Dolorosa, the route of Jesus' final journey from Pilate's house to Golgotha. Some of these encounters, such as Jesus' meeting with Veronica, were legendary, but others had scriptural warrant. The devotions of pilgrims were not systematic, nor were they performed in any special order. When Margery Kempe, that extraordinarily lachrymose visionary from Norfolk, visited Jerusalem around 1413, she visited places associated with the passion, but in a random way as many still do today. Indeed, it seems that her devotions were confined within the walls of the Church of the Holy Sepulchre rather than performed in the open streets of the city, where the Ottomans had imposed restrictions on the public devotions of Christians.

By 1342, the Franciscans were given responsibility for the holy places of Jerusalem and it was they who popularized this form of devotion by erecting tableaux to aid visitors. The affective devotion of these custodians of the holy places, who had invented the custom of assembling a crib at Christmas, complete with suitable animals, now also produced Stations of the Cross. It was probably at the prompting of the Franciscans that indulgences were attached to prayers said at specific places along the route. This "encouraged" the popularity of the devotion, though the indulgences corresponded only in part with the way the Stations are now observed. By the fifteenth century the custom of setting up occasional "stations" in churches was widespread in much of western Europe, though the events they featured and the devotional exercises they inspired continued to vary in content and number. It was not until the seventeenth century that the custom of erecting stations ranged at intervals around the walls of Catholic churches became established. These took the form of wooden crosses, with a representation of the events in the passion story—either a picture or sculpture—placed underneath. Some of these, such as Eric Gill's series for Westminster Cathedral, are outstanding pieces of art.

The Stations of the Cross has proved to be a curiously tenacious Christian devotion. It seems to belong to a piety of another era, but it continues to be rehearsed faithfully by individuals and congregations across the world, particularly during Lent and on Good Friday evening—and not just in Roman Catholic churches. It offers an intimate and immediate way for ordinary people to reflect on the crucifixion. The usual way of doing them is for a person (or congregation) to genuflect at each station and recite the prayer "We adore you, O Christ, and we bless you, because by your holy cross you have redeemed the world." This may be accompanied by a reading from the Bible, the reciting of the Lord's Prayer, Hail Mary, or Gloria Patri. When the number of participants make movement impossible, only the priest moves around the church, with the congregation turning in order to face a particular station.

The number of "stations" was finally fixed at fourteen in 1731 by Clement XII, as follows:

1. Jesus is condemned to death by Pilate.
2. Jesus receives the cross.
3. Jesus falls for the first time.
4. Jesus meets Mary, his mother.
5. Simon of Cyrene is made to carry his cross.
6. Veronica wipes Jesus' face with her veil.
7. Jesus falls for the second time.
8. Jesus is met by the women of Jerusalem.
9. Jesus falls for the third time.
10. Jesus is stripped of his garments.
11. Jesus is nailed to the cross.
12. Jesus dies.

13. Jesus' body is removed from the cross (Pietà).
14. Jesus is laid in the tomb.

In 2007, following the changes instituted by his predecessor John Paul II, Pope Benedict XVI authorized a reform of the devotion to exclude legendary material (such as Veronica wiping Jesus' face) and to ensure that the stations follow Scripture more closely. The reformed rite is as follows:

1. Jesus in the Garden of Gethsemane
2. Jesus is betrayed by Judas and arrested.
3. Jesus is tried before the Sanhedrin.
4. Jesus is denied by Peter.
5. Jesus is condemned to death by Pilate.
6. Jesus is scourged and receives the crown of thorns.
7. Jesus takes up his cross.
8. Simon of Cyrene is made to carry his cross.
9. Jesus is met by the women of Jerusalem.
10. Jesus is nailed to the cross.
11. Jesus promises the kingdom to the penitent thief.
12. Jesus speaks to his mother and the beloved disciple.
13. Jesus dies.
14. Jesus is laid in the tomb.

The recovery of the primitive understanding of liturgically commemorating the death and resurrection of Christ together has also led some to include a fifteenth station of the resurrection, particularly when the devotion is used outside Lent and Passiontide.

As with many liturgical observances, the Stations of the Cross have inspired musicians to compose settings for the *Stabat Mater*, a poem on the grief of the Virgin as she stood at the foot of the cross watching her son die. Its title comes from its opening words:

At the cross, her station keeping,
stands the grieving Mother weeping,
close to Jesus to the last.

The poem is passionate and highly charged. It was intended to evoke tears of sorrow from the penitent for the sins that had crucified Christ, as is clear from its closing verses:

O Holy Mother! Grant that my heart
may be pierced through
with the wounds of my Savior crucified:

Let me share with you his pain,
who for my sins was slain,
and who for me died in torment.

Let me mingle my tears with yours,
mourning him who was crucified,
all the days of my life.

Let me stand with you beside his cross,
in mourning your dying Son
for this is my desire.

O Virgin of all virgins!
do not be bitter to me
let me share your grief;

Grant that I may share his death,
inebriate me in this way with his cross,
bathe me in the blood of your Son.

Written in the thirteenth century, *Stabat Mater* is variously attributed to Innocent III and Jacopone da Todi, and has been set to music by many composers, including Mozart, Pergolesi, and Dvořák, as well as medieval and Tudor composers. The fifteenth century was captivated by the thought of Mary's sorrow, the grief of a mother weeping for her dead child. Her grief resonated with the experience of ordinary men and women for whom such bereavements were commonplace events. This is the era in which the image of the Pietà, Our Lady of Pity, caught the lay imagination, and statues of it appeared in many churches across Europe, the most famous of which is by Michelangelo in St Peter's, Rome.

Mystery Plays

The vernacular religious dramas known as the "mystery plays," notably the English Corpus Christi plays and the French passion plays, are the other great flowering of medieval popular devotion. They are commonly believed to have developed from the dramatic parts of the Holy Week and Easter liturgy, though the influence of early vernacular paraphrases of the Bible and Gospel harmonies is clear. In the Middle Ages, liturgical celebration, as we have noted, was invariably dramatic, if not theatrical, with stylized dialogues and the use of choirs of men and boys to impress upon the congregation the significance of the events being commemorated. As early as the tenth century we find the monks of St. Gallen in Switzerland writing sequences, hymns, litanies, and tropes—elaborations of parts of the liturgy, particularly the introit—and setting them to music.

Nowhere is this seen more clearly than in the drama of Easter Day, where the gathering of the women at the sepulchre at dawn was embellished with an imagined conversation between them and the angel(s) guarding the tomb. Over time this was further elaborated, with clerics dressed in albs going to a previously prepared "sepulchre tomb" in the church and seating themselves in representation of the angels. Then three other priests, vested in copes and carrying censers, arrive, representing the three Marys. Upon their arrival, the "angel" questions them and directs them to proclaim the news of the resurrection.

In their day, these Easter plays constituted the highest development of medieval drama. The popular taste for them was fed by the clergy, who introduced the characters of Pontius Pilate, the Jews, and the soldiers guarding the tomb. With the increased length of the plays, it became necessary to separate them from church services. In a non-literate age, people wanted to see representations of the whole life of Jesus, particularly his passion. The passion plays were by far the most impressive of the so-called mystery plays, but there were also cycles of plays that dealt with the major events of the Christian calendar, from the creation to the day of judgment. In the north of England, such as at York and Chester, these dramas were performed out of doors on wagons or on decorated carts called "pageants." In East Anglia, London, and Europe, they were performed on temporary or fixed stages.

The Reformation was inimical to mystery plays, partly because performances were often occasions for public disorder, but also because legendary and apocryphal material distorted the purity of the scriptural account of Christ's life. With the spread of religious conflict across Europe, uneasiness with liturgical drama in general increased, and mystery plays gradually ceased to be performed.

Conclusion

Crucifixion lifted up its victims to display them naked and immobilized before a terrified populace. In St. John's Gospel, Jesus addressed those who had come up to Jerusalem to celebrate the Passover, saying, "And I, when I am lifted up from the earth, will draw all people to myself" (12:32-33). John says that Jesus said this, "to indicate the kind of death he was to die." Jesus' words indicate that he had a premonition about the fate that awaited him but, for Christians, they have always had a deeper meaning. The lifting up of Jesus on the cross is part of a single movement of his self-offering and exaltation to God. Jesus is the victim who is being put down, but inadvertently the soldiers are actually lifting him up into his victory and glory.

The purpose of the Christian liturgy is to draw people into this movement of grace, and to allow them to be irresistibly drawn by the attractiveness of God. There is no adequate way of commemorating the death of Jesus, and in the end probably only silence and penitence will suffice. To truly remember is a complex thing because it involves more than simply drumming up a memory of an event, even something as horrific as the crucifixion of Christ. Remembrance is more than a feat of memory. To remember means to put something back together that has become disconnected. To truly remember requires that we turn back to past actions and events and recognize our place within what has happened. In the case of the passion of Christ, Christians believe that when they do this, they are inwardly transformed because they encounter not the condemnation of God, but salvation.

5

Musical Settings of the Passion Texts

Andrew Shenton

The principle question concerning the setting of any text to music is: What does the music actually do to the text? How does it change or transform it? The answer is twofold: first, music provides increased expressivity, and second, it seeks to interpret the text. It is difficult to express in words the additional depth of emotion achieved by adding music to any text, let alone a story that concerns cruelty and death and is directly related to religious beliefs. It is even harder to describe how a composer might seek to contribute to our understanding of this story by highlighting certain words, reordering the events, or even by adding innovative elements to the traditional narrative. Nonetheless, the developmental history of musical settings of the passion is directly concerned with increased expressivity and is intimately linked with developments in musical style. Study of musical settings requires reference to manuscript and source studies, reception history, performance practice, cultural studies, and to changing theological concerns, all of which demonstrate how composers have sought to make the death of Jesus engaging to their audiences.[1]

Establishing the Text

The texts of most musical settings of the passion are based on the narratives found in the four canonical Gospels, Matthew, Mark, Luke, and John. Three of these, known as the Synoptic Gospels, give similar accounts. The Gospel of John differs slightly and includes additional details. Though some musical settings use elements from all four Gospels, most focus on one. As singing the gospel texts during the mass replaced reading them, a tradition developed that Matthew was sung on Palm Sunday, Mark on Tuesday in Holy Week and Luke on Wednesday, and finally John on Good Friday.[2] The passion story is inherently dramatic and was often told by actors as a non-liturgical drama. In medieval times, the passion play, like its counterparts the mystery play and the miracle play, were told on the streets and were an effective method of religious instruction and evangelizing. All musical settings share these functions and have often moved the passion out of the liturgy and into the concert hall so that the story may be more widely heard.

As musical settings became more complex, two additional texts were frequently set as part of the story: the "Seven Last Words" and the *Stabat Mater*. The Seven Last Words are a collection of short phrases taken from the four Gospels that were uttered by Jesus

1. Factual information in this essay has been collated from articles in *Grove Music Online*, ed. L. Macy, www.grovemusic.com, especially the article "Passion Music" by Kurt von Fischer and Werner Braun, and from the other books cited in these endnotes.
2. Basil Smallman, *The Background of Passion Music: J. S. Bach and His Predecessors* (London: SCM, 1957), 22.

immediately before he died on the cross. They are frequently used as part of a meditation liturgy during Lent and Holy Week, usually on Good Friday. The traditional order of the sayings is

1. Father, forgive them, for they know not what they do. (Luke 23:34)
2. Truly, I say to you, today you will be with me in paradise. (Luke 23:43)
3. Woman, behold your son: behold your mother. (John 19:26-27)
4. *Eloi, Eloi lama sabachthani?* ("My God, My God, why have you forsaken me?" Matt. 27:46; Mark 15:34)
5. I thirst. (John 19:28)
6. It is finished. (John 19:30)
7. Father, into your hands I commit my spirit. (Luke 23:46)

There are several well-known and important musical settings of the Seven Last Words by composers such as Heinrich Schütz, Joseph Haydn, César Franck, Théodore Dubois, Sofia Gubaidulina, and James MacMillan.[3] Our present interest in them, however, is only as accretions to the Gospel narrative as texts for passions.

The *Stabat Mater* is a thirteenth-century Roman Catholic sequence of verses variously attributed to Innocent III or Jacopone da Todi. Its title is an abbreviation of the first line, *Stabat mater dolorosa* (the sorrowful mother was standing). The hymn meditates on the suffering of Mary, Christ's mother, during his crucifixion. It is a popular text and has been set to music by many composers, among them Palestrina, Haydn, Rossini, Poulenc, and Verdi, as well as the French black metal band Anorexia Nervosa (1995–2005). The

3. Heinrich Schütz, *Sieben Worte Jesu Christi am Kreuz*, SWV 478 (1645); Joseph Haydn, *Die sieben letzten Worte unseres Erlösers am Kreuze* (1787); César Franck, *Les Sept Paroles du Christ sur la Croix* (1859); Sofia Gubaidulina, *Sieben Worte* (1982); James MacMillan, *Seven Last Words from the Cross* (1993).

addition of this text and the Seven Last Words adds variety, perspective, drama, characterization, and emotion to the traditional passion narrative.

The Plainsong Passion

History does not relate exactly when passion texts began to be chanted instead of spoken, though it is likely related to the building of large basilical churches and the discovery that words could be better heard at a distance from the reciter if they were sung and not spoken. This probably happened as a gradual process from the fifth to tenth centuries. According to the Roman Ordines, the collection of documents that contain the rubrics for the medieval mass of the Roman rite, originally just one person (the *diakon*) chanted the passion using a single reciting tone. Music notation developed gradually, beginning in the ninth century with the addition of *litterae significativae* (letters of signification) to manuscripts. These letters indicate a different way of delivering certain words that affect pitch, tempo, and dynamic. For example, *s* by a word or passage denotes *suaviter*, meaning softly, and *c* stands for *celeriter*, meaning quickly. These letters indicate that, even in a liturgical setting, the dramatic power of the words could be enhanced with careful presentation.

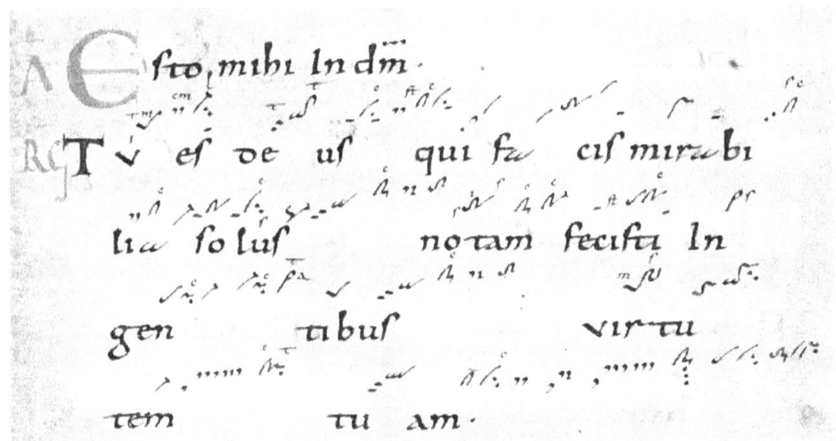

Tu es deus, with litterae significativae, from the Cantatorium of St. Gallen, Codex Sangallensis 359.

By the twelfth century, specific pitches were indicated for reciting the passion that in total had a range of just over an octave. This range is within the capability of a single singer, suggesting that just one person did the chanting. The different pitch ranges helped the lone singer to identify the different people in the drama, thereby clarifying the plot. By the thirteenth century, there is evidence of more than one person taking part and this led to the tradition of Jesus being sung by a bass, the Evangelist by a tenor, and the *synagoga* (the minor characters) and *turba* (crowd) being sung by an alto. The earliest extant manuscript that shows the use of multiple voices is the Dominican *Gros livre* of 1254. According to musicologist Kurt von Fischer, "this move towards greater expressivity is rooted in the theological developments of the time, especially the influence of St. Bernard of Clairvaux, whose followers sought to depict the agony of Christ with increasing realism."[4] Early manuscripts do not contain much information regarding "performance practice," the manner in

4. Paul Hillier, *Arvo Pärt* (Oxford: Oxford University Press, 1997), 124.

which the music is sung. A source in the British Museum, however, indicates that a cleric called Durandus (d. 1296) directed that "the words of Christ should be sung with sweetness, those of the Evangelist in the formal Gospel tone, and those of the 'most impious Jews' in a loud and harsh manner."[5]

The Polyphonic Passion

It is widely agreed among scholars that the earliest extant elaboration from the basic chant version of the passion is found in a manuscript in the British Museum known as Egerton MS 3307 (compiled between 1430 and 1444). It contains anonymous settings of Matthew and Luke in which monophonic chant is retained for the words of the Evangelist, but three-part polyphony is used for the *synagoga* parts and the words of Christ.[6] This type of passion became known as the "Responsorial Passion."

The earliest extant setting that can be accurately identified as the work of a known composer is the four-part setting of Matthew by Richard Davy (c. 1465–1507), a former organist at Magdalen College, Oxford. Davy's version survived as part of the collection known as the Eton Choirbook (Eton College MS 178). Like the anonymous versions in Egerton MS 3307, Davy adds polyphonic settings of the crowd parts to the traditional plainsong passion tones, an innovation that became the standard format for many decades.

5. Smallman, *Background of Passion Music*, 22.

6. Gwynn S. McPeek and Robert White Linker, eds., *The British Museum Manuscript Egerton 3307* (London: Oxford University Press, 1963).

Bach's *St. Matthew Passion*, Exordium, system 1-2. Davy edition.

Roughly parallel to the development of the responsorial passion, a different type arose called the "Motet Passion," in which the complete text, including the crowd parts, is set polyphonically. Kurt von Fischer notes that from the sixteenth century onward Motet Passions can be divided into three types according to the sources of the text:

1. Those that set the complete text according to one evangelist;
2. The *Summa Passionis*, which utilizes texts from all four Gospels, the Seven Last Words, usually an opening phrase called an *exordium* ("here begins the Gospel according to . . ."), and a

concluding phrase called a *conclusio* (which may, for example, be an elaborate "amen");

3. A version found only in Protestant Germany that sets a shortened version of just one Gospel.

With the sixteenth century, the history of the passion settings can be divided by denomination. For Catholics, the most widespread type was the Responsorial Passion to which there was one important innovation, the setting of the *vox Christi* (voice of Christ) polyphonically. The earliest extant examples of this are a setting of Matthew and two of John by the Italian composer Gasparo Alberti (c. 1489–1560). The Protestant passions were largely monophonic and polyphonic settings of the *Summa Passionis* type.

The most famous passion setting from the early-sixteenth century, *Passio Domini nostri Jesu Christi* (The Passion of our Lord Jesus Christ), was originally thought to have been composed by Jacobus Obrecht but has now been attributed to Antoine de Longueval (or Longaval) (fl. 1498–1525), a French singer and composer contemporary with Josquin des Prez. Longueval most likely composed his *Passio* for Holy Week in 1504, while a singer at the Court of Ferrara. The setting is a *Summa Passionis* in three sections, utilizing variation in texture, rhythmic character, and scoring for dramatic effect. The words of the Evangelist are in two, three, or four parts, while those of the other characters are generally in three parts, and the turba sections mainly in four parts. Longueval's setting was evidently very popular, since it survives in more than thirty manuscripts.

Another important and influential composer of this period was Martin Luther's principal music adviser, Johann Walther (1495–1570), who, probably between 1525 and 1530, composed two passion settings that enjoyed wide popularity in Germany. His

Matthew Passion, which was used in the Thomaskirche in Leipzig until J. S. Bach replaced it with his own version in 1729, is notable because it is the first setting to place a dramatic pause after the death of Jesus, echoing current liturgical custom. Walther used a monophonic reciting tone for the Evangelist and other characters, and a simple type of polyphony called *fauxbourdon* for the crowd and disciples.

During the sixteenth century, many notable composers set passion texts, including Lassus, Vittoria, and Byrd. The texts were in Latin, and, as musicologist Basil Smallman correctly notes, these settings were "stereotyped in form and conceived in a manner which was ritualistic rather than realistic."[7]

Heinrich Schütz (1585–1672) wrote one of the earliest German-language oratorios under the (abbreviated) title *Historia der Aufferstehung Jesu Christi* (The Story of the Resurrection of Jesus Christ, 1623, which is not a liturgical piece), a setting of the Seven Last Words from the Cross (1645), and a Luke Passion (c. 1664). His most well-known setting, however, is the *Historia des Leidens und Sterbens Jesu Christi nach dem Evangelisten St. Matthaeus* (The Story of the Suffering and Death of our Lord Jesus Christ according to the Evangelist St. Matthew) composed in 1666 for the Court of Dresden. It is scored for unaccompanied choir, thus adhering to an ancient custom that disallowed musical instruments during Holy Week as a sign of penance and renunciation. Schütz's *St. Matthew Passion* opens with a short *introitus* that sets a serene and contemplative mood, while for the main text Schütz devised an unaccompanied recitative in a plainsong style. It is largely syllabic and unmetered, with only occasional use of more than one note per syllable (melismas), frequently to emphasize a word like *gekreuziget* (crucified).

7. Smallman, *Background of Passion Music*, 24.

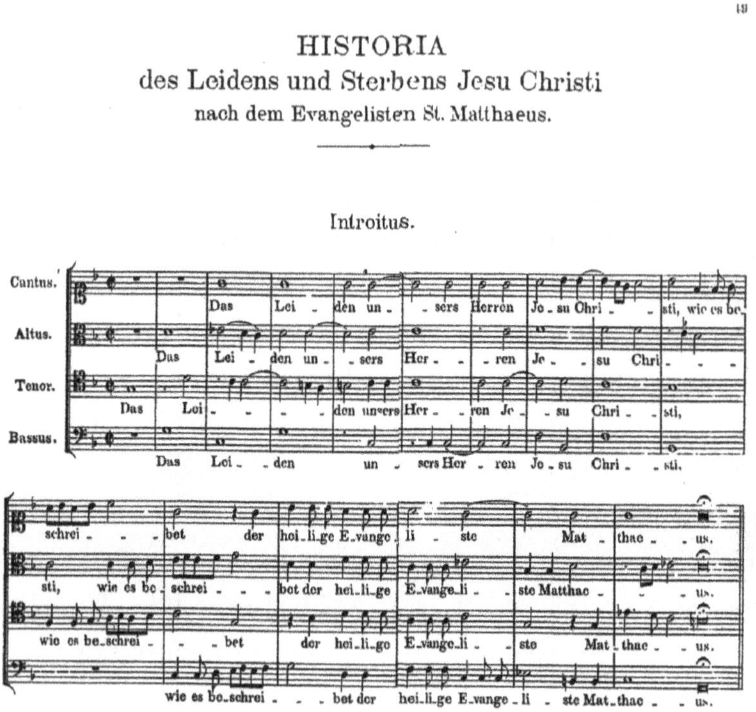

HISTORIA
des Leidens und Sterbens Jesu Christi
nach dem Evangelisten St. Matthaeus.

Introitus.

Introitus (opening) of Schütz's *St. Matthew Passion* (SWV 479). Spitta edition.

The Baroque Passion

Around 1600 there was a significant development in music history that radically changed the way drama was set to music. The new style, called "monody," set a melody to simple harmonic accompaniment. It was developed in the 1580s by a group of men called the Florentine Camerata, who wanted to restore Greek ideals of declamation. In contrast to music of the Renaissance, which was polyphonic, this new style sought to give precedence to the text, taking the side of those who admonished composers whose overly elaborate settings obscured the words in a piece—a frequently recurring debate about musical settings of religious texts.

One of the most significant early developers of monody was Giulio Caccini (1551–1618), who wrote an important description of the new style in his collection of madrigals and songs for solo voice and *basso continuo* called *Le nuove musiche* (*The New Music*, 1601–1602).

LE NVOVE
MVSICHE
DI GIVLIO CACCINI
DETTO ROMANO.

IN FIRENZE
APPRESSO I MARESCOTTI
MDCI.

Cover of Caccini's *Le nuove musiche* (*The New Music*, Florence, 1601–1602).

The introduction to this volume outlines the purpose of monody and includes instruction on performance practice, giving musical examples that show how a specific passage can be ornamented in different ways, depending on the emotion the singer wishes to convey. His argument that monodies could have passages that were more melodic or more declamatory led to the development of two musical forms, the recitative and the aria that would be important in later passion settings. The advantages of these two new forms in the presentation of dramatic action are many. First, recitative moves through the text very quickly and can therefore propel the action forward. *Secco* (dry) recitative uses only a bass instrument (such as the cello) and a harmony instrument (such as the harpsichord) in a technique called *basso continuo*, which is designed to allow the words to be heard clearly. Accompanied recitative uses more instruments and therefore adds more levels of emotion and interpretation to the text. In contrast, the aria is much more melodic. It offers the opportunity for reflection on the action and may utilize the full orchestral resources and showcase the technique and expressivity of the singer.

These new forms allowed for both greater diversity and more expressivity so that longer texts could be set more effectively. This in turn led to the rise of opera and its sacred counterpart, the oratorio, of which the passion became a subset. During Lent, when opera could not be performed, composers turned to non-staged dramatic religious works such as the stories of Jephtha and Jonah, and set them to music that was in many ways similar to opera, utilizing a combination of recitative and aria. Both sacred and secular works also used duets, trios, ensembles, and often a chorus for dramatic effect. In the Baroque period, the use of arias and recitatives became the norm for passion settings, although there were many hybrid varieties.

In addition to radical changes in musical style there were also significant changes to texts at this time. Under the influence of pietism, a new kind of passion text appeared in 1706 with *Der blutige und sterbende Jesus* (The Bleeding and Dying Jesus, 1704) by Christian Friedrich Hunold (known as Menantes). In his librettos Hunold freely paraphrased the biblical narrative but sought to achieve a sense of realism by emphasizing the details of the torture and crucifixion.

J. S. Bach: *Matthäuspassion*

Passion settings reached a new height of length and expressivity with J. S. Bach. Two of the four or possibly five settings of the passion that Bach wrote have survived: the *St. Matthew Passion* and the *St. John Passion*. A setting of Luke (formerly BWV 246) was attributed to Bach but is now listed as apocryphal or anonymous. The libretto by Christian Friedrich Henrici (known as Picander) of Bach's *St. Mark Passion* BWV 247 is still extant; the musical score, however, is lost.

The *Matthew Passion*, BWV 244, was composed in 1727 and is scored for solo voices, double choir, children's choir, and double orchestra. It sets chapters 26 and 27 of the Gospel of Matthew in German, interspersing chorales and arias written by Picander. It was probably first performed on Good Friday 1727 in the Thomaskirche in Leipzig, where Bach was the kapellmeister.[8]

Bach's setting is in two parts, which would have been sung before and after an extended sermon. This passion is set in scenes that are comprised of recitatives, chorales, arias (sometimes with chorus), and occasional duets. The first part begins with Jesus' anointing in Bethany and ends with his arrest in Gethsemane. The second part continues with Jesus before Caiaphas and concludes with his entombment. The degree of subtlety of the piece and the skillful use of the entire ensemble is evident right from the prologue, "Kommt,

8. Robin A. Leaver, "St. Matthew Passion," in *Oxford Composer Companions: J. S. Bach*, ed. Malcolm Boyd (Oxford: Oxford University Press, 1999), 430. "Until 1975 it was thought that the St. Matthew Passion was originally composed for Good Friday 1729, but modern research strongly suggests that it was performed two years earlier."

ihr Töchter, helft mir klagen" ("Come ye daughters, share my mourning"), which utilizes both choruses and a children's choir singing the chorale "O Lamm Gottes unshuldig" ("O Lamb of God unspotted").

Though congregations commonly sang in Protestant services, it is unlikely the chorales in Bach's settings of the passion were sung by the congregation, since they are unannounced and occur frequently, though irregularly, throughout the whole piece. They would have been familiar to congregations in Bach's time, however, and emphasized Bach's understanding of Lutheran theology, with its emphasis on salvation through Jesus by God's grace.

There are many other notable examples of Bach's genius as a musician and storyteller in the *St. Matthew Passion*, though they do not always occur where one might expect. For example, in the scene with Jesus before Pilate that comprises numbers 43 through 50 of the score, Bach sets out the text in thirteen sections:

#	Form	Singer(s)	Opening text
43	Recitative	Evangelist & others	And they took counsel together
44	Chorale	Chorus	Commit thy way [to Jesus]
45a	Recitative	Evangelist & others	Now at the feast
45b	Chorus	Chorus	Let him be crucified!
46	Chorale	Chorus	O wond'rous love
47	Recitative	Evangelist & Pilate	And the governor said
48	Recitative	Soprano	To us He hath done all things well
49	Aria	Soprano	For love my savior now is dying
50a	Recitative	Evangelist	But they cried out the more
50b	Chorus	Chorus	Let him be crucified!
50c	Recitative	Evangelist & Pilate	When Pilate saw he could prevail nothing
50d	Chorus	Chorus	His blood be on us
50e	Recitative	Evangelist	Then released he Barabbas

Most of the sections are short recitatives that divide the text up by character. A chorale verse, "Befiehl du deine Wege" (Commit thy way [to Jesus]), breaks up a long passage of recitative and reaffirms the Lutheran desire to commit to Jesus. The narration includes Pilate's wife, who warns him not to interfere with Jesus because she had a dream. Both choruses join in the cry for Barabbas to be released and then call for the crucifixion of Jesus in a short passage that mounts in tension using a twisted (and some say cruciform) motif. Another chorale verse, "O wond'rous love," leads into a two-measure recitative in which Pilate asks the crowd why Jesus should be crucified. Then, in a remarkable stroke of genius, Bach does not continue with shouts from the crowd but inserts an accompanied recitative, sung by an unnamed woman, who lists the positive things Jesus has done. This in turn leads to an aria, "For love my savior now is dying," of sublime pathos, sung by the same woman. What Bach has contrived is a gradual removal from the action to the interior monologue of one of the crowd. He has slowed down time and blurred the background action in an aria that is both well placed and well controlled. The effect is stunning, especially since immediately after the aria the narrator returns to announce the second call for Christ's crucifixion by the choir and the story resumes.

J. S. Bach *Matthäuspassion*, opening words of aria "Aus Liebe will mein Heiland sterben."

Surprisingly, the *Matthäuspassion* was probably not heard outside of Leipzig until 1829, when Felix Mendelssohn performed an abbreviated and modified version of it in Berlin to great acclaim.

The Romantic Passion

In the nineteenth century, the musical passion was not an important genre, partly because of changes in the liturgy and partly because of Romantic philosophies that were expressed in new musical forms, such as the symphonic poem. During this period, however, there are two notable attempts to set the passion to music, one by Beethoven and one by Liszt.

Ludwig van Beethoven's *Christus am Ölberge* (*Christ on the Mount of Olives*) premiered on April 5, 1803. It sets a libretto in German by the poet Franz Xaver Huber, in six sections, using three soloists: Jesus (tenor), an angel (soprano), and Peter (bass). The chorus takes the parts of angels, soldiers, and disciples, with a comparatively large orchestra accompanying the whole. The work is notable for its musical evocation of both scenes and moods, and for the humanism of the text, though it is now commonly regarded as one of Beethoven's lesser and rarely performed works. *Christus* (S. 3 1862–66) is a three-hour, three-movement oratorio by Franz Liszt, scored for large chorus and orchestra. The three movements cover the life of Christ in chronological order: I Christmas Oratorio (five movements); II After Epiphany (five movements); and III Passion and Resurrection (four movements, including a setting of the *Stabat Mater* text). Musical themes are connected throughout the three movements, providing musical and theological unity. The last movement, *Resurrexit!*, is famous for its long fugue based on a rising fifth motif. The work, too, is rarely performed, however, because of its length and scale—and changing aesthetic tastes.

John Stainer: *The Crucifixion*

Two works from the Victorian era have been validated by time and are still regularly performed, especially in the United Kingdom: John Stainer's *The Crucifixion* (1887) and *Olivet to Calvary* (1904) by John Henry Maunder.[9]

9. Other works include Arthur Somervell's *The Passion of Christ* (1914), Charles Wood's *Saint Mark Passion* (1921), and Eric Thiman's *The Last Supper* (1930). These works are all passion cantatas.

Stainer's *Crucifixion* is typical of Victorian treatments of the passion. It is in English and uses texts from all four Gospels and the Lamentations of Jeremiah, interspersed with five hymns sung by the choir and congregation. There are two soloists, tenor and bass, and both take the part of narrator. The bass usually sings the words of Jesus, but at the end of the work (which finishes at his death), the words of Jesus are given to the tenors of the chorus in four-part harmony as his character takes on a more spiritual dimension.

The librettist was the Reverend William J. Sparrow Simpson, and while some of the language (and perhaps some of the music) seems dated, one of the choruses "God so loved the world," and two of the hymns, "Cross of Jesus" and "All for Jesus," are regularly performed or sung as separate pieces. Sparrow's text is succinct and beautiful:

Cross of Jesus, Cross of Sorrow,
Where the blood of Christ was shed
Perfect man on thee was tortured,
Perfect man on thee has bled,

Here the King of all the ages,
Throned in light ere worlds could be
Robed in mortal flesh is dying
Crucified by sin for me.

O mysterious condescending!
O abandonment sublime!
Very God Himself is bearing
All the sufferings of Time!

The popularity of *The Crucifixion* and other settings of the period owe much to the relative simplicity of the music, which can easily be sung by an amateur choir. The use of organ as the sole accompaniment, with a part that is also not technically difficult, means that performances of the piece are relatively inexpensive and do not present the logistical problems of choir and orchestra placement. Congregational hymns actively engage the congregation in the drama.

The Twentieth Century

In general, the passion was not a popular genre in the twentieth century either, though two settings caused sensations when they were first performed: the 1965 setting of Luke's passion by the Polish composer Krzysztof Penderecki (b. 1933) and the 1982 setting of John's passion by the Estonian composer Arvo Pärt (b. 1935).

On the Wednesday evening of Holy Week, March 30, 1966, the world premiere of Penderecki's *Passio et Mors Domini Nostri Jesu Christi Secundum Lucam* took place in Münster, Germany. Prior to the performance Penderecki told the press, "The Passion is the suffering and death of Christ, but it is also the suffering and death at Auschwitz, the tragic experience of mankind, in the middle of the twentieth century. In this sense, it should according to my intentions and feelings have a universal, humanistic character like *Threnody*."[10] Penderecki chose to set the text in Latin rather than his native Polish or German because of its universal comprehensibility. The text comprises ten passages from Luke, three from John, excerpts from five Psalms, and the Lamentations of Jeremiah. He also includes four non-biblical interpolations that include a Latin hymn and the *Stabat Mater* sequence. This setting is largely atonal, using extended techniques for the chorus, including shouting, hissing, and giggling. Its two parts feature twenty-seven sections, scored for three choruses, boy choir, and large orchestra. Although the score is typified by tone clusters in the orchestra and dense writing, Penderecki has great command over his resources and balances the onslaught of the

10. The Threnody to which he refers is his own piece for 52 string instruments, composed in 1960, entitled *Threnody to the Victims of Hiroshima*.

combined choruses and orchestra with passages for smaller ensembles. One of the most effective of these comes toward the end of the work when a choir sings an excerpt from the *Stabat Mater* sequence, emphasizing the grief of the bereaved woman. Penderecki's passion is a powerful piece that continues to perplex and amaze.

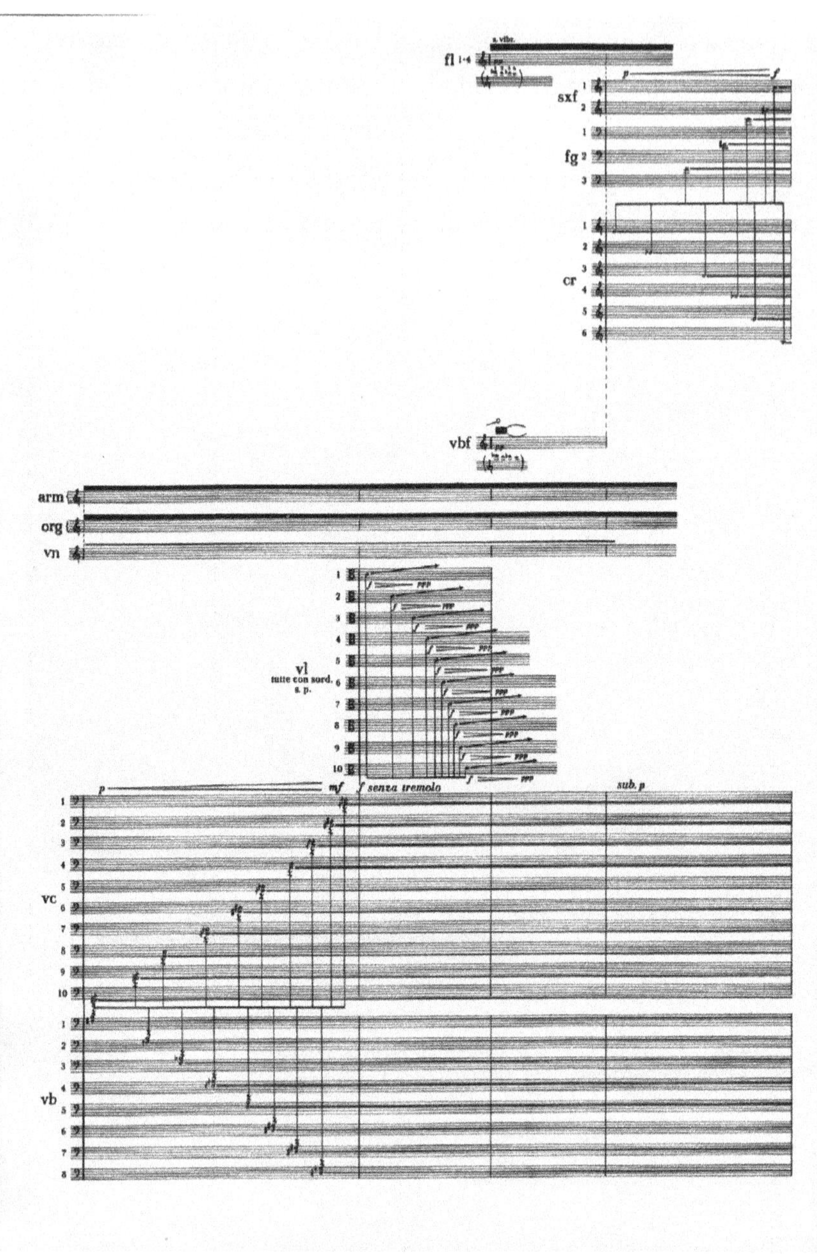

Excerpt from Penderecki's *Passio et Mors Domini Nostri Jesu Christi Secundum Lucam* (Universal).

Arvo Pärt: *Passio*

Musical development in the twentieth century was marked by rapid and significant change, including the abandonment of tonality, the emancipation of the bar line, the adoption of serial techniques that use all twelve pitches in the equal-tempered system, incorporation of music from non-Western traditions, and the use of electronic and amplified instruments.

One composer, Arvo Pärt, found a highly original voice and used it to set a number of significant Christian texts, including the *Te Deum* and *Stabat Mater*. In 1976, Pärt developed a new creative process reminiscent in some ways of sounding bells, hence its appellation, "tintinnabula." The technique is seemingly simple, comprising just two musical lines, one moving in largely stepwise motion and the other employing the notes of a principal triad. In his *Passio*, Pärt used this technique to set John's account of the passion in Latin in a single movement lasting some seventy-five minutes. *Passio Domini Nostri Jesu Christi Secundum Joannem* is scored for choir and soloists, accompanied by an instrumental ensemble of violin, oboe, cello, bassoon, and organ. Following tradition, Pärt assigns the role of Jesus to a bass, and that of Pontius Pilate to a tenor, but the role of the Evangelist (commonly sung by a tenor), Pärt assigns to a quartet of singers accompanied by four instruments. The choir, sometimes doubled by the organ, sings the roles of the High Priest, Peter, and the minor characters.

Tintinnabula as a musical style does not use harmony in the same way as the "common practice" harmony of Haydn, Mozart, and others, where a tonic key is presented as the "home" key at the beginning and end of a piece. In Pärt's new technique, however, there is no modulation to new keys or use of chromatic pitches. Silence is an important compositional device for Pärt, frequently used between short musical phrases. There are also rhythmic innovations in the tintinnabula style. For *Passio*, Pärt created a rhythmic scheme of three-note values—short, medium, and long—which are ascribed to each syllable of the text depending on its position in a phrase and in the relationship of one phrase to another. Pärt distinguishes different voices in his passion by ascribing to them different relative values. Some of his compositional process is mathematical. For example, the text he used for the Evangelist has 210 phrases, grouped into four sections of fifty phrases each, with a concluding set of ten. Each of the four main sections begins with a different solo voice that sings two phrases. There is then a change of texture every two phrases, so that after the solo voice has begun, the other voices and instruments are added one by one until all eight are heard together; this pattern is then reversed back down to a single voice, and the process begins again.[11] Most listeners will not notice this process but, as Paul Hillier notes, on close study "it is impossible to account in prose for the numerous subtleties within this pattern, which consists in several layers of interconnecting, perfectly balanced details, operating both within each section and from one section to another, so that at comparable phrases in each section a variation of the same idea is taking place."[12] I cannot undertake a full discussion of *Passio* here, but in my estimation it is a work of such remarkable genius that it will take its place in history alongside the passions of Bach.

11. Hillier, *Arvo Pärt*, 131.
12. Ibid., 132.

Excerpt (system 3) from Arvo Pärt's *Passio Domino Nostri Jesu Christi Secundum Joannem*.

Passion music has by no means been limited to classical music genres. The early 1970s witnessed Andrew Lloyd Webber's rock opera *Jesus Christ Superstar* (with lyrics by Tim Rice) and Stephen Schwartz's *Godspell* (in collaboration with John-Michael Tebelak). Although both contain elements of traditional passions, they are much more widely known than most classical settings, in large part because of the style of their music and the non-liturgical formats in which they have been presented. Their popularity raises several interesting questions. First, it is striking that earlier musical settings of the passion were not written for the stage. Medieval passion plays, for example, died out in the Renaissance without giving rise to staged musical performances. Largely because the church prohibited drama during Lent, composers continued to set the passion story to music, but without stage action. Instead, they concentrated on developing character and drama solely by musical means. Only late in the twentieth century do we begin to find examples of operatic settings for the passion, such as Jonathan Harvey's *Passion and Resurrection*, a church opera in twelve scenes (1981).[13] Second, part of the work of the evangelists—the writers of the Gospels—was to evangelize. But although the move from church to concert hall can certainly help broaden the audience for the passion story, to be truly engaging to contemporary audiences on a global scale it must also be presented in modern language *and* style. Third, the church constantly struggles to be relevant to contemporary audiences, which are constantly changing. Thus, while the settings from the 1970s may seem dated now, their use of electric guitars and drum sets, and their emphasis on rock-style vocals have paved the way for the multimedia, fusion settings by composers of the late-twentieth and early-twenty-first century, such as Tan Dun and Osvaldo Golijov.

Passion 2000 and Beyond

Dun (b. 1957) and Golijov (b. 1960) were two of the composers commissioned by the Internationale Bachakademie in Stuttgart, Germany to compose musical settings for the passion narratives in the Gospels. They were jointed by Sofia Gubaidulina (b. 1931) and Wolfgang Rihm (b. 1952). The four composers were each asked to write a piece in commemoration of the 250th anniversary of the death of Johann Sebastian Bach for what became known as the Passion 2000 project. They were each assigned an evangelist and encouraged to engage the text in innovative ways.

The contributions by Gubaidulina, Dun, and Golijov are all syncretic, combining different forms of beliefs and practices into new patterns of meaning. Gubaidulina's contribution was the *Johannes-Passion.* In 2002, she followed this with the *Johannes-Ostern* (Easter according to John), commissioned by Hannover Rundfunk. Originally the *Passion* was in Russian, but she has revised it in German so that now the two works together—her largest works to

13. This piece, like its predecessor the Latin Church drama, invites congregational participation in the singing of the plainsong hymns.

date—form a diptych on the death and resurrection of Christ. The *Passion* is scored for four soloists, two choirs, and large orchestra. The music is dark and dramatic and reflects her Russian heritage with prominent use of bells and orthodox chants.

In considering the text, Gubaidulina was determined to include the resurrection so that the work would look not only to Christ's past but also to his future. She therefore used both the Gospel according to John and the Revelation of John the Divine. One of the most significant events in her *Passion* is the death of Christ, here described by Gubaidulina herself:

> I sensed that the narration of Jesus' earthly life path must in no case be allowed to end with a "solution of the dramatic conflict"; after such a dramatic process, there could only be one thing—a sign from the Day of Judgment. This meant an extreme dissonance, a kind of cry or scream. And following this final scream, only one thing was possible—silence. There is no continuation and there can be no continuation: "It is finished."[14]

Tan Dun, a Buddhist, titled his setting *Water Passion after St. Matthew* and described it as "musical metaphysics and drama based on the story of Jesus's Passion according to St. Matthew."[15] Dun, who grew up in China under Mao, was twenty when he first heard Bach's music. It was a transformational and cathartic experience: "You are standing on the ruins. Everything's been destroyed. Family's been destroyed, culture [has] been destroyed. And nobody [was] allowed to touch anything Western or ancient. And suddenly you heard Bach. It's like a medicine curing everything you were suffering."[16]

14. "Sofia Gubaidulina: Passion and Resurrection of Jesus Christ," *Sikorski*, 2002, http://www.sikorski.de/3028/en/sofia_gubaidulina_passion_and_resurrection_of_jesus_christ.html.
15. "Dialogues with Tan Dun," 2000, http://tandun.com/composition/water-passion. Dun's website also has the libretto and images from performances of his *Water Passion*, as well as information about his other works.

He describes his *Water Passion* as an answer to Bach's *St. Matthew Passion*, with "the water representing the tears, the resurrection, the circling, incarnation." As its title implies, water is an important feature of the piece. A "Water-Instruments-Orchestra"—seventeen transparent water bowls played by members of the ensemble using cups and flicking—produces a wide variety of pitched and unpitched water sounds. Dun thought of water as "a metaphor for the unity of the eternal and the external, as well as a symbol of baptism, renewal, re-creation and resurrection."[17] Water is not the only unusual part of the aural experience, however. Dun has fused a number of diverse elements: the fiddling of the Silk Road cultures, the solo and choral vocalizations from his "Sound Map of One World Tradition" (which include chanting), Tuvan (Mongolian) overtone singing, and the high-pitched "calligraphy" (Dun's term) of Eastern Opera traditions, and four-part chorales that recall Bach's passions. The choir also plays stones, Tibetan bells, and other small instruments.

Dun's work starts and ends with the sound of water. He set his text in English and includes the Baptism of Jesus and the temptation in the wilderness. *Water Passion*'s two parts comprise a total of nine sections, plus a short "water cadenza." The penultimate movement, entitled "Death and Earthquake," is a devastating response to the crucifixion. It includes an ominous chant and the emotional cry of the xun, a Chinese ceramic vessel flute in the shape of an egg. Unusually, Dun chose to end *Water Passion* with the resurrection, so the devastation of the death and earthquake is superseded as the scene turns from dark to light, and, as is perhaps befitting of a Buddhist interpreting Christian Scripture, Christ sings "a time to love, a time of peace."

16. Davis Schulman and Jeffrey Freymann-Weyr, "Tan Dun's Cultural Evolution," *NPR*, June 15, 2006, http://www.npr.org/templates/story/story.php?storyId=5148259.

17. "Riveting 'Water Passion' at SummerFest," *San Diego Story*, August 6, 2012, http://www.sandiegostory.com/riveting-water-passion-at-summerfest.

Osvaldo Golijov also sought to extend the musical boundaries beyond the limits of the traditional Western concert choir and orchestra. His *Pasión Según San Marcos* weaves South American, Cuban, and Jewish musical influences into the Western tradition. It is scored for female and male vocalists, soprano solo, up to eight soloists from the choir, one Afro-Cuban dancer, one Capoeira dancer (a Brazilian blend of martial arts and dance), choir (with a minimum of sixty singers), and an orchestra that includes such exotic instruments as the berimbau (a single string instrument used in Capoeira), the accordion with efx (sound effects), and the *tres* (a Cuban guitar). He not only uses Mark's Gospel but also texts from the Kaddish, the Lamentations of Jeremiah, Psalms 113–119, and poems by the Spanish writer Rosalía de Castro (1837–1885).

Golijov explained that he wanted to record the Christians like Rembrandt recorded the Jews:

> My great grandmother had a picture of *Jeremiah Lamenting the Fall of Jerusalem* by Rembrandt—it's the greatest Jewish picture ever. He was not a Jew, but he lived amongst them. I cannot aspire to be Rembrandt but if at least one section of the passion has the truth about Christianity that Rembrandt's paintings have about Judaism, I'll be all right—that's enough.[18]

Golijov's *Pasión* represents an enormous cultural shift not only in its orchestration but also in its setting: a South American Lenten street scene celebration where news of the trial and crucifixion is spread by voices and drums. Singers and dancers, both male and female, portray the major characters, and Jesus is portrayed by both male and female performers of color, which can only serve to enhance and broaden the appeal of the story. The success of the Passion 2000 project owes much to this huge diversity of musical styles, and the gospel, which

18. http://www.osvaldogolijov.com/wd1.htm.

might otherwise be lost to many non-Christians, is thus perpetuated outside the liturgy.

These innovative and syncretic versions of the passion are not the only successful ones, however. Wolfgang Rihm and more recently Francis Grier have used more traditional musical resources to great dramatic effect. Both of their settings rely on the work of accomplished poets who have sought to re-envision the story. Rihm set Luke's passion narrative supplementing it with a text by Paul Celan (1920–1970) to modernize the narrative and give it relevance. His contribution to the Passion 2000 project, *Deus Passus*, is scored for five soloists, mixed chorus, and large orchestra. According to critic Christian Eisert, Rihm's music uses the text to "retrieve the Passion history from the noncommittalism of times past and bring it in line with today's expectations. He places 'suffering humanity' next to the 'suffering God' [the *Deus Passus* of the title], thus radically refashioning the hitherto prevalent conception of a Passion."[19] Musically, this setting is the least radical of the early-twenty-first-century passions, though the text does endeavor to reengage the listener with the story by using a modern voice.

The Passion of Jesus of Nazareth, by Francis Grier and Elizabeth Cook, a co-commission of VocalEssence and the BBC Singers, premiered in 2006. The Grier-Cook passion is particularly effective, combining elements from different versions of the traditional story with elements of their own devising, and a children's chorus that lends authenticity and another dimension to the drama of the story. The piece requires a large orchestra, more than twenty soloists, and SATB chorus with many divisions. Its scale and uncompromising technical difficulty will inhibit frequent live performance, so most listeners will be dependent upon recordings for access to the piece.

19. Liner note to Rihm's *Deus Passus*, Stuttgart Bach Collegium, Helmuth Rilling (conductor), Hanssler Classics, B00005MLLQ.

The Passion of Jesus of Nazareth is a significant piece because it tells a very human story, grounded in several realities with libretto and music that are both poetic and memorable.

Conclusion

As with other pieces of classical music, it is hard to explain why certain passion settings have survived. Most are validated by time, in spite of changing fashion and tastes. Though live performances are constrained by financial and technical limitations, recording technology and the Internet have vastly expanded listening options, so that the passion story can still be heard anew year after year. Even if listening to passion settings has become a largely solitary experience, the transformative power of the music can nonetheless lead listeners through the narrative, constantly inspiring them to reengage Christ's passion.

Glossary

cantata: a composition for one or more voices usually comprising solos, duets, recitatives, and choruses and sung to an instrumental accompaniment

***conclusio* or *gratiarum actio*:** the closing chorus (often an "'amen'")

***exordium* or *introitus*:** the opening chorus (e.g., "Here begins the gospel according to . . .")

***historia*:** an umbrella term for a musical setting based on a biblical narrative, such as the Christmas story; the most important type, however, being the passion

motet passion: sung throughout; characterization is achieved by changing the number of voices singing different texts

oratorio: a lengthy choral work, usually religious in nature, consisting chiefly of recitatives, arias, and choruses, without action or scenery

oratorio passion: employs recitatives, arias, ensembles, choruses, and instrumental pieces

passion: an oratorio based on a gospel narrative of the passion

plainsong passion: originally intoned on a single pitch, then to the passion tone, then to plainsong with different pitches for characterization

responsorial passion: late-fifteenth-century plainsong passion with polyphony for the *synagoga* parts

***summa passionis* (also called passion harmony):** utilizes texts from all four Gospels and the Seven Last Words, and usually includes an *exordium* and *conclusio*

***synagoga*:** the minor characters

***turba*:** the crowd

***vox Christi*:** the voice of Christ

Suggested Recordings

Bach, J. S. *Matthäuspassion*, English Baroque Soloists, Monteverdi Choir, John Eliot Gardiner (conductor), Archiv Produktion, B0000057DG, 1989.

Beethoven, Ludwig van. *Christus am Ölberge*, Deutscher-Symphonie-Orchester Berlin, Kent Nagano (conductor), Harmonia Mundi Fr., B0000CEWVC, 2004.

Dun, Tan. *Water Passion after St. Matthew*, Rias-Kammerchor Berlin, Tan Dun (conductor), Sony, B0000787FZ, 2002.

Golijov, Osvaldo. *Pasión Según San Marcos*, Schola Cantorum de Caracas, María Guinand (conductor), Hanssler Classics, 98404, 2000.

Gubaidulina, Sofia. *Johannes-Passion*, St. Petersburg Mariinsky Theatre Orchestra, Valery Gergiev (conductor), Hanssler Classics, B00005QE11.

Liszt, Franz. *Christus*, Stuttgart Radio Symphony Orchestra, Helmuth Rilling (conductor), Brilliant Classics, B00008UANN, 2003.

Pärt, Arvo. *Passio et Mors Domini Nostri Jesu Christi Secundum Joannem*, The Hilliard Ensemble, Paul Hiller (conductor), ECM Records, B0000031UP, 1994.

Penderecki, Krzysztof. *Passio et Mors Domini Nostri Jesu Christi Secundum Lucam*, Polish Radio Orchestra & Chorus Katowice, Sigune von Osten (conductor), PolyGram, B000004CVQ, 1990.

Rihm, Wolfgang. *Deus Passus*, Stuttgart Bach Collegium, Helmuth Rilling (conductor), Hanssler Classics, B00005MLLQ.

Schütz, Heinrich. *St. Matthew Passion*, Württemberg Chamber Choir, Dieter Kurz (conductor), Ent. Media Partners, B000002X7S, 1997.

Stainer, John. *The Crucifixion*, BBC Singers, Brian Kay (conductor), Chandos, B000000B1E, 1997.

PART III

Literature

In some ways, reading literature based on the passion narratives of the gospels is simply an extension of reading the narratives themselves. After all, when we read the gospels, we are reading literature and, as the first section of this book argues, the gospels themselves are interpretations of earlier oral or written sources. To be sure, for many the experience of reading (or hearing) the passion is tied closely to a religious service or is part of a spiritual exercise (Lenten devotions, for example), so that certain expectations are at play in the reading. And even those who read the narratives outside of any religious or spiritual context also take them up with expectations—sometimes the same, sometimes different from religious readers. For all readers, therefore, engaging the passion is challenging because of what we bring to it.

Biblical commentaries, devotional books on the passion, or reflective essays are commonly the first place many readers will go for guidance in reading the passion narratives. The essays in this section invite readers to look at novels and poems as another source for more engaging encounters with the passion.

John McWilliams's essay surveys the passion in American literature. After setting his themes in the writings and history of early America, he turns to poems by Walt Whitman (1819–92), Edwin

Arlington Robinson (1869–1935), and Emily Dickinson (1830–86). In each instance, he reads the poems themselves with keen insight and sets them in the context of their authors' lives and the changing shape of American history. McWilliams next turns to three novels, examining them under the rubric of "imitatio Christi" (the imitation of Christ), borrowing the phrase from the title of Thomas à Kempis's widely read meditations on the life of Christ (first published anonymously in 1418). The novels are Harriet Beecher Stowe's *Uncle Tom's Cabin* (1852), Herman Melville's *Billy Budd* (posthumously published in 1924), and Nathaniel West's *Miss Lonelyhearts* (1933). Here, too, McWilliams offers deep readings of the texts and sets them in the context of American religious and political history. McWilliams's survey concludes with a reading of Countee Cullen's poem "The Black Christ (Hopefully Dedicated to White America)" (1929), in which the author compares the lynching of his black hero to the crucifixion of Jesus and refers to the cross of the biblical passion as "the first leaf in a line / Of Trees on which a Man should swing / World without end." McWilliams's survey points to a strain in American literature that, though influenced in significant ways by the piety that was common in the nation's religious history, is far from sentimental and at times prophetic in its critique of American culture.

Michael Katz writes on the Russian novelist Fyodor Dostoevsky, many of whose works explore "how the life of faith is to be imagined" in the face of many reasons not to believe.[1] Dostoevsky's novels are not easy reads. But as Katz demonstrates in his treatment of Dostoevsky's "fiery 'Furnace of Doubt,'" they are worth the effort. He also shows how Dostoevsky returns to important questions again and

1. This is the theme of Rowan Williams's *Dostoevsky: Language, Faith, and Fiction* (Waco, TX: Baylor University Press, 2008). The phrase first appears in the introduction (p. 5), but is addressed in various ways throughout the book.

again, having his fictional characters wrestle with the issue of faith (and with one another) from many perspectives, never allowing his characters or his reader easy answers. In setting up his treatment of Dostoevsky's wrestling with issues of faith, Katz offers a brief synopsis of Russian Orthodoxy, emphasizing its linking of the passion with the resurrection and its use of icons to draw worshippers into the gospel stories. This will provide important background for readers unfamiliar with this form of Christianity. Katz next draws on Dostoevsky's personal correspondence, notebooks, and novels to show how he wrestles with belief in the resurrection and the reality of the crucifixion. In the first part of the essay Katz explores scenes in which Dostoevsky treats the story of the raising of Lazarus (John 11) and then turns to Dostoevsky's fictional treatment of a moment in his own life—seeing Hans Holbein's painting "The Body of Christ in the Tomb" (1521). Katz's conclusion to the essay ends with a stark question, one that invites readers to engage the passion.

The last essay in this section treats J. R. R. Tolkien's *The Lord of the Rings*. In the essay, Matthew Dickerson, the author of numerous books and essays on Tolkien and C. S. Lewis, explores how Tolkien's imaginative portrayal of Frodo Baggins reflects his deep Catholic faith. Drawing on Tolkien's essays, personal correspondence, and the novels themselves, Dickerson argues that Tolkien does not make his point with a simplistic allegorical identification of Frodo and Jesus but with a complex narrative that uses multiple characters and plotlines to explore both the theological significance of the gospel and its moral applicability. In developing his argument, Dickerson examines the "passions" of Gandalf, Aragorn, and Frodo, finding in Frodo's journey, with its wounds, stripes, and burdens, an evocation of Isaiah's Suffering Servant psalms and the gospels' use of them. Dickerson concludes that Tolkien's story does not treat Frodo as a symbol of Christ, but of all Christians whose journeys—like Frodo's—have both triumphs and failures.

Readers of these essays—and the novels and poems they discuss—will find new approaches to reading the passion and greater insight into the questions it raises.

6

The Passion in American Literature

John McWilliams

And though I may not guess the kind—
Correctly—yet to me
A piercing Comfort it affords
In passing Calvary—

To note the fashions—of the Cross—
And how they're mostly worn—
Still fascinated to presume
That Some—are like My Own—
—Emily Dickinson (1863)[1]

In 1787, the United States of America was politically constituted as a secular republic, soon to be without establishment of religion;

1. Emily Dickinson, *The Poems of Emily Dickinson*, ed. R. W. Franklin (Cambridge, MA: Belknap Press of Harvard University Press, 1998), 249–50.

but there was every expectation that the republic would remain a nation of Christians, if not a Christian nation. Not only was the white population by 1800 still 99 percent Christian, but the Continental Congress had, during the Revolutionary War, issued proclamations seeking the blessing of Christ for forgiveness of the sins of the people.[2] Immediately after George Washington was sworn into office as the first president, an Episcopalian bishop and a Dutch-Reformed chaplain conducted a church service attended by Washington and the joint houses of Congress. Christian services would continue to be held in the Hall of the House of Representatives until the 1850s. They were conducted first by Presbyterian, Episcopalian, or Congregationalist ministers, and later joined by Catholic priests, by Baptist, Methodist and evangelical ministers, and then, beginning in the late 1830s, by more controversial denominations like the Unitarians (Jared Sparks) or Swedenborgians. Sermon subjects included the "Second Coming of Christ" and "Christ's Body the Bread of Life, Christ's Blood the Drink of the Righteous." Among the regular attendees of Christian services in the halls of Congress during the first decade of the century was then-president Thomas Jefferson, the self-acknowledged Deist who famously wrote, in 1802, that there should be a "wall of separation between Church and State." To be sure, Holy Communion was not permitted in the Capitol, but the Eucharist was intermittently offered at lengthy services held in two of the executive office buildings, the Treasury Building and the War Office.[3] Neither in legislative ceremony nor in bricks and mortar was Jefferson's "wall of separation" much in evidence.

2. Richard W. Fox estimates that "in 1800 there were only fifty thousand Catholics and two thousand Jews in a population of five million" (Richard W. Fox, *Jesus in America* [San Francisco: HarperCollins, 2005], 160).
3. See James H. Hutson, *Religion and the Founding of the American Republic* (Washington, DC: Library of Congress, 1998), 75–97.

What was meant by "Congress shall make no law respecting an establishment of religion, or prohibiting the free exercise thereof"? There were probably as many answers as there were people who spoke or thought about the phrase. How far did the individual's right to life and liberty, as sanctioned by the laws of nature and nature's God, extend? According to the Preamble, the Constitution pledged the Republic to "secure the Blessings of Liberty to Ourselves and our Posterity" but surely none of the ratifiers of the First Amendment ever believed that "free exercise" of religion should be extended to witchcraft (now protected as Wicca) or to atheism. Nor, however, would the signers have agreed with John Winthrop who, influenced by his reading of Paul, had famously argued before the General Court of Massachusetts in 1645 that "civil liberty" is "the proper end and object of authority . . . a liberty to that only which is good, just and honest . . . a liberty maintained and exercised in a way of subjection to authority . . . the same kind of liberty wherewith Christ has made us free."[4]

In addition to issues of separating church and state, there were the multiple possible meanings of the phrases "Christian nation" or "nation of Christians." Did one's identity as a "Christian" require the Trinitarian faith specified in both the Nicene Creed and the Shorter Westminster Catechism? Or, as many a Puritan descendant believed, was worship of the triune nature of God less important than justification by faith in Christ Jesus, with the doing of good works as sequential evidence of one's regenerative faith? Could a person who joined a Protestant church, who believed in the Great Commandment and the Sermon on the Mount, but who kept silent about Christ's singular divinity as the Son of God, possibly be a

4. John Winthrop, "Speech to the General Court at Hingham, Massachusetts, July 3 1645," in *The Journal of John Winthrop, 1630–1649*, ed. Richard S. Dunn and Laetitia Yeandle (Cambridge, MA: Harvard University Press, 1996), 280–84.

Christian? What if, as some evangelicals exhorted, a person chose to love Jesus and one's fellow man with the whole heart, regardless of any church affiliation, sacraments, or the law? Did such unchurchly attitudes qualify or disqualify their adherents as members of Christ's body? And what was the highest reach of Christian conduct? Was it an act of pride or humility to believe that an imperfect human being could, in Thomas à Kempis's phrase, live one's life in imitation of Christ? If imitation of Christ were possible, must every true Christian, as Charles Grandison Finney urged, continuously strive to embody the perfection of love?

Consider the problem posed by Jefferson, whose ideas left such an impress on the nation's founding. Jefferson urged a wall of separation between church and state at the same time he was attending Christian services in Congress. As he assembled the so-called Jefferson Bible (*The Life and Morals of Jesus of Nazareth*), he stripped away not only Acts, Revelation, and the letters of Paul, but all Gospel chapters and verses describing Christ's miracles, as well as every mention of the virgin birth, of Christ's resurrection, the Second Coming, the kingdom, and the millennium. And yet there is no reason to doubt Jefferson's sincerity when he wrote to Benjamin Rush: "I am a Christian, in the only sense he [Christ] wished any one to be; sincerely attached to his doctrines, in preference to all others; ascribing to himself every human excellence; and believing he never claimed any other."[5] Very few Americans in Jefferson's day would have accepted this definition of a Christian. How many would do so today?

Of the many points at issue in assessing America as a "Christian nation" or "nation of Christians," response to the crucifixion had to remain crucial. Christ's prophetic words at the Last Supper, "This

5. Thomas Jefferson, *The Jefferson Bible: The Life and Morals of Jesus of Nazareth* (Boston: Beacon, 1989), 30.

is my blood of the covenant, which is poured out for many for the forgiveness of sins. I tell you I shall not drink again of this fruit of the vine until that day when I drink it new with you in my Father's kingdom" (Matt. 26:27-29), foretell the blood of bodily crucifixion yet bind crucifixion inseparably to the everlasting life of resurrection embodied in the surety of the new covenant. Without the resurrection, as many including Jonathan Edwards have noted, the crucifixion becomes intolerable, especially so in light of the benign assumptions about human nature advanced by Jeffersonian Deists and latter-day Armenians. The disciples' complete abandonment of Christ to his lonely agony on the cross presents a view of our ordinary human nature—cowardly, unfaithful, forgetful and self-serving—that is wholly at odds with the Enlightenment faith in man's reason, intelligence, and underlying regard for good. When, therefore, Jefferson chooses to end his redaction of the Gospels with John 19:41-42 ("Now in the place where he was crucified, there was a garden; and in the garden a new sepulcher, wherein was never man yet laid. There laid they Jesus. And rolled a great stone to the door of the sepulcher, and departed."), Jefferson chooses to forgo assurance of the triumph of good for the sake of avoiding what he regards as the superstition of miracle. No resurrection, no kingdom. Jefferson leaves us with a code of sublime morals sanctioned and authenticated by no authority beyond the human being who spoke them. By what power the meek could ever inherit the earth, or God's chosen could ever go toward Jubilee, or even toward some form of apocalypse beyond the western frontier, the Jefferson Bible cannot tell us. Jefferson's *Life and Morals of Jesus of Nazareth* provides a secular faith for a secular republic by assembling the words of Jesus Christ into a code of ethics that deprives them of any covenantal fulfillment.

My purpose in the following pages is to explore a range of American literary responses to the conundrum of the crucifixion posed by the example of Jefferson. Valuing self-reliance and individuality, canonical American writers, mostly Protestant, confronted the significance of the crucifixion without the assurances of theological belief or sectarian dogma. I choose my texts partly with regard to canonical status, partly because of their influence, and partly because of my personal sense of their literary quality, but without any claim to be comprehensive, and without pre-selection according to authors' personal religious heritage. My groupings are determined by chronology and genre, hopefully in an orderly sequence. It is my conviction that most scholars of American literature, for whom the biblical heritage of American literature is no longer a central concern, have not been in a position to address the problems I hope to clarify.

I. Six Poems

During the middle decades of the twentieth century, as a canon of American literature was first established, and then hardened before its current implosion, no poet was deemed as central as Walt Whitman. He was repeatedly accepted, on his own terms, as the bard of democracy and equality, celebrator of the individual and the masses, singer of the soul and the body. His leaves of grass attested to life's possibilities growing everywhere and in everyone; his faith in a divine life force was thought to be particularly American because it accepted all faiths while rejecting all dogma, remaining resilient enough to defy death and to survive civil war. "Song of Myself" (1855), Whitman's signature poem, proclaimed that all selves live in all other selves; reciprocal patterns of inspiration and respiration lead the "I" (Walt Whitman) to project himself into all others, and then lead the "you" (the reader, all others) to project our selves back into the poet, who could thus proclaim one universal human identity.

This process required Whitman to celebrate the pains of the past as well as its glories, to proclaim a living Christ within his self and our selves. If "Song of Myself" has a climactic passage, it is surely the sections later numbered 37–39 of the 52 sections that were to comprise a kind of weekly liturgy for democratic believers. After imagining celebrated historical tragedies and everyday individual sufferings, the narrator experiences the crisis of feeling himself suddenly reduced from "Walt Whitman a cosmos" to the meanest of beggars:

> Askers embody themselves in me, and I am embodied in them,
> I project my hat, sit shame-faced, and beg.
>
> Enough! enough! enough!
> Somehow I have been stunn'd. Stand back!
> Give me a little time beyond my cuff'd head, slumbers, dreams, gaping,
> I discover myself on the verge of a usual mistake.
>
> That I could forget the mockers and insults!
> That I could forget the trickling tears and the blows of the bludgeons and hammers!
> That I could look with a separate look on my own crucifixion and bloody crowning.
>
> I remember now,
> I resume the overstaid fraction,
> The grave of rock multiplies what has been confided to it, or to any graves,
> Corpses rise, gashes heal, fastenings roll from me.
>
> I troop forth replenish'd with supreme power, one of an average unending procession,
> Inland and sea-coast we go, and pass all boundary lines.[6]

Well aware that many of his contemporaries would still have regarded Christ as the Son of Man, separate and above fallen humankind, Whitman affronts his readers with customary heresy, but

6. Walt Whitman, "Song of Myself," in *Leaves of Grass and Other Writings*, ed. Michael Moon et al. (New York: Norton, 2002), 63. "Song of Myself" was first published in 1855 in the first edition of *Leaves of Grass*. The Norton edition reprints the so-called Deathbed Edition of 1891–92.

this time without comic overtones. His "usual mistake," as explained in the next stanza, is to have forgotten that his truest identity is indeed to be Christ. Through his empathy with the suffering of the world ("trickling tears"), he bears the blows of crucifixion and he wears the bloody crown, as presumably do we in reading these lines ("what I shall assume, you shall assume"). His lowest moment ("sit shame-faced and beg") is his highest moment; he has saved himself by losing himself. And the consequence is his certain, sure resurrection, the falling away of his shroud, his rising from the grave of rock in order to then lead the "average unending procession" of his fellow citizens inward and presumably westward to the Pacific, hindered by no boundary.

How implausibly easy these transformations are said to be! Whitman's reciprocal rhetoric (I am you and you are me) allows him to claim identity with Christ, to proclaim his own resurrection, and then to assert his own prophetic leadership, all within a mere nine lines. There is here no cry of human pain ("My God, my God why hast thou forsaken me"), no vinegar, and no spear, only the distant alliterative evocation of "trickling tears and the blows of the bludgeons." No one is watching and no one is absent because the experience, despite its claim to facticity, is wholly visionary, not actual. Whitman's resurrection follows his crucifixion immediately, without surprise and apparently without joy. Again, there is no one there to witness. As we read, the entire nine lines slide quickly by as in a remembered dream, and for good reason. Once Whitman has established that he can *be* anyone he chooses to be at any point on his journey, his identity with Christ becomes, like all his other identities, a momentary convenience, a trope he can call upon in a moment of crisis, then pass on to a different identity serving his next need. For purposes of wish fulfillment, for invoking an American yet to be, no rhetoric could be more powerful than Whitman's, but it has precious little to do with the immediacy and specificity of the passion in the Gospel narratives.

An Afro-American spiritual, probably sung at the same time Whitman was writing "Song of Myself," could hardly be more different:

Were you there when they crucified my Lord?
Were you there when they crucified my Lord?
Sometimes it causes me to tremble, tremble, tremble,
Were you there when they crucified my Lord?

Were you there when they nailed him to the tree?
Were you there when they nailed him to the tree?
Sometimes it causes me to tremble, tremble, tremble,
Were you there when they nailed him to the tree?

Were you there when they pierced him in the side?
Were you there when they pierced him in the side?
Sometimes it causes me to tremble, tremble, tremble,
Were you there when they pierced him in the side?[7]

The singer can have no illusion that he or she might actually be Christ in the self-authenticating manner of Walt Whitman. The repeated phrase "Were you there" is an insistent question, not a claim. To label such a phrase "anaphora" is to demean it into the rhetoric of literary critics. "Were you there" challenges all listeners to bear witness to the central defining experience of their spiritual world. The underlying assumption of the lines may be that the life of a slave is a form of crucifixion, but the import of its phrasing is to question whether the listeners will be able to raise their souls to fully appreciate and participate in its meaning. The slow pace with which the song works its way through its seven stanzas, always attending to the chronological sequence of the gospel account, and broken only

7. For the seven-stanza version of "Were You There When They Crucified My Lord," see Gwendolin Sims Warren, *Ev'ry Time I Feel the Spirit* (New York: Henry Holt, 1998), 99–100.

by the triple falling cadence on "tremble, tremble, tremble," suggests that the bearing of true witness is no easy process. "Sometimes" the speakers and listeners will be able to rise to trembling, but sometimes, evidently, they will not.

When the resurrection is invoked in the last stanza, the diction of the repeated lines changes, but not the underlying rhetorical form:

Did you know He is risen from the dead?
Did you know He is risen from the dead?
Sometimes I want to shout "glory, glory, glory!"
Did you know He is risen from the dead?

Both the questioning of true witness ("Did you know") and the acknowledging of insufficiency ("Sometimes") are still here. It is striking that three widely known recordings of "Were You There When They Crucified My Lord?"—by Marion Anderson, Harry Belafonte, and Johnny Cash—all eliminate the stanzas referring to Christ's burial and resurrection. Like Jefferson, they leave us the crucifixion only. Whether there has been a need to shorten the song for a three to four minute recording, or whether reference to a sure resurrection might arouse the disbelief of twentieth-century listeners—or both—is not clear.

Walt Whitman, little known until late in his life, was to be celebrated for a full century after his death. Edwin Arlington Robinson, highly regarded in his early maturity, has become nearly forgotten. Among many possible reasons for Robinson's eclipse is his preference for traditional pre-modernist verse forms through which he expresses unwelcome, accusatory thoughts:

CALVARY

Friendless and faint, with martyred steps and slow,
Faint for the flesh, but for the spirit free,
Stung by the mob that came to see the show,

The Master toiled along to Calvary;
We gibed him, as he went, with houndish glee,
Till his dimmed eyes for us did overflow;
We cursed his vengeless hands thrice wretchedly,—
And this was nineteen hundred years ago.
But after nineteen hundred years the shame
Still clings, and we have not made good the loss
That outraged faith has entered in his name.
Ah, when shall come love's courage to be strong!
Tell me, O Lord—tell me, O Lord, how long
Are we to keep Christ writhing on the cross![8]

To Whitman, every democratic self could lay claim to crucifixion and resurrection. To Robinson, poet as well as reader are implicated in the "we" who remain mere onlookers, "come to see the show," and gibe and curse the "Master" from our safe distance. Nineteen hundred years have evidently brought no resurrection, no Second Coming, and not even guilt for our callousness, only the "shame" of being recognized as a people who lack "love's courage" to protest injustice.

Instead of the expected solitude of Calvary, Robinson surrounds Christ with "the mob that came to see the show," a mob surely meant to recall "the crowd" (Romans and Jews) before Pontius Pilate who twice shout "Let him be crucified" (Matt. 27:22-23). Today, as in 1895, Americans who believe themselves members of a Christian nation, if not bound toward salvation, surely do not like to be included among cowardly, sadistic crucifiers, any more than readers of modernist poetry readily grant stature to contemporaries who write Petrarchan sonnets, however finely turned. Robinson risks both sentimentality ("Till his dimmed eyes for us did overflow") and empty exclamation ("Ah, when . . .") but concludes his poem with the forceful plea "Tell me, O Lord, how long" and with an inversion of the Petrarchan rhyme scheme that enables his last phrase to be "keep

8. Edwin Arlington Robinson, "Calvary," in *Selected Poems of Edwin Arlington Robinson*, ed. Morton Dauwen Zabel (New York: Macmillan, 1965), 10–11.

Christ writhing on the cross." No handy Whitmanesque shape-shifting here. Because we lack the love, the will, and the courage to be worthy of the cross, our crucifying of the "Master" can only continue indefinitely.

A poem so unequivocally judgmental as "Calvary" would seem to leave little room for ambiguity of any kind. And yet we should pause over the evasive vagueness of the lines ". . . we have not made good the loss / That outraged faith has entered in his name." Is it Christ's faith, or ours, that has been "outraged" by centuries of unchristian conduct, despite all our lip service? Some hint of a violation of the covenant of grace seems to lie behind the phrase "made good the loss," but the lines remain tantalizingly unspecific. Quite possibly, Robinson's personal inability to believe that Christ's death assured forgiveness of sin enables him vividly to imagine Christ still "writhing on the cross," but not to imagine any good arising from it. Repentance for sin, even if it were to occur, would yield no salvation. The poet's final pleading question, adapted from Ps. 13, "Tell me, O Lord, how long," seem to carry with it the implied answer "forever."

As the epigraph to this essay shows, Emily Dickinson was well aware that there have been many "fashions—of the Cross," each fashion worn as a garment, although most of them are now "worn" with age. To "note" the changing fashions affords her "piercing Comfort," as if her body could be both pierced and comforted in passing by all the changes in meaning that Calvary has undergone. By poem's end, however, she has moved beyond noting fashions, choosing instead to be "fascinated" by the realization that "some" fashions are like her own. Her passion is one among many, yet of singular and unapologetic importance.

We will never be certain whether Emily Dickinson embraced the idea of suffering, or furthered her occasions for suffering, in order to create great poetry out of vicarious pain. We do know that by imagining her own crucifixion, her marriage to Christ, she could exalt her inner emotional suffering once human love had failed her. The best known of her crucifixion poems begins, not by revealing the cause of her suffering, but by imagining herself entitled to be "Empress of Calvary":

> Title divine—is mine
> The Wife—without the Sign—
> Acute Degree—conferred on me—
> Empress of Calvary—
> Royal—all but the Crown—
> Betrothed—without the Swoon
> God gives us Women
> When You hold Garnet to Garnet—
> Gold—to Gold—
> Born—Bridalled—Shrouded—
> In a Day—
> Tri-Victory
> "My Husband"—women say—
> Stroking the Melody—
> Is this the way—[9]

Only metaphorically could the Empress of Calvary be the bride of Christ, even on her cross; she might be titled the bride of Christ, but could never be crowned King of the Jews, nor does she desire to be. To title herself "Empress" is instead to embrace a subversive, pagan alternative to "Son of God."

To be the uncrowned Empress is, however, far preferable to the earthly alternative of being brided. The marvelous double meanings of the line "Born—Bridalled [Brided, Bridled]—Shrouded" with its implied references both to Christ's burial ("shrouded") and to the Trinity ("Tri-Victory"), belittle the tokens of an earthly marriage,

9. Dickinson, *Poems of Emily Dickinson*, 92.

garnet and gold, by comparison to an imagined marriage of Christ and his empress on the cross—without, of course, either woman's swoon or the dogma of theology. Absent any ceremonial "sign," the "degree" conferred upon the Empress of Calvary will be her very own "crown" of thorns. Only in the last three lines do Dickinson's multiple ironies drop away, replaced by frontal satire on the complacency of contemporary brides who believe that, by stroking the melody of marriage, as if their husbands were domesticated cats, they have somehow found "the way." It would hardly surprise us to learn that Emily Dickinson was fully aware that, in the decades immediately following Christ's death, the Christian movement was frequently called "the Way."

The difficulty of accepting or relinquishing mid-nineteenth-century doubt of scriptural revelation here receives acute expression. A less successful poem, written two years later, suggests a suspect overconfidence about Whitmanesque universality of crucifixions:

One Crucifixion is recorded—only—
How many be
Is not affirmed of Mathematics—
Or History—

One Calvary—exhibited to stranger—
As many be
As Persons—or Peninsulas—
Gethsemane—

Is but a Province—in the Being's Centre
Judea
For Journey—or Crusade's Achieving—
Too near—

Our Lord—indeed—made Compound Witness
And yet—
There's newer—nearer Crucifixion
Than That—[10]

The poem arises from the popularity of American pilgrimages to the Holy Land that arose in the 1850s and would attract Herman Melville and Mark Twain, among others. The notion of there being but one holy land, one Gethsemane, and one crucifixion is taken to task by Dickinson's citing of the empty spaces in mathematics and history, the provinciality of Gethsemane and Judea, the similarity of today's pilgrimage to yesterday's crusade, and, most tellingly, the claim that any visitor to Calvary will always remain a "stranger."

Both Gethsemane and Judea, far across the ocean from Dickinson's home in Amherst, Massachusetts, are thus "Too near" to our attentions, especially because, as the poem's closing lines proclaim, "There's newer—nearer Crucifixion / Than That—." This last crucifixion is, of course, her own, one of the many crucifixions to which Jerusalem travelers pay no attention. But this perplexing poem has a forbiddingly jagged quality—syntax continually broken across the lines, lines of one or two words, unrelenting dashes forcing us to work out the punctuation—that impedes the force of her statement. This abrasive quality climaxes in the last quatrain when Dickinson breaks the *abcb* rhyme scheme with an off rhyme (Yet/That), which seems to convey her full-throated contempt for "That" crucifixion (Christ's). Doth the lady protest too much?

The metaphoric subtlety with which Emily Dickinson approached the crucifixion could not be more unlike the direct narrative simplicity of Ezra Pound's "Ballad of the Goodly Fere" (1917). Simon Peter, speaking after the crucifixion, recalls Christ as the good companion, "mate of the wind and sea," and "a man o' men." After the Last Supper, during which, as Peter recalls, "we drank his 'Hale' in the good red wine," Christ vowed he would soon show his disciples "How a brave man dies on the tree":

10. Ibid., 299.

> He cried no cry when they drave the nails
> And the blood gushed hot and free,
> The hounds of the crimson sky gave tongue
> But never a cry cried he.[11]

Here the blood of the new covenant is recalled only as hearty wine drinking among good fellows, and the torturing of Christ brings forth no *"consummatum est,"* no cry of "Why hast thou forsaken me?" Instead, Pound's imagined "goodly fere" presages the tough stoicism, the silent bearing of pain, which was soon to characterize the Hemingway hero. As the modernist simulator of a medieval oral ballad, Pound endows the voice of Simon Peter with the rowdy tones of the then-recent but short-lived movement called "Muscular Christianity," while conveniently forgetting the guilt Simon Peter felt for having denied Christ three times.

What can be concluded about the disparate, often contradictory views of the crucifixion emerging from these six poems, all published within a sixty-year period? Probably no more, but no less, than that their contradictions reflect the bewildering cross currents of their cultural era. Darwinism, the higher criticism, biological and environmental determinism, sudden awareness and concern over T. H. Huxley's word *agnosticism*, half-believing liberal ministers in mainline protestant churches, the social gospel, masculinist reaction against such publications as Elizabeth Cady Stanton's *Women's Bible* (1895), the ecumenicism of the Chicago World's Fair sponsoring a "World's Parliament of Religions" (including Hinduism and Buddhism), immigration of millions of Catholics and Jews into America, shifting of evangelical activities toward new factories and rapid growth of new cities. The list could obviously be much extended; today we could extend it many times over.

11. Ezra Pound, "The Ballad of the Goodly Fere," in *Selected Poems of Ezra Pound* (New York: New Directions, 1964), 11.

All six poems search for spiritual meaning in the crucifixion, even though their creators are as unchurched as their assumed readers. Singularity of truth remains as desired as it is denied. The passion narratives in the Synoptic Gospels retain for these poets an emotional and cultural importance despite the lost authority of scriptural revelation and churchly theology. As poets, they would make music from the Gospels; as creative writers, they wish to think outside the box of any creed; as Americans they feel a special need to escape past traditions. None of these independencies, however, frees them from confronting the death of the Christ whose identity as humankind's singular Savior they can no longer accept. Only the singers of "Were You There When They Crucified My Lord" acknowledge a spiritual dependency quite different from slavery.

II. Uncle Tom, Billy Budd, and Miss Lonelyhearts: *Imitatio Christi*

In all three Synoptic Gospels, Jesus knows long before Calvary how his earthly ministry will end:

> And he called to him the multitude with his disciples, and said to them, "If any man would come after me, let him deny himself and take up his cross and follow me. For whosoever would save his life will lose it; and whoever loses his life for my sake and the gospel's will save it. For what does it profit a man, to gain the whole world and lose his own soul?" (Mark 8:34-36)

These verses, together with their variants in Luke 9:23-24 and Matt. 16:24-25, pose problems of no easy solution. Does Christ's command to take up the cross and follow him require an excruciating death for those who would follow Him? Or is Christ's word "cross" meant as a metaphor for any and all forms of suffering endured for the faith? "Whosoever loses his life" suggests that bodily death is necessary for our taking up the cross, yet the heart revolts at the notion that we mortals, born of merely earthly fathers, are called upon to suffer a bodily end similar to the Son of God. For whom, therefore is Christ's command exactly intended: for the disciples or, as Mark claims, for the "multitude" as well?

Thomas à Kempis struggled to resolve these problems, while making Christ's words universally applicable, by rendering the cross as a metaphor and then emphasizing the benefit of losing life in order to save it. Book two, chapter 12 of *The Imitation of Christ*, titled "The Road of the Holy Cross," reminds us that "our whole mortal life is full of misery and surrounded by crosses."[12] Thomas à Kempis explicitly associates bearing the cross with chastising the body, avoiding earthly honors, and being "ready to suffer any trials and much trouble in this wretched life."[13] He thus implies, but does not directly state, that it is the Christian life, not crucifixion, that entitles those who "in their lifetime, conformed themselves to Jesus Crucified" to have everlasting salvation.[14] The cross, therefore, is everything that the true Christian must bear along the royal road of life.

Thomas à Kempis knows, however, that Christ's command, even in its less demanding form, will elicit few true followers. No matter how eloquent Christ's universal urgings may be, they can never be realized: "Jesus has many lovers of his heavenly kingdom, but few of them carry his cross. . . . Many follow Jesus up to the breaking of the bread, but few go on to drinking of the chalice of his passion. Many admire his miracles, but few follow in the ignominy of His cross."[15] Thomas à Kempis did not account for Christian failing merely by citing the authority of Christ's Word: "Many are called but few are chosen." Instead, he based his skepticism upon his sense of our

12. Thomas à Kempis, *The Imitation of Christ*, trans. Joseph N. Tylenda (New York: Random House, 1998), 67. *The Imitation of Christ* first circulated in manuscript about 1425.
13. Ibid., 68.
14. Ibid., 65.
15. Ibid., 63.

daily world, riven as it is by the foolish distractions of vanity fair. In this regard, his observations often seem to anticipate Henry David Thoreau. "We mourn our temporal losses and for a trifling gain we work long hours and dash about every which way," Thomas à Kempis observes. "We are totally unmindful of the injury it causes our spiritual life, and later on we rarely think about it."[16] For Thoreau, John Brown's martyrdom for the cause of abolition earned him a Christ-like stature Thoreau was willing to ascribe to few if any other countrymen.[17]

More than a century after *Uncle Tom's Cabin* was published, Uncle Tom remained, as James Baldwin put it, "a figure of controversy yet."[18] During the civil rights movement, to call an African-American "an Uncle Tom" was to condemn him for cringing submission to the white man: black on the outside, white on the inside. Baldwin largely concurs with this judgment, describing the Uncle Tom of Mrs. Stowe's novel as "phenomenally forbearing," "robbed of his humanity and divested of his sex," washed white in Mrs. Stowe's "the robes of grace."[19] We know, of course, that although the cultural figure of Uncle Tom originated in Mrs. Stowe's dimly remembered novel, Uncle Tom had been remade by the legacy of the Uncle Tom plays and by accusatory memories of accommodating negro behavior during the decades of Jim Crow. We have not fully recognized, however, how unfair (if convenient) a distortion it is to confuse Stowe's Uncle Tom with the Uncle Tom of cultural memory. No

16. Ibid., 32.

17. In the essay "A Plea for Captain John Brown," first delivered as a lecture in 1859 shortly before Brown was hung, Thoreau challenged his audience to recognize that John Brown was savior to the slave: "You who pretend to care for Christ crucified, consider what you are about to do to him who offered himself to be the savior of four millions of men" (Henry David Thoreau, *The Major Essays*, ed. Jeffrey L. Duncan [New York: E. P. Dutton, 1972], 167).

18. James Baldwin, "Everybody's Protest Novel," in *James Baldwin: Collected Essays* (New York: Library of America, 1998), 14. "Everybody's Protest Novel" was first published in *Partisan Review* in 1949.

19. Ibid.

portion of Mrs. Stowe's novel shows the difference more clearly than her portrayal of the climactic sequence of Tom's death; Tom's way of dying gives the lie to the cultural mythology that would be made from him.

Tom's death in imitation of Christ could hardly be more explicit. Simon Legree first whips and then beats Tom to death both in the fields and in the waste room of the cotton gin house. There seems to be no one present at Tom's torturing except Cassy, who serves as a Mary Magdalene, and Sambo and Quimbo, who are transformed from sadistic Roman soldiers into the two thieves on the cross. When Cassy, reading the passion narrative to Tom, arrives at Christ's words "Father forgive them," both break down weeping until Tom grasps what is being asked of him: "If only we could keep up that ar'! . . . it seemed to come to him so natural, and we have to fight so hard for't. O, Lord help us, O blessed Jesus do help us!"[20] While Sambo and Quimbo whip Tom nearly to unconsciousness, Tom cries out "I forgive ye, with all my soul," whereupon the narrator observes "There stood by him ONE—seen by him alone—'like unto the Son of God.'"[21] The chapter describing Tom's crucifixion is titled "The Victory." No literary subtlety here: we are dealing with an evangelical author certain that love of Jesus is the essence of Christianity and that, by following Christ's love even unto death, bearing one's cross will give the victory even to the most downtrodden of slaves.

Tom has been brought to the cross, not by his submission, but by his defiance. He has refused to obey his master's order to whip fellow slaves. He has refused to tell his master the whereabouts of Cassy and Emmeline. He has refused to kill Legree, though he has had

20. Harriet Beecher Stowe, *Uncle Tom's Cabin*, ed. Elizabeth Ammons (New York: Norton, 1994), 313. First published in 1852.
21. Ibid., 359. The biblical verse is Heb. 7:3.

the opportunity. Most importantly, Tom has repeatedly challenged Legree's claim that he has "bought" Tom body and soul, by exclaiming that Christ's blood has bought his soul for eternity. Uncle Tom is no Uncle Tom. Like Thoreau in Concord jail, Charles Sumner on the Senate floor, and Theodore Parker in the Boston Melodeon, Tom is testifying for passive resistance against slavery in the name of the higher law.

The problematic decision Mrs. Stowe faces is how to account for the agency of God in providing Tom the strength to die so miserable and unseen a death within the hell of Legree's Red River plantation. If divine providence rules in the affairs of men, it must play a part in so important a victory; if the hand of providence intervenes directly, however, many a reader would no longer be able to suspend his or her disbelief. Walking an epistemological tightrope, Mrs. Stowe renders Tom's "dread soul crisis" with these words:

> The atheistic taunts of his cruel master sunk his before dejected soul to the lowest ebb; and, though the hand of faith still held to the eternal rock, it was with a numb despairing grasp. Tom sat, like one stunned, at the fire. Suddenly everything around him seemed to fade, and a vision rose before him of one crowned with thorns, buffeted and bleeding. Tom gazed, in awe and wonder, at the majestic patience of the face; the deep pathetic eyes thrilled him to his inmost heart; his soul woke, as, with floods of emotion, he stretched out his hands and fell upon his knees—when, gradually, the vision changed; the sharp thorns became rays of glory; and, in splendor inconceivable, he saw that same face bending compassionately towards him, and a voice said, "He that overcometh shall sit down with me on my throne, even as I also overcame, and am set down with my Father on his throne."[22]

Just as Christ's bodily suffering, his bleeding head, is transformed into Christ's strength of soul ("the majestic patience of the face"), so Christ's thorns of crucifixion become the rays of resurrection,

22. Ibid., 339–40. The biblical verse is Rev. 3:21.

and the floor of Legree's cotton gin house holds out the promise of a heavenly throne. The paradoxes in such visualizing of Christ are remarkably close to the words of Jonathan Edwards, whom Mrs. Stowe so resented and so admired. Futilely adding phrase upon phrase to try to describe moments in which he hoped to have experienced grace through Christ Jesus, Edwards wrote of a "sweet conjunction: majesty and meekness joined together: it was a sweet and gentle, and holy majesty; and also a majestic meekness; an awful sweetness; a high, and great, and holy gentleness."[23]

Throughout the passage, Mrs. Stowe is careful to maintain consistency of fictional point of view. We see Tom's "vision" through his eyes only. Yet the question remains: what exactly is the source of Tom's spiritual experience when he "gazed, in awe and wonder, at the majestic patience of the face"? Has Christ crucified, sent to save, appeared before Tom? Or is the face a visual embodiment of the Christian love still ruling Tom's spirit? Or is Tom experiencing a hallucination? Needing to settle these possibilities, but desiring to reach readers who do not share her faith in providential intervention, Mrs. Stowe needed to proceed cautiously:

> The psychologist tells us of a state, in which the affections and images of the mind become so dominant and overpowering that they press into their service the outward senses, and make them give tangible shape to the inward imagining. Who shall measure what an all-pervading Spirit may do with these capabilities of our mortality, or the ways in which He may encourage the desponding souls of the desolate? If the poor forgotten slave believes that Jesus hath appeared and spoken to him, who shall contradict him? Did He not say that his mission, in all ages, was to bind up the broken-hearted, and set at liberty them that are bruised?[24]

23. Jonathan Edwards, "Personal Narrative," in *Letters and Personal Writings*, ed. George S. Claghorn, in *The Works of Jonathan Edwards*, ed. Harry S. Stout (New Haven, CT: Yale University Press, 1998), 14:793.
24. Stowe, *Uncle Tom's Cabin*, 340.

In 1852, some thirty years before William James wrote the first textbook of psychology, the very word "psychologist" would surely have puzzled many a careful reader. Mrs. Stowe's first sentence, written from the psychologist's point of view, renders Tom's vision of the crucified Christ as an "inward imagining." Her second sentence then renders Tom's "vision" as an intervening act of Christ's "all pervading Spirit." Her third attempts to shame a skeptical reader who would deny Tom his consolation simply because it might have been imagined. But her last sentence, instead of resolving earlier possibilities, renders them less important than the spiritual effect of such visions: they "set at liberty" both the bodies and souls of those who are bruised, especially, surely, chattel slaves.

There is more argumentative subtlety here than first appears. Such passages force us to recognize that James Baldwin's attack on *Uncle Tom's Cabin* as "a very bad novel, having, in its self-righteous, virtuous sentimentality, much in common with *Little Women*" is relentlessly one-sided.[25] After this salvo, Baldwin continues to define "sentimentality" in literature, concisely and cogently, as "the ostentatious parading of excessive and spurious emotion."[26] And yet, Mrs. Stowe's concluding words about Uncle Tom, as George Shelby buries Tom's bodily remains on a knoll just beyond Legree's plantation, are "Pity him not! Such a life and death is not for pity! . . . Blessed are the men whom [God] calls to fellowship with him, bearing their cross after him with patience."[27] For Baldwin, to evoke pity for a slave who loved the enemy who beat him to death is a "sentimentality" that serves neither black nor white. For Stowe, no pity need be extended to the slave who bore his cross and rose to eternal victory. Beyond their common outrage against racial

25. Baldwin, "Everybody's Protest Novel," 11–12.
26. Ibid., 12.
27. Stowe, *Uncle Tom's Cabin*, 365.

oppression, Baldwin and Stowe share no common ground; these are two authorial mentalities that do not meet.

Neither the just God nor the loving Jesus in whom Mrs. Stowe believed so fervently was to be understood through irony. To Melville, the idea of God and the possibility of a Christ-like contemporary could not be considered apart from an ironic perspective that would shroud all stereotypes, all received notions, in ambiguity. *Billy Budd, Sailor (An Inside Narrative)* can be read as an inversion of Mrs. Stowe's rendering of a trusting man suffering injustice unto crucifixion.[28] Tom's Christianity, based upon the Beatitudes and the Golden Rule, is first gained from an evangelical Methodist minister, then bolstered by constant listening to the word he cannot read. However blessedly childlike Tom may be in his faith, he also serves as a "patriarch" showing the way of salvation to St. Clare as well as to fellow slaves.

As an impressed sailor, Billy Budd too is a slave, forced from *The Rights of Man* into the necessarily autocratic world of the *Bellipotent*. Introduced as "The Handsome Sailor," Billy is first likened to an "intensely black" seaman whom the narrator once saw on the Liverpool docks; Billy is soon revealed to be, in physique and in character, a "Baby Bud," the most blond-haired and blue-eyed of sailors, an Anglo-Saxon "angel" whose Adamic innocence shades into naiveté.[29] Whereas Tom unequivocally becomes a Black Christ, Melville relishes the plausible multiplicity of Billy's likenesses (Aldebaran, Alexander, Apollo, Hercules and Achilles, as well as Adam and Christ). Billy's unconscious ministry to other sailors consists of his unfailing good cheer and comradely seamanship. Although he is as illiterate as Tom, Billy cannot seem ever to attend

28. Herman Melville, *Billy Budd, Sailor (An Inside Narrative)*, ed. Harrison Hayford and Merton M. Sealts Jr. (Chicago: University of Chicago Press, 1962), 26.
29. Ibid., 43, 70, 120.

to biblical wisdom, even at the moment of his death. Whereas Christ sent forth his disciples into a wolfish world with the command to be "as wise as serpents and as harmless as doves" (Matt. 10:16), Billy Budd, has "little or no sharpness of faculty or any trace of the wisdom of the serpent, nor yet quite a dove."[30]

As the crucifier within a slave system, a more blatant exemplar of obtuse human cruelty than Simon Legree would be hard to conceive. In characterizing the deceitful John Claggart, first as Satan, then as an accusatory witness before a hastily convened court, Melville restores something of the complexity of the Gospel account of Christ's crucifiers, while emphasizing differences among them. Just as Christ was falsely accused first of heresy and then sedition, so Claggart falsely accuses Billy of conspiracy and treason. Christ chooses to be silent; Billy is physically unable to speak in his defense. Claggart's ability to cloak self-serving malice underneath a reasonable exterior more closely resembles the caution of the Sanhedrin and of Pilate rather than the savage outbursts of Simon Legree. Mrs. Stowe isolated Tom and Legree inside a shed in darkest Arkansas in order to dramatize human cruelty; Billy is accused by Claggart in public, questioned and tried before fellow officers, then hung before the eyes of every sailor aboard the ship. Melville's public rendering, in which crucifixion is inseparable from the rationalizing of murderous injustice, seems to be at once the more modern and the more biblical.

For the sailors who have witnessed Billy's hanging, the event would soon acquire a simple, unequivocal meaning. They have watched Billy ascend to the yardarm and saw how his "pinioned figure . . . ascending, took the full rose of the dawn."[31] They then heard Billy's last words at the yardarm—"God bless Captain Vere!"[32]—but they seem to have sensed only a similarity of tone, not

30. Ibid., 52.
31. Ibid., 124.

any difference in acumen, between Billy's "God bless Captain Vere!" and Christ's "Father forgive them, for they know not what they do" (Luke 23:34). Because their minds' eye treasures images of the Handsome Sailor crucified and transfigured, if not resurrected, they treasure the chips of the yardarm "as a piece of the Cross."[33] Although the sailors sense that Captain Vere has condoned an injustice, they can neither define it nor act upon it. They therefore sentimentalize it—in James Baldwin's sense of the term.

The sailors' need to see Billy's death as a crucifixion, however understandable, is but one instance of the "outside narratives" with which Melville's novella concludes. To treasure Billy as a Christ-like memory is, in its way, as simplistic as the British naval records, which eulogize Claggart and villainize Billy, or as the concluding poem "Billy in the Darbies." The impossibility of regarding Billy as a modern Christ, or even as a Christ figure, is indicated by Melville's rendering of the crucial moment when Billy's death becomes, not only likely, but inevitable. As soon as Claggart has falsely accused Billy of mutiny, Captain Vere, knowing of Billy's stutter, tries to calm him by saying, "There is no hurry, my boy. Take your time, take your time":

> Contrary to the effect intended, these words, so fatherly in tone, doubtless touching Billy's heart to the quick, prompted yet more violent effort at utterance—efforts soon ending for the time in confirming the paralysis, and bringing to his face an expression which was as a crucifixion to behold. The next instant, quick as the flame from a discharged cannon at night, his right arm shot out, and Claggart dropped to the deck.[34]

In these two sentences, the controlling biblical analogy for Billy shifts from Adam to Christ. Claggart's lies, together with Billy's inability

32. Ibid., 123.
33. Ibid., 131.
34. Ibid., 99.

to refute them, lend Billy's face a crucified expression because he instinctually senses his victimization, and his death. Melville, however, instantly undermines the connotations of the word "crucifixion" by picturing Billy as a killer, his right arm shooting forth like the cannons that line the *Bellipotent*'s deck.

The ironies here are surely intended to be irresolvable. Unlike Billy Budd, Jesus Christ killed no one. On one level, therefore, the sailors who see Billy's death as a crucifixion are trying to conflate a sailor who has killed his superior officer with the Son of God, prince of peace. But, on another level, Billy's killing of Claggart must be seen as both admirable and purgative. From the moment Claggart was first described as an example of "Natural Depravity,"[35] the narrator has likened him to Satan, to the serpent, and to "the scorpion for whom the Creator alone is responsible."[36] To kill John Claggart is therefore, on a symbolic level, to rid the *Bellipotent* of evil; perhaps Melville implies that contemporaries need reminding that, in addition to the Beatitudes, Christ once said, "I have not come to bring peace but a sword" (Matt. 10:34).

How then, is Billy to be judged? Over Claggart's body, which the narrator likens to a "dead snake," Captain Vere mutters "Fated Boy,"[37] thus suggesting that Vere has already decided the outcome of Billy's forthcoming trial. Because the *Bellipotent* is a microcosm for the world, and Starry Vere is captain of the ship, Vere is allegorically placed in the position of God passing judgment upon a killer who in significant ways resembles both a fallen Adam and a victimized Christ. The naval code, based upon the Articles of War, is at least clear; as the captain of His Majesty's ship, Vere must enforce the death penalty. Yet it is Vere himself who acknowledges to the court that

35. Ibid., 75.
36. Ibid., 78.
37. Ibid., 99.

Billy is, according to natural and divine justice, "a fellow creature innocent before God" and that, "at the Last Assizes" the plea of unintentional homicide "shall acquit."[38] But on the allegorical level, Vere cannot escape his Godlike responsibilities so easily. Just as the Creator is responsible for the scorpion, so Starry Vere rewards Adam/Christ with hanging as just punishment for ridding his ship of the essence of evil.

An understandable silence has recently fallen upon decades of debate over "the meaning" of *Billy Budd.* Every plausible assertion only arouses an equally plausible objection. The human level and the scriptural level of the narrative are usually inconsistent, but always there. We are never allowed to forget that a British naval trial, a retelling of Genesis 2–3, and a modern day passion are all occurring together. Melville's subtitle, *An Inside Narrative*, infers that the fiction we will read, not the trial's naval record, provides the inside truth, but Melville's ultimate irony is that the "inside narrative" provides no inside truth at all, only the fullest possible range of questions. I advance here only one conclusion: viewed narrowly, as an imitation of Christ, Billy's life leads him along no *via crucis*. As Thomas à Kempis knew, to take up one's cross and follow him is a decision every follower must deliberately and knowingly undertake; Billy Budd never formulated any such Christ-like intent.

As an American Jew who had discarded his family's faith, Nathanael West (born Nathanael von Wollenstein Weinstein) became fascinated with contemporary Christian thought, in particular with bogus searches for various kinds of Messiahs to regenerate the surreal wastelands of modern urban life. West's vantage point made him aware of the thin line between the hope of acting like Christ (Uncle Tom) and the folly of believing one could

38. Ibid., 110, 111.

succeed in consciously imitating Christ. The nameless protagonist of West's *Miss Lonelyhearts* (1933), who writes an advice column under that name, has become his own pseudonym. Revolted by the irredeemable bodily, marital, mental, and spiritual disfigurements of his desperate correspondents, he daily dispenses hastily typed palaver about faith, hope, charity, and a dawning tomorrow until he becomes consumed with rage against his own hypocrisy as well as the world's unchanging miseries. Only his determination to see the dark humor of the grotesque, fortified by alcohol from Delehanty's speakeasy, saves Miss Lonelyhearts from immediate spiritual despair.

Understandably drawn to Dostoevsky's *The Brothers Karamazov*, Miss Lonelyhearts is moved by Father Zossima's exhortations to "Love all God's creation," to "love a man even in his sin, for that is the semblance of Divine Love."[39] Believing that helplessness, not sin, is the modern condition love must overcome, Miss Lonelyhearts is increasingly drawn to fantasize Christ-like acts, but then to denigrate them. Whether from fear of ridicule or simple uncertainty, he keeps his fantasies private. Reading three of his correspondents' letters leads him immediately to conclude, "Christ was the answer, but if he did not want to get sick, he had to stay away from the Christ business."[40] The son of a Baptist minister, Miss Lonelyhearts retains only one image on the bare walls of his Brooklyn room: a cross from which he has removed the figure of Jesus, but then "nailed it [the figure of Jesus] to the wall with large spikes."[41] So perverse an act suggests that, in his confusion, Miss Lonelyhearts imagines himself as the crucified, but acts as crucifier. Literal crucifixion cannot be the end of any twentieth-century life, but in order to fix the image of a living Christ daily within sight, he must drive the nails through Christ's body.

39. Nathanael West, *Miss Lonelyhearts & The Day of the Locust* (New York: New Directions, 1962), 8.
40. Ibid., 3.
41. Ibid., 8.

Asserting his Christ-like identity, then retracting it, becomes a debilitating psychological pattern. When his fiancée, Betty, who is in denial both of the world's disorder and of spiritual torment, asks Miss Lonelyhearts whether he is "sick," he responds, "'I'm not sick. I don't need any of your damned aspirin. I've got a Christ complex. Humanity. I'm a humanity lover. All the broken bastards.' He finished with a short laugh that was like a bark."[42] After envisioning the world as a gigantic pawnshop, where all selves and all objects are pawned in desperation, he imagines that a "gigantic cross" is growing from within its midst until it fills the entire pawnshop.[43] When the vision proves intolerable, Miss Lonelyhearts abruptly extracts the cross from his fantasy, then discards the cross into an imagined ocean in order to reduce the pawnshop to manageable mental proportions.

Eventually, the pattern must extend beyond both Miss Lonelyhearts's room and his dreaming into his writing. The entirety of his last quoted column reads as follows: "Christ died for you. He died nailed to a tree for you. His gift to you is suffering and it is only through suffering that you can know Him. Cherish this gift for . . ." At this moment, Miss Lonelyhearts snatches the paper out of the typewriter, suddenly sensing, perhaps plausibly, that for such as he "even the word Christ was a vanity."[44]

Throughout these moments, the presiding spirit within Miss Lonelyhearts remains the inner voice of Shrike, his boss and his devil. To Shrike, all words are weapons, all sacredness is folly, and all ideals idols. The blasphemies for which Shrike first gains attention are his jeering parodies of the Lord's Prayer and the Catholic prayer to Mary. Once his audience is captive, Shrike proceeds to the kill implied in his

42. Ibid., 13.
43. Ibid., 31.
44. Ibid., 39.

name by jeeringly conflating Christ with Miss Lonelyhearts, and then offering himself, Shrike, as the modern Messiah: "Oh, so you don't care for women, eh? J.C. is your only sweetheart, eh? Jesus Christ, the King of Kings, the Miss Lonelyhearts of Miss Lonelyhearts . . . Haven't you ever heard of Shrike's Passion in the Luncheonette, or the Agony in the Soda Fountain?"[45] Shortly after Miss Lonelyhearts feels that the shadow of a passing lamppost "pierced him like a spear," Shrike compares "the wounds in Christ's body to the mouths of a miraculous purse in which we deposit the small change of our sins."[46] Our pathetic sins, Shrike believes, are our only currency, readily collectible in his body, while we dwell sentimentally on the stigmata. Blasphemy so grotesquely cynical risks forfeiting the black humor that is Shrike's and West's trademark.

Unless West's reader risks crediting Shrike's cynical nihilism, West would seem to be exposing the folly of believing that a human being might act like Christ in the midst of a world of scoffers, hedonists, and their helpless victims. Miss Lonelyhearts, admittedly, is no Jesus Christ. Because he cannot bring himself to believe that adultery is a sin, he commits adultery. Instead of blessing the poor and the meek, he explodes in futile rage at their helplessness. As a boy, he thought it cute to sacrifice a Paschal lamb, but then mangled both the ritual and the lamb's body. As an adult, he takes fleeting sexual pleasures from his pregnant fiancée, while excusing his indifferent cruelty by imagining that Betty is but a "party dress" whereas he is "the Rock."[47]

Despite these differences, there proves to be tragedy beyond cynicism in West's working out the impulsive fantasies of Miss Lonelyhearts's "Christ complex." Only Miss Lonelyhearts is tormented by the irredeemable miseries of the wretched of the earth.

45. Ibid., 6–7.
46. Ibid., 4, 7.
47. Ibid., 56.

In the novel's concluding scenes, the voice of Shrike recedes, to be replaced by the voice of the cripple Doyle, whom Miss Lonelyhearts has cuckolded. Doyle's thoughtful letter to Miss Lonelyhearts reaches beyond the disaster recitals of previous correspondents to inquire, five times, what the meaning of life's misery may be, to wonder what or who causes such misery, and, especially to ask "what is it all for?"[48] Reduced to silence by such Job-like questions, Miss Lonelyhearts reaches out, in the first controlled act of empathy in the novel, to hold Doyle's hand. The comedy of hiding their handholding under the table, for fear of arousing homoerotic suspicion, only adds to the intimacy of the moment.

Affected by this moment of touching, but sure of "the triumphant thing that his humility had become,"[49] Miss Lonelyhearts determines to be the savior for Doyle and his wife. As both a writer and a minister's son, his first attempt to do so inevitably proceeds through words:

> "Christ is love." He screamed at them. It was a stage scream, but he kept on. "Christ is the black fruit that hangs on the crosstree. Man was lost by eating of the forbidden fruit. He shall be saved by eating of the bidden fruit. The black Christ-fruit, the love fruit. . . ."[50]

There is nothing here but rhetoric: dimly remembered biblical and churchly tags, the fall and the crucifixion jumbled together, linked only metaphorically by the word "fruit," probably recalled from the opening phrases of *Paradise Lost* ("Of Man's first disobedience and the fruit / Of that forbidden tree . . ."). To his credit, Miss Lonelyhearts recognizes that "this time he had failed still more miserably."[51] Scriptural or no, words have become for Miss Lonelyhearts, no less

48. Ibid., 46–47.
49. Ibid., 47.
50. Ibid., 49.
51. Ibid., 50.

than for Shrike, only the coin of self-importance, an attempt to evoke salvation into being.

At the physical center of Christ's crucifixion is bodily pain, blood, and near-silent endurance. Newly determined to be a "rock" in a better way than he has ever been to Betty, Miss Lonelyhearts now seeks Doyle's salvation through deeds. Lying on his bed, "he fastened his eyes on the Christ that hung on the wall opposite his bed. As he stared at it, it became a bright fly, spinning with quick grace on a background of blood velvet."[52] The entire "world of things" around him, suddenly transformed into a fish, rises to snatch the Christ-fly, thus foreshadowing, if not determining, his own end. Sure that "the room was full of grace," and bent on converting the cripple by embracing him, "Miss Lonelyhearts rushed down the stairs to meet Doyle with his arms spread for the miracle."[53] Instead of achieving a "miracle," he is killed by a bullet accidentally fired from Doyle's pistol. As Miss Lonelyhearts rushes lovingly to his death, his arms are spread in the posture of crucifixion. Deliberately cartoonish and ironically terse to novel's end, West titles this last chapter "Miss Lonelyhearts has a religious experience."

To describe the effect of such an ending, the word *nihilism* will not suffice. No matter how many ironies may accumulate, Miss Lonelyhearts ultimately responds with love, even with grace; his blood is shed in order to try to save another. The novel's outcome is thus terrifyingly pitiable. Modern man, in the midst of all his confusion and failings, can rise to try to imitate Christ. But the consequence, as West would have it, involves no trace of renewal for others. Mistaken motives, destructive passions, and the conditions of modern urban life all play their part in the perversity of Miss Lonelyhearts's crucifixion, but as West's last sentence notes, it is

52. Ibid., 56.
53. Ibid., 57.

accident that seals up the fruitless outcome: "They rolled *part of the way* down the stairs" (emphasis added).

III. Afterword: "The Black Christ"

Countee Cullen, once regarded as the major poet of the Harlem Renaissance, could not rest content with being—or not being—a Christian. Like James Baldwin, for whom he would serve as first literary mentor, Countee Cullen was raised by a dominant pastor father against whose authority and preaching he half-guiltily rebelled. In his many references to himself as a "pagan," Cullen's pride in establishing his own church-free and father-free identity conflicted both with anxiety about his disbelief and with his comfort in traditional Christian imagery and traditional English verse forms. Compounding these problems was Cullen's awareness that, for white American churches, God and Christ were conceived to be white, whereas for Negro churches, insofar as they embraced separatism and tolerated bitterness against whites, any claim to be a universal church had to remain hollow.

At the height of his fame, Cullen completed, during his Guggenheim year in Paris, an ambitious thirty-page poem that attempts to resolve these problems. "The Black Christ (Hopefully Dedicated to White America)," published in 1929, begins as if Cullen were penning a proposition for an undeclared epic poem. The poet proposes four subjects: 1) "God's glory and my country's shame"; 2) how any man who curses Christ can be pardoned only by Christ; 3) how God has picked the "stark soul" of the poet up from the mire; and 4) most importantly:

> How Calvary in Palestine,
> Extending down to me and mine,
> Was but the first leaf in a line
> Of Trees on which a Man should swing

World without end, in suffering
For all men's healing, let me sing.[54]

The problem of proposing four subjects (Homer, Virgil, and Milton had proposed only one) is how to combine the uncovering of his "country's shame," with an account of personal spiritual growth, while also convincing the reader that crucifixion is both unending and universal.

Cullen's narrative is designed starkly to expose the shame of American racism. After Cullen's hero, "that proud nigger, handsome Jim" of "imperial breed," is seen lying with a white girl, a white mob vilifies the two lovers and strikes Jim down, provoking Jim (very like Billy Budd) to kill his chief tormenter by an instinctive retaliatory blow. Jim's subsequent lynching by the mob is rendered as a reenactment of Christ's passion, with contemporary representations of Pontius Pilate, Christ's bloody crowning, the sorrow of the three Marys, and a mutilated body twisting on the rood. Not even Harriet Beecher Stowe was as prepared as Cullen to validate the reality of a contemporary resurrection. Dead three days, Jim appears before his mother in the family cabin and then allows his brother, a doubting Thomas, to reify his resurrected body through touch. For so explicit a narrative, a title more appropriately blunt than "The Black Christ" would be hard to imagine, even though Cullen's subtitle, "hopefully dedicated to White America," reflects wariness of the readings that white Americans are likely to give his poem.

Despite Cullen's explicit narrative parallels, ambiguity and evasion are everywhere in the significance ascribed to Jim's crucifixion and resurrection. From the poem's outset, the submissive and hopeful Christianity of Jim's mother, who supports her family at every turn, and tries to love her enemies, is granted great authority. So, however,

54. Countee Cullen, *My Soul's High Song: The Collected Writings of Countee Cullen, Voice of the Harlem Renaissance*, ed. Gerald Early (New York: Doubleday, 1991), 207.

is the secular skepticism of Cullen's narrator, Jim's brother, who denounces Southern racism in general and lynching in particular, and who is well aware that his mother's piety only allows the "line of trees on which a Man should swing" to lengthen. ("But Christ who conquered Death and Hell / What has He done for you who spent / Bleeding life for His content?")[55]

Cullen was clearly determined upon resolution of these conflicting beliefs. Jim's crucifixion and resurrection are to be the cause of the narrator's conversion from skepticism to piety, bitterness to love. "Recalling now His agonies," the narrator claims to be prepared to pray with his mother "forever on my knees, / Ever to praise her Christ with her."[56] But the Christ to which the narrator prays is explicitly described as *his mother's* Christ. Similarly, the passage that most fully conveys spiritual experience is the narrator's summary of Jim's thoughts when, after his resurrection, Jim prays to his crucified predecessor, Jesus:

> O Form immaculately born,
> Betrayed a thousand times each morn.
> As many times each night denied,
> Surrendered, tortured, crucified!
> Now we have seen beyond degree
> That love which has no boundary;
> Our eyes have looked on Calvary.[57]

The narrator's claim to a transformative inner conversion, never rendered for us, is based upon his observing Jim's crucifixion and his attesting to the vicarious spiritual experiences of others involved in it.

At the end of the poem's proposition, Cullen had promised to sing "For all men's healing," but his poem concludes, not with signs of

55. Ibid., 231.
56. Ibid., 235.
57. Ibid., 234.

healing, but with the hope that the blood Jim shed on the lynching tree, now flowering in next year's green, will not be entirely forgotten:

> And those who pass it by may see
> Naught growing there except a tree,
> But there are two to testify
> Who hung on it . . . we saw him die.
> Its roots were fed with priceless blood.
> It is the Cross; it is the Rood.[58]

So insistent and overemphatic a last line suggests that Countee Cullen wished spiritually to engage in a crucifixion and a conversion that he could not feel. His overwrought language and contradictory beliefs seem signs of a poet trying somehow to will both his major poem and his faith in the blood of the new covenant into existence simultaneously.

With few exceptions, creative writers address biblical subjects from a vantage point outside the structure of profession and the stricture of creed. Accordingly, we should not expect any creative writer to respond to the crucifixion with the stylistic and spiritual assurance of a Jonathan Edwards, who could unequivocally proclaim, in exact parallel phrases: "It was in Christ's last sufferings, above all, that he was delivered up to the power of his enemies, and yet by these, above all, he obtained victory over his enemies."[59] Even so, the particularly jagged extremities of style and tone with which American writers of the next century would render Christ's crucifixion, and the problem of his resurrection, remain striking. American writers are interested in the ironies, tensions, interstices, and implausibilities within the

58. Ibid., 236.
59. Jonathan Edwards, "The Excellency of Christ" (1736), in *Sermons and Discourses: 1734–1738*, in *The Works of Jonathan Edwards*, ed. M. X. Lesser (New Haven, CT: Yale University Press, 2001), 19:579.

gospel accounts, and how they may find their counterparts in contemporary life. With the important exception of Harriet Beecher Stowe, they are bent on transforming the gospel account for personal or present cultural purpose, not in reaffirming it. The legacies of Jeffersonian Deism, Darwinism, and the higher criticism leave their mark upon this process, but perhaps the overdone intensity of tone, from Whitman's limitless egoism to West's agonized cynicism, is ascribable to a particularly American belief in the right and duty of individual self-determination, for the writer as well as the citizen.

7

Dostoevsky's Fiery "Furnace of Doubt"

Michael R. Katz

> When we hear the old bells ringing out on a Sunday morning, we ask ourselves: can it be possible? This is for a Jew, crucified two thousand years ago, who said he was the son of God. The proof for such a claim is wanting.
>
> —Friedrich Nietzsche, *Menschliches, Allzumenschliches* (*Human, All Too Human*) (1878)

In his final notebook (1880–81), the renowned Russian novelist Fyodor Dostoevsky confessed that his own religious faith had been severely tested on more than one occasion. Referring to the "Pro and Contra" section of his last novel, *The Brothers Karamazov*, he acknowledged:

> And so I believe in Christ and confess Him not like some child; my *hosanna* has passed through a vast *furnace of doubt.*[1]

In fact, in the late 1860s, this most devout of all major nineteenth-century Russian writers had planned to write a great work entitled "Atheism." It was never completed, and once Dostoevsky left Florence (he had been forced to live in Europe to escape his creditors), there were no further references to this idea. But it is clear from another project he described in greater detail that the plan for that novel was subsumed into another called "The Life of a Great Sinner." In a letter written in 1870 to his good friend, the poet Apollon Maikov, he described the new project as follows:

> The main question that will run though all parts of the novel is the question that has tormented me either consciously or unconsciously all my life—the existence of God. In the course of his life, the hero [of "The Life of a Great Sinner"] turns from atheism to faith, to fanaticism and sectarianism, and then back to atheism. . . . For God's sake, don't tell anyone about the contents. . . . (I never tell anyone about my themes in advance—I feel embarrassed, somehow, in doing so, but to you I confess).[2]

But this work was never completed either. Instead, Dostoevsky used the components for his last three major novels: *Devils* (*Demons* or *The Possessed*), *The Adolescent* (or *The Raw Youth*), and *The Brothers Karamazov*.

Somewhat earlier, in 1854, from the remote Siberian town of Omsk where he was serving out his sentence of exile for his alleged revolutionary activities, Dostoevsky wrote to one of his correspondents, Natalya Fonvizina,[3] characterizing his own idiosyncratic version of Russian Orthodoxy as follows:

1. "Zapisnaya tetrad' (1880–1881)," in *Literaturnoe nasledstvo*, ed. V. R. Scherbina (Moscow: Zhurnal'noe-gazetnoe obedinenie, 1971), 83:696.
2. Joseph Frank and David Goldstein, eds., *Selected Letters of Fyodor Dostoevsky*, trans. Andrew McAndrew (New Brunswick, NJ: Rutgers University Press, 1987), 331–32.
3. The wife of a rebel, Natalya Fonvizina, had selflessly followed her husband to Siberia after he had participated in and been arrested for the aborted rebellion of December 14, 1825.

> . . . God sends me moments of great tranquility, moments during which I love and I find I am loved by others; and it was during such a moment that I formed within myself a symbol of faith in which all is clear and sacred for me. The symbol is very simple, and here is what it is: to believe that there is nothing more beautiful, more profound, more sympathetic, more reasonable, more courageous, and more perfect than Christ; and there not only isn't, but I tell myself with a jealous love, there cannot be. More than that—if someone succeeded in proving to me that Christ was outside the truth, and if, *indeed*, the truth was outside Christ, I would sooner remain with Christ than with the truth.[4]

This is an extraordinarily powerful statement, especially from someone who considered himself an Orthodox Christian believer.

The theology of Eastern Orthodoxy is rich and elaborate, with its doctrine of the hypostatic Trinity, its belief in the incarnation of Logos as the Son of God, its veneration of holy tradition, its original ecclesiology, and so on. The resurrection of Christ is the center of the Orthodox liturgical year and is understood as a real historical event. Jesus Christ, the Son of God, was crucified and died, descended into Hades (where he rescued all the souls being held there), and then, because Hades could not restrain the infinite God, rose from the dead, thus saving the entire human race. Through these events, Christ released men from the bonds of Hades and then came back to the living as both man and God. According to Orthodox tradition, each human being can partake of this immortality, which would have been impossible without the resurrection.

Every holy day of the Orthodox liturgical year relates to the resurrection, directly or indirectly. Each and every Sunday is dedicated to celebrating this momentous event and the triune nature of God.[5] Thus, in Russian commemorations of the passion of Christ

4. Frank and Goldstein, *Selected Letters*, 68.
5. The Russian word for Sunday (*voskresenie*) means "resurrection."

during Holy Week, there are frequent allusions to the ultimate victory at its completion.

Orthodox Christians also believe in the dual nature of Christ. He is both divine and human, Perfect God and Perfect Human. Throughout the ages this has been a point of contention between Christian breakaway groups (heterodox) and mainstream believers (orthodox). This means that Christ had both a divine will and a human will. He had a human body and was able to suffer as we do, but at the same time, He was perfectly divine and could not suffer corruption.

Two extraordinary scenes, one in each of Dostoevsky's first two major novels, *Crime and Punishment* (1866) and *The Idiot* (1868), present an astonishing demonstration of the extremities of Dostoevsky's profound Orthodox faith on the one hand, and his troublesome disbelief on the other. While each of these moments has been described and analyzed separately, the juxtaposition of these two scenes presents an opportunity to grasp them more fully and appreciate both the zeal and the depth with which the author himself passed through that "furnace of doubt," not unlike his hero the "great sinner" who vacillated from passionate belief to despairing atheism.

In *Crime and Punishment* (part III, chapter 5), when the hero Raskolnikov goes to his first interrogation with the examining magistrate Porfiry Petrovich, the conversation soon turns from a discussion of the hero's published article on his theory of the "ordinary" and "extraordinary" man to the question of Raskolnikov's own religious convictions. After summarizing his cherished ideas and referring, in a rhetorical flourish, to the coming of the New Jerusalem (Rev. 21:2), Porfiry challenges Raskolnikov on his faith:

> "So you still believe in the New Jerusalem?"
>
> "I believe," Raskolnikov answered firmly. . . .

> "And . . . and . . . and do you also believe in God? Excuse me for being so curious."
>
> "I believe," Raskolnikov repeated, looking up at Porfiry.
>
> "And . . . and do you believe in the raising of Lazarus?"
>
> "I be-believe. What do you need all this for?"
>
> "You believe literally?"
>
> "Literally."
>
> "I see, sir . . . just curious."[6]

This exchange serves several functions, not the least of which is introducing the theme of Lazarus into the narrative.[7]

A little over fifty pages later, in part IV, chapter 4, when Raskolnikov first goes to visit the heroine Sonya Marmeladova, primarily to test her to see if she is capable of hearing his confession of double murder, he questions her about her faith and even suggests the possibility that it may be misplaced. When Sonya assures him that God will protect her younger brothers and sisters from poverty and prostitution, Raskolnikov smugly replies, "But maybe there isn't any God."

> Sonya's face suddenly changed terribly: spasms ran over it. She looked at him with inexpressible reproach, was about to say something, but could not utter a word and simply began sobbing all at once very bitterly, covering her face with her hands.[8]

As so often happens in Dostoevsky's world, the only reply to such elemental doubt is silence. Words can never convey the essence of belief. It is not only Sonya who is speechless: after all, she is a poor,

6. Fyodor Dostoevsky, *Crime and Punishment*, trans. Richard Pevear and Larissa Volkhonsky (New York: Random House, 1993), 261.
7. The story of the raising of Lazarus appears in John 11:1-44 and 12:9-11.
8. Dostoevsky, *Crime and Punishment*, 321.

simple, uneducated girl who has resorted to prostitution to support her ailing mother, drunken father, and impoverished siblings. Even Christ himself utters not a single word in reply to Ivan Karamazov's devastating attack on faith in the celebrated chapter "The Grand Inquisitor"; he merely plants a warm kiss on Ivan's lips and departs in silence.

But if the words of men and women can never provide a rejoinder to fundamental doubt, the word of God can certainly be introduced into the "debate." Raskolnikov suddenly requests, and then peremptorily commands, that Sonya read to him from the copy of the New Testament he spies on her chest of drawers. And it's not just any copy of the Gospel, of course. It is the personal, well-worn copy that had belonged to Lizaveta Ivanovna, the pawnbroker's sister; Raskolnikov had murdered both women as part of his plan to determine whether he himself was one of the "extraordinary men" described in his article. That fact serves to link the two women, Lizaveta and Sonya, in an elemental way. The hero makes this connection explicit in his ill-mannered remark about Sonya's "mysterious get-togethers" with Lizaveta: "two holy fools."[9]

In the Russian tradition, a "holy fool" or "fool for the sake of Christ" denotes a person who assumes "madness or folly as an ascetic feat of self-humiliation."[10] This figure possesses both special status in the culture as well as distinct characteristics as he or she pursues a sanctified life in Orthodox Christianity.[11] Most important, the Russian "holy fool" is someone who always tells the truth, even if in strange ways, and is protected, even if "speaking truth to power." The best-known example is the sixteenth-century "holy fool" who tells

9. Ibid., 325.

10. Harriet Murav, *Holy Foolishness: Dostoevsky's Novels & the Poetics of Cultural Critique* (Stanford, CA: Stanford University Press, 1992), 2.

11. Western Christianity has analogies, such as St. Francis of Assisi, and various figures in Ireland, France, and elsewhere.

Boris Godunov that he murdered the legitimate heir to the Russian throne to become tsar.

Sonya Marmeladova possesses many of the traits of the archetype: she is a homeless wanderer and seems to have no fixed abode. It is she who passes judgment on Raskolnikov and selects his punishment—instead of urging him to confess to a priest in church, she advises him to expiate his sin publicly in the marketplace, bowing down, kissing the earth, and proclaiming his sin for all to hear.[12]

Before Sonya begins her Gospel reading, Raskolnikov inquires about the connection between these two fanatic believers. Sonya replies that Lizaveta, whom she knows was recently "killed with an axe," used to come and visit her on occasion: "She and I used to read and . . . talk. She will see God."[13] After this surprising admission Raskolnikov thinks to himself, "One might well become a holy fool oneself here! It's catching!"

Before she begins the reading, Sonya echoes the crucial question Porfiry had posed to the hero, but she implies a negative response: "You don't believe, do you?" Unlike the previous catechism with the examining magistrate, this time the hero refuses to answer and merely insists that she read to him.

The ensuing scene is one of the most powerful in all of Dostoevsky's work. Sonya begins reading from John 11:1-45, as commanded, and Raskolnikov not only listens, but also notes in detail her volume, intonation, expression, body language, and gestures as she proceeds. What is most astonishing is that Sonya moves from a timid and self-conscious reading of the raising of Lazarus to a confident recitation, since she knows almost all the words by heart. From this recitation, she advances to an inspired performance of

12. See Ewa M. Thompson, *Understanding Russia: The Holy Fool in Russian Culture* (Lanham, MD: University Press of America, 1987), 144.
13. Dostoevsky, *Crime and Punishment*, 325.

the narrative, and finally to a virtual reenactment of the miracle before the hero's incredulous eyes. The narrator describes her as "trembling in a real, true fever"; Sonya experiences a feeling of "joy and triumph," which is reflected in her tone of voice; finally, she trembles and grows cold "as if she were seeing it with her own eyes." In fact, what Dostoevsky presents to the reader is no ordinary narration of the raising of Lazarus, but a symbolic reenactment of the great miracle: resurrection from the dead. The only compelling reply to doubt can never be found in human speech, but only in ineffable miracle. Christ's own passion, foreshadowed by Lazarus's emergence from the tomb after four days, is, as stated above, the most significant event of Orthodox Christianity.[14] Sonya has undoubtedly passed the test, with flying colors, one might even say. She certainly has the spiritual strength to withstand the imminent confession of Raskolnikov's heinous crime.

The raising of Lazarus foreshadows yet another symbolic resurrection that takes place in the epilogue to the novel. In Dostoevsky's notebooks to *Crime and Punishment* there is one line that makes this connection explicit, a line that was included in the final version of the novel: Raskolnikov says, "I myself [was] a dead Lazarus, but Christ resurrected me."[15] Indeed, after several more critical events transpire that include the death of the hero's mother, displays of Sonya's loyal devotion, the hero's severe illness and gradual recovery, his extraordinary nightmare ("senseless delirium") of the pestilence that infects the entire world and drives everyone mad to such an extent that each man "thought that truth was contained in himself

14. Cf. J. Børtnes, "The Function of Hagiography in Dostoevsky's Novels," in *Critical Essays on Dostoevsky*, ed. Robin Feuer Miller (Boston: G. K. Hall, 1986), 191: "The Resurrection of Lazarus has complex symbolical meaning in the Orthodox tradition—it is an expression of the divine power of Christ to restore man to his original immortality and as a prefiguration of the imminent death and resurrection of Christ."

15. Fyodor Dostoevsky, *The Notebooks to Crime and Punishment*, trans. and ed. Edward Wasiolek (Chicago: University of Chicago Press, 1967), 231.

alone," Raskolnikov undergoes his long-awaited and much anticipated epiphany.

It is early morning on a clear warm sunny day in spring, shortly after Holy Week and Easter Sunday, and Raskolnikov goes out for a walk along the river. He is presented with a scene on the opposite bank that reveals to him a glimpse of the promised land, "as if the centuries of Abraham and his flocks had not passed." Suddenly (the author's favorite temporal adverb), Sonya appears at his side:

> How it happened he himself didn't know, but suddenly it was as if something lifted him up and flung him down at her feet. . . . Infinite happiness lit up in her eyes; she understood, and for her there was no longer any doubt that he loved her, loved her infinitely, and that at last the moment had come. . . .[16]

They cannot speak: just like true faith, real love cannot be expressed in words. The next lines drive this point home:

> . . . in those pale, sick faces there already shown the dawn of a renewed future, of a complete resurrection into a new life. They were resurrected by love. . . . But he was risen and he knew it, he felt it fully with the whole of his renewed being. . . .[17]

Lazarus, Christ, and Raskolnikov: the circle is complete at the novel's end. It is human love that has accomplished the miracle, but it was divine love that inspired Sonya and may yet come to conquer the hero's heart:

> Under his pillow lay the Gospels. . . . It belonged to her [Sonya], it was the same one from which she had read to him about the raising of Lazarus. . . . A thought flashed through him: "Can her convictions not be my convictions now? Her feelings, her aspirations, at least. . . ."[18]

16. Dostoevsky, *Crime and Punishment*, 549.
17. Ibid., 549–50.
18. Ibid., 550. Even at this epiphanic moment, the last qualifier ("at least") seems to allow just a smidgen of doubt.

The gospel has now come full circle—from the innocent victim to the sacrificial lamb and finally to the repentant murderer, from one "holy fool" to another and ultimately to the hero.

One final aspect of this scene deserves comment, namely, its iconographic nature. Eastern Orthodoxy ascribes a special place to icons. Churches are filled with them: the iconostasis dividing the sanctuary from the body of the church is a solid screen covered with them; icons stand in special shrines around the church; the walls of the church are decorated with icons, frescoes, or mosaics; believers prostrate themselves in front of them, kiss them, place lit candles before them; they are censed by priests and carried in processions.[19] The icons themselves are never worshipped—they are merely reverenced or venerated. In the Russian tradition, icons are viewed not merely as sacred paintings, but as images, "dynamic manifestations of man's spiritual power to redeem creation through beauty and art. . . . The icons were part of the transfigured cosmos."[20]

The raising of Lazarus was a frequent subject for icon painters, especially Russian icon painters. There are numerous portrayals of the scene, each following the general pattern set out for Orthodox iconography.

19. See Timothy Ware, *The Orthodox Church* (New York: Penguin, 1997), 31; "Orthodoxy regards the Bible as a verbal icon of Christ, the seventh Ecumenical Council laying down that the Holy Icons and the Book of the Gospels should be venerated in the same way" (201).

20. Nicolas Zernov, *The Russians and Their Church* (Crestwood, NY: St. Vladimir's Seminary Press, 1978), 34.

Icon. *The Raising of Lazarus*. Fifteenth century.

This scene in Dostoevsky's novel is iconographic in two ways: first, it calls to mind the numerous Orthodox icons depicting the raising of Lazarus. As Sonya reenacts the crucial moment, the image comes into clear focus, both for her and for the reader:

> "And when He thus had spoken, He cried with a loud voice, Lazarus, come forth. *And he that was dead came forth. . . .*"
>
> (she read loudly and rapturously, trembling and growing cold, as if she were seeing it with her own eyes:)
>
> ". . . bound hand and foot with grave clothes: and his face was bound with a napkin. Jesus saith unto them, 'Loose him and let him go.'"[21]

Sonya is seeing the scene with her own eyes in part because she has venerated so many icons portraying this event; Dostoevsky's readers would also know the icons from their own churches.

But there is yet another iconographic image in this scene, which has occasioned comparisons to various Western etchings, including a work by Rembrandt,[22] as well as fierce objections by critics such as Vladimir Nabokov, who describes it as "sheer stupidity."[23] Dostoevsky describes the moment following the Gospel reading as follows:

> The candle-end had long been burning out in the bent candlestick, casting a dim light in this destitute room upon the murderer and the harlot strangely come together over the reading of the eternal book.[24]

Before the reading of Lazarus, just after Sonya had declared her faith in God and her certainty that he would protect her siblings, the hero reacts to her confession in a strange way: "With a sudden, quick movement he bent all the way down, leaned towards the floor, and kissed her foot."[25] A few pages later Sonya is described as having a "pale, thin, and angular little face" with "meek blue eyes

21. Dostoevsky, *Crime and Punishment*, 328.
22. Joseph Frank, *Dostoevsky: The Miraculous Years, 1865–1871* (Princeton, NJ: Princeton University Press, 1995), 131.
23. Vladimir Nabokov, *Lectures on Russian Literature* (New York: Harcourt Brace, 1991), 110: "But then comes this singular sentence that for sheer stupidity has hardly the equal in world-famous literature."
24. Dostoevsky, *Crime and Punishment*, 328.
25. Ibid., 321.

capable of flashing with such fire, such severe energetic feeling."[26] That evening, after Raskolnikov leaves her room, promising that if he returns the next day, he would tell her who killed Lizaveta, Sonya dreams "of Lizaveta, of reading the Gospel, and of him . . . him, with his pale face, his burning eyes. . . . He was kissing her feet, weeping. . . . Oh, Lord!"[27] These characters are portrayed as having faces similar to those in Russian icons, and the dramatic action depicted, the kissing of Sonya's feet, is a familiar iconographic motif: in the raising of Lazarus his two sisters, Martha and Mary, typically demonstrate in icons their gratitude for their brother's restored life by kissing Christ's feet. These images correspond closely to the iconographic details in the final scene in the epilogue, when Sonya suddenly appears by the hero's side on the riverbank that spring morning in Siberia: "Her face still bore signs of illness; it had become thinner, paler, more pinched." When he notices her presence, Raskolnikov is flung down at her feet: "He wept and embraced her knees."[28] Moments later, they both want to speak, but words fail them:

> They were both pale and thin, but in those pale, sick faces there already shone the dawn of a renewed future, of a complete resurrection into a new life.[29]

Once again, the description of faces, particularly Sonya's, and the dramatic action, namely Raskolnikov's, are identical to the features and figures in Russian icons.

26. Ibid., 324.
27. Ibid., 330.
28. Ibid., 549. Note the absence of personal agency. Raskolnikov is "flung down"—he does not "fling or hurl himself" down. Supernatural force is acting upon or from within him.
29. Ibid., 549.

In his monumental and definitive five-volume study of Dostoevsky's life and works, Joseph Frank wrote about Sonya's reading of Lazarus:

> Nowhere perhaps do we come closer to Dostoevsky's own tortuously anguished relation to religious faith than in the mixture of involuntary awe and self-conscious skepticism with which Raskolnikov reacts to Sonya.[30]

That is ultimately the value of this spectacular scene: not only is it the turning point in the novel foreshadowing the hero's figurative resurrection from spiritual death in the last pages of the epilogue, but it is the most dramatic and poignant display of the author's lifelong struggle with the demon of disbelief as he made his way through his fiery "furnace of doubt" and gave fictional life to his struggle in his remarkable writing.

Turning from Dostoevsky's first novel to *The Idiot* (1868), we find an equally dramatic scene, completely antithetical to the raising of Lazarus.

In her book of *Reminiscences*, the writer's second wife, Anna Grigoryevna Snitkina, describes in detail an overnight stop the couple made in Basel, Switzerland, on their trip from Baden-Baden to Geneva in August 1867. Her husband was eager to visit the art museum to see a painting he had heard about, a work by Hans Holbein the Younger (c. 1497–1543), the German artist and printmaker who was one of the most distinguished exponents of the Northern Renaissance style, especially in the realm of realistic portraiture. The painting in question was one of his most famous works, *Der Leichnam Christi im Grabe* (*The Body of Christ in the Tomb*), a startling work still on display in the Kunstmuseum in Basel.[31]

30. Frank, *Miraculous Years*, 131.
31. This painting is also known as "Dead Christ" and "The Body of the Dead Christ in the Tomb."

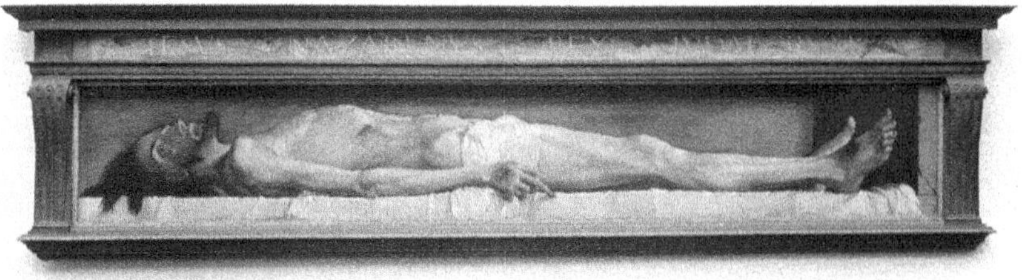

Hans Holbein the Younger, *The Body of Christ in the Tomb*, 1521. Kunstmuseum, Basel.

It is likely that Dostoevsky first learned about the painting from a brief reference to it by Nikolai Karamzin (1766–1826), an early-nineteenth-century Russian poet, writer, and historian. His *Letters of a Russian Traveler* (1791–92), modeled on Lawrence Sterne's popular *Sentimental Journey*, met with great success. In it Karamzin writes about Holbein's painting:

> Although there is nothing divine in the Christ taken from the cross, He is portrayed with remarkable naturalness as a dying man. According to legend, Holbein took a drowned Jew as his model.[32]

Dostoevsky's wife recalls the painting in greater detail:

> This painting, by Hans Holbein, depicts Jesus Christ after his inhuman agony, after his body has been taken down from the Cross and begun to decay. His swollen face is covered with bloody wounds, and it is terrible to behold.[33]

More significant was her husband's reaction to this strange work:

> The painting had a crushing impact on Fyodor Mikhailovich. He stood before it as if stunned. . . . When I came back after fifteen or twenty

32. N. M. Karamzin, *Letters of a Russian Traveler, 1789–90: An Account of a Young Russian Gentleman's Tour through Germany, Switzerland, France, and England*, trans. and abr. Florence Jonas (New York: Columbia University Press, 1957), 113.
33. Anna Dostoevsky, *Dostoevsky: Reminiscences*, trans. and ed. Beatrice Stillman (New York: Liveright, 1975), 133–34.

> minutes, I found him still riveted to the same spot in front of the painting. His agitated face had a kind of dread in it, something I had noticed more than once during the first moments of an epileptic seizure. . . . He calmed down little by little and left the museum, but insisted on returning once again to view this painting which had struck him so powerfully.[34]

In her diary for that day Anna noted these events as follows:

> In the city museum there [Basel], F.M. saw Hans Holbein's painting. It struck him with terrific force, and he said to me then, "A painting like that can make you lose your faith."[35]

That overwhelming experience and that astonishing formulation of the impact of this one painting on the writer's imagination will become the central motif of *The Idiot*.

This painting has been described in graphic detail by one of the foremost art historians of the Northern Renaissance:

> Holbein's dead Christ is at first sight frightening and repulsive. Stretched out before us, seen slightly from below, is the lifesize cadaver of a dead man [6' x 1'] recognizable as Christ only by the marks of the lance and nail wounds. Rigor mortis has set in with the gruesome head twisted backward so that the teeth in his gaping mouth and the eerie half-closed eyes are vividly close to the viewer. The body [is] painstakingly painted in morbid tones and exacting detail. . . . Even the low tomb chamber is as cold and barren as a shelf in a morgue with only a thin shroud spread beneath the body.[36]

Holbein's image is the most powerful image of total and unrelenting death imaginable: the emaciated body is bruised, bloody, and broken,

34. Ibid., 134.
35. Quoted in Dostoevsky, *Reminiscences*, 393. According to several art historians, Dostoevsky misinterpreted the meaning of the painting and reached the "wrong conclusion" about the creator's intention in painting it. Rather than being the product of an atheist, the image is a "work of piety" and an aid to devotion.
36. James Snyder, *Northern Renaissance Art: Painting, Sculpture, the Graphic Arts from 1350 to 1575* (New York: Prentice Hall, 1985), 386–87.

mutilated after what seems to be a prolonged and severe period of physical punishment. Christ's chest bears a bloody spear wound; the hands show the stigmata, while the feet reveal the imprint of nails. The enormous size and unusual shape of this work, its unrelenting horizontality (a huge rectangle six feet by one foot), reinforce a sense of claustrophobia resulting from the entombment. Holbein's ultra-naturalistic image lacks any physical beauty and is devoid of all supernatural connotations or spiritual transcendence: a rotting corpse, jaw dropped, flesh spotted with a blue-green decay, eyes rolled upward. The Bulgarian-French linguist, philosopher, and critic Julia Kristeva has written movingly about this work in a collection of essays entitled *Black Sun*.[37] She comments on the total isolation of the body (as opposed to other representations of the scene); it is stretched out alone, lying above its viewers, completely separated from them. This is Christ at his lowest point: forsaken by his Father and set apart from all of us. Yet, she argues, Holbein attempts to include us in this final moment of Christ's life: the hair and hand extend beyond the base, almost reaching outside the picture, as if they might slide over toward us and invade our personal space: it is as if the frame of the picture could not hold back its corpse.[38]

In part II, chapter 4 of *The Idiot*, Dostoevsky's hero, Prince Lev Myshkin, whom the author was later to describe as a "positively beautiful man," a combination of Christ and Don Quixote, pays his first visit to the home of a wealthy merchant, the mysterious Parfyon Rogozhin, whom he had happened to meet in the first scene of the novel on his way back home from Europe to Petersburg:

> They came to a big reception room. Here there were several paintings

37. Julia Kristeva, *Black Sun*, trans. Leon Ruodiez (New York: Columbia University Press, 1989), 105–38.
38. Ibid., 244.

> on the walls, all portraits of bishops or landscapes in which nothing could be made out. Over the door to the next room hung a painting rather strange in form, around six feet wide and no more than ten inches high. It portrayed the Savior just taken down from the cross. The prince glanced at it fleetingly, as if recalling something, not stopping, however, wanting to go on through the door. He felt very oppressed and wanted to be out of the house quickly. But Rogozhin stopped in front of the painting.[39]

After Rogozhin explains the history of the reproduction, the guest recalls having seen the original during his time in Switzerland: "I'm no great expert," Myshkin confesses, but "it seems to be an excellent copy. I saw the painting abroad and cannot forget it." Obviously, Dostoevsky has ascribed his own reaction to his hero.

Almost immediately Rogozhin changes the subject and asks Myshkin a question; actually, in Dostoevsky's world, it is not merely a question, but *the* question: "I've long wanted to ask you something, Lev Nikolaich: do you believe in God or not?" (Recall Porfiry Petrovich's unexpected question to Raskolnikov after the discussion of the hero's article.)

Myshkin doesn't answer. As if "forgetting his question," Rogozhin turns back to the Holbein: "But I like looking at that painting." At this prompting, the hero suddenly cries out: "At that painting! . . . At that painting! A man could even lose his faith from that painting!"[40] Rogozhin quickly replies, "Lose it he does." The discussion returns to the original question posed by Rogozhin; again the Prince doesn't answer, but he narrates four recent encounters with Russians, all demonstrating the presence or absence of religious conviction. A more abstract and somewhat perplexing discussion of faith and disbelief follows. The scene concludes with a series of bizarre actions:

39. Fyodor Dostoevsky, *The Idiot*, trans. Richard Pevear and Larissa Volkhonsky (New York: Random House, 2002), 217–18.
40. Ibid., 218.

the men exchange crosses, Rogozhin's deranged mother gives her blessing to the Prince, the two men embrace as they bid farewell, and finally, Rogozhin renounces his attachment to Nastasya Filippovna (the ravishing, "fallen woman"), ceding her to Prince Myshkin: "Take her, then, if it's fate! She's yours! I give her up to you!" All this in reaction to the reproduction of Holbein's painting in Rogozhin's reception room—"that painting," which could lead a man to lose his faith.

As quoted above, Joseph Frank argued persuasively for the enormous significance of the scene in which Sonya Marmeladova read the Gospel account of the raising of Lazarus to Raskolnikov in *Crime and Punishment*. Similarly, he writes the following about the implications of the Holbein painting in *The Idiot*:

> No greater challenge could be offered to Dostoevsky's own faith in Christ the God-Man than such a vision of a tortured and decaying human being, whose face bore not a trace of the 'extraordinary beauty' with which, as Dostoevsky was to write in the novel, Christ is usually painted.[41]

The similarities to the former scene are many. Myshkin is a "holy fool," actually described by one critic as Dostoevsky's "most stylized holy fool."[42] He is simpleminded in a touching kind of way, lacking in social graces. Before the novel begins, he had been a patient at a mental institution in Switzerland; at the end, after reverting to madness, Myshkin returns to the same institution. Like Sonya, he shares the rootlessness of that type, wandering from place to place, even in his own country; in the final chapter, he leaves Russia and returns to the West.

Not only does the theme of "holy foolishness" connect these two crucial scenes, but iconography also comes back into play. If the

41. Frank, *Miraculous Years*, 221.
42. Thompson, *Understanding Russia*, 146.

raising of Lazarus was a frequent motif of icon painters, and the scene of Sonya reading to the hero by candlelight was also cast in iconographic form, Holbein's *The Body of Christ in the Tomb* serves as a consummate "anti-icon."[43] Unlike Dostoevsky's other novels, genuine icons are rarely mentioned in this second novel. The placement of this painting over a door in Rogozhin's large reception room, hanging among other portraits (and landscapes), has suggested to more than one reader the distorted image of a chapel or church, complete with mock iconostasis and royal doors.[44]

Rogozhin's house had already attracted the Prince's attention: it is large, "cluttered," "grim," "gloomy," and "without any architecture"; it is sturdily built, with thick walls and "extremely few windows." Everything is somehow "inhospitable and dry and everything seems to hide and conceal itself." Most symbolically significant, however, is the fact that the house has a history of intimate connection with the Russian castrates, an underground sect that split off from the Orthodox Church in the eighteenth century. One of the founding members of that sect, a peasant by the name of Kondratii Selivanov, had proclaimed himself none other than the Son of God incarnate in the person of the late Tsar Peter III (who was allegedly assassinated and succeeded by his wife, Catherine II, in 1762). For eighteen years Selivanov lived in Petersburg in the house of one of his disciples and received double homage as both Christ and the Tsar. Rogozhin, whose father always "had great respect for the castrates," still rents part of his house to members of this sect.

In Rogozhin's large reception room, Russian Orthodoxy seems to be turned upside down, or at least, on its side. Genuine icons are

43. The phrase is borrowed from Murav's study *Holy Foolishness*, 132.

44. See, for example, Tomas Baran, "The Window Closes: The Disappearance of Icons from Dostoevsky's *Idiot*," in *Depictions: Slavic Studies in the Narrative and Visual Arts*, ed. D. M. Greenfield (Dana Point, CA: Ardis, 2000), 35–41; and Carol Apollonio, *Dostoevsky's Secrets: Reading against the Grain* (Evanston, IL: Northwestern University Press, 2009), 94–95.

usually oriented vertically, with a victorious Savior portrayed above the royal or holy doors leading to the altar. Theologically these doors represent the gates of Jerusalem through which Christ entered on Palm Sunday, as well as the entrance to the Heavenly Jerusalem. But in Rogozhin's house, the "anti-icons" are nothing like "windows into the invisible world," or "images of the living word," or bold assertions of Christ's victory over mortality: it is quite the opposite. Holbein's Christ depicts and represents the inevitability and finality of death in the most naturalistic, disconcerting, and grotesque manner imaginable.

"A man could even lose his faith from that painting!"

Holbein's strange work appears a second time in *The Idiot*. One critic has argued that given the central importance of the iconographic tradition in Dostoevsky's fiction and in the Russian Christian tradition, Holbein's painting is the novel's "central mystery physically, narratively, and symbolically."[45] In part III, a key figure in the secondary plot, Ippolit Terentyev, an acutely conscious, terminally ill young nihilist, reads aloud his "Necessary Explanation" at Prince Myshkin's birthday celebration. In fact, it is a lengthy, rambling suicide note in which he expresses both his despair at having failed to find any meaning in life and his lack of faith in any form of afterlife. Just as the Holbein painting is an "anti-icon," this reading can be seen as an "anti-Gospel" and is analogous to Sonya's inspired reading of Lazarus.

In his narrative, Ippolit describes his visit to Rogozhin's house and his own (long-winded) reaction to the Holbein print that had so riveted the prince:

> This picture portrays Christ just taken down from the cross. . . . In Rogozhin's picture there is not a word about beauty; this is in the fullest sense the corpse of a man who had endured infinite suffering before the

45. Apollonio, *Dostoevsky's Secrets*, 94.

> cross, wounds, torture, beating by the guards, beating by the people as he carried the cross and fell down under it, and had finally suffered on the cross for six hours. . . . But, strangely, when you look at the corpse of this tortured man, a particular and curious question arises: if all his disciples . . . if all those who believed in him and worshipped him had seen a corpse like that . . . how could they believe, looking at such a corpse, that this sufferer would resurrect? Here the notion involuntarily occurs to you that if death is so terrible and the laws of nature are so powerful, how can they be overcome?[46]

Ippolit even refers in passing to the image of the raising of Lazarus:

> How overcome them . . . by the one who defeated nature while he lived, whom nature obeyed who exclaimed . . . 'Lazarus, come forth' and the dead man came out?[47]

Condemned to die by his terminal illness, unable to believe in God or any form of afterlife, Ippolit decides in his despair to kill himself before his listeners as a final act of his own volition. But his revolver doesn't fire and his attempt fails. After this scene of great bathos, he fades out of the novel and this secondary plot comes to naught.

Myshkin, on the other hand, remains at the center of our attention as he struggles against the dark forces, embodied primarily by the nonbeliever Rogozhin with Holbein hanging in his house: "But I like looking at that painting," he declares to Myshkin on their first entering the large reception room in his house. The dark forces in *The Idiot* prove to be too powerful for Prince Myshkin. Ultimately his Quixote-like nature and his Christ-like goodness cannot withstand the onslaught of evil.

The heroine of the novel, the "fallen woman" Nastasya Filippovna, agrees to marry the prince, but on her way to the church, convinced that she will ruin Myshkin, whose ideals and innocence are so unlike

46. Dostoevsky, *The Idiot*, 407–408.
47. Ibid., 408.

the cynicism and corruption around her, she suddenly decides to run off with Rogozhin. Realizing that he can never fully possess her body and soul, Rogozhin murders her. The novel concludes with an extraordinary scene of the two rivals keeping a vigil over her body, eventually lying side by side in a made-up bed:

> [Myshkin] finally lay down on the pillows, as if quite powerless now and in despair, and pressed his face to the pale and motionless face of Rogozhin; tears flowed from his eyes onto Rogozhin's cheeks, but perhaps by then he no longer felt his own tears and knew nothing about them. . . .[48]

The metaphysical forces of evil, the strength of doubt and disbelief, the power of death, and the strain of all these traumatic events have combined to shatter Myshkin's fragile psyche. The prince returns to the asylum in Switzerland from whence he came. *The Idiot* is without a doubt the most despairing of Dostoevsky's works and the one that he himself regarded as an artistic failure.

This then is yet another compelling restatement of Dostoevsky's lifelong dilemma presented in terms of the same iconographic opposition: the raising of Lazarus vs. Christ in the tomb, the miracle of resurrection vs. the mystery of death, sincere faith vs. profound disbelief, or, as he succinctly expresses the idea of opposition in Book V in *The Brothers Karamazov*, the "Pro and Contra."[49]

Just as in *Crime and Punishment* the reader was invited to participate in, or was implicated in the miracle of resurrection as Sonya reads/recites/performs/reenacts the raising of Lazarus, so too in *The Idiot* the reader is compelled to experience the temptation of such powerful human emotions as gloom, despair, anguish, and doubt when confronted with the image of the definitively dead Christ in the

48. Ibid., 611. I have modified the translation slightly.
49. This section contains Dostoevsky's most famous attack on Christ, Ivan Karamazov's "Grand Inquisitor."

tomb.[50] For Ippolit the laws of nature had gained complete domination over beauty, over Christ's divinity, and over the possibility of life everlasting.

Here then is the crux of the matter: Dostoevsky spends his entire personal and artistic life engaged in a most arduous spiritual journey, navigating between Porfiry Petrovich's leading question to Raskolnikov, "And . . . and do you believe in the raising of Lazarus?" and Prince Myshkin's heartrending confession, "A man could even lose his faith from that painting!" This is surely the quintessence of the man and the writer—his own personal search reflected so brilliantly in his inspiring art; and this surely is also the nature of our own quest.

50. See Olga Meerson, "Ivolgin and Holbein: Non-Christ Risen vs. Christ Non-Risen," in *Slavic and East European Journal* 39, no. 2 (1995): 200–13.

8

Frodo and the Passion in J. R. R. Tolkien's *The Lord of the Rings*

Matthew Dickerson

He came from a lowly people in a forgotten land, ignored by the mighty of the earth. He had no great social stature, nor any wonderful appearance—nothing to make him important in the eyes of the world. Yet to bring salvation to a world that thought little of him, he became the afflicted one: a man of suffering, familiar with pain, imprisoned. When his captors struck him, bruised him, beat him, and crushed him, he did not fight back, but went like a lamb to slaughter. He walked a lonely road, betrayed by one he trusted and abandoned by others, cut off from the land of the living. In the end, though he knew it would cost him all, he willingly and humbly laid down his life for those he loved.

Then, when all was done—when he had faced death to break the power of the evil one—he came back in triumph to the world of the living. He saw again the light of life and was given a portion among the great, walking in the world for a time before leaving the mortal plane and journeying to the undying lands.

A description of Jesus, the Christ? It could be, taken from the messianic prophecy of Isaiah or from the passion narratives of the Gospels. But it could also be a description of Frodo Baggins, the hero of J. R. R. Tolkien's great mythopoeic work *The Lord of the Rings.*[1]

Of course the forgotten land from whence Frodo came is the Shire, a peaceful country tucked away in an unimportant corner in the northwest of Middle-earth, far from the ruling realm of Gondor and all its glory. Frodo's people are the diminutive race of hobbits, who—for the most part—dwell in holes in the ground. They are not powerful among the races of Middle-earth. Indeed, they are so insignificant in the politics of the world that they are either ridiculed for their size and weakness or, more often, ignored altogether.

Yet it is on Frodo, one of the Little People, that the task falls of saving Middle-earth from enslavement by its demonic foe Sauron, a monster of angelic origin who long ago rebelled against the creator and lost his place in heaven. Frodo accepts the burden, and Middle-earth is saved, but only after the hero experiences his own sort of passion, which includes betrayal, abandonment, captivity, torture at the hands of his enemies, and a lonely climb up a desolate mountain where he forfeits his life.

Indeed, Frodo makes a journey through the earthly equivalent of hell itself: the Plains of Udûn in the land of Mordor. But even as he ultimately experiences something akin to a death, so too does

1. Citations from *The Lord of the Rings* are from the Houghton Mifflin second edition, published in 1965. Thanks to Ralph Wood for the many comments, suggestions, observations, and insights that helped shape this chapter.

he experience a sort of resurrection and ascension. This is Frodo Baggins's story. And author J. R. R. Tolkien's imaginative portrayal of him reflects his deep Catholic faith and the passion of Christ.

J. R. R. Tolkien, Allegory, and a Threefold Portrayal of Christ and the Passion

As soon as one makes such a close and explicit connection between the biblical narrative of Christ and a work of fantasy, however, the question of allegory arises. For those familiar with Tolkien and his writings, this is troublesome. Tolkien was notorious for his dislike of intentional allegory, and he publicly and adamantly expressed that distaste more than once. Unlike the children's fantasy novel *The Lion, the Witch and the Wardrobe*—written by Tolkien's close friend C. S. Lewis—which has strong allegorical elements (including a clear Christ figure in Aslan the Lion, son of the great Emperor-over-the-Sea), Tolkien's Middle-earth writings do not fit well into an allegorical framework, and attempts to force such interpretations fail. In particular, Frodo is not an allegory for Christ, at least not in any strict sense of the word *allegory*.

The most obvious point where an allegorical interpretation fails is that Frodo, unlike Aslan, is not portrayed as the Son of God, the incarnate Creator. This is evident on many levels. Unlike Jesus, Frodo does not perform miracles. And while he willingly gives up his life, and comes *near* to physical death, he does not actually die; he is brought back from a comatose state at the *edge* of death, but isn't resurrected. Furthermore, while his sacrifice does have temporary salvific power in the immediate war against a tyrannical and satanic foe, Frodo does not give himself for the *sins* of others; his sacrifice does not provide salvation for all time. Most importantly, though, he himself is not without sin. Not only does he lack mercy (early in the book) and gives in to self-pity (later in the story) but also on more than one occasion he succumbs to the temptation to use the Ring. And ultimately he fails in his quest: the Ring is destroyed (though not by Frodo).

Nonetheless, while readers do well to resist the temptation to allegorize *The Lord of the Rings,* at the same time we need to understand that Tolkien considered his writings to be deeply Christian (and, in many of the particulars, specifically Catholic). More generally, he argued that myth, fantasy, and fairy tales *must* contain both religious truth and moral applicability. He makes this case in a variety of ways in essays, personal letters, and even within his fiction. Among the most important truths that fairy tales should reflect, as Tolkien explained in his essay "On Fairy-Stories," is the truth of the Christian gospel of the incarnation, death, and resurrection of Jesus. He refers to the gospel as the *eucatastrophe* of human history: a sudden joyous turn of events coming at a moment when all seems hopeless; divine grace revealed in a miraculous victory that does not deny the horror of suffering, but does deny universal final defeat.

We also need to keep in mind that Middle-earth was not intended by its author to be some otherworldly fantastic setting disconnected from the *real* world; it was meant to be *our* world, the world inhabited by humankind, albeit an imagined episode in the history of this world. Even the name Middle-earth derives from the Old English word *middangeard,* which refers simply to the world where the race of Men dwell. The word appears in the Old English poem, "Christ I," which with its mysterious reference to the name Earendel speaks of Christ entering into this Middle-earth, and was one of the most important early literary and mythical inspirations for Tolkien's own writings about Middle-earth and his imagined tale of Eärendil, the great hero of the First Age of Middle-earth.[2]

It should not be surprising, then, that Tolkien's account of the journey and suffering of Frodo was inspired—at some levels perhaps unconsciously, but at other levels consciously—by the Gospel accounts of the passion of Christ. Understanding how Tolkien drew on the passion can lead to a deeper understanding of his works. Perhaps more importantly, though, those narratives in *The Lord of the Rings,* which flow from a deeply Christian imagination, can lead to a greater appreciation for the role of the passion in the Christian life.

The Passions of Gandalf and Aragorn

In presenting elements of the Christian story in *The Lord of the Rings,* Tolkien created three different types of heroes and gave to each of them different elements of the character and story of Christ. They are the wizard Gandalf, the human hero Aragorn, and the hobbit Frodo. Taken individually, none serves as a Christ figure. Taken together, however, they provide a much broader and more complete picture of Christ.

Gandalf is the most obvious candidate to be an allegorical Christ figure. In Tolkien's mythology, Gandalf is the equivalent of an incarnate angel, a spiritual being who, like Christ, assumes a flesh-and-blood body vulnerable to hunger, injury, temptation, and, eventually, mortality. Like Jesus in the Garden of Gethsemane, Gandalf also anguishes over whether or not to follow a path that will lead to death. For the wizard, it is the path into the Mines of Moria, where his friend Aragorn has prophetically foreseen his death. This ancient dwarf kingdom, as readers learn, has become a place ruled by an evil demonic spirit known as a Balrog. Just as Jesus' disciple Peter seeks to dissuade Jesus from following that path, so too does Aragorn urge Gandalf not to follow the path into Moria.

2. Tom Shippey, *J. R. R. Tolkien: Author of the Century* (London: HarperCollins, 2001), 257–59.

Again like Christ, Gandalf refuses such safe counsel. He chooses to descend into Moria, where he battles the demonic Balrog in order to save his friends. Though he defeats the Balrog in battle, he himself plummets into a hellish abyss and also dies. He is then miraculously sent back to life.

Gandalf uses his power to confront—or cast out—other demonic foes, too, including his fellow wizard Saruman in Isengard and the dreaded Lord of Nazgûl at the gates of Gondor, whom he addresses with the words, "Go back to the abyss prepared for you! Go back! Fall into the nothingness that awaits you and your Master." His dealings with the Balrog, Saruman, and the Nazgûl, especially the words of power he speaks in these confrontations, bear striking resemblance to accounts of Jesus casting out demons or healing people of demonic possession.

Despite all this, Gandalf is not a strict allegory for Jesus. Though more powerful than Frodo, he is nonetheless still a finite created being, and not the Creator himself. He does not even appear to be more powerful than the demonic foes he casts out. Indeed, he is not even the most powerful member of his own order. Early in the story the wizard Saruman is shown to be *more* powerful than Gandalf. The Balrog is nearly an even match for him. The Lord of the Nazgûl might be, as well, but readers never find out. Sauron is unquestionably more powerful than Gandalf. Though less so than Frodo, Gandalf is also prone to both moral failures and errors of judgment. At the Council of Elrond he acknowledges mistakes of judgment, and though he passes his greatest moral test by refusing the temptation to take the Ring, he fails smaller moral tests. Careful readers will note that Gandalf is given to pride and that he can be short-tempered. On at least one occasion, out of desperation he gives in to the temptation to torture the prisoner Gollum to gain information from him—an act that Tolkien in one essay describes as immoral. And so, though he reflects some aspects of Christ, Gandalf is not himself intended to *be* Christ.[3]

A second aspect of Tolkien's threefold portrayal of Christ is found in the person of Aragorn, who is also finite, mortal, fallible, and human. He is not intended to be divine, an allegorical stand-in for Christ. Nonetheless, like Jesus, Aragorn is a descendant of the famous kings of old—one who is prophesied to take up the throne of his ancestors. He is also a healer, and it is because of his gifts that he is recognized as king. While Aragorn's healing is often based more on knowledge of medicinal herbs than on miraculous power, at least in the healings of Éowyn, Faramir, and Merry, Aragorn also relies on his inner spiritual strength to call them back to life.

Like Christ—and Gandalf—Aragorn also faces a difficult choice. His friend Legolas describes the scene in which Aragorn spends the night alone in a high chamber agonizing over whether he should travel the Paths of the Dead: "He has neither rested nor slept, I think. He went thither some hours ago saying that he must take thought, and only his kinsman, Halbarad, went with him; but some dark doubt or care sits on him." This description echoes Jesus' own wrestling with the hardest of choices as he prays in Gethsemane, asking the Father to take the cup from him.

We also see that, just as Peter sought to turn Christ away from the cross, and Aragorn sought to keep Gandalf from entering Moria, so too do Aragorn's small group of friends seek to dissuade him from taking the Paths of the Dead. When Aragorn does start down

3. Tolkien wrote numerous essays, reflections, and notes about Middle-earth as he sought to understand and clarify philosophical and theological concerns arising from his imagined mythology, cosmology, and cosmogony. In one such essay on the origin of orcs, he writes about torture ("torment") and the ethical treatment of orc prisoners, stating clearly, "Captives must not be tormented, not even to discover information for the defence of the homes of Elves and Men. If any Orcs surrendered and asked for mercy, they must be granted it, even at a cost. This was the teaching of the Wise, though in the horror of the War it was not always heeded" ("Orcs," in *Morgoth's Ring: The Later Silmarillion, Part One*, in *The History of Middle-Earth*, ed. Christopher Tolkien [New York: Houghton Mifflin, 1993], 10:419).

this perilous road, the narration leaves him for a time. Those who love him but cannot follow (along with readers of the tale) are then left in doubt, fear, and despair, assuming they will never see him again—much as Jesus' followers must have felt on Good Friday.

What readers eventually learn is that the Paths of the Dead lead to the place where oath-breaking souls are held captive in a sort of living death. Aragorn releases them from their bondage on the condition that they atone for their earlier betrayal by joining the war against Sauron. Tolkien may have been thinking here of Paul's Letter to the Ephesians (4:8-10), which speaks of Jesus descending into the lower places, and then ascending with a host of newly freed captives. And as a Catholic, Tolkien is likely to have had Purgatory in mind, since it is the post-earthly realm through which all Paradise-bound sinners must pass in order to purge their remaining sins before being granted the Beatific Vision. Aragorn is the Christ-like provider of release to these captives.

Leading Up to the Passion

It is in Frodo, however, where I see the narrative elements most clearly drawn from traditional aspects of the passion story of Christ, and it is to Frodo's passion narrative that we now turn.

The first and perhaps most significant element is that nothing less than salvation is at stake in Frodo's calling to destroy the One Ruling Ring of power. Frodo himself uses that terminology to describe his own quest. "I should like to save the Shire," he states, when he takes on the burden of the Ring. And at the end, as he remembers these words to his friend Sam, he proclaims that "it has been saved." Frodo's use of the word *save* brings to mind the gospel story and connects his mission to that of Jesus, bringing salvation to our world. Now Frodo was initially speaking only of saving the Shire, and not all of Middle-earth. But, in fact, all of Middle-earth *is* saved when the demonic power of Sauron is shattered.

We also consider the words spoken by the great Elven king Elrond some time after Frodo expresses his desire to save the Shire, and realizes that the stakes are far greater than just his beloved homeland; he will be saving Rivendell and Lothlórien and many other places of beauty and worth. "But it is a heavy burden," Elrond tells Frodo. "So heavy that none could lay it on another. I do not lay it on you. But if you take it freely, I will say that your choice is right." Like the Christ depicted in Philippians 2, Frodo was not coerced into this enormous sacrifice; though Gandalf may have told him that the path was laid out before him, Frodo freely chose that path.

Near the start of his quest, Frodo also experiences, like Jesus, a temptation from demonic foes. Jesus' temptation near the start of his public ministry is threefold, coming in the wilderness as Satan seeks to entice him with various forms of power and authority: bread from stones to satisfy his hunger, miraculous rescuing by angels to prove his authority, and all of the wealth of the world. Frodo is tempted by a similar demonic foe: a Ringwraith. And the temptation for Frodo is also to seek power, in his case by putting on the One Ring. Unlike Jesus, however, Frodo gives in, justifying his sinful act by declaring that he should save himself even if his friends die. And throughout the tale, he repeatedly faces—and sometimes gives in to—that same temptation.

The desire for power, or the means to power, also comes into Frodo's story in another way. It might be tempting to view Boromir as a Judas character: a trusted follower who betrays the savior. But Boromir is much more like Peter. In Matt. 16:21-23, Peter does not *betray* Jesus to his enemies, as Judas will later do. Rather, Peter *rebukes* Jesus and tries persuade him against his divinely appointed destination. Peter was presumably trying to help Jesus—to protect him and steer him on the best path toward fulfilling his destiny as the Messiah, the Christ. "Surely you need not die," Peter tells Jesus. "May it never be that this should happen." In Peter's way of thinking, the way of the Messiah could not possibly be the way of the cross; the cross is the way of defeat, not of victory. Thus later on it is Peter, famously, who also draws his sword and cuts off the ear of one of those who comes to arrest Jesus. And then on the day of his Lord's death, Peter denies Christ not once but thrice.

As it was with Peter and Jesus, so it is with Boromir and Frodo. Surely the way to victory, Boromir tells Frodo, is not to walk into Mordor and certain death. The way to victory is with the sword: to seize the Ring and with it to rise up in power and throw down the enemy. In many ways, the temptation to follow the way of Peter and Boromir—to battle earthly evil on its own terms with physical and military might—is a far greater danger than Judas's outright betrayal and repudiation. Like the eventually forgiven Peter, Boromir is finally pardoned of his terrible attempt to take the Ring from Frodo. He dies only while slaying many orcs in order that Sam and Frodo might escape them. Acting like a priest administering the last rites over the dying Boromir, Aragorn assures him that in such a death he has found victory rather than defeat.

It is Boromir who ultimately pushes Frodo to his Gethsemane moment at Amon Hen, when in great anguish Frodo wrestles over his decision to enter Mordor and destroy the Ring. In Gethsemane, Jesus was free to bear the cross or to refuse it. "Not my will be done," he says. So Frodo was free to bear, or to refuse to bear, his burden. Though the will of Sauron bears down on him with nearly irresistible force—turning him into a virtual puppet of Evil—we learn Frodo finally recovers his freedom and thus his real person. "He was aware of himself again. Frodo . . . free to choose."

Wounds, Stripes, and Burdens

Frodo's choice, however, does not lead him to the cross on the next day, nor even the day after. It is many days before he will bear his burden up the mountain, there to be betrayed by the one whom he had so riskily yet faithfully trusted. Gollum. His own Judas.

Frodo's acceptance of Gollum as a fellow traveler along the path to Mount Doom, and his eventual trust in him, is an indispensable part of the story. The ever-suspicious Sam never musters such trust in Gollum. But Frodo, though he has reason to distrust Gollum, is persuaded by Gandalf to have mercy on this wretched creature, just as Bilbo had many years earlier shown mercy even at great personal risk. Gandalf's saying—"The pity of Bilbo may rule the fate of many"—is repeated three times, becoming the virtual leitmotiv of the entire epic. And so Frodo chooses to place his own life in Gollum's hand. There is reason to believe that, for a time, Gollum really has been transformed into one of Frodo's loyal followers, trying to help his "master" accomplish the quest to destroy the Ring. But, in the end, just as Judas betrays Jesus out of an unbridled lust for political power, so also does Gollum betray Frodo out of his own desire to possess a similar kind of coercive strength.

And when Frodo is betrayed into the hands of his enemies, he suffers greatly. It is clear that Frodo is scourged and receives wounds similar to those of Jesus. And, like Christ, he has been abandoned at the time. It is the only time in the story when even his most loyal follower, the determined and faithful Sam, has temporarily left him, thinking him dead. The narrator does not describe firsthand Frodo's torture by these minions of the Evil One. He does not describe the depths of Frodo's torment as it is happening, but only gives one brief vision of the whip raised over him and cracking down. Later, however, there are several more hints, as we see through Sam's eyes the results of Frodo's torture.

What Tolkien also once again does so powerfully (as he did earlier with both Gandalf and Aragorn) is to leave the reader (as well as Frodo's companion Sam, and later Gandalf, Aragorn, Pippin, Gimli, and Legolas) in doubt and despair as, for a time, Frodo is thought to be dead. And even when Sam is given hope that Frodo still lives, many hours (and many pages) pass with Frodo in torment before any hope can be restored.

When Sam finally discovers that Frodo is sorely wounded but not dead, we learn that Frodo "was naked, lying as if in a swoon on a heap of filthy rags: his arm was flung up, shielding his head, and across his side there ran an ugly whip-weal." The images of torture, and particular of scourging by whips, are all too clear. So is the humiliation and physical suffering from being stripped. Readers may be moved to reflect on the similar experience endured by Jesus, described so poignantly in Matt. 27:27-31. Among the worst humiliations visited upon malefactors by the Romans was the final degradation of being stripped naked as they were crucified.

Following his own torture at the hands of the orcs, Frodo must then carry his own burden—his cross, as it were—across Mordor and up Mount Doom. He must journey to his own death, the place where he must make the final sacrifice to save Middle-earth. Yet Frodo, by his own choice, continues on. He does not turn back. Yet neither does he bear his burden alone. Wasted in both body and spirit by his long bearing of the Ring, he becomes physically unable to ascend Mt. Doom. He must be carried by his dear friend Samwise Gamgee, who thus serves as a virtual Christopher, a Christ bearer.

But now we come to where Frodo's own passion is an imperfect one. Not only does Frodo not literally die, but he also fails in his quest. Just as he failed to resist temptation at his earlier testing—and perhaps in part *because* he fails that earlier testing—so he fails again at the Cracks of Doom. He does not surrender the Ring, but cries out instead: "I do not choose now to do what I came to do. I will not do this deed. The Ring is mine!" This is a final, desperate act of utter self-deception, for the Ring can never really be Frodo's. But in this self-deception Frodo fails to surrender the Ring. It seems clear that his own will has been usurped by the power of the Ring. Yet for Tolkien the Christian, Frodo would have ceased to be human if he had become merely a tool of Sauron.

In any case, this final failure may seem to negate all comparison with Christ's own passion. Yet while it removes Frodo's story from being a strict allegory, it does not negate the significance of his passion. One of the most ancient ways of narrating the redemption was to liken Christ to a baited hook that Satan fatally swallows. In this case, it is Gollum who does so, for in an act of his own worst deceit, Gollum bites the Ring from Frodo's finger and dances a jig of demonic joy, until he falls backward into the molten lava of the volcanic mountain that alone is sufficiently hot enough to melt the Ring. In this sense, Frodo becomes the unwitting instrument by which the quest is won in spite of his own collapse.

Thus we return again to Frodo's statements mentioned earlier. "I should like to save the Shire," he states at the start of the quest, and then later, "it has been saved." The first is phrased in the active voice, whereas the second in the passive. Frodo is no longer the subject of the verb, for he cannot claim himself to have saved the Shire, only that the Shire *was saved*. He knows he has not accomplished this great deed of his own autonomous will, but that he is the grateful recipient of grace and power far exceeding his own strength. For just as the first statement is in the active voice and the second passive, the earlier passage is only a statement of his wish, while the second is a statement of a completed action, a realized fact; salvation has already been accomplished, but not by Frodo.

Thus there is a hope to be found in Frodo's imperfect passion. If he had succeeded in destroying the Ring by his own will and strength, he would no longer have been a fallen hobbit akin to his fallen readers: he would instead have become the Christ of Middle-earth, thus displacing Jesus as its one true King and Lord and Savior. For Tolkien, as for all other Christians, there could be no worse horror. That Frodo's efforts finally fail, and yet in that failure he is shown grace, is what makes him a true analogue, not of the one Christ, but of all Christians. Like him, our own imitation of Christ will always be imperfect until Christ himself wins the victory that, as Tolkien said, lies "beyond the walls of the world." Until then, we travel the One Road in the assurance that the one true passion enables all our lesser versions of it.

PART IV

Images

The art of the passion is vast and appears in many forms—public and private, intimate and monumental. The essays in this section explore some of the ways artists engage moments of the passion from the betrayal by Judas to Mary Magdalene's encounter with the recently risen Jesus; the section concludes with an essay on the treatment of the passion in cinema.

The first essay in this section treats one of the earliest images depicting crucifixion—the Alexamenos graffito, a second- or early-third-century drawing of a human figure with the head of an ass crudely etched into the plaster of slave quarters in an imperial palace complex on the Palatine Hill in Rome. It examines popular anti-Jewish and anti-Christian slanders that may have contributed to the making of the image and how one critic of the gospels rejected the worship of a crucified god.

The second essay illustrates how the cross could become a symbol of power and prestige, a process that began with the story of Constantine's using the chi-rho symbol to promote his victory at the Milvian Bridge (312 C.E.) that established him as the sole emperor of Rome and made the cross a symbol of power throughout the ages of empire. Eliza Garrison, a medievalist, looks at one example—the

Lothar Cross, a bejeweled and intricately etched cross that came to be used in both church and court processionals for the Saxon kings and emperors who ruled much of Europe from 919 to 1024. She explores how the cross reveals tensions between religion and politics, image and substance, the past and the present.

Christopher Kent Wilson looks at two of the numerous etchings Albrecht Dürer produced to illustrate biblical stories during the early period of the reformation in Europe. A great admirer of Martin Luther, Dürer completed two sets of illustrations for his "Small" and "Great" passions (1509 and 1510), which reflected Luther's emphasis on the death of Jesus. Wilson suggests that the differences between the two versions of Judas's betrayal reveal the artist to be a close and insightful reader of the Bible, especially as evidenced in the way he treats the moment of Judas's kiss.

Katherine Smith Abbott and her student Elizabeth Oyler examine the painting *Noli Me Tangere* ("Do not touch me") by the Italian renaissance artist Titian (c. 1487/90–1576). Paintings depicting Jesus' appearing to Mary Magdalene in the Garden of Gethsemane (John 20:11-18) appear frequently in the history of Christian-influenced art. This essay argues, however, that Titian rendered it in a particularly intimate way, drawing not only on the scene in John but also on the annunciation scene in the Gospel of Luke—a scene that was especially important in Titian's Venice, said to have been founded on the Feast of the Annunciation.

In the next essay, John Hunisak asks why Édouard Manet (1832–83), a "secularist and non-believer," would take up a traditional scene from the Gospels when he was so committed to "a radically modern style." Teasing out the meaning of the inscription Manet placed in the lower right hand corner of the painting, Hunisak argues that Manet's approach to the scene was in fact very much part of his modernist agenda, combining as it does a traditional scene and a new way to "see" its narrative sources—in keeping with new trends in the biblical scholarship of his time. With Hunisak's reading, Manet's *Dead Christ with Angels* is a striking contrast to Titian's *Noli Me Tangere* treated in the previous chapter.

Margaret Steinfels's "Marc Chagall's Jewish Jesus," the next essay, also poses a question: Why did a Jewish artist from an East European *shtetl* paint so many crucifixions? The question has been asked, she writes, by both Christians and Jews, many of whom find this and other aspects of Chagall's use of the New Testament deeply perplexing, if not insulting. Firmly rejecting the notion that Chagall had converted, Steinfels finds at least a partial answer to the question in his life and times, which saw pogroms in his hometown of Vitebsk and the holocaust that swept Europe. She examines examples of Chagall's crucifixions from 1912 (the earliest) to the ones he continued to work on after moving to the United States in 1941 and then after returning to France in 1948 until his death in 1985. While pointing out that Chagall himself never explicitly answered his Jewish and Christian critics, Steinfels concludes that "he saw Jesus not as the resurrected savior of Christian faith but as the quintessential Jewish martyr, the cross representing Jesus' own suffering as well as that of the Jewish people."

Kymberly Pinder's essay "Can You Feel Me?: The Passion in the Public Art Ministries of Damon Lamar Reed" and Emmie Donadio's "Banksy's Christmas Passion" bring the treatment of the passion in art up to the twenty-first century. Reed, Pinder shows, is a contemporary painter, poet, and rapper who works in inner-city churches in Chicago, but has a much wider following on the Internet and through other social media. He proclaims the gospel through murals, vernacular translations of Scripture, music, graffiti, and T-shirts. Pinder writes that Reed and others like him are "'making church' for the churchless in the most secular corners of their cities."

The way he places young African American men in biblical scenes of the passion is one of the most powerful aspects of Reed's art.

Emmie Donadio writes on a provocative piece by an anonymous street artist who goes by the pseudonym *Banksy*. Though *Christ with Shopping Bags* is in some ways like the Alexamenos graffito in Rome, Banksy's target is more political than theological—in that he uses the figure of a crucified Jesus who carries shopping bags filled with gifts to attack the commercialism of Christmas—and the capitalist system that encourages it. Donadio "reads" the image for us and sets it in the context of Banksy's other works that make use of traditional images of Jesus (and other figures) to condemn bigotry, violence, and oppression with visual irony. She also sees irony in the commercial success Banksy has gained from his attack on commercialism, noting at the same time that he has given away much of what he has made.

In the last essay in this section Adele Reinhartz explores the treatment of the passion in cinema—the "moving pictures." After briefly looking at medieval passion plays, the forerunners of cinematic dramatizations, Reinhartz discusses themes and developments in Hollywood productions that feature the passion—whether in the concluding scenes of a "biopic" on the life of Jesus or as the slowly developed and graphically explicit central theme in Mel Gibson's 2004 film *The Passion of the Christ.* Reinhartz concludes her essay with a film of a very different kind, Denis Armand's *Jesus of Montreal* (1989). This film, she shows, is a subtle but powerful exploration of the passion, since it develops the story as a play within a play, forcing viewers to ask what the real story is.

Art also figures prominently in other sections: Michael Katz, for example, examines Dostoevsky's fascination with a painting of Jesus in the tomb by Holbein the Younger and his use of icons to set scenes in several of his most important novels. Jeremy Cohen draws attention to stylized images of the church and synagogue in medieval art to explore the ways Christians stigmatized Jews. And Katherine Sonderegger's essay on the theology of the passion references paintings of Gauguin, Rembrandt, and Chagall.

9

The Alexamenos Graffito

Street Art in Ancient Rome

Oliver Larry Yarbrough

Graffiti—street art—was a common site in ancient Roman cities, just as it is in most urban settings today. Then, as now, street artists advertised, promoted, incited, or ridiculed anyone and everything.[1] Even so, it is surprising that a street artist in Rome provides one of the earliest graphic representations of crucifixion. Dateable to the second century C.E., the drawing is composed of two crudely rendered figures and an inscription etched between and below them, in equally crude letters[2] (See image on p. 232). The more prominent figure has a human body with the head of an ass. Seen from the rear

1. See the Introduction to J. A. Baird and Claire Taylor, *Ancient Graffiti in Context* (London: Routledge, 2011) for a review of recent approaches to the study of ancient graffiti. On modern street artists, see the essays by Kymberly Pinder and Emmie Donadio in this volume.
2. The Alexamenos graffito was removed shortly after discovery and is now in the Palatine Museum. The preserved piece of plaster with the graffito measures 33.5 x 38 cm (13.2 x 15 in). I have treated this image more fully in "The Shadow of an Ass," in *Text, Image and Christians in*

(as evidenced by the exposed buttocks), it is attached to a T-shaped cross with arms outstretched and feet resting on a short crossbeam. The head of the figure is turned to the left, in the direction of (and perhaps looking toward) the other figure.

The Alexamenos Graffito from the Domus Gelotiana, Palatine, Rome. Second–third century C.E.

The second figure appears to be standing level with the bottom of the vertical post of the cross. He is slightly shorter than the central figure

a Graeco-Roman World: A Festschrift in Honor of David Lee Balch, eds. Carolyn Osiek and Aliou C. Niang (Eugene, OR: Wipf & Stock, 2011), ch. 15.

and also appears to be seen from the rear, though the buttocks are not exposed beneath the garment he is wearing. The head, which is large for the body, is turned and raised slightly toward the crucified figure, so that it is seen in profile. His right arm is raised in a salute.

The inscription runs to four lines, with the first word being divided. It reads ALE / XAMENOS / SEBETE / THEON, which may be translated either "Alexamenos, worship God" or "Alexamenos worships God," with the latter being more likely.[3]

The Alexamenos graffito was discovered during excavations of a building adjacent to the imperial palace designed for the emperor Domitian (ruled 81–96 C.E.). Originally completed in 92 C.E., it went through several renovations over the course of the next century and underwent a significant expansion during the reign of Septimius Severus (ruled 193–211 C.E.). Though not enough of the original building survives to allow certainty in assessing the full range of its functions, the building's scale, proximity to the palace, and the types of graffiti in its various rooms suggest that it served as living and working quarters for imperial slaves and freedmen.[4]

The Alexamenos etching is one of 369 graffiti to have been recovered from the slave complex. Though the vast majority of them are simply the names of slaves and freedmen who occupied the building, there are also twenty-five drawings, most of which are even more crudely rendered than the figures in the Alexamenos graffito. Two, however, are clearly better. In the same room as the Alexamenos graffito someone drew a horse that is more detailed, anatomically correct, and aesthetically pleasing; and a drawing of an ass turning a millstone that is more competently and realistically rendered appears in an adjoining room. Like the Alexamenos graffito,

3. In Greek the subject and verb do not agree, so that the grammar is as crude as the drawing.

4. The building, its uses, and the graffiti in it are discussed in Heikki Solin and Marja Itkonen-Kaila, *Graffiti del Palatino. I. Paedagogium*, AIRF 3, ed. V. Väänänen (Helsinki: AIRF, 1966). For the Alexamenos graffito, see pp. 40–41 and 209–12.

this one also has a taunting inscription: "Work, little ass, as I have worked—and it will go well for you."[5]

If we wonder how a graffito admonishing an ass to work hard ends up in the slave quarters of an imperial palace, how many more questions arise with regard to the appearance of the Alexamenos graffito in such a context. For whereas the exhortation in "the little ass" graffito seems generalized and moralistic, the Alexamenos graffito is pointedly direct, so that its target is almost certainly a real person—and one whom the artist knew.

Still, the artist who composed the graffito spoke not only to Alexamenos but also to everyone else who worked in the complex. This makes the question of the artist's purpose all the more challenging. Did he simply want to embarrass Alexamenos or was he after something more sinister? Was the artist exposing Alexamenos's religious practices, or did everyone know of them already? Does the graffito give vent to anger? Frustration? Fear? Was it the product of a private feud or was it commentary on larger social questions? What did the artist know about the iconography he uses in his drawing? And how did he come by his knowledge?

Most of these questions cannot be answered with certainty. But there are hints for some of them, not only in the naming of the figures but also in the identification of the action. The artist, that is, makes sure everyone who sees his creation will know:

1. That Alexamenos is worshiping his god;
2. That Alexamenos's god has the head of an ass; and
3. That this ass-headed god is crucified.

Whatever else the artist may have known (or meant to convey) about Alexamenos and his god, these three things are fundamental. They

5. The Latin reads *labora aselle quomodo ego laboravi/et proderit tibi.* Translations in the essay are my own, unless otherwise indicated.

are what give the graffito its punch. As absurd as the image seems, the artist may well have been playing on popular anti-Jewish and anti-Christian rhetoric of the time.

The Roman historian Tatian, the Jewish historian (and apologist) Josephus,[6] and the Christian apologists Minucius Felix and Tertullian refer to popular characterizations of the Jewish and Christian god with the head of an ass or with other asinine features. Minucius Felix, for example, reports that his opponent Caecilius slanders Christians by claiming they "worship the head of an ass" and by suggesting they have the morals of an ass.[7]

Tertullian rebuts the ass-worshiping slander in two of his apologetic works *Apology* 16:1-3 and *To the Nations* 1:14. In both passages, he also refers to a rumor he has heard regarding a charlatan who had been parading around Rome carrying "a picture with the explanatory inscription 'The ass-begotten God of the Christians.'" The image on the picture, he reports, has the ears of an ass and a hoofed foot; it also carries a book and wears a toga. In *To the Nations*, he adds that "the ass-begotten god was proclaimed throughout the city (*in tota civitate*)."[8] Though the description of the picture paraded through Rome does not match the Alexamenos drawing exactly, its combination of human and asinine features suggests variations on a theme. Tertullian's linking the picture to the slander directed at Christians for worshiping an ass-headed God makes it clear he would have recognized what the street artist was doing—and refuted it vigorously.

Celsus, a second-century critic of the early Christian movement, would have recognized—and appreciated—the intent of the

6. On Tacitus and Josephus, see Peter Schäfer, *Judeophobia: Attitudes toward the Jews in the Ancient World* (Cambridge: Harvard University Press, 1997), ch. 1–2.

7. *Octavius* 9-10. Caecilius gives a long list of shameful practices he associates with Christians.

8. The phrase could also mean that the picture was *displayed* throughout the city.

Alexamenos graffito also, even though he never refers to the claim that Christians worship the head of an ass. Having studied their Gospels carefully, Celsus examined Christian belief and practice in his treatise *The True Doctrine*, offering an extensive refutation at many different levels.[9] One of his sharpest attacks was on their worship of "a crucified god." The rhetorical range of criticisms was broad. At times, he speaks of the "shame" of the cross.[10] At other times, he resorts to humor. He writes, for example,

> And everywhere [Christians] speak in their writings of the tree of life and of resurrection of the flesh by the tree—I imagine because their master was nailed to a cross and was a carpenter by trade. So that if he had happened to be thrown off a cliff, or pushed into a pit, or suffocated by strangling, or if he had been a cobbler or stonemason or blacksmith, there would have been a cliff of life above the heavens, or a pit of resurrection, or a rope of immortality, or a blessed stone, or an iron of love, or a holy hide of leather.[11]

More substantively, he argues that Christian claims that Jewish prophets predicted Jesus' suffering and death on the cross meant nothing, since it was "wicked and impious" to suggest such an idea. Celsus's strongest argument, however, derives from his understanding of God:

> So we should not consider either whether [Jewish prophets] did or whether they did not foretell [the manner of Jesus' death], but whether the act is worthy of God and is good. And we should disbelieve what is disgraceful and evil, even if all men should seem to predict it in a state of frenzy. How, then, is it anything but blasphemy to assert that the things done to Jesus were done to God.[12]

9. Though Celsus's own writings have not survived, the Christian writer Origen (c. 185–254) quoted him extensively in his treatise *Against Celsus*. References here are to Henry Chadwick's *Contra Celsum* (Cambridge: Cambridge University Press, 1965).
10. See 2.35 and 39, for example.
11. 6.4.
12. 7.14.

If Jesus had been a god, Celsus writes elsewhere, "he ought, in order to display his divinity, to have disappeared suddenly from the cross" (2.68). Celsus, that is, defends the notion of "the highest God" of the philosophical tradition.[13] Consequently, he refutes Christian claims, arguing that they "worship not a god, nor even a daemon, but a corpse" (7.68).

It is not at all clear the Alexamenos artist would have understood Celsus's theological arguments against Christian belief and practice. They may have been overly subtle for him. There is no doubt, however, that he would have appreciated Celsus's satirical humor. After all, biting satire informs every aspect of his art, crude though it may be. Celsus may well have appreciated the Alexamenos graffito, had he ever chanced to see it. It would certainly fit his ridicule of Christians who worship a crucified god.

Interestingly, the Christians themselves were better prepared to respond in kind to Celsus's verbal attack than they were to develop their own art of the passion, at least until they had gained a more secure position in Roman society. In the early-fifth century, not far from the Palatine Hill where the Alexamenos graffito was drawn, Christian artists (or, at least, artists employed by Christians) would decorate the doors of the Santa Sabina basilica with panels depicting scenes from the passion narrative, including one of the first representations of Jesus on the cross.[14] These scenes resemble the visual narratives of the passion on the Junius Bassus Sarcophagus and Maskell caskets of the same period, both of which were commissioned by people of high social status. All three works have been the subject of important recent studies, which promise to revise

13. See Chadwick's comments in *Contra Celsum*, xvi–xxii and Robert Wilken, *Christians as the Romans Saw Them* (New Haven, CT: Yale University Press), ch. 5.
14. Other scenes from the passion include Jesus before Pilate, Pilate washing his hands, Peter's denial, and various resurrection and ascension scenes. The crucifixion panel is in the upper left corner of the doors, scarcely visible from floor level.

our understanding of the origins of the art of the passion—and perhaps provide new ways to see the Alexamenos graffito.[15]

The Crucifixion of Christ, upper-left panel of the main entrance door to the Santa Sabina Basilica, Rome. Fifth century C.E.

15. See the important essays by Mary Charles-Murray and Robin M. Jensen in *Picturing the Bible: The Earliest Christian Art*, ed. Jeffrey Spiers (New Haven, CT: Yale University Press, 2007). The catalogue reproductions and notes in section 4–6 are excellent. Additional important articles include Felicity Harley McGowan, "Death is Swallowed Up in Victory: Scenes of Death in Early Christian Art and the Emergence of Crucifixion Iconography," *Cultural Studies Review* 17 (2010): 101–24, and Allyson Everingham Sheckler and Mary Joan Winn Leith, "The Crucifixion Conundrum and the Santa Sabina Doors," *Harvard Theological Review* 103 (2010): 67–88.

10

Engaging the Lothar Cross

Eliza Garrison

Early medieval liturgical crosses, especially those created in the late tenth and early eleventh centuries in association with Ottonian patrons, are remarkable for their rich beauty and for the complex ways in which their religious and political meanings were activated.[1] In what follows, I will offer a brief analysis of the visual and theological tensions that are revealed in the imagery and materials of the early-eleventh-century Lothar Cross (see images on pp. 241-42). Such tensions, I propose, derive much of their significance from Christian notions of transformation, and from the dialectical relationships between life and death and between the world of Christ

1. The Ottonians were a line of Saxon kings and emperors who ruled much of Europe between 919 and 1024: Henry I, 919–36; Otto I, 936–73; Otto II, 973–83; Otto III, 983–1002; Henry II, 1002–1024.

and the world of the emperor.[2] On this cross, the political and spiritual concerns that would have been activated in its use were tied directly to the commemoration of its donor, Emperor Otto III (983–1002), who presented the work to the treasury of the Palace Chapel of Aachen at his celebration of the feast of the Pentecost in the year 1000. The Lothar Cross was intended to recreate salient aspects of Otto III's official presence during his lifetime, and the work would have served a memorial function after his death in January 1002. There can also be no doubt that the work played an important role in funeral services for Otto III at the Palace Chapel on Easter Sunday, 1002, after the imperial corpse had been transported all the way from Rome to Aachen so that the young ruler could be buried at the church's altar to Mary.

2. While I am presenting a slightly different line of argumentation here, I encourage those readers who are interested in learning more about the Lothar Cross to consult my book, *Ottonian Imperial Art and Portraiture: The Artistic Patronage of Otto III and Henry II* (Farnham: Ashgate, 2012), especially pp. 39–86. Many of the propositions that I made in that chapter are also contained in my article "Otto III at Aachen," *Peregrinations* 3, no. 1 (Spring 2010): 83–137. Both of these analyses contain numerous references to the broader scholarship on the Lothar Cross.

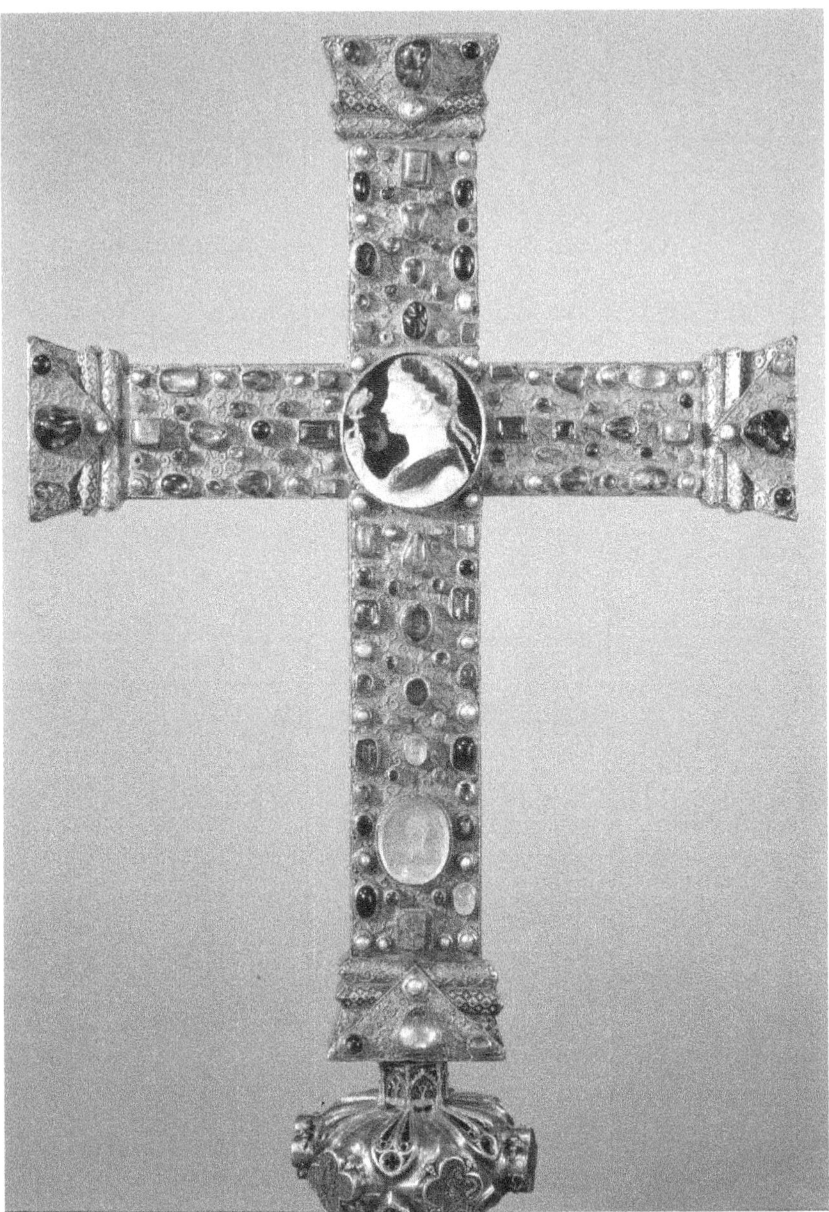

Lothar Cross, jeweled side front.

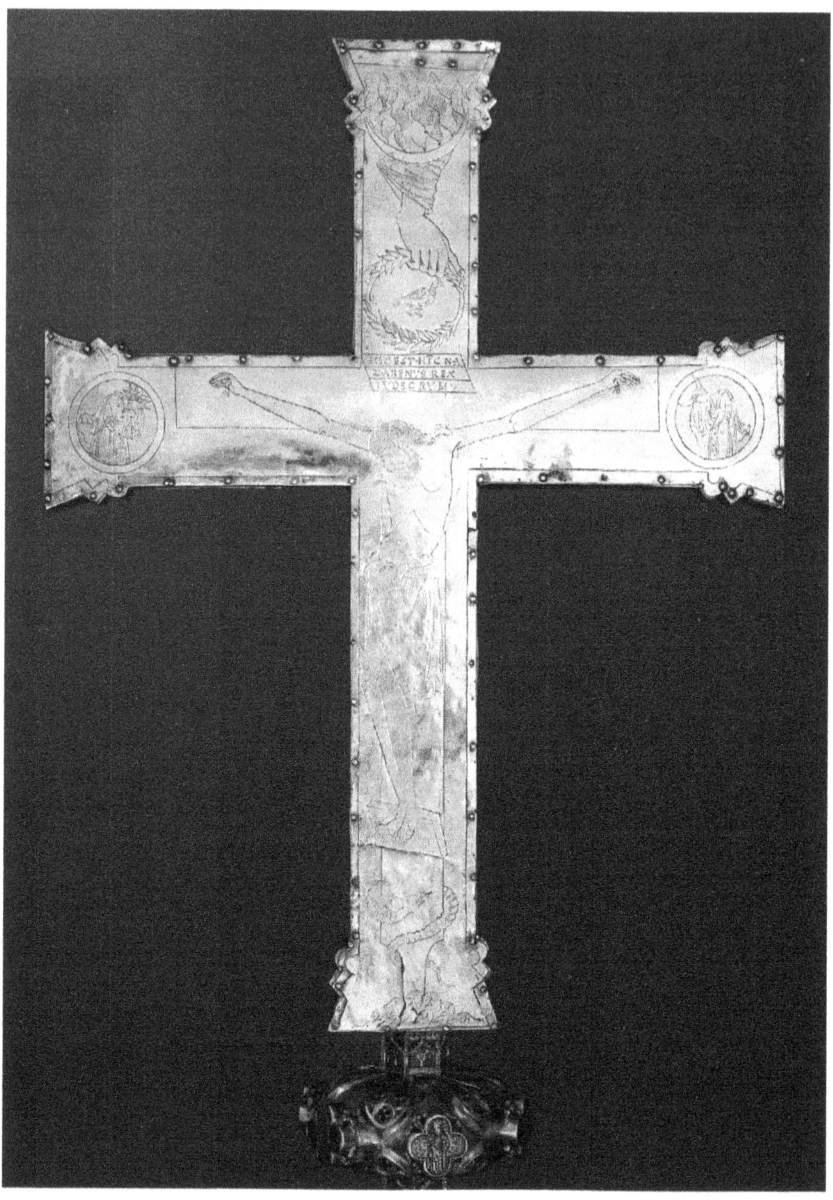

Lothar Cross, engraved side back.

The Lothar Cross is a richly beautiful object, and its monumental size enhances its stunning appearance: not including the late gothic stand, it is roughly twenty inches tall, fifteen inches wide, and about an inch thick. The large, slightly oval cameo of the emperor Augustus that sits at the center of the cross's obverse side measures three inches tall by slightly less than three inches wide. The cameo is arguably the cross's most striking element, and the smaller stones, intaglios, and gold filigree that surround it provide it with movement. Augustus is shown from the left; he is crowned with a laurel wreath whose ribbons appear to flutter in the wind. The eagle scepter that Augustus lightly grips with his right hand resembles an official portrait of Otto III contained in a gospel book that he donated to the Aachen Cathedral treasury along with the Cross. A smaller crystal seal matrix of the Carolingian ruler Lothar II (reigned 855–69) is nestled among the gems in the lower arm of the cross; both rulers cast their respective gazes in the same direction, as if Lothar is clearly following the cues of his Roman model, and as if Otto III, as Augustus, likewise relies on the physical support of his Carolingian predecessor.[3]

The reverse contains a dramatic, naturalistic image of the crucified Christ, who hangs limply from the cross as personifications of the sun (Sol) and the moon (Luna) weep for him. If the jeweled "front" of the cross is decidedly sculptural, therefore, with the materials and their colors animating it, this niello engraving of the crucifixion on the reverse more closely resembles a two-dimensional sketch. Indeed, this quality is used to illusionistic effect on this side: the cross of Christ's Crucifixion is indeed separate from the actual body of the cross as an object, and, as is especially clearly visible at the bottom of the incised crucifix, its shape intentionally evokes that of a processional cross. The telescoping of cruciform shapes here enhances the numerous symbolic aspects of the cross as a form, and this combination also creates a visual distinction between the cross as an object and the cross as an image.

3. See Genevra Kornbluth, "The Seal of Lothar II: Model and Copy," *Francia* 17 (1990): 55–68.

The broader contrast between the jeweled side of the cross and the side containing the Crucifixion is ultimately in keeping with other visual antitheses between life and death in works created for the Aachen treasury. Perhaps we are also to imagine that the jeweled side of the cross speaks to the material world and the world of the emperor, while the reverse evokes the most holy death in Christian history. In the upper arm of the "reverse" side, the Hand of God appears, bearing a laurel wreath that encircles the Holy Spirit in the form of a dove; this bears a deliberate resemblance to the eagle on Augustus's scepter on the work's jeweled side. In combination, these symbols suggest the equal importance of political and spiritual victories, and both sides of the cross can be understood to represent two successive moments in the act of a triumphal coronation, where Christ's coronation is succeeded by the appearance of the crowned Augustus. On the Lothar Cross, therefore, it is an imperial figure that completes the story that the Crucifixion set in motion. This symbolic narrative was well suited to the Palace Chapel as a site of royal coronations, and this work was used in such ceremonies. Certainly the various references to coronation on this object recalled Otto III's own coronation at the Palace Chapel in 983, when the king was just three years old; in the year 1000, when the Cross was likely created, this iconography would have commemorated Otto III's imperial coronation in Rome in 996.

While in its ritual use these implied narratives and layered symbols could vacillate among references to the past and the present and to the embeddedness of the past in the present, let us consider closely the "Christ side" of the Cross. Representations of the Crucifixion and images of its related feasts often relied on dialectical imagery to convey seemingly opposed ideas. Here, the deep sorrow that we see in Christ's figure and in those of Sol and Luna is echoed by their postures and positioning: the two personifications buckle under the weight of their sadness. As his side wound indicates, Christ appears before us just after his physical death (John 19:34-37). Placed in clear and dramatic contrast to Sol and Luna's mournful figures below, the Hand of God swoops down from above to place a triumphal laurel wreath on Christ's head; this wreath encircles the Dove of Holy Spirit. A writhing serpent twists around the base of the cross from which Christ hangs; it hisses as an embodiment of the sin that Christ's death removed from the world. If Sol and Luna offer us a horizontal axis that would seem to refer to the passage of time, as these figures typically do in other representations of the Crucifixion, the vertical axis of the Crucifixion scene reveals a dynamic opposition between the Trinity above and the vestiges of sin on earth below. The death that we witness on this side of the Lothar Cross is visually rife with the promise of rebirth and renewal.

A similar dialectical relationship between life and death also lends meaning to the objects on the jeweled side of the Cross; together, these precious materials offer the viewer a visualization of the majesty of Christ's sacrifice and of the glory of heaven. Certainly the gems and gold do much of the visual work here, but one of the most curious aspects of the Lothar Cross is that it is a decidedly pagan Roman imperial object that is the material and visual focus of this side. Indeed, the legibility of the inscription on the smaller crystal seal matrix of Lothar II was sacrificed so that the ruler's profile could align with that of the larger figure above. Ottonian artists integrated *spolia*—older, often non-Christian objects—into new works because they were useful in giving form to abstract spiritual concepts. And, of course, spolia were also prized for their aesthetic and material value. Although the cameo originally referred to and represented the Emperor Augustus and his political triumphs, on this object the cameo's field of reference was expanded to include Emperor Otto III. Located directly at the center of the cross and thus directly opposite the image of Christ's face on the reverse of the object, the cameo also refers to Christ as the king of heaven. On the jeweled side of the cross, we see the transformation of a pagan work to suit Christian imperial ideals, and we are enjoined to consider the numerous transfigurations and transformations that gave meaning to the story of Christ's life, death, and resurrection; all of these stories hinge on notions of liminality and duality and, ultimately, the transformative power of faith and the promise of salvation. Not least, Otto III's memory and the self-conscious *romanitas* of his reign appear here as entirely informed by Augustus's visual and ideological legacy.

This brief analysis of the Lothar Cross can only skim the surface of its multivalent meanings, and yet I hope to have drawn attention to some of the dynamic visual and material tensions that informed the ways in which the work's privileged medieval viewers interacted with it. As is the case with most liturgical artworks, the spiritual and political work that the Lothar Cross had to perform at the Palace Chapel of Aachen could only be effectuated by the people who viewed and used it in a ritualized setting. That is, in the moments of its use at the Palace Chapel, viewers not only became witnesses to the glory of heaven and the Christ-like imperial grace of the ruler, but they were instrumental in making those connections come to life.

11

Albrecht Dürer's *The Kiss of Judas* or *"der heyligen schryfft studiren"*

Christopher Kent Wilson

The embodiment of the Renaissance man, Albrecht Dürer (1471–1528) excelled as a master engraver and painter renowned for his portraits, landscapes, and biblical illustrations, including such masterpieces as *The Four Horsemen of the Apocalypse*, *St. Jerome in His Study*, *Melancholia*, and *Knight, Death and the Devil*. In addition to his art, Dürer possessed a passion for mathematics, architectural design, and theology and also wrote several treatises on proportion, perspective, and anatomy. As a citizen of Nuremberg and as a man of art and intellect, Dürer traveled widely throughout Germany and

Italy, befriending Raphael, Bellini, and Leonardo, as well as Erasmus, Friedrich the Wise, Melanchthon, and Martin Luther. Although he never met Luther, Dürer greatly admired his integrity and reforming zeal. In turn, upon Dürer's death, Luther wrote, "It is natural and right to weep for so excellent a man . . . still you should rather think of him blessed, as one whom Christ has taken in the fullness of his wisdom and a happy death from these most troublous times. . . . May he rest in peace. Amen."[1] After his death, Dürer's wife established an educational endowment in his name at the University of Wittenberg to support theological study and specifically to fund the sons of artisans (like Dürer) in their pursuit of biblical research or "der heyligen schryfft studiren."[2]

Through his associations with the leaders of the German Reformation, Dürer embraced the new theology focusing on Christ's passion (as opposed to church ritual and indulgences) as the only true path to the forgiveness of sins. Christ's death and suffering had always been a passion for Dürer. In 1509-11, he published the Large and Small Passion series of woodcuts that he had begun as early as the 1490s. In each series, he fashioned a different version of the betrayal scene, reflecting the creative and intellectual genius of the artist (see images on pp. 249-50).

1. See the unsigned article "Albrecht Dürer" in *Church Quarterly Review* 31 (1891), 314-339. The quotation is from p. 339. For Dürer's admiration of Luther, see 338–39.
2. David Hotchkiss Price, *Albrecht Dürer's Renaissance* (Ann Arbor: University of Michigan Press, 2003), 7–8, 283.

Albrecht Dürer, Betrayal of Christ (Small Passion), 1509-11, woodcut.

Albrecht Dürer, The Kiss of Judas from The Great Passion, 1510, woodcut on paper.

In *The Betrayal* woodcut from the Small Passion dating from 1509–11, Dürer created a *traditional* representation depicting the dramatic moment of the kiss of Judas (see image on p. 249). Virtually every painting and print of *The Betrayal* in western art prominently portrays Judas kissing Christ. From Giotto to Caravaggio, Christ and Judas are shown in dramatic profile, highlighting the undisguised, open betrayal of Christ while emphasizing the guilt and treachery of Judas. In his famous fresco from the Arena Chapel, Giotto depicts Christ as a Greek god with noble profile and high forehead while Judas is rendered with a low brooding forehead and apelike features, capturing in a single image the nobility and depravity of life.

To underscore the evil intent of Judas, Dürer subtly points the sword of the disciple in the foreground directly at Judas's moneybag with its thirty pieces of silver. Surrounded by the violence of the arrest, a calm and composed Christ confronts Judas illustrating his response to the betrayal: "Judas, betrayest thou the Son of Man with a kiss?" (Luke 22:50).[3] Serene in the midst of the storm, Christ is fully aware of what is happening ("Verily I say unto you, that one of you shall betray me" [Matt. 26:21, Mark 14:18]) and realizes that the divine imperative of the Scriptures must be fulfilled (Matt. 26:56, Mark 14:49, Luke 22:16, John 18:9).

In his 1510 woodcut of *The Betrayal* from the Large Passion, however, Dürer creates a striking and unusual *variation* on the traditional depiction Judas' kiss (see image on p. 250). The intensity and passion of the scene with its extraordinary visual energy—the thrusting, tugging, resistance, rage, and hatred—all contribute to a disturbing but beautiful chaos that underscores the anger and violence of the scene itself.

Most unusual is Dürer's rendering of Judas, who instead of being prominently displayed in the foreground lurks in the shadows barely visible behind an anguished Christ. Although Dürer carefully

3. Unless noted, all quotations are from the KJV.

positions the lips of Judas and Christ (clearly alluding to the kiss), the woodcut is more of an arrest than a betrayal. To understand this most unusual illustration, we have to return—as Dürer did—to the biblical text.

Although there are several textual similarities in the Gospels—the kiss, Christ's response, the armed multitude, and the cutting off of the servant's ear—there are some important differences that are at the heart of Dürer's woodcut for the Large Passion. The most obvious and telling detail is the naked young man in front of the house in the background who flees the scene. This strange narrative moment is recorded only in the Gospel of Mark:

> And there followed him, a certain young man, having a linen cloth cast about his naked body; and the young men laid hold on him: And he left the linen cloth, and fled from them naked. (14:51-52)

This peculiar verse has generated many diverse and equally peculiar interpretations ranging from resurrection and baptism to homosexuality and the weaknesses of the flesh. Although forever analyzed and interpreted, in the end, this naked young man will, in the words of Raymond Brown, "always be wrapped in mystery."[4] As an isolated, biblical non sequitur, the naked young man should be viewed not in a narrative sense but rather from a broader symbolic perspective.

Although Judas has become the focus and embodiment of betrayal, it is important to note that in the Gospels and especially in Mark, all of the apostles are portrayed in a negative light, reflecting the ancient prophecy and God's plan that the Scriptures must be fulfilled: "I was daily with you in the temple teaching, and ye took me not: but the scriptures must be fulfilled. And they all forsook him, and fled" (Mark 14:49-50). Mark immediately continues with the story of the naked

4. Raymond E. Brown, *The Death of the Messiah* (New York: Doubleday, 1994), 1:310.

young man who in a single image embodies the shame of the apostles as they desert and betray Christ. Even Peter, the rock and future foundation of the church, denied Christ not once but three times:

> But he began to curse and to swear, *saying*, I know not this man of whom ye speak. And the second time the cock crew. And Peter called to mind the word that Jesus said unto him, Before the cock crow twice, thou shalt deny me thrice. And when he thought thereon, he wept. (Mark 14:71-72)

In the Gospel of Mark, Judas and *all* the apostles forsake Christ: "And Jesus saith unto them, All ye shall be offended because of me this night: for it is written, I will smite the shepherd, and the sheep shall be scattered" (Mark 14:27; cf. Jer. 25:34; Zech. 13:7). Mark's unusual description of the young man was not included in any of the later three Gospels. In striking contrast, Dürer read the same strange description of the fleeing young man in the Gospel of Mark, but unlike Matthew, Luke, and John, he chose to include the scene in his 1510 woodcut.

Excluding biblical voyeurism, Dürer included this strange vignette to provide a broader context for the kiss and betrayal and to indicate to the viewer that Mark is the textual inspiration for the woodcut. In addition to the naked young man, there is one other key difference between Mark's description of the betrayal and the other Gospel accounts. And as always, we begin with a question: What was Judas thinking when he betrayed and identified Christ to the authorities? At the Last Supper, prior to the betrayal, Christ announced to the apostles that one of them—one of the twelve—would betray Him: "And they began to be sorrowful, and to say unto him one by one, Is it I." Christ then declared,

> The Son of man indeed goeth, as it is written of him: but woe to that man by whom the Son of man is betrayed! Good were it for that man if he had never been born. (Mark 14:21)

In spite of the admonition, Judas would soon betray Christ not because of choice and free will but in fulfillment of the Scriptures—"as it is written," which Mark repeatedly states throughout the betrayal and arrest narrative (Mark 14:18, 21, 27, 31, 41, 49).

As for Judas, Mark provides no explanation or motive (other than scriptural fulfillment) for his betrayal. Brown in his classic study *The Death of the Messiah* notes that the Greek verb *paradidonai* means "to give over" and not "to betray."[5] Through the later Gospels and especially through art and literature, Judas became the embodiment of evil, greed, and betrayal—a biblical and artistic stereotype without redemption, humanity, or textual justification. Sadly, over the centuries, by demonizing Judas we have unknowingly diminished ourselves. If we strip away the cultural hatred and religious bigotry and return to the biblical text, we encounter a very different Judas suffering in shame and seeking forgiveness:

> Then Judas, who betrayed him, seeing that [Christ] was condemned, repenting himself, brought back the thirty pieces of silver to the chief priests and ancients, Saying: I have sinned in betraying innocent blood. But they said: What is that to us? Look thou to it. And casting down the pieces of silver in the temple, he departed: and went and hanged himself with an halter. (Matt. 27:3-5)

The Gospel of Mark does not describe the suicide, but Mark does provide another intriguing glimpse into the mind and humanity of Judas that is often overlooked or denied. In identifying Christ to the authorities, Judas declares in the Latin Vulgate that they should lead him away *caute*.[6] The Douay-Rheims translation (1582 for the NT) renders the verse, "Whomsoever I shall kiss, that is he; lay hold on him, and lead him away *carefully*" (Mark 14:44). The later King James Version (1611) arrived at a slightly different but equally revealing

5. Ibid., 1:211, 2:1399.
6. The Greek text of Mark reads *asphalos*—ED.

translation: "Whomsoever I shall kiss, that same is he; take him, and lead him away *safely*," which is the same translation (*fuhret ihn sicher*) found in Martin Luther's German Bible. It appears that in all these translations, Judas is not betraying Christ but rather identifying him in the hope that Christ will be judged but not harmed. If this were not the case, then why would Judas want Christ to be led away carefully and safely?

Interestingly, the modern Revised Standard Version has presented a different translation: "Now the betrayer had given them a sign, saying, 'The one I shall kiss is the man; seize him and lead him away under guard." However the kiss and arrest are described and interpreted, this is a powerful biblical scene of conflicting emotions and intentions that are at the heart of human drama and suffering—and Dürer's 1510 woodcut.

Unlike the pictorial tradition, Dürer creates a subtle portrait of Judas rather than the stereotype. Dürer has shown Judas as he might like to be portrayed or viewed—remote, out of the way, barely visible. Quickly (or immediately) identifying Christ with little fanfare or attention, Judas wants to disappear into the shadows as Christ is safely taken away. Both Christ and Judas, however, are involved in a much larger divine plan that transcends human understanding. In spite of his best intentions, by identifying Christ, Judas sets violence and chaos into motion, which ends in passion and death.

In a subtle but clear allusion to both of their deaths, Dürer carefully frames the heads of both Christ and Judas against the backdrop of a dead tree, a powerful and poignant symbol of both hanging and crucifixion: "The God of our Fathers raised up Jesus, whom ye slew, hanging him on a tree" (Acts 5:30; cf. Deut. 21:23; Gal. 3:13). To further underscore the crucifixion, Dürer cleverly alludes to the instruments of the passion by juxtaposing a large spiked weapon or nail carefully aligned with the dead tree and a large spear recalling the spear that pierced the side of Christ in the Gospel of John (19:34). To complete the visual foreshadowing of the crucifixion, an imploring Christ, now stripped of his dignity and nobility, looks to the heavens (framed by the dead tree) recalling the final anguished words of the crucified Christ: "My God, my God, why hast thou forsaken me" (Mark 15:34), or in the words (and fulfillment) of the Scriptures: "My God, my God, why hast thou forsaken me? Why art thou so far from helping me? (Ps. 22:1-2).

In his *Death of the Messiah*, Brown captures the very essence of the Gospel of Mark while, at the same time, indirectly describing the artistic and interpretive genius of Albrecht Dürer:

> The Marcan Jesus who faces Judas does so with a resolve born of obedience, but with the taste of suffering in his mouth and the sense that in this struggle he will stand alone without human companionship and without visible help from God.[7]

Both as an artist and as a biblical interpreter, Albrecht Dürer understood the underlying power of the Gospel of Mark—a gospel of action and immediacy, of prophecy and fulfillment, of foreshadowing and passion, and above all, human suffering and divine wisdom. Viewed from another perspective, Dürer's 1510 woodcut of *The Kiss of Judas* would have been both instructional and inspirational for any young artisan beginning his biblical studies or *"der heyligen schryfft studiren"* in either Wittenberg or Nuremberg.[8]

7. Ibid., 1:215.
8. Dürer's woodcut *The Kiss of Judas* from the Large Passion has never been thoroughly analyzed either visually or textually. My interest in this provocative print grew out of an annual art history discussion section exploring the relationship between a biblical text and a work of art. Over the years, Dürer's woodcut from the Middlebury Art Museum has stimulated many fascinating discussions among my students, and it is for that reason that I dedicate this article to them and, of course, to Albrecht Dürer and *"der heyligen schryfft studiren."*

12

Titian's *Noli Me Tangere*

Katherine Smith Abbott and Elizabeth Oyler

Titian's *Noli Me Tangere*, dated to c. 1511 and now in the National Gallery, London, reflects the kind of experimentation that occurred early in the artist's career.[1] Not only was the subject of the Noli Me Tangere rare in Venetian Renaissance painting, but also in this case, the artist interpreted a pivotal moment in the resurrection story in surprisingly intimate terms. The scale of the painting, coupled with the highly personal interaction between Christ and the Magdalene, suggests that this work was intended for a private audience for placement in a domestic setting.[2] As with some of his early portraits, Titian seems either to have developed the *Noli Me Tangere*

1. "Noli me tangere" is the Latin for Jesus' words to Mary in John 20:17. The KJV renders it "Touch me not"; the NRSV reads, "Do not cling to me."
2. Paul Joannides, *Titian to 1518* (New Haven, CT: Yale University Press, 2001), 175.

composition for his own satisfaction or at the behest of an adventurous and trusting patron who gave the artist latitude in developing his singular approach to the subject.[3] The result is a composition that draws on multiple models, both direct and inferred, to emphasize Mary Magdalene as the embodiment of transcendent belief, in opposition to the expression of human doubt as played out in the story of the apostle Thomas. Titian accomplished this by referencing representations of both John the Baptist and the Annunciation, suggesting that he understood the Noli Me Tangere as an "incarnation moment" in its own right.

3. David Alan Brown and Sylvia Perino-Pagden, *Bellini, Giorgione, Titian, and the Renaissance of Venetian Painting* (New Haven, CT: Yale University Press, 2006), 131.

Titan (Tiziano Veccellio), *Noli Me Tangere.*

Set against a rolling, bucolic backdrop, with a contemporary village or farm estate visible in the near distance, Titian's Christ and Mary Magdalene encounter each other next to what appears to be a small, tilled garden. While sheep graze behind Christ's back, the hoe on which he leans suggests that there is farm work to be done close at hand. Clothed only in a loincloth and a billowing white cape that we understand as the binding cloth used in his recent burial, Christ gazes down at Mary Magdalene while arching his body away from her outstretched hand. She, in turn, approaches Christ on bended knee, her left hand propped on an ointment jar, one of her defining attributes. Her right hand extends outward in a gesture that simultaneously communicates recognition, longing, and restraint. Pushed so far forward as to appear almost at the picture plane, the two human figures are echoed in the middle ground by a standing tree and a low bush. Like the human forms before them, bush and tree are proximate to each other, but do not touch. This profound connection to the natural world has been noted by others as both a keynote of the painting and of Titian's career moving forward.[4] Christ's graceful, upright form intersects with that of the tree. In turn, the branches of the tree reach almost to the upper edge of the canvas, to the sky, and by extension to the heavenly realm invoked by the gold-tinged clouds. By contrast, Mary Magdalene is rooted to the earth, her signature red dress flowing across and even into the dirt of the garden. This dichotomy is Titian's visual shorthand for the central tension of the narrative; while Christ appears to Mary as of this world, he anticipates his ascension to God and may not physically connect with her.

Titian's composition is an interpretation of the narrative found in John 20:11-18. Brief, yet potent dialogue anchors this passage, and it fell to Titian to discern the most effective means of translating words into paint. The artist's additional challenge was to communicate the liminal moment in which Christ is first seen (re)incarnate—resurrected from the dead but not yet ascended to God. To accomplish both ends, Titian creates an intersection of three

4. George Richter, "The Problem of the Noli Me Tangere," *The Burlington Magazine for Connoisseurs* 65, no. 376 (1934): 4–16, 19. See also Cecil Gould, "A Famous Titian Restored," *The Burlington Magazine for Connoisseurs* 100, no. 659 (1958): 44, and Joannides, *Titian*, 175.

senses: sight, hearing, and touch. The Gospel writer notes that "Jesus said to her, 'Woman, why are you weeping? Whom do you seek?' Supposing him to be the gardener, she said to him, 'Sir, if you have carried him away, tell me where you have laid him and I will take him away.'"[5] As Edward Olszewski has noted, "Christ's hoe becomes a signifier of Mary's confusion,"[6] and it is only when she *hears* her name spoken that she recognizes Christ. Mary's reliance on visual cues proves faulty; as viewers, we understand Mary's outstretched hand in part as documentation that Christ's words and their meaning have reached her. X-rays of the painting reveal that at an earlier stage, Christ may also have worn a gardener's hat, suggesting that Titian worked to find the most effective means of communicating Mary's natural inclination to collapse setting with the identity of the stranger she encounters.[7]

Remarkably, Titian's *Noli Me Tangere* also succeeds in conveying the story's complex emotional charge. The painting isolates a specific moment with an imagined extension: Titian depicts Mary reaching for Christ, who avoids her grasp and cautions, "Do not touch me," as translated in the Latin Vulgate Gospels that the artist would have known.[8] Mary obeys and goes on to proclaim Christ's resurrection. In the Gospel, Christ's reprimand directly follows Mary's exclamation of recognition, "Rabboni," or "teacher"; there is no mention of an attempted touch.[9] But Titian, like several of his contemporaries, chose to illustrate Mary's implied gesture, to which he envisions Christ responding verbally and physically. Titian therefore makes visually explicit a theme merely suggested by the text: the

5. John 20:15, NRSV.
6. Edward Olszewski, "The Sexuality of Mary Magdalen in Renaissance Oblivion and Modern Recollection," *Source Notes in the History of Art* 27, no. 1 (2007): 14–21, here 19.
7. For more on the x-ray discoveries, see Gould, "A Famous Titian Restored," 44–50.
8. Olszewski, "Sexuality of Mary Magdalen," 19.
9. John 20:16, NRSV.

significance of physical contact in these biblical moments of disbelief and incarnation. At the same time, he encourages a comparison of this scene with the story of Thomas that follows. John's narrative goes on to describe Christ's encounter with the apostle Thomas, who declares that he "will not believe" until he sees and, crucially, *feels* the wounds of Christ's crucifixion. Christ allows this and then announces, "Blessed are those who have not seen and yet believe."[10] Even as Thomas refuses to acknowledge Christ's resurrection without physical contact, Christ affirms the type of faith and restraint Mary Magdalene so recently modeled.

This juxtaposition of scenes suggests Mary's favor with Christ, which helps us understand the strength and affection of the relationship Titian portrays, but it also draws attention to another distinction between the two stories. Whereas Thomas requires tactile confirmation of Christ's identity, Mary's gesture is less straightforward. She already knows that the figure before her is Christ; she reaches for him perhaps to confirm his presence—an impossible hope—or perhaps simply because she has missed him and longs to be nearer to him. While Thomas's desire for contact reveals his humanity and capacity for doubt, Mary's seems to emphasize love, even as her compliance confirms her belief. The association of this moment with the story of Thomas expands the evocative power of this image, allowing for a more complete expression of Mary's yearning and profound faith.

Titian portrays the Magdalene reaching with her whole body, the fabric of her gown spread out behind her. While other Renaissance depictions of the Noli Me Tangere present Mary Magdalene in a somewhat similar position, Titian narrows the distance between teacher and devoted follower, intensifying the tension and

10. John 20:29, NRSV.

underscoring the figures' gestures. Mary Magdalene's right hand, bent back at the wrist with palm facing Christ, is met with Christ's arched form and downward glance, the affirmation and admonition to which she responds. We have explored the remarkable economy of meaning found in Mary's gesture, but when coupled with the exaggerated sway of Christ's torso, it carries an even greater significance. A brief comparison with Fra Bartolommeo's painting of the same subject reveals the extent to which Titian's compositional choices impact the painting's meaning. Fra Bartolommeo also includes the hoe as signifier of Mary's confusion, but he presents the two figures as directly confronting each other, with Christ's right hand reaching out in a gesture that suggests blessing, rather than avoidance. Similarly, Mary rises off the ground and lifts both hands toward Christ in a manner that emphasizes her desire to confirm what she has seen and heard.[11]

Various models have been proposed for Titian's depiction of Christ. Of these, the most convincing is the St. John the Baptist (in reverse) from Sebastiano del Piombo's c. 1509 altarpiece for the church of San Giovanni Crisostomo in Venice. This figure's twisting contrapposto, crossed legs, and gesture of grasping at the drapery that surrounds him was undoubtedly known to Titian, and was easily accessible as a template.[12] Though not easy to establish with certainty, it is worth considering whether Titian was drawn specifically to the Baptist as a model for a painting focused on the intersection of faith and rebirth. What has not previously been proposed is the possibility that Titian relied on images of the Annunciation to compose the

11. Although Tuscan by birth, Fra Bartolommeo spent time in Venice in 1508, working on a commission for the church of San Pietro Martire on Murano. In an undated preparatory drawing for this painting, Fra Bartolommeo depicts Mary Magdalene with just one hand extended. In the same drawing, however, Christ has an even greater formality, his right arm and hand extended in blessing as he turns away to his left.
12. Brown and Perino-Pagden, *Bellini, Giorgione, Titian*, 128.

core of the scene. By depicting Mary Magdalene low on the ground, her dress trailing behind, her right hand upheld in greeting, with Christ's body arching away from her, Titian seems to deliberately invoke the gestures and arrangements so often found in images of Gabriel appearing to the Virgin Mary. The gender roles are reversed, as is the composition: Mary Magdalene appears in the position of Gabriel (who most often approaches from the left), Christ in that of the Virgin Mary. As noted earlier, images of the Noli Me Tangere were rare in Venice, but the Annunciation was extremely prominent: tradition confirmed the foundation date of the Venetian Republic as March 25, 421, on the same date given for the Annunciation. From an early date, images of the Annunciation were located on the facades of important buildings, in the Sala del Maggior Consiglio—the heart of Venice's civic identity—and on altarpieces. It was an image whose contours and resonance were well understood by the young Titian. This offers a partial explanation for how the Annunciation—found in Luke, but not in John—may have appeared as a ready, logical model for the young Titian.

On a broader level, contemporary theological discussions of the Annunciation focused on the Virgin's physical being and her function as the means of Christ's incarnation.[13] Mary's inverted compositional counterpart in Titian's *Noli Me Tangere* is Christ, whose corporeal nature is similarly emphasized: the central gesture of the painting, Mary Magdalene's reach, draws attention to the physical manifestation of Christ and the miracle of his presence. In the Annunciation, Mary's movement away from Gabriel conveys awe, humility, and disbelief that she has been chosen by God. Titian's Christ inhabits the same form in the *Noli Me Tangere* and embodies Mary Magdalene's disbelief transformed through faith. Even the

13. Gail L. Geiger, "Filippino Lippi's Carafa 'Annunciation': Theology, Artistic Conventions, and Patronage," *The Art Bulletin* 63, no. 1 (1981): 62–75, here 64.

painting's emotional power can be interpreted as an attempt to further realize Christ, as the evocative interaction depicted reminds us of our own humanity and therefore also his. The idea of incarnation can therefore be seen as fundamental to both scenes. If Titian did consciously reference Annunciation images in his composition, his bold association would have served to accentuate this shared theme, provoking considerations of the two narratives and the definitions of faith they present.

13

Manet's *Dead Christ with Angels*

John Hunisak

During the 1860s, Édouard Manet (1832–83) was the most important and innovative artist working in Paris, the international capital of art, and the magnitude of his achievement continued until his death. Insistence on contemporaneity was his fundamental contribution to Western art: he achieved greatness by choosing modern subjects, capturing fleeting appearances, and embracing the material world in which he lived. Manet was "the painter of modern life," but this designation implies more than subject matter. He also invented a radically modern style that epitomized his historical milieu and challenged avant-garde artists for more than a century. Why would a secularist and nonbeliever like Manet choose to paint two large canvases with Christ as his protagonist, a subject matter alien to his sensibility and utterly inconsistent with his other works? Why would he apply his radically new vision to traditional subjects that had virtually disappeared from the history of art?

Before addressing these questions, I will offer a brief consideration of historical antecedents. From the fourteenth until the end of the seventeenth century, religious images had been central to the enterprise of making art in the Western world. They served to educate the illiterate and enhance the devotion of the educated; they conveyed the narratives of sacred history and concretized the teachings of the church. Even creators who specialized in secular images usually established their credentials with sacred subjects. Practically and economically, religious commissions were the primary source of income for most artists.

During the eighteenth century, when pleasure and reason challenged piety and faith for dominance in the cultural arena, Western society witnessed a concomitant decline of significant art based on religious themes. Political revolutions, democratic ideals, and secularization exacerbated this trend, even as they further undermined the hegemony of Christian Europe. Religious art as a category of vibrant artistic creativity diminished to a trickle by the nineteenth century. Commissions had become exceedingly scarce; and artists had little incentive to create such works on speculation.

Whereas traditional modes of representation and religious subject matter had meshed symbiotically, with the former enhancing the credibility and communicative power of the latter, stylistic changes that defined modernity in art were intrinsically at variance with religious sensibility. With few exceptions, great artists from the time of Giotto (1266/7–1337) until the early-nineteenth century had created a mode of illusionist representation in which the canvas, panel, or wall mural acted like a window revealing fictive realities where illusions were believable. Figures and objects arranged in proper perspective occupied space that mimicked the real world.

Brilliant highlights, deep shadows, and a full range of intermediary gradations generated from a single light source gave forms a consistent and rational appearance. How we actually see is far more complex, but painters had developed and enshrined this mode of illusionist representation, and the audience for painting had accepted it as objective reality for centuries.

Manet made a momentous choice early in his career when he rejected these traditions and conventions. The surface upon which he painted ceased to be a window. He abandoned one-point perspective, which is based on monocular vision, as if one eye is closed and the world of perceived reality is reduced to eternal stasis in clear focus. He often juxtaposed two or more competing systems so that his illusion of depth vacillated between readable and irrational, as did his modeling. He also often, and jarringly, juxtaposed the most intensely illuminated highlights and the darkest shadows without gradated, intermediate tones. Looking back from our vantage point, we realize that Manet's radical departures mimic, at least in part, the way we actually see: with complex binocular vision and changeable focus. Manet's alternative, fictive world was inherently unstable. His new pictorial realm—so effective at conveying the uncertainties of modern, secular existence—was, at best, inhospitable to religious representations; his paintings neither comforted nor reassured viewers with eternal verities rendered concrete.

We may never be sure why Manet chose to paint images of Christ, but we know that he never chose a subject without a reason and a purpose. He always insisted that an artist must "be of his time." Why would he abandon this cardinal rule when his cast of characters included Jesus? He must have felt that he could revive an outmoded religious subject, while maintaining his unshakable commitment to the present moment.

Édouard Manet, *The Dead Christ with Angels*, Metropolitan Museum of Art, 1864.

When Manet began *Dead Christ with Angels* (see image directly above) in the late fall of 1863, he was already a notorious celebrity in the art world. At the scandalous *Salon des Refusés* the previous summer, his *Le Déjeuner sur l'herbe* had become the prime focus of a hostile public's derision, the epitome of everything detestable about new art: an unacceptable contemporary subject painted with apparent technical ineptitude. Although Manet always insisted that the Salon was "the true battlefield" where he would one day win acceptance and renown, his early career had not unfolded according to plan. He had gained few supporters since his Salon debut in 1861. The public laughed in 1863, and critics attacked him viciously; almost everyone questioned his competence and sincerity.

In the wake of this debacle, Manet decided to create a painting with a religious theme for submission the following year; to serve his programmatic needs in the present, he chose a devotional subject, especially popular in the northern Italian art of the fifteenth and sixteenth centuries. The "dead Christ with angels" had once provided a hospitable vehicle for creating great art, but no painter had submitted a version of this theme to the Salon jury in generations. Manet chose an anachronistic subject that he intended to metamorphose into a contemporary masterpiece. An image with Christ as the protagonist might even neutralize some of his detractors, who had been horrified by the shocking newness of earlier subject matter.

The *Dead Christ with Angels* is one of the strangest and most remarkable works of Manet's career. The Salon jury accepted the painting, but critics and the public loathed it; his few supporters were baffled by this new direction. It features the internal contradictions that characterize his earlier work: the coloring of the angels is unexpectedly brilliant, while the rest of the canvas abounds in neutrals. One angel kneels, but the other is incongruously airborne. Draperies behave like cloth in certain passages, but act according to an abstract schema in others. Jesus seems alternatively dead and revived, depending on where we concentrate our gaze. His mouth and eyes are partially opened. The blurring of his left hand and the toes of both feet suggest spasmodic movement. The entire pictorial system is in flux, and the iconography is equally disconcerting. In the foreground we encounter living creatures that have no place in traditional images of the "dead Christ with angels": a number of snails on our left and a snake on the right. Although the snails lie on the ground, obeying the laws of gravity, the serpent is in motion, as if slithering across a flat surface, but we see it—incongruously—from above.

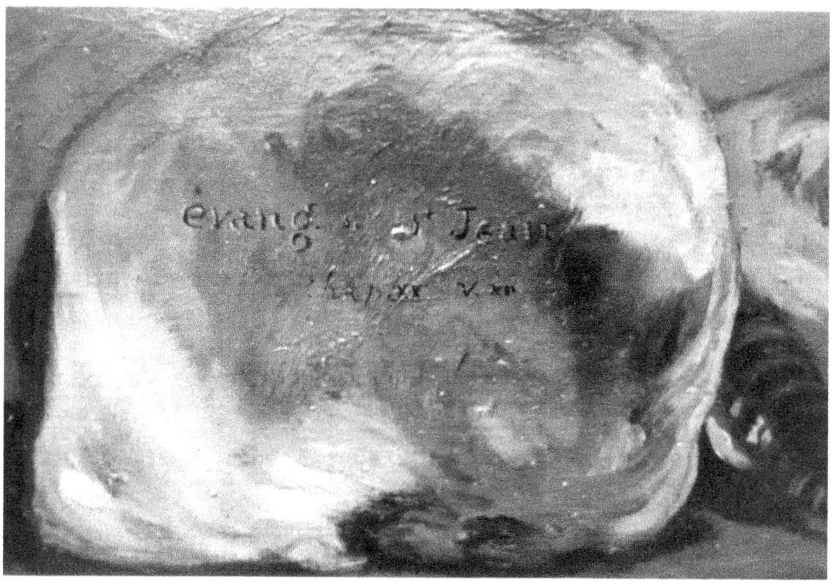

Manet, *The Dead Christ with Angels*, close-up.

Most puzzling is the inscription on the larger of two rocks (see image directly above). The first line is straightforward: *évang. sel. St Jean* ("the Gospel according to St. John"), but the second seems willfully ambiguous: *chap. XX V.XII.* This has been transcribed as "chapter twenty, verses five through twelve," but normal French syntax would require a hyphen between "five" and "twelve," if that were what Manet had intended. Another interpretation is that "V. XII" should be read as a lowercase "v" and a period (the abbreviation for *vers* [verse]), thereby indicating "verse twelve." Since the supposedly small letter "v" is considerably larger than the Roman numeral for twelve, this assertion is not especially compelling.

The biggest paradox, however, is that neither reading of the numerals corresponds to the image, as inscriptions traditionally do. Christ and two angels together are inimical to the scriptural passage in its entirety, beginning with verse five and ending with twelve, and to verse twelve alone: "two angels in white sitting, one at the head and one at the feet, where the body of Jesus had been laid." Manet's painting is a "dead Christ with angels," based on traditional devotional imagery with the body of the Savior dominating the pictorial field, not the scriptural "two angels in white" in an otherwise empty tomb. Manet understood the difference between a devotional image and a literal reading of the narrative, but he purposely confused the two, announcing in November 1863: "I am going to do a dead Christ with angels, a variation on the scene of the Magdalen at the sepulcher according to Saint John." These two traditional themes are, and had always been, incompatible. Manet never explained his works or offered clues to their meaning. This statement is without precedent in his career.

Intense controversies that divided Parisian society provide the context in which Manet conceived and executed the *Dead Christ with Angels*. In June 1863, the eminent historian Ernest Renan published his *Life of Jesus*, which became an instant bestseller. His central thesis was sensational: the historical Jesus was merely mortal; an exceptional man, perhaps, but certainly not the son of God, or any other kind of divine being. Renan wrote this biography according to modern historical method, incorporating multiple sources of evidence. He insisted that there had been no resurrection. This "miracle" had occurred only in the mind of a hysterical, hallucinating Mary Magdalen. Concluding his chapter entitled "Jesus in the Tomb," Renan wrote, "Divine power of love! Sacred moments when the passion of a hallucinating woman gave to the world a resuscitated god!"

The book had an instant and incendiary impact. Catholic polemicists mounted a relentless negative campaign from pulpits and in the press. Renan's followers counterattacked with equal vehemence. In early October, Georges Darboy, the newly appointed archbishop of Paris, convened a pastoral retreat for his clergy at Saint-Sulpice. A key topic on his agenda was the condemnation of Renan and his book. On October 9, the day of his official installation at Notre-Dame, Darboy sent a letter to Pope Pius IX, reporting on the circulation of "odious blasphemies against Our Lord Jesus Christ" contained in Renan's text, and announcing that his clergy had their pens in hand, ready to engage in a "sacred cause." Manet's decision to paint a "dead Christ with angels" coincided precisely with this controversy that pitted faith and belief against reasoned, historical argument.

Manet intended to call attention to the twentieth chapter of the Gospel of St. John with his inscription, but not in the traditional manner of a literary source and its illustration. He singled out verses five and twelve to be considered individually (the inscription shows V and XII with a period separating them) and then in opposition. These verses describe differing perceptions of the same phenomenon, the empty tomb. In verse five, John peers inside and sees prosaic visual evidence: the linen cloths in which Christ's body had been wrapped, nothing more. In verse twelve, Mary Magdalen sees extraordinary things: first, two angels, and then the resurrected Jesus. In Renanesque terms, verse twelve marks the beginning of her hallucination, which intensifies over time.

With Renan as his inspiration, Manet had indeed fused a scriptural narrative and devotional type. In other representations of the scene at the sepulcher, Mary saw Jesus fully animated and mistook him for a gardener, but Manet ignored that tradition altogether. No one had ever seen "a dead Christ with angels," except through the imaginative power of artists, but Manet animated the devotional image as if it were a narrative. In the thrall of hysteria, Mary peered into the tomb and saw a dead body returning to life, accompanied by two angels. Her vision was baseless, but it became the source of Christian belief in a "resuscitated God." Thus, two very different perceptions of the empty tomb corresponded to faith-based belief and empirical perception. According to Renan, the resurrection had never occurred; Mary's hallucination and inclination to believe were the sole evidence that it had. This painting's viewer witnesses Christ's return to life, not as historical fact, but through Mary's overheated imagination.

The *Dead Christ with Angels* is a powerful and disconcerting work of art. By grafting his personal formal language, invented to convey the complexities of modern existence, onto a religious subject, he created a hybrid without precedent. In earlier, secular works Manet had embedded meanings beneath casual appearances and references to art of the old masters; for his first religious subject he followed suit. He understood that the past could never be duplicated, but that it could convey a disturbing, powerful relevance when revived and updated.

14

Marc Chagall's Jewish Jesus

Margaret O'Brien Steinfels

Jesus is Jewish. Could there be a more basic fact about him than that?[1] By all accounts, nothing has altered contemporary Christian perceptions of Jesus in his own time more than the attention of Scripture scholars, theologians, and historians to his Jewishness. Yet the actual image of Jesus garbed in Jewish garments hanging on a cross and surrounded by Jewish images in a Jewish context still gives pause to Jews and Christians alike. What is such an image of an explicitly Jewish Jesus meant to convey?

Marc Chagall (1887-1985) painted many such images, many more than either Jews or Christians would expect of the son of a Hassidic family, and certainly more than most of us will have ever seen. That

1. A briefer version of this essay appeared in "Painting the Jewish Jesus," in Commonweal, November 15, 2013, p. 8.

gap in our knowledge and understanding was filled by an exhibit at New York's Jewish Museum: "Chagall: Love, War, and Exile" (September 15, 2013–February 2, 2014).[2] More than twenty-five of these images were displayed in a single room, one right next to the other. What do they mean?

Chagall's representation of a Jewish Jesus is very different in intent and outcome, of course, from that of modern biblical scholars and others who quest after the historical Jesus. They strive to portray the Jewish Jesus before Christianity. Chagall portrays a Jewish Jesus after Christianity. This Jesus is identified not only with the Jewish people of Exodus and temple but also—and especially—with the Jewish people, medieval and modern, who lived within the bosom of Christian Europe, sometimes at peace, too often in pain.

Modern scholars put Jesus into the context of Roman occupation, Hellenistic culture, Herodian rulers, Pharisees, Sadducees, and messianic insurgents. Chagall puts Jesus into the context of rabbinic Judaism, Talmudic sages, medieval expulsions, and modern pogroms and attempted extermination. This crucified Jewish Jesus typically has a striped and fringed loincloth, which represents the medieval and modern prayer shawl that stems ultimately from Moses' ancient command (Num. 15:37-41) that the Israelites wear ritual fringes or tassels on the corners of their garments. In the background are the Torah-wielding rabbis, fiddlers, and Sabbath candlesticks of daily life and the burning buildings and assaulted victims of the pogroms that so affected *shtetl* (traditional Jewish town and village) life in Eastern Europe. Modern scholarship put Jesus into a rapidly changing

2. Susan Tumarkin Goodman, "The Fractured Years of Marc Chagall: The 1930s and 1940s," in *Chagall: Love, War, and Exile*, ed. Susan Tumarkin Goodman (New Haven, CT: Yale University Press, 2013). The catalog includes a second insightful essay, Kenneth E. Silver, "Fluid Chaos Felt by the Soul: Chagall, Jews, and Jesus," along with poems by Chagall and reproductions from the exhibit.

Judaism of two millennia ago. Chagall puts Jesus into a quintessential Judaism of all ages but especially of our own.

Chagall was not the first Jewish artist to adopt Christ as a subject. Russian sculptor Mark Antokolsky's *Ecce Homo* (1876) and German painter Max Liebermann's *Jesus in the Temple* (1879), among others, are often cited examples of works created in the generation before Chagall.[3] For Jewish artists, the lure of European art, especially in Paris, and the prospect of assimilation were part of the nineteenth-century shift from isolation in a subculture to the opportunities opened to all artists by the growing secularization of art. "The disenchantment of the world," in Max Weber's phrase, included the desacralization of iconic images of Christian devotion and piety once reserved for religious settings and purposes.

Like these other Jewish artists, Chagall deployed images from Christian Scripture. His included the Annunciation, the Madonna and Child, the Flight into Egypt, and the Angel of Judgment, as well as the Crucifixion. Unlike them, Chagall accepted—indeed seemed to embrace—the spiritual significance of these New Testament images. While benefitting from modernity's secularizing agenda, his was not a secularizing project, but a reconfiguring of the Christian Christ into a Jewish Jesus, an expression of spiritual affinity with Jesus without a theological affirmation of the Christian savior.

Chagall's multiple paintings of the crucified Jesus conceived not as a Christian but as a Jew was, nonetheless, unprecedented. Chagall was a Russian émigré in Paris when he first painted the crucifixion (*Calvary*, 1912). He turned to the image again with *White Crucifixion* (1938), as Kristallnacht signaled Nazi Germany's increasing persecution of its Jewish citizens. A steady succession of such

3. Olga Litvak, "Rome and Jerusalem: The Figure of Jesus in the Creation of Mark Antokol'skii," in *The Art of Being Jewish in Modern Times*, eds. Barbara Kirshenblatt-Gimblett and Jonathan Karp (Philadelphia: University of Pennsylvania Press, 2008), 228–53.

paintings followed, most of them created in the late 1930s and 1940s, when Chagall had permanently left Russia and lived, first in France and then, during and after World War II, in the United States.

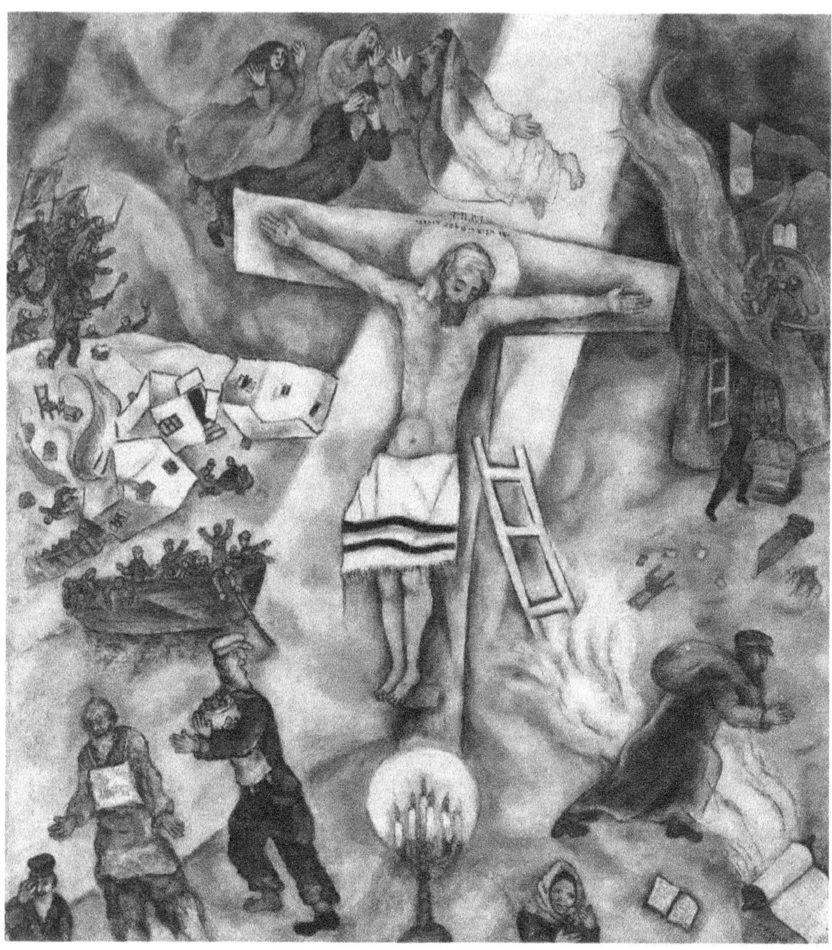

Marc Chagall, *White Crucifixion*, 1938.

The sheer variety and number of examples in the Jewish Museum exhibit emphasize the degree to which the crucifixion of a Jewish Jesus became a central focus for Chagall not simply as a thematic scheme but as an emotional and spiritual encounter. In *My Life*

(1921–22), written in his early thirties, he professes a fascination "about Christ, whose pale face had been troubling me for a long time."[4] One of his poems from the late 1940s evokes Jesus' dying words on the cross, "My God, my God, why have you forsaken me?" Chagall writes, "Already the dark of night surrounds me / You keep your distance, my God. Why."[5] The variety of settings, surrounding images, and self-portraits in these painting underlines his preoccupation and fascination with the crucified Jesus. Chagall came to regard him as the supreme example of Jewish suffering and martyrdom and perhaps made him the embodiment of the artist's own heterodox spirituality.

Standing before this array, the viewer encounters a Jewish Jesus who is more than a representation of secular adaptation or scholarly revisionism. Chagall has placed the facticity of the Jewish Jesus at the center of these works—in our face, so to speak. Having first seen such paintings only piecemeal and sporadically (*The White Christ* at the Art Institute of Chicago and *Calvary* at the Museum of Modern Art), I found Chagall's work a disorienting curiosity. Why did a Jewish artist paint the crucifixion (when not even Protestant artists were accustomed to placing a corpus on the cross)? Once in my young life I wondered if, like his friend Raïssa Maritain, Chagall had become a Catholic. No, he had not. He remained firmly rooted in his Jewish tradition.

More than a curiosity, the exhibit at the Jewish Museum was an epiphany. In *The Crucified* (1944), Chagall evokes the pogroms of pre-Revolutionary Russia: a Jesus on the cross presides over Vitebsk, the artist's native village, in flames. Deep in the background, two crosses with hanging figures evoke the two who hung with Jesus

4. Marc Chagall, *My Life*, trans. Elizabeth Abbott (Cambridge: Da Capo, 1994), 128. Chagall wrote his autobiography in 1921–22. It was first published in English in 1960.
5. Goodman, *Chagall*.

on Golgotha. The "Triptych," which Chagall worked on from 1937 to 1952, depicts in two panels crucifixion scenes amid references to the 1917 Russian Revolution and the resistance of Russian soldiers to Hitler in World War II, while the third pictures a post-war scene of peace and harmony without a cross. In some paintings, Jesus wears a loincloth patterned on the tallith (Jewish) while a halo circles his head (Christian); others have Mary and the disciple John at the foot of the cross; in yet another, Mary Magdalene. In almost all of these works, dreamlike figures typical of Chagall—some mythical and mystical, others earthly and folkloric—float around and above the crucified figure. Angels, animals, Torah scholars, bearded rabbis, the Wandering Jew, Madonna and child, Joseph of Arimathea with a ladder, and sometimes the artist himself—upside-down beside the cross—populate the paintings. Drawing on yet another tradition, Chagall renders many of these scenes in the vibrant, deeply saturated colors typical of Russian icons, which he likely first saw in the Orthodox churches of Vitebsk, now in Belarus. Titles like *Martyr* and *Christ Carrying the Cross* underline the appropriation of both Christian imagery and language.

The viewer's perplexity at the variety and richness of Chagall's crucifixions is mirrored in *The Artist with Yellow Christ* (1938), wherein the artist appears to share our bafflement. The studio background is dominated by a painting of a crucifixion, *The Yellow Christ*; in the foreground, the artist himself with palette and brushes turns away from the picture toward the viewer as if to ask, "What have I done?" Given the topsy-turvy positions and the self-portraits in so many of these works, Chagall may well have asked that question many times. Could he have answered his own question, much less ours? Probably he would not have tried.

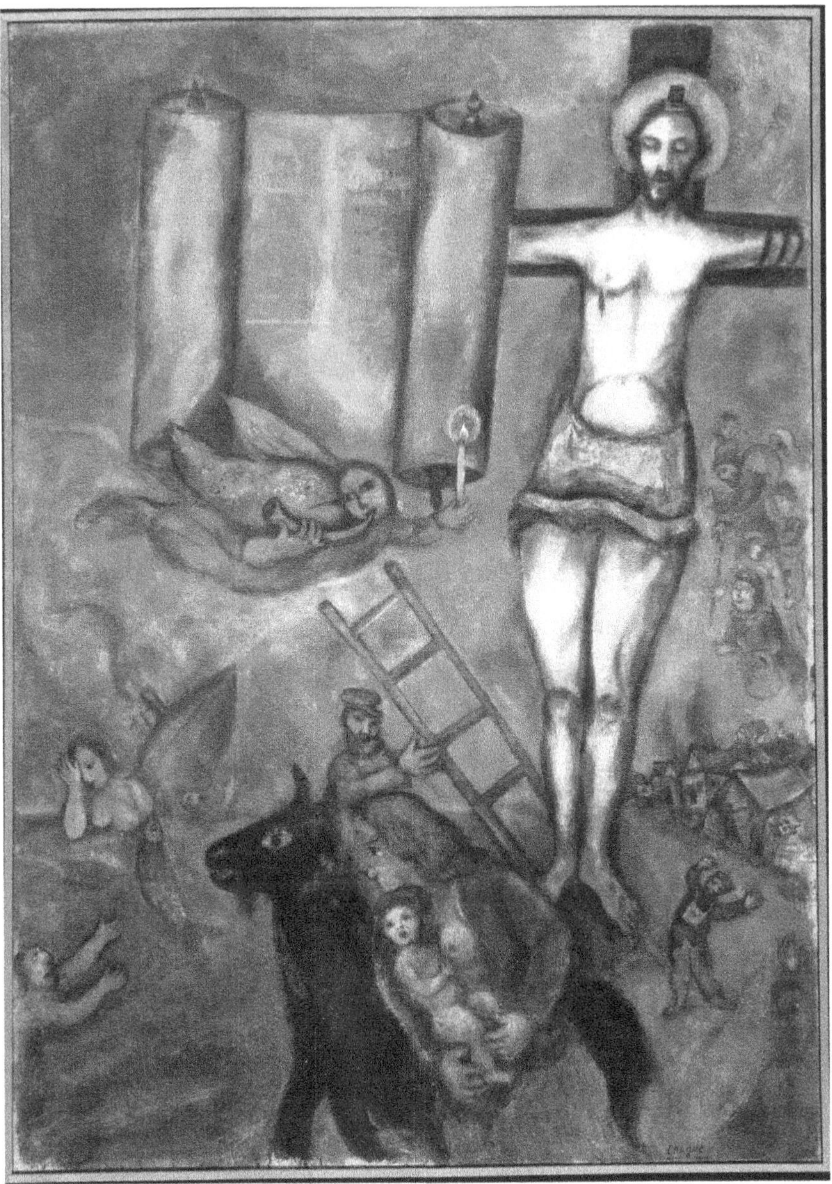

Marc Chagall, *The Yellow Crucifixion*, 1942.

He was not an analytic thinker, nor did he seem to think in linear or logical terms. *My Life*, like the floating images of his paintings, wanders from dream to image to incident without framework or context or even topic sentences. Things happen! Objects float! Nor is it likely that Chagall had a theological response to the perplexity his viewers might feel. Philosopher Jacques Maritain, a friend of the artist and Raïssa Maritain's husband, observed that his "art has none of the restraints of Greek form, but rather the extreme opposite. It's a kind of fluid chaos felt by the soul, from whence are born symbols all the more moving for their uncertainty."[6]

Nor did Chagall stop with that theological ambiguity. More startling still, and more unexpected, the crucified Jesus dominates scenes from Hebrew Scripture: a crucifixion oversees *The Exodus* (1952–66). Moses is relegated to the lower right corner, carrying the stone tablets, while the Jewish people cross the Red Sea under the gaze of Jesus. If the Christian viewer is disconcerted, how much more a Jewish one? What did Chagall intend? Kenneth Silver, writing in the exhibit catalog, speculates that Chagall, rather than identifying with the patriarchal Moses, identified with the rebel Jesus, placing the flight from Egypt under his protection.[7] The title of the painting may also be a reference to the ship, *Exodus*, carrying Jewish refugees to Palestine in 1947, and turned back by the British Mandate authorities.

Though the crucifixion was for centuries the source of anti-Judaism and Jewish persecution, Chagall saw Jesus not as the resurrected savior of Christian faith but as the quintessential Jewish martyr, the cross representing Jesus' own suffering as well as that of the Jewish people. During World War II, as rumors of the extermination of European Jews made their way to the United States, Chagall held out the hope his images of the suffering Jesus would elicit from Christians some reaction, some response. But, as he wrote, "with few exceptions, their hearts are silent."[8]

6. Ibid., 114.
7. Silver "Fluid Chaos," 128–29.

Marc Chagall, *The Exodus*, 1952/1966.

Chagall acknowledged the transgressive nature of combining images sacred to Jews or Christians. He "deliberately chose the most contested visual expression possible to articulate a specifically Jewish crisis. That some viewers might not understand this, or might assume that Jesus was being depicted as Christ, the Christian Messiah, did not disturb him. Indeed, as in all of Chagall's symbolism, such ambiguities were left to the viewer to resolve."[9] His fellow Jews in the United States, however, were critical, while some Christians regarded his use of "Christian symbolism as naïve and misguided."[10] He paid little attention to these critics. In words and images, he identified himself

8. John A. Coleman, "Mel Gibson Meets Marc Chagall: How Christians & Jews Approach the Cross," *Commonweal*, July 4, 2004, www.commonwealmagazine.org/mel-gibson-meets-marc-chagall-0.
9. Goodman, *Chagall*, 43.
10. Ibid., 51.

with the man on the cross: in "Christ and the Artist," gazing up at the cross with palette in hand, or substituting his own name, Marc, for the inscription INRI, at the top of the cross.

Even now, these paintings, though perhaps offering Christians a salutary meditation on Jewish suffering, could be an affront to Chagall's fellow Jews. Today, post-Holocaust and after Vatican II, the history of Christian persecution still shadows efforts to reconcile and overcome centuries of hostility, as Jeremy Cohen poignantly shows elsewhere in this volume.[11]

However each viewer chooses to interpret these beautiful paintings, the exhibit catalog for "Chagall: Love, War, and Exile" locates Chagall and his images in a specifically Jewish context: "The Crucifixion images were not—or not primarily—an expression of Christian theology. For him the cross was a symbol of persecution and oppression rather than a sign of redemption and hope."[12] And yet, it is also a symbol reminding us that memory is at the heart of both Christian and Jewish faith.

11. See chapter 18 of the present volume.
12. Goodman, *Chagall*, 37.

15

Can You Feel Me?

The Passion in the Public Art Ministries of Damon Lamar Reed

Kymberly Pinder

Damon Lamar Reed is a contemporary artist who uses painting and music in a comprehensive arts ministry associated with the House Covenant Church in the Lawndale neighborhood of Chicago, Illinois. As part of this ministry, Reed creates murals, rap music, and T-shirts that reflect his devout Christian principles. Images of a black Christ feature prominently in his work; his use of images from the passion story is strikingly bold. A native of Phoenix, Arizona (b. 1978), Reed moved to Chicago, where he received a Bachelor of Fine Arts from the School of the Art Institute of Chicago (SAIC) in 2000. At SAIC he met the artist Bernard Williams (b. 1964), with whom he apprenticed as a mural restorer at the Chicago Public Art Group (CPAG) in the late 1990s.

When his own work gained greater recognition, Reed became an active member of the Chicago Public Art Group as both a lead artist on restorations and recipient of original commissions. In 2003, his career was boosted when MacArthur Fellow Kerry James Marshall invited Reed to exhibit with him at the Museum of Contemporary Art in Chicago.[1]

Though Reed includes images of young people of all races in his art, African-Americans dominate his work because he wants to speak to his generation of young people:

> I get inspiration from a number of sources: The Bible, old photographs from family albums, songs with a message that align with my beliefs, my own lyrics (which I have started to incorporate into my paintings), and everyday life. My aim is to show the world that this "Hip-Hop" generation is not completely lost. In my paintings I uplift people, showing them there is a way out of the darkness. If one person or child can look at one of my creations or at my life as an example and decide to empower him or herself, then I have made my mark on the world.[2]

Reed's arts ministry is directed toward inner-city Christians, predominantly African-American, Latino, and young adults under thirty, who participate in Reverend Phil Jackson's hip-hop services at the House Covenant Church, where Reed is an active participant. Services at "The House" frequently feature Reed's rapping, emceeing, and graffiti-writing as spiritual acts performed in real time for and with the congregation. He has also created two large murals for this congregation and others that adorn the Firehouse Community Arts Center, an integral part of the arts ministry just down the street from The House.

1. Marshall invited to each venue of this exhibition one artist from a generation that influenced him and one emerging artist. It was his way of acknowledging some black artists who have not received the attention they deserve.
2. "Damon Reed," *Chicago Public Art Group*, www.cpag.net/home/artistbios/reed.html.

Mural on the Firehouse Community Center run by the House Covenant Church in the Lawndale neighborhood of Chicago, Illinois.

Like the sculptural program on a Renaissance cathedral, his paintings on the façade of the old firehouse (now used as a youth arts and worship center) draw on Scripture and traditional religious iconography, but in a very different idiom. In this mural, Reed uses the main elements of hip-hop arts to interpret Isa. 43:19, which in the King James Version reads:

> Behold, I will do a new thing;
> now it shall spring forth; shall ye not know it?
> I will even make a way in the wilderness,
> and rivers in the desert.

The DJ scratching LPs, the lanky rapper with his mouth obscured by the microphone, and the break-dancer suspended upside down on one hand pulse with color, together representing the racial demographic of the Lawndale neighborhood, which is mainly black and Latino. Above the dancers is a young black woman wearing headphones and looking heavenward. In the context of this ministry, she hovers at the apex like a black Madonna. The text below her renders the Isaiah passage:

> And Yo! I'm doing a new thang.
> Can you feel me?
> I'm making a new way out of the wilderness of life.
> I am bringing out rivers from the desert.

The colloquial, urban vernacular translation of the text here in Reed's mural echoes the voice of the neighborhood and ministry of The House where Pastor Phil Jackson uses the informality of hip-hop speech to reach a demographic that he feels traditional churches are losing.

In their book, *The Hip-Hop Church: Connecting with the Movement Shaping Our Culture*, Jackson and Efrem Smith present "holy hip-hop" culture as an opportunity to create a wide-reaching spiritual movement among contemporary black and Latino youth.[3] Moving against church stereotypes, these services feature multiple presentations ranging from traditional readings to slam poetry, none lasting more than fifteen minutes. In the language and liturgy of holy hip-hop, emcees are "Theolyricists," while the step-dance team and "One Voice" rappers provide another praise element within a service structured like any traditional one. Yet this barrage of "eye candy," according to Smith and Jackson, appeals to the visual sensibilities

3. Efrem Smith and Phil Jackson, *The Hip-Hop Church: Connecting with the Movement Shaping our Culture* (Downers Grove, IL: InterVarsity, 2005).

of an at-risk urban audience that is hardly traditional and never static. Thus, Reed's hip-hop art on the firehouse wall draws on and illustrates clearly the main elements of the new movement described in *The Hip-Hop Church.*

Reed also composes Christian rap songs, sometimes using their lyrics in his paintings.[4] In one small painting, he places a rapper in the foreground with an image of Christ bearing the cross behind him; their arms mirror each other—the wordsmith holding his mike, the black Christ his cross. This work illustrates the lyrics to Reed's song "Bold as A Lion":

> I tell the storm, calm down, I know that I'm heard
> I don't have to think twice, I believe in His word
> He made me a king; I got to be bold
> He made me a kingdom, it's got to be gold, I'm bold
>
> *Chorus:*
>
> I'm as bold as a lion,
> I Fear no man.
> Bold as a lion,
> Mic in my hand.
> Bold as a lion.
> You got to understand,
> I'm as bold as a lion.

The racial empathy provided by Reed's image of a black Christ draws on Black Theology, one form of liberation theology. As defined by its creator, James H. Cone, "Black Theology must uncover the structures and forms of the black experience, because the categories of interpretation must arise out of the thought forms of the black experience itself."[5] African-Americans in the United States and black

4. For more on rap and religion, see Anthony B. Pinn, *Noise and Spirit: The Religious and Spiritual Sensibilities of Rap Music* (New York: New York University Press, 2003).
5. James H. Cone, *God of the Oppressed* (New York: Seabury, 1975), 18.

Christians all over the world have frequently tried to reconcile European Christian traditions with their own cultural contexts in different ways, such as emphasizing the African presence in the Bible. Fashioning a Christ in one's own image is not a new phenomenon in art or religious history as evidenced in this volume. Christians of color have been making dark-skinned Christs and saints for centuries.

Reed's images are not unusual in the contemporary United States, as black imagery in African-American churches has become increasingly more common in the last few decades. The black Christ has been a powerful trope in political rhetoric for more than a century. Depictions of a Jesus with dark skin and the conflation of the crucified Christ with a lynched black man present Christ as a symbolic device charged with racial-religious meaning. Political and religious leaders in the last century, such as Henry McNeal Turner, Marcus Garvey, Martin Luther King Jr., Father Divine (George Baker Jr.), and Jesse Jackson, have deployed the conflation of Christ's suffering with racial oppression, sometimes as a Black Christ, in their activism. Black public figures from President Barack Obama to Kanye West have been depicted as Christ. Many African-American artists, such as Jacob Lawrence, William H. Johnson, Aaron Douglas, Archibald Motley Jr., Frederick C. Flemister, Romare Bearden, John Biggers, David Hammons, and Renee Cox, have addressed this struggle in their art by depicting racialized biblical subjects in the twentieth century.

Reed also reaches millions on the Internet through social media. His interviews, recorded rap performances, and video tours of his murals all extend the reach of his visual and musical gospel to people who will never set foot in Chicago or purchase one of his CDs or T-shirts. This immediate access is just another way his work is relevant to his young audience.

Another painting by Reed shows a young man with a cornrow hairstyle taking the bleeding body of a brown Christ with dreadlocks down from a glowing cross. The cropped head of one man and the shoulder of another in the foreground make the viewer part of the crowd of contemporary spectators who wear baseball caps and jeans at the crucifixion. Many of Reed's paintings focus on a single black man, often a self-portrait, in a plain white T-shirt wearing a cross around his neck. The centrality of the devout man in the white T-shirt often reads as a Christ figure, especially when others pray and lift up their hands around him. In the mosaic outside Lawndale Community Church at Central Park and Ogden, a dove hovers inside the halo above the central figure and empties bottles of water over his head—an allusion to baptism.

With his street aesthetic and fine art training, Reed is part of a larger, national movement of devout graffiti artists. The most well known of these religious "taggers" goes by the name "Jesus Saves" and has been spray-painting this phrase/moniker in Manhattan and the surrounding boroughs since 1995, although he has also tagged in Europe. He calls his work a "graffiti ministry":

> As I write it on the walls, it preaches for me 24/7, it is a message I leave behind for many people to see it and realize that salvation is found through Jesus Christ not through church, religion or being a goody goody.[6]

In additions to his murals and rap music, Reed also uses the ubiquitous T-shirt as public art and ministry to his community.

6. Jesus Saves describes himself as a man of God and a graffiti evangelist who led Bible studies and counseled fellow inmates while serving at Riker's Island. His tags sometimes include other biblical passages. A 2009 interview with Jesus Saves is available at www.bombingscience.com/index.php/blog/viewThread/1772.

"Listen Up." Image for embossed T-shirts.

"He Gave." Image for embossed T-shirts.

His shirt designs merge the painted image of Jesus and a real black body—the one wearing the T-shirt. On Reed's T-shirts the figure of Jesus fills the entire "frame" of the shirt: the head nears the edge of collar and the outstretched arms reach toward the sleeves, melding the body of Christ with the body of its wearer. In this he is part of trend over the last decade that makes the extra large "white T" an iconic symbol in hip-hop culture, so that spray-can artists have come to consider the body as a "wall" for messaging and memorializing celebrities or loved ones. With his shirts, Reed has used this popular practice to create a new religious icon celebrating Christ's sacrifice.

The fluidity in Reed's music, painting, and spiritual witness conforms to many of the traditional passion themes discussed in this volume, despite the vernacular urban forms he uses. Reed is a self-proclaimed messenger of the good work that he raps and paints for his audience of young Christians of color in Chicago. The devotional graffiti by anonymous taggers serves the same purpose: "making church" for the churchless in the most secular corners of their cities. Their ministries are unfettered, unexpected, and, therefore, boundless.

16

Banksy's Christmas Passion

Emmie Donadio

The international celebrity and street artist who conceals his identity under the pseudonym *Banksy* adopted the crucifixion a decade ago for one of his characteristically provocative volleys against capitalism. *Christ with Shopping Bags*, his version of a Christmas passion, is aimed precisely at the commercialism that in the Western world marks the holiday season surrounding the birth of the Savior.[1]

1. See www.complex.com /style /2013 /11 /banksy-greatest-works /consumer-jesus.

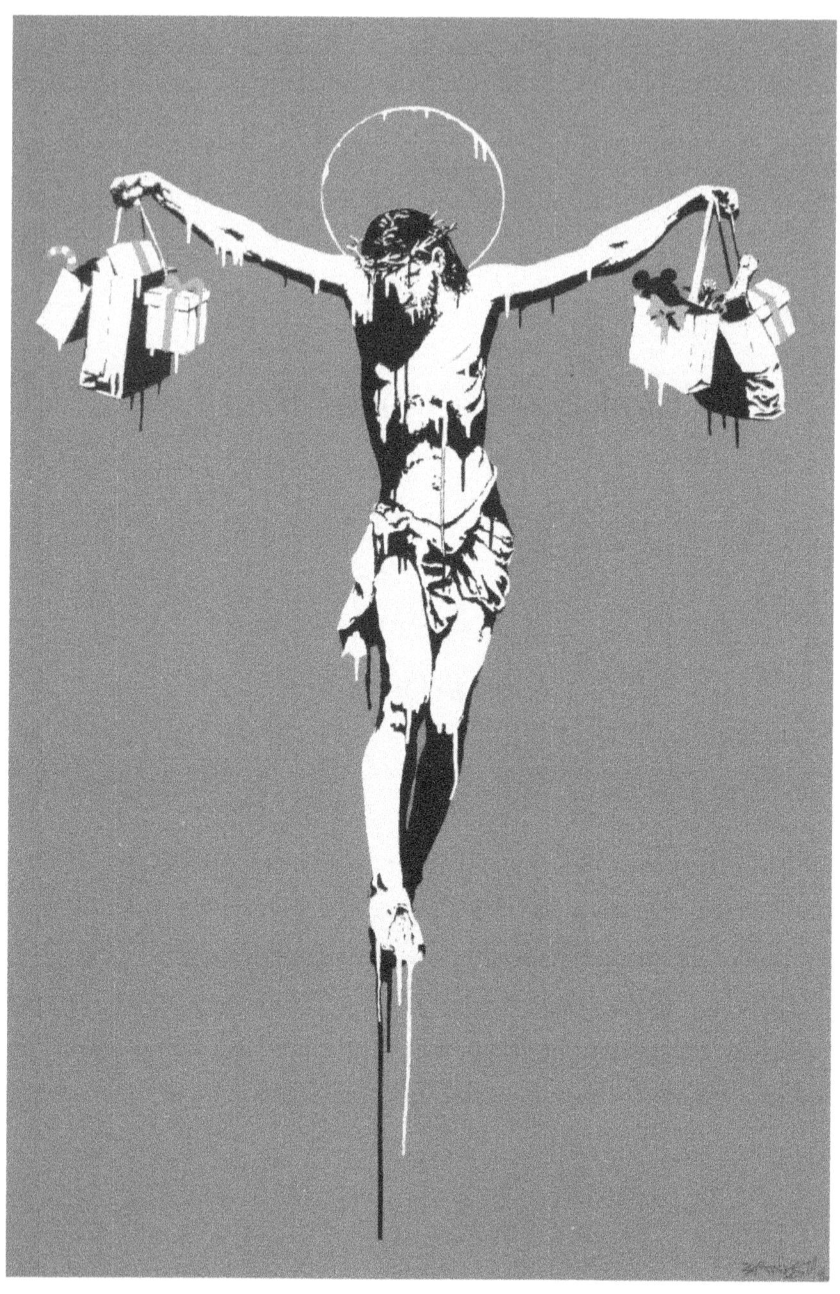

Banksy, *Christ with Shopping Bags*, 2004.

While the traditional iconography of Christmas depicts the infant Jesus in his mother's lap (or in a manger) attended by Joseph and surrounded by the three kings, a group of shepherds, and various animals, Banksy's Jesus is the martyred, crucified savior. A silkscreen in stark tones of white and black—a grisaille with the addition of a few bright fuchsia ribbons—*Christ with Shopping Bags* presents a bearded and manly Jesus, adorned with a halo and a crown of thorns. Although his arms are fully extended, there is no cross in the depiction, and no sign of the nails that pinned his hands to it. Rather, at the implied extremities of the instrument of torture his limp fists grasp the handles of shopping bags and gift boxes. These dangle symmetrically to the right and left of his contorted torso. A toy doll, the silhouette of Mickey Mouse, a candy cane, and what appears to be a bottle of spirits emerge from these sacks. All of these items, with bows and ribbons around them, are unmistakable signs of the Christmas shopping season that marks the fourth quarter of the annual financial cycle.

If we look more closely at the body of the dead Christ, we also detect a slight trace of fuchsia at the spot where the wound inspected by the doubting St. Thomas traditionally appears. This exceedingly subtle detail is almost invisible to the naked eye. Its inclusion, however, indicates that the artist is fully aware of all the defining symbolic elements of the passion he has appropriated, giving expression to every ironic twist. And while there is no other sign of blood, the image itself is literally dripping, as if it had been painted by an overloaded brush; gravity-bearing drops of "paint" drag the representation down, enhancing the sense of weight that the flutter of pink ribbons is intended to counter. These distended drips alter the proportion of the figure, elongating it and nearly filling the overall space allotted to it on the page. Even the halo has sloppy tendrils that attenuate its crisp delineation.

In this iconographic marriage, this conjunction of commercialism and the crucifixion, Banksy has struck one of his unerring bull's-eyes, taking aim at capitalism, religion, and hypocrisy all at once. His graphic designs are meant to be broad-edged, legible, and of high impact. He has created many such contradictory images. If this image evokes the passion, it is the passion for shopping.

Included among the artist's other emphatic designs are a pair of bobbies groping each other, a notice that "the Future has been cancelled," and a surveillance camera aimed at the legend "What are you looking at?" His appropriation of the famous Vietnam War news photo of a naked little girl running toward us, the screaming victim of a napalm attack, shows her hand in hand with towering representations of Ronald McDonald and Mickey Mouse stepping along beside her, waving to the crowd as if they were marching in the Macy's Thanksgiving Day parade.[2] In another nod to popular culture, Banksy depicts John Travolta and Samuel Jackson in their roles in the film *Pulp Fiction* aiming bananas instead of guns toward an imagined target.

Indeed, Banksy's particular power as an artist lies in his ability to juxtapose worlds of meaning through the calculated manipulation of signs and well-established icons of our culture. He deploys these bearers of cultural information with an unsettling equivocation in images that through his tightly focused intervention contradict one another. This ability to turn symbols against each other is also what accounts for the shock value of his works, and for the following he has attracted. Still, it is not necessary to comprehend his subtler references to art history in order to see the dark humor in his art.

2. Banksy, *Wall and Piece* (London: Century, 2006), 191. Of the several books that Banksy has self-published to illustrate his works, this is the most useful. It incorporates three earlier, smaller books: *Banging Your Head Against a Brick Wall* (2001), *Existencilism* (2002), and *Cut It Out* (2004). Banksy, *You Are an Acceptable Level of Threat* (Darlington, UK: Carpet Bombing Culture, 2012).

When the artist made a one-month visit to New York in October 2014 there was a media circus, as his graphics and various street actions popped up in locations that were announced on his Facebook page and then tweeted and instagrammed to followers who showed up with their iPhones poised to take selfies before the eagerly awaited outbreaks of art.[3]

But although he is often seen simply as a manipulator of the media, Banksy is in fact a consummate artist—if he is not, indeed, a conglomerate of artists—a highly productive and widely followed figure who has been at the top of his game for more than twenty years. Despite his well-guarded anonymity, an indelible and essential facet of his persona, he has been nearly continuously in public view. He is said to employ a full-time PR firm—in part to protect his privacy as well as to disseminate information blasts about his activities. In many ways, he can be said to operate as if he were a business foundation.[4]

And yet he is perhaps the most widely recognized descendant of the corps of fugitive street artists who arose in New York in the 1970s and '80s. The enterprise of street art provided a means of claiming power for disenfranchised youth who had little hope of finding meaningful work or adequate incomes and who were staring at a bleak future but possessed a terrific energy and graphic skill. They drew to show their presence in the world.[5]

Most significantly in this regard, Banksy is said to have emerged from the Barton Hill Youth Club in Bristol, England, where "at risk" youths learned the tools of a trade.[6]

3. See *Banksy Does New York*, www.hbo.com/documentaries/banksy-does-new-york#.
4. Will Ellsworth-Jones, *Banksy: The Man Behind the Wall* (New York: St. Martin's, 2012). See the chapter entitled "Welcome to Team Banksy," 155–80.
5. "My first impression of why other people were writing was because I felt people were angry . . . upset that they didn't have a voice in the world. . . . Writing was a way of saying, 'Don't make a decision without consulting us.'" Artist LSD OM, quoted by Roger Gastman and Caleb Neelon, *The History of American Graffiti* (New York: HarperCollins, 2010), 23.

Paradoxically, though the club's offerings may have kept the boys off the street for a time, some of them soon began active lives as public artists and many of them achieved notoriety by establishing their careers on the streets and on the run. Other alumni of the club have also become bona fide graphic artists.[7] But it is Banksy's career that has left the brightest meteoric trail.

Because they operate as guerrilla warriors of a sort, regularly flouting laws that protect private property, street artists are also—and often avowedly—identified as vandals. Many have been arrested and charged for trespassing and/or destroying property. This insistent challenge to legal restrictions accounts in no small way for their implicit antiestablishment credentials. The thrill of risking life and limb to "tag" subway cars, storefronts, and other urban surfaces with their designs is a significant aspect of their activity. According to their own testimony, it gives them a genuine sense of exhilaration and freedom.

Anonymity has served Banksy exceptionally well. Because graffiti artists made their reputations by more or less "hit and run" strategies, and placed their signatures, or "tags," in difficult to reach but highly visible locations, they usually adopted short names, or pseudonyms. It would have been unthinkable for them to leave verifiable personal information.

In recent years, however, whether despite of or because of its subversive cachet, this renegade art has become mainstream. Books and museums have devoted their efforts to documenting and tracing it; there have been comprehensive exhibitions at the Tate Modern in London, the Los Angeles County Museum of Art, and the Museum of the City of New York.[8] Related publications have routinely

6. Ellsworth-Jones, *Man Behind the Wall*, 26.

7. Ibid., 30.

8. Cedar Lewisohn, curator of the Tate Modern exhibition in 2008, is the author of *Street Art: The Graffiti Revolution* (New York: Abrams, 2008). Jeffrey Deitch, Roger Gastman, and Aaron Rose,

emphasized the antiestablishment roots of the enterprise: *The Art of Rebellion, Urban Guerrilla Protest,* or *Trespass* are typical in this respect.[9]

If we trace the chain of developments that culminate in Banksy's work, we note that the first weapon in the well-documented invasion of public space was the aerosol spray can. The best of the early graffiti artists could handle this tool with great skill and control, making swooping gestures and elaborately delicate squiggles that earned the individual practitioners recognition and widespread reputations. Like the mark of Zorro, or the skull and crossbones of a pirate flag, their tags told the world that they had struck again. The early outlaw stages of what can legitimately be considered an art movement have been recorded in such films as *Wild Style,* which show the connection between the New York graffiti artists, hip-hop, and the music and dance style of urban America. *Style Wars* (1983), which won the Grand Jury Prize for documentaries at the Sundance Film Festival, surveys the breadth of talent unleashed in aerosol attacks on the city of New York.[10]

The creator of our Christmas passion himself began as a hit-and-run spray-can artist of this kind until the night he found himself underneath a parked boxcar, hiding from the British transport police. He has written that it was while lying on his back, staring up at a metal plate that bore the name of its manufacturer, that he had the

Art in the Streets (New York: Skira Rizzoli, 2011), accompanied the eponymous Los Angeles County Museum of Contemporary Art exhibition. Martin Wong, Sean Corcoran, and Carlo McCormick, *City as Canvas: New York City Graffiti from the Martin Wong Collection* (New York: Museum of the City of New York, 2013).

9. Christian Hundertmark, *The Art of Rebellion,* 3 vols. (*I: The World of Street Art* [Berkeley, CA: Gingko, 2005]; *II: The World of Urban Art Activism* [Mainaschaff: Publikat, 2006]; *III: The Book about Street Art* (Mainaschaff: Publikat, 2010). Ake Rudolf, *Urban Guerrilla Protest* (Brooklyn: Mark Batty, 2008). Carlo McCormick, *Trespass: A History of Uncommissioned Urban Art* (Cologne: Taschen, 2010).
10. Charlie Ahearn, *Wild Style* (1983). Tony Silver, *Style Wars* (1983). See also Martha Cooper and Henry Chalfant, *Subway Art,* 25th anniversary ed. (New York: Chronicle, 2009).

"epiphany" that led him to adopt the silkscreen process for installing his art in the world.[11] A stencil permitted him to execute his designs on a variety of surfaces with great speed (sometimes in less than sixty seconds). Working this fast provided him safety as he pursued his public career under cover.[12]

Not only did this process shorten his forays onto the street—and make his getaways quicker— but they also made his art eminently reproducible. Silkscreen technology makes T-shirts, posters, and indeed any artifact available for distinctive branding and mass production. Widely used for high art since Andy Warhol adopted it in the early 1960s for portraits of the rich and famous (as well as Campbell's Soup cans), silkscreen printing has become one of the standard and most common techniques of postmodern artistic production. Banksy himself has sent thousands of ersatz CD covers (of *Paris*, Paris Hilton's debut CD) and banknotes ("tenners" with Princess Diana in place of the Queen) into circulation.[13]

If *Christ with Shopping Bags* had been a unique image existing in only a single incarnation, it might have disappeared into the world of ephemeral street phenomena and not come to our attention at all. But the image has become ubiquitous. In addition to the eighty-two numbered screenprints signed by the artist (the smallest number of copies associated with his editioned prints, making this one of the rarest), it is available for purchase online and can be obtained in a range of products, sizes, and prices.[14] One can choose whether to

11. Banksy, *Wall and Piece*, 13. The story is often repeated in accounts of Banksy's career.

12. According to Ellsworth-Jones, however, the real story is more complicated: *Man Behind the Wall*, 57ff.

13. See www.complex.com/style/2013/11/banksy-greatest-works/paris-hilton-reworked-album-dangermouse-collabor and www.complex.com/style/2013/11/banksy-greatest-works/di-faced-tenner.

14. Many of these are available on eBay. Also see www.picturesonwalls.com. Banksy's website features reproductions of *Christ with Shopping Bags*. The mechanics of selling prints by street artists is a complex story, and for Banksy a tale unto itself. Most of his editioned prints—those he signs and numbers—number in the hundreds, and their value depends among other things

purchase the image on a T-shirt, on paper, or stamped on canvas. That there is actually a shopping bag emblazoned with the image adds an almost surreal level of irony. But to apprehend the full spectrum of ironies that Banksy's Christmas passion embodies, it is necessary to trace its genesis in more detail and to take account of the context of its original appearance.

The image of *Christ with Shopping Bags* was originally a painting on canvas.[15] It made its first appearance in a pop-up store launched for the benefit of its participating artists in Kingly Court on Carnaby Street, London. Called "Santa's Ghetto," a sly oxymoron considering the linguistic origins and history of the term *ghetto*, the shop opened for the Christmas holiday season in 2003.[16] According to Banksy, "the Ghetto [was] partly a shameless commercial enterprise and partly about promoting art. But basically it [was] a piss-take on Christmas."[17]

The original canvas was offered for sale among prints and artworks created by a number of artists, including the cult comic-book artist Jamie Hewlett and the New York street artists known as Faile and Bäst. The price of their works ranged from "forty odd quid screen prints and five pound stickers, to the four figure bracket."[18]

Whatever one chooses to make of its ostensible celebration of the Christmas spirit—here reduced to the imperative to go out and buy—the image itself can be seen as emblematic of Santa's Ghetto, if not in fact an advertisement for it. After the success of its first

on rarity and condition. Any unnumbered, unsigned work is of course far less valuable. Because of a brisk business in forgeries, a website, PestControl, has emerged to authenticate Banksy's prints in order to protect their value.

15. E-mail to the author from PestControl, January 6, 2015. The image appears at www.artofthestate.co.uk/Banksy/Banksy_Santas_Ghetto_Christ_shopping.htm.
16. A precursor, in Shoreditch, is mentioned by Ellsworth-Jones, *Man Behind the Wall*, 125.
17. "It is also a great place to buy presents," he added, referring to the Carnaby Street installation. Banksy quoted in *The Independent*, www.artofthestate.co.uk / Banksy / Banksy_Santas_Ghetto_Christ_shopping.htm.
18. Ibid.

incarnation, Santa's Ghetto was resurrected the following year on Charing Cross Road, near the Tottenham Court Road tube stop. It was also in 2004 that the printed edition of *Christ with Shopping Bags* appeared. The print was offered for sale by the same enterprise that launched and supported Santa's pop-up Ghetto: Pictures on Walls (or POW), the London print shop and art gallery started by Banksy and his then-agent Steve Lazarides. POW, no longer associated with either Banksy or Lazarides, continues to print and sell works by street artists to a global public.[19]

All accounts of the Ghetto suggest that it was an extremely successful commercial enterprise and a great hit with the public. Lines of eager customers formed at its doors in advance of its opening. The most likely beneficiaries of the profits were POW and the artists themselves, yet to someone as presumably hostile to capitalism, whose pseudonym was originally a contraction of "Robin Banx," there is something clearly paradoxical about the staging of such an unabashedly commercial enterprise.[20]

Indeed, one cannot imagine that the artist once known as Robin Banx would admit to being behind the counter himself. For him the Robin Hood persona looms large. Not only the moniker Banksy, but the very modus operandi of the brigand who steals from the rich and gives to the poor serves as a paradigm of the actions of the street artist, who instead of placing art on gallery walls places it all over the built-up environment. That said, for Banksy to lend his outlaw credibility to such a clearly and unambiguously commercial venture as Santa's Ghetto, nestled at the holiday season amid one of London's busiest shopping neighborhoods, hardly qualifies as an

19. See www.picturesonwalls.com. Lazarides maintains a gallery in Knightsbridge. His relationship with Banksy is discussed by Ellsworth-Jones in *Man Behind the Wall*, 155–80.

20. Lynn Barber, "The Secrets of Art's Mystery Man; His Street Art Makes Millions, He Donates Thousands, but Does Anybody Know Anything Concrete About Banksy?" *The Sunday Times*, May 13, 2012.

anti-capitalist gesture. Indeed, it places Banksy—the proponent of the counterculture—squarely behind the counter.

After all, Banksy has succeeded in selling his anti-capitalist message to countless willing buyers. Perhaps a few embrace *Christ with Shopping Bags* because they see a similarity in it to the message of Christ casting the moneychangers out of the temple. And Banksy *is* an unabashed enemy of profiteers and moneychangers. If anything upsets him, it is purchasers of his works who acquire them as investments only to flip them via eBay or auctions to make a good return.[21] And yet his remarkable degree of commercial success has made the artist wealthy. He has been questioned about this evident conflict and has gone on record more than once to call attention to the difficulty of maintaining a counterculture persona while benefiting so handsomely from the moneyed classes.[22]

As if in recognition of his highly ambiguous status as an anonymous and very wealthy Robin Hood, Banksy has practiced public philanthropy on numerous occasions.[23] In one of his most ambitious projects he brought global attention to a site of international contention—and one in which it seemed an underdog could readily be identified. In 2007, he set up a Santa's Ghetto in Manger Square in Bethlehem, flying in nearly twenty street artists

21. In an effort to keep his work affordable he would release prints by warning in advance that they would be made available at a particular time and place to be announced, but there would be no telling when the announcement would come. Consequently he had collectors who would wait in line for hours in the hope of being able to acquire a work. Ellsworth-Jones, *Man Behind the Wall*, 181–204, esp. 189.

22. In an e-mail interview with Lauren Collins, he was asked whether "accusations of hypocrisy had worn on him" and answered that it had been "easier when he was the underdog. . . . The money that my work fetches these days makes me a bit uncomfortable, but that's an easy problem to solve—you just stop whingeing and give it all away. I don't think it's possible to make art about world poverty and then trouser all the cash, that's an irony too far, even for me." See Lauren Collins, "Banksy was Here," *The New Yorker*, May 14, 2007, http://www.newyorker.com/magazine/2007/05/14/banksy-was-here.

23. In one notable instance he posted bail for a Russian art collective, Voina, who perform acts of public protest, to be released from prison. Ellsworth-Jones, *Man Behind the Wall*, 197–98. See 201–203 for additional charitable activities.

from around the world to contribute their work. They created a market to lure shoppers and tourists to this troubled scene. He turned his commercial skills to use in this situation by donating the considerable funds raised in the market to create scholarships for Palestinian children who might not otherwise have had the opportunity to seek a college education.[24]

In doing this Banksy joined a corps of celebrities who have made a point of using their fame and fortune to do good. Like his fellow street artist JR—and a succession of entertainers like Sting, Bono, Madonna, and Angelina Jolie (who with Brad Pitt has often been counted among Banksy's loyal fans and collectors)—Banksy has established himself as a prominent philanthropist. Whether or not he winks at the mechanical operations of philanthropy—which begin, after all, by acquiring great wealth amassed from others—he has put his money to good use, supporting causes widely judged to be worthwhile.

Operating in the vicinity of Bethlehem—as opposed to Knightsbridge or Los Angeles, where he was likely to attract the glitterati—marked Banksy's return to a distressed urban environment at the same time it signaled his entry onto a wider world stage. It also brought him another opportunity to put his mark on walls and to focus global attention on graffiti. The existence of the Separation Wall that Israel began to erect in 2002 during the Second Intifada, in the hope of keeping terrorists from the West Bank from wreaking havoc on the Israeli civilian population, has provided scores of artists, both famous and not, with a tempting canvas on which to practice their craft. Not since the Berlin Wall was rendered obsolete and subsequently razed has there been such an irresistible fortification to

24. Ibid., 203–204. See also Brie Schwartz, "Artists Draw Attention to Bethlehem," December 12, 2007, www.cnn.com/2007/WORLD/meast/12/03/banksy.bethlehem, and Eric Westervelt, "Graffiti Artists Decorate Bethlehem Barrier," December 24, 2007, www.npr.org/templates/story/story.php?storyId=17497631.

attract them. JR, Blu, Faile, and scores of others with less familiar names have flocked to leave their designs on one of the world's newest and most controversial walls.[25]

In 2007, the same year he set up Santa's Ghetto in Bethlehem Banksy painted what has been referred to as "a Christmas Card for Bethlehem." On the separation wall near the city, he depicted Mary and Joseph as seen on their iconic flight from Egypt. But instead of entering the city where Jesus would be born, they are literally walled out—giving the "site-specific" aspect of his performance piece a new, dramatic burst of meaning.[26]

In other charged depictions of the Holy Family, included in the "Altered Images" series, Banksy took liberties with images of the Madonna and Child. In order to bring them "up to date" for our time, he depicted the Madonna tuned out and wearing earbuds, apparently listening to her iPod instead of communing with her child. In another (less potentially amusing) image, the Christ Child has an IED strapped to his chubby chest, its timer clearly visible.[27]

If it is true, as has been reported, that Banksy is well educated—the product of a private school, if not university—it makes sense that his knowledge of both Christian iconography and art history is more than skin deep, and that his calculatedly irreverent icons may be seen as a kind of running commentary on more traditional ones. Perhaps because of his mysterious background, and certainly by virtue of his cloak of anonymity, he has maintained his fame for far longer than the "fifteen minutes" Andy Warhol's famous dictum would have allotted him. As the artist who created *Christ with Shopping Bags* he

25. "Segregation Wall, Palestine," in Banksy, *Wall and Piece*, 136–45.

26. "A Spray in a Manger: Banksy at Christmas," www.bbc.co.uk/programmes/articles/2fnrV0PQQDkDqJ6VNv6/a-spray-in-a-manger-banksy-at-Christmas, and Ahram Online, "Banksy's Christmas Card: Israel/Palestine Strife Blocks Holy Family from Bethlehem," December 11, 2012, english.ahram.org.eg/NewsContent/5/25/60241/Arts--Culture/Visual-Art/Banksys-Christmas-card-IsraelPalestine-strife-bloc.aspx.

27. "Art," in Banksy, *Wall and Piece*, 164–65.

may continue for some time to reap the benefits of his anti-capitalist persona, and in this way succeed in regularly biting the very hand that feeds him.

17

Dying for Our Sins

Jesus' Passion on the Silver Screen

Adele Reinhartz

The dramatic reenactment of Jesus' passion is by no means a modern innovation. Indeed, passion plays have been performed in Christian countries since the Middle Ages, and perhaps long before. The most famous dramatic rendition of Jesus' last days is the passion play at Oberammergau, Germany, a tradition that dates back to 1633. During a deadly outbreak of the plague, in the midst of the Thirty Years' War, the residents of Oberammergau swore an oath that they would perform the "Play of the Suffering, Death and Resurrection of Our Lord Jesus Christ" every ten years and on the century anniversary. The first performance took place at Pentecost 1634, on a stage erected in the cemetery above the fresh graves of plague victims. Miraculously, the plague stopped.[1]

Since the advent of cinema, viewers do not have to travel to Oberammergau once each decade in order to be spectators to the drama of Jesus' passion. Instead, we can go to the cinema down the street and, since the invention of VHS and DVD technology, we can take part in Jesus' passion from the comfort of our own homes. Like the passion dramas, and perhaps, the passion itself, passion films from the very beginning drew a big crowd. The very first Jesus movie, released in 1898, was itself a passion film. Its title, *The Passion Play at Oberammergau*, suggested that it was a filming of the famous German passion play. Even the revelation that it was staged and filmed on the roof of the Grand Central Palace in New York did nothing to deter audiences.[2]

Since those beginnings, Jesus' passion has been dramatized in dozens of films, sometimes as the exclusive subject, as in Mel Gibson's 2004 *The Passion of the Christ*, but more often as the lengthy and dramatic climax to a "biopic" narrating Jesus' life from birth to death. While the production has not been steady—no feature films were produced during the period of the censorship code (1927–61) or, less explicably, between the years 1989 (*Jesus of Montreal*) and 2003 (*The Gospel of John*)—it has been prodigious. Jesus' passion has proven to be both popular and controversial. Jesus movies occupied the general public in the period leading up to the release of Martin Scorsese's *Last Temptation of Christ* in 1988, and, more intensively, for at least six months preceding the release of Gibson's film.

These movies are made for the same reasons that have given birth to most other films: the artistic vision of the director and the entire filmmaking team, and the commercial vision, or dream, of box office

1. The year 2000 saw the fortieth performance of the play. For an excellent discussion of the passion play at Oberammergau, see James S. Shapiro, *Oberammergau: The Troubling Story of the World's Most Famous Passion Play* (New York: Pantheon, 2000).
2. Roy Kinnard and Tim Davis, *Divine Images: A History of Jesus on the Screen* (New York: Carol Publishing Group, 1992), 20.

success. But Jesus movies, like the passion play at Oberammergau, often claim even loftier goals: to continue the work of the evangelists by providing a vehicle for spreading the good news of salvation and redemption throughout the world.

The biblical support for such a mission is found most clearly in Matt. 28:19-20, in which the Matthean Jesus commands his disciples to "go therefore and make disciples of all nations, baptizing them in the name of the Father and of the Son and of the Holy Spirit, and teaching them to obey everything that I have commanded you."[3] Cecil B. DeMille hoped his audiences would view his highly popular 1927 silent film, *The King of Kings*, as a fulfillment of this very commandment, as noted in the scrolling text that opens the film:

> This is the story of Jesus of Nazareth . . . He, Himself, commanded that His message be carried to the uttermost parts of the earth. May this portrayal play a reverent part in the spirit of that great command.

Even more explicit is the 1979 film simply called *Jesus*. Produced for evangelical use, it presents itself as a two-hour docudrama about the life of Christ based on the Gospel of Luke. According to its website:

> The film has been seen in every country of the world and translated into hundreds of languages since its initial release in 1979. Our goal is to reach every nation, tribe, people and tongue, helping them see and hear the story of Jesus in a language they can understand. So whether a person speaks Swahili, French, or a language whose name is extremely difficult for most to pronounce, he or she will encounter the life and message of Jesus in a language "of the heart." . . . [T]his powerful film has had more than 6 billion viewings worldwide since 1979. . . . As a result, more than 200 million people have indicated decisions to accept Christ as their personal Savior and Lord.[4]

3. All direct quotations from the New Testament are taken from the New Revised Standard Version.
4. "About the JESUS Film Project," The Jesus Film Project, www.jesusfilm.org/aboutus/index.html.

Most Jesus films do not declare any evangelical intentions. But the camerawork, which tends toward long and extreme close-ups of Jesus' face, the heavy use of direct quotation from the Gospels, the visual references to iconic paintings, and the attempt to recreate the stations of the cross, all suggest that these films are intended not so much to entertain as to create a liturgical experience for their viewers that will transform them, move them to faith, perhaps, or at least to provide a powerful spiritual as well as emotional experience.

The possibility that a film based on Jesus' life might have a transformative effect on the viewers is not at all far-fetched. In the first place, the film medium in general exerts a powerful force. A good film transports us into another life and can take us through a range of emotions that feel real and significant, at least for the two or so hours we are in the theater, and, in some cases, for much longer. Second, and just as important, the Jesus movies by and large are cinematic adaptations of the Christian Gospels of Matthew, Mark, Luke, and John. In the Christian tradition, the canonical Gospels are viewed as powerful agents of transformation. Indeed, the evangelists themselves recognized that most of their audience lived after Jesus' death and had no opportunity for a direct encounter with the earthly Jesus. Thus the Johannine Jesus' comment to doubting Thomas in John 20:29: "Have you believed because you have seen me? Blessed are those who have not seen and yet have come to believe." The Gospels, as written accounts of Jesus' life, words, and works, became vehicles through which audiences could experience Jesus. This is expressed clearly in John 20:30-31, commonly seen as the Gospel's conclusion and statement of purpose:

> Now Jesus did many other signs in the presence of his disciples, which are not written in this book. But these are written so that you may come to believe that Jesus is the Messiah, the Son of God, and that through believing you may have life in his name.

If the Gospels themselves have transformative potential, then surely films that dramatize the Gospels must have the same, if not more, given the visceral power of the cinematic medium.

Not surprising, then, many Jesus filmmakers declare their fidelity to Scripture, a fidelity that is often equated with historical authenticity and accuracy.[5] Cecil B. DeMille begins his silent epic with an assertion that "the events portrayed by this picture occurred in Palestine nineteen centuries ago, when the Jews were under the complete subjection of Rome—even their own High Priest being appointed by the Roman procurator." A half-century later, Roberto Rossellini, the director of the 1975 Italian film *Il Messia* (*The Messiah*), states,

> I do not want to invent, or to interpret the Old and New Testaments—but just to present it in "quotes." I attempt to reconstruct everything accurately—you have to do this precisely and objectively in order to portray the truth. *The Messiah* will thus present the historical Jesus as portrayed in the Four Gospels through an accurate development of the principal events of his life.[6]

The equation of fidelity to Scripture with historical accuracy and authenticity is itself highly problematic from the point of New Testament scholarship. But setting scholarly objections aside, the question remains as to whether dramatizing the Gospel narratives

5. The discrepancies among the Gospels with regard to the reconstruction of the life of the historical Jesus have been noted and grappled with by scholars for centuries, with widely varying results. For a good treatment of the challenge, see Michael Grant, *Jesus: An Historian's Review of the Gospels* (1977; New York: Macmillan, 1992), and, more recently, Mark Allan Powell, *Jesus as a Figure in History: How Modern Historians View the Man from Galilee* (Louisville: Westminster John Knox, 1997). See also William E. Arnal and Michel Desjardins, ed., *Whose Historical Jesus?* (Waterloo, ON: Wilfrid Laurier University Press, 1997); Paula Fredriksen, *Jesus of Nazareth, King of the Jews* (New York: Knopf, 1999); and W. Barnes Tatum, *In Quest of Jesus*, rev. ed. (Nashville: Abingdon, 1999). For an excellent exploration of Jesus' Jewishness and its relevance to Jewish-Christian relations in our own time, see Amy-Jill Levine, *The Misunderstood Jew: The Church and the Scandal of the Jewish Jesus* (San Francisco: Harper, 2006).
6. Rossellini's words are quoted on the box of the VHS version.

can provide a spiritually transformative viewing experience. As I will argue below, the power inherent in the passion story gets lost when the Gospels are turned into biographical films. Further, it is precisely those films that stray the furthest from the Gospel accounts that are the most successful at conveying Jesus' transformative power.

Biographical Jesus Movies

Most Jesus films fall into the genre of the biopic or biographical film[7] and essentially follow the same pattern as the biographies of entertainment barons, country and western singers, American presidents, and other heroes. The narrative template of the biopic situates its subject socially within a familial, societal, and political context. It describes the subject's emerging capabilities and mission, creates conflict between the subject and other individuals or groups (or perhaps society as a whole), and resolves the conflict—often through the device of a judicial trial that allows the subject to proclaim his or her philosophy and mission to the movie-going audience as well as to the judge and jury.[8] Cinema packages Jesus' life story into the same template: Jesus is born into a loving family of Galilean Jews and a society oppressed by Roman soldiers on behalf of the colonizing empire.[9] This template dovetails nicely with the narrative structure of the Gospel accounts. It is particularly serendipitous that Jesus' canonical biographies also culminate in a highly dramatic trial scene.

One of the key features of the biopic narrative structure, as in most other realistic movies, is the principle of causality.[10] Most often, the

7. For detailed treatment of the Jesus movies as biopics, see Adele Reinhartz, *Jesus of Hollywood* (New York: Oxford University Press, 2007).
8. George F. Custen, *Bio/Pics: How Hollywood Constructed Public History* (New Brunswick, NJ: Rutgers University Press, 1992), 144.
9. For detailed analysis of the Jesus movies and more detailed discussion of the points made in this essay, see Reinhartz, *Jesus of Hollywood*.

plot revolves around the relationship between the protagonist and the antagonist. It is the antagonists' very antagonism toward the hero that propels the plot forward to its climax in the hero's trial. The Jesus movies on the whole follow this pattern very closely. They collectively blame one or more characters in the Gospel narrative for the sequence of events leading to Jesus' death and propose a number of reasons for their animosity.

The Agents of Jesus' Passion

Caiaphas

Both the Gospels and the Jesus biopics assign key roles in Jesus' passion to the religious and political authorities of Jesus' time. In all four canonical Gospels, Caiaphas has a particular interest in Jesus and is deeply involved in the plot against him. According to Matt. 26:3-5,

> the chief priests and the elders of the people gathered in the palace of the high priest, who was called Caiaphas, and they conspired to arrest Jesus by stealth and kill him. But they said, "Not during the festival, or there may be a riot among the people."

In John, Caiaphas's role is expanded further. While the Jewish authorities have been persecuting Jesus from chapter 5 onward,[11] their activities intensify after the raising of Lazarus:

> So the chief priests and the Pharisees called a meeting of the council, and said, "What are we to do? This man is performing many signs. If we let him go on like this, everyone will believe in him, and the Romans will come and destroy both our holy place and our nation." But one of them, Caiaphas, who was high priest that year, said to them, "You know nothing at all! You do not understand that it is better for you to have

10. On the centrality of causality in the "classical paradigm" of cinematic narrative (to which most films, including Jesus films, belong), see Louis Giannetti, *Understanding Movies*, 8th ed. (Upper Saddle River, NJ: Prentice Hall, 1999), 353.
11. Cf. John 5:16-18.

> one man die for the people than to have the whole nation destroyed." (11:41-44)

The narrator explains that Caiaphas "did not say this on his own, but being high priest that year he prophesied that Jesus was about to die for the nation, and not for the nation only, but to gather into one the dispersed children of God. So from that day on they planned to put him to death" 11:51-53).

In all the Gospels, Jesus is brought to the house of the high priest before he is taken to Pilate. In Matthew, after an interrogation before the Sanhedrin, Caiaphas asks Jesus under oath: "Tell us if you are the Messiah, the Son of God." Jesus responds, "You have said so. But I tell you, From now on you will see the Son of Man seated at the right hand of Power and coming on the clouds of heaven." Hearing these words, the high priest rends his clothes and declares that Jesus has blasphemed, and the Sanhedrin delivers the guilty verdict (26:63-66).

The trial before Caiaphas and his council is dramatized in the major Jesus biopics, with the notable exception of DeMille's *The King of Kings*, which follows John (18:24) in simply showing that Jesus was brought before Caiaphas without dramatizing the proceedings. Franco Zeffirelli's marathon made-for-television series, *Jesus of Nazareth* (1977), presents this sequence at great length, depicting the high priest's delicate situation as the liaison between the Jewish nation and the Roman governor Pilate, as well as Caiaphas's genuine and profound distress upon hearing Jesus' blasphemous claim.

Other films, however, attribute baser motives to the high priest. Most egregious is DeMille, who exculpates the Jewish people as a whole but amplifies the role of Caiaphas by suggesting that he harbored tremendous animosity toward Jesus out of greed for money and power. Caiaphas's first introduction into the story is accompanied by an intertitle that identifies him as "the Roman appointee Caiaphas, the High Priest—who cared more for Revenue than for Religion—and saw in Jesus a menace to his rich profits from the Temple." Later, the film informs us that the temple, which the "Faithful of Israel" considered to be "the dwelling place of Jehovah," was for Caiaphas "a corrupt and profitable market-place." Thus, DeMille's Caiaphas will not rest until Jesus is brought down.

Pilate

Jesus movies made in the two decades or so after the Holocaust era tend to focus on Pontius Pilate, the Roman governor. This shift may be due both to sensitivity to anti-Semitism and to the growing interest in Jewish-Christian dialogue and rapprochement. Many movies follow the Gospels in absolving Pilate of moral responsibility as he washes his hands of Jesus' blood;[12] others, such as the animated film *The Miracle Maker* (2000), portray Pilate as bearing animosity toward the Jews in general and their high priest in particular. Nicholas Ray's 1961 epic *King of Kings* (not to be confused with DeMille's silent film *The King of Kings*) portrays Pilate as being quite interested in getting rid of the Galilean troublemaker. Ray's Pilate is suspicious of Jesus but feels constrained by Roman law to conduct a proper legal process. Pilate lays out the charges as follows:

> You have just been interrogated by Caiaphas. They have judged you guilty on two counts: blasphemy and sedition. This court takes no cognizance of your blasphemy, but the charge of sedition is a major offense. The rules of Roman law will prevail. I, Pontius Pilate, Governor of Judea, by grace of the Emperor the divine Tiberius of Rome will judge your case. No matter what you've done up to this moment, no matter what others have accused you of doing, I and I alone have authority to sentence you to be crucified or flogged or to set you free. How you conduct yourself here and now will determine your fate. Do you understand?

12. Cf. Matt. 27:24.

Ray's Pilate then provides judicial representation for Jesus in the form of a fictional character named Lucius, who becomes ever more convinced of Jesus' innocence, but to no avail.

Judas

Whether it is Caiaphas who is blamed, or Pilate, or both, Judas Iscariot invariably plays the role of betrayer to which the Gospels have consigned him. Evangelists and filmmakers alike consider Judas's motivation and arrive at two explanations: greed and politics. The Gospels indicate that the chief priests paid Judas thirty pieces of silver for betraying Jesus (Matt. 26:14–16), and almost every film dramatizes the scene in which the silver changes hands. DeMille seats Caiaphas and Judas across a small table. Caiaphas leans toward Judas, asking, "Dost thou swear to betray to us His secret place of prayer, that we may destroy him?" Judas does not meet Caiaphas's eyes; he is distressed and unresponsive but does not refuse or walk away. The camera slows as it focuses on the money changing hands. (Gibson also uses slow motion in this scene.) As Caiaphas tosses the moneybag toward Judas, the coins fall out and scatter. Judas stares at Caiaphas, stoops, and hurriedly gathers them up. Both films emphasize Judas's inner turmoil, in which his greed finally outweighs loyalty to his master. Pier Paolo Pasolini's *The Gospel According to Saint Matthew* (1964), by contrast, exhibits only glee. It is he who initiates the agreement, by asking Caiaphas what he will give him for betraying Jesus to them. He smiles when Caiaphas offers him thirty denarii; the soundtrack plays the melody of Kol Nidre, from the liturgy of the Jewish Day of Atonement.

Films from the 1960s, such as George Stevens's *The Greatest Story Ever Told* (1965) and Ray's *King of Kings*, portray Judas in a more sympathetic light, though even they cannot rewrite the script that requires Judas to betray Jesus. In these epics, Judas is a well-meaning but misguided young man who believes the salvation Jesus preaches is not primarily spiritual in nature but rather military and political. He sees his role as helping Jesus fulfill his promise to liberate Judea from Roman rule.

The most detailed exposition of this plot line is found in Zeffirelli's six-and-a-half-hour marathon, released in 1979. In order to avoid blaming Caiaphas or any other historical Jewish figure, Zeffirelli creates a fictional Jewish scribe named Zerah as Jesus' principal antagonist and the one who actively plots Jesus' death. In his naiveté, Judas approaches Zerah in the hope that Zerah will agree to set up a meeting between Jesus and the Sanhedrin, in which Jesus can explain how he plans to liberate Judea. Zerah is only too pleased, though for reasons rather different from those proposed by Judas. We viewers easily detect Zerah's hypocritical and duplicitous nature, which becomes clear to Judas only when he realizes, too late, that he himself has been betrayed into revealing Jesus' whereabouts, thereby setting the stage for Jesus' trial, condemnation, and execution.

The Jewish People

No doubt the most disturbing line in the Gospel passion accounts is Matt. 27:25, in which the Jewish crowd cries out, "His blood be on us and on our children!" The outcry occurs in response to Pilate's ritual hand washing, by means of which he cleanses himself of moral responsibility for Jesus' fate. Jesus films treat this scene in a variety of ways. In the little known German silent movie *Der Galiläer* (1917), for example, the large crowd, incited by Caiaphas, demands Jesus' death and in doing so takes Jesus' blood upon themselves and their children, not once, as in Matthew, but twice. A decade later, DeMille silenced the crowds and transferred their words to Caiaphas. In doing so, he no doubt wished both to sharpen the dramatic conflict between

Jesus and Caiaphas and to insist that the Jews as a whole were not culpable. When Pilate asks, "Shall I crucify your king?" it is Caiaphas, not the people, who declares, "We have no King but Caesar." After Pilate washes his hands of the affair, the high priest tells him "If thou, imperial Pilate, wouldst wash thy hands of this man's death, let it be upon me and me alone!" Pilate declares, "I am innocent of the blood of this just Man; see ye to it." The Roman governor then retreats to his throne room, nearly sobbing in despair, while Caiaphas remains outside in a pose of smug self-satisfaction.

Later epics simply omit the problematic line. In Stevens's *The Greatest Story Ever Told*, for example, Pilate washes his hands but does not declare his innocence; neither does the crowd take Jesus' blood upon themselves. In Pasolini's *The Gospel According to Saint Matthew*, the line is uttered by a single, unidentified voice. Gibson preserves the line in Aramaic dialogue, but after some deliberation, agreed to remove it from the English subtitles. It remains audible, and comprehensible, however, to anyone who understands a Semitic language.

Satan

While there is no doubt as to the human agency that led to Jesus' death, in the Gospels, Jesus' greatest antagonist is Satan. It is Satan, say Luke and John, who was ultimately responsible for Judas's act of betrayal (Luke 22:1-5; John 13:2, 13:21-30). Gibson's film is the one that places the most emphasis on Satan's role in the passion drama by inserting Satan in the background of many scenes. Satan floats smoothly and quietly among the crowds of priests and Roman soldiers who watch intently as Jesus is flogged and tortured within an inch of his life. This presentation implies Satan was working through Jews and Romans alike, and indeed, perhaps through us, the viewers, who are also passively bearing witness to Jesus' suffering displayed so graphically on the screen before us.

As these brief examples show, the biographical Jesus movies present a chain of causality that leads from Jesus to his antagonists, in the figures of Pilate, Caiaphas, Judas, the Jewish people, and finally Satan, each of whom plays a role in the events that lead to Jesus' passion and crucifixion. The sequence, while based on scriptural sources, is also required by the biopic genre to which these films belong.

Jesus' Passion in the Divine Plan of Salvation

We all know how the story ends, of course. Yet despite our familiarity, the biographical films engage us emotionally in the tale of an innocent man, divinely begotten and beloved, who is unjustly hounded, betrayed, convicted, and executed by the powers of evil in the world. Jesus' passion is a tragedy in the classic sense of the term. Its dramatization can make for an emotionally powerful viewing experience, but can it succeed in conveying the spiritual power that the Gospels, the letters of Paul, and later Christian theology assign to Jesus' passion?

For the Gospel writers, Jesus' death is not only the inevitable, tragic consequence of his enemies' schemes, but also the essential component of God's divine plan for human salvation and redemption.[13] As the narrator of the Gospel of John so famously declared,

> No one has ascended into heaven except the one who descended from heaven, the son of Man. And just as Moses lifted up the serpent in the wilderness, so must the Son of Man be lifted up, that whoever believes in him may have eternal life. For God so loved the world that he gave his only Son, so that everyone who believes in him may not perish but may have eternal life. (3:13-16)

13. Cf. Mark 8:31.

It is difficult for a visual medium like film to convey the role of an invisible deity in orchestrating the death of his only son. Nevertheless, some films do try. The whiny Jesus in the 1973 film version of Andrew Lloyd Webber's musical *Jesus Christ Superstar* momentarily sets aside his own ego to expound upon his role in God's plan and announces to his puzzled followers that "To conquer death / You only have to die."

According to the Gospel of John and other New Testament texts, Jesus was the lamb of God who removes sin from the world. Like the Paschal Lamb, his death marks the salvation of others (John 1:29). This point is hinted at by the scrolling text that introduces Gibson's *The Passion of the Christ*. The text quotes from the "Suffering Servant song" in Isa. 53:3–5: "He was wounded for our transgressions, crushed for our iniquities; by His wounds we are healed. Isaiah 53–700 B.C." In Isaiah, the full passage reads as follows:

> He was despised and rejected by men, a man of sorrows, and familiar with suffering. Like one from whom men hide their faces he was despised, and we esteemed him not. Surely he took up our infirmities and carried our sorrows, yet we considered him stricken by God, smitten by him, and afflicted. But he was pierced for our transgressions, he was crushed for our iniquities; the punishment that brought us peace was upon him, and by his wounds we are healed.

Gibson's scrolling text indicates that Jesus' suffering, culminating in death, was foreseen, indeed was planned by God many years before his son took on human flesh and came into the world as a man. By the time the movie is over, however, the introductory text is long forgotten. The gallons of blood spilled in this movie suggest, to this viewer at least, the hand of Gibson far more strongly than the hand of God.

Fictional Jesus Movies

Despite efforts to define Jesus' divine identity, the biopics largely focus on the human and political aspects of the passion sequence, remaining bound to the narrative conventions of their genre. Ironically, perhaps, it is those films that explicitly deny both historicity and fidelity to Scripture that come closer to making us feel the power of the divine imperative. Martin Scorsese's *The Last Temptation of Christ* is a film adaptation of Nikos Kazantzakis's novel of the same name. The fictional nature of the film is brought to the viewer's attention by an introductory scrolling text:

> The dual substance of Christ, the yearning, so human, so superhuman, of man to attain God . . . has always been a deep inscrutable mystery to me. My principle [sic] anguish and source of all my joys and sorrows from my youth onward has been the incessant, merciless battle between the spirit and the flesh . . . and my soul is the arena where these two armies have clashed and met. . . . This film is not based upon the Gospels but upon this fictional exploration of the eternal spiritual conflict.

Despite its explicitly fictional nature, the film created a stir almost as intense as that caused by Gibson's film. In Scorsese's case, the furor was caused by a report that the film depicts Jesus having sex with Mary Magdalene and other women, and fathering children. When the film was finally released, it was immediately apparent that these scenes were not "historical" but rather occurred in what can be referred to as a dream sequence—a hallucination or fantasy that Jesus experiences while on the cross. Far more interesting, and theologically profound, however, is the film's depiction of the relationship between Jesus and Judas and the role that Jesus assigns Judas in his life and death. Here, and only here, is God depicted as a player in the passion drama. Those who protested Scorsese's depiction of Jesus' relationship with Mary Magdalene missed what is surely the most intense and intimate of this Jesus' relationships: his friendship with Judas. Whereas Jesus avoids all physical contact with Mary Magdalene, he seeks out the company of Judas, who, as in Zeffirelli's film, is a Zealot who believes that Jesus will start the revolution against Rome. Jesus gradually reveals to Judas that he must die on the cross in order to fulfill God's plan of salvation, a message that Judas finds difficult to absorb, let alone to accept.

The final piece of the plan, and the most difficult, is Judas's own role. Yet without Judas, salvation will not come. The revelation occurs after a tumult in the crowded temple area. Judas has urged Jesus to give a sign for the revolution: "They are all waiting for your signal. If you don't give the sign now they'll kill us. . . . This is the way, do it." Jesus is silent, holds out his hands, showing the blood flowing from the holes that the nails will soon make in them. The silence continues. Jesus looks down, as if he is already dead. He calls Judas to help him: "Stay with me. Don't leave me." They walk away, Judas supporting Jesus, who is so depleted of energy that he can barely walk. They stop and sit down in a passageway, away from the noisy crowd. Judas checks Jesus' forehead, with concern, to see if he has fever:

> Jesus: I wish there was another way; I'm sorry, but there isn't. I have to die on the cross.
>
> Judas [vehemently]: I won't let you die.
>
> Jesus: You have no choice; neither do I. We are bringing God and man together. I'm the sacrifice. Without you there can be no redemption.
>
> Judas [dismissive]: Get somebody stronger.
>
> Jesus: You promised me . . . You once told me if I moved one step from revolution you would kill me. . . . I have strayed, haven't I?
>
> [Judas, softly, reluctantly, agrees.]

> Jesus: Then you must keep your promise. You have to kill me.
>
> Judas: If that's what God wants, let God do it. I won't.
>
> Jesus: He will do it, through you. The temple guards will be looking for me—go to Gethsemane, make sure they find me there.
>
> [Judas is silent, unhappy.]
>
> Jesus: I am going to die. After three days I'll come back in victory. You can't leave me. You have to give me strength.
>
> Judas: If you were me would you betray your master?
>
> Jesus: No. That's why God gave me the easier job, to be crucified.

In agony, Judas sobs into his hands as Jesus sits close by and clasps his shoulder in sympathy. Judas finally calms down and asks, "What about the others?" Jesus replies, "I'll tell them tonight."

Scorsese's Judas shares some superficial features with his counterpart in the biographical movies in that he is politically motivated. Here, too, he misinterprets Jesus' intentions, and it is Jesus' task gradually to convince him that the true way is not revolution but something much more difficult. And while the film is indeed fictional, in the sense that it strays freely from the Gospels in terms of the events it portrays, it is far truer to their spiritual message than the biographical films can be when it comes to God's role in salvation through Jesus.

The theological message comes through, more subtly but still palpably, in what is no doubt the most secular Jesus movie, Denys Arcand's *Jesus of Montreal*. Strictly speaking, this 1989 Quebecois film is not a Jesus movie. Rather, it falls into a subgenre of films that focus on a group of actors in a village or city preparing to stage a passion play. Such films typically portray the contemporary story as a frame narrative in which the passion itself is also viewed.[14]

Arcand's film initially mocks the very idea that Jesus died on account of human sin. This can be seen in an early scene, in which Daniel, the actor who plays Jesus in the passion play that he and his troupe create, views a videotape of the overwrought passion play that he has been asked to revitalize. The scene is humorous, but the dialogue expresses precisely the connection between Jesus' passion and the sin of humanity and the role of the passion play as an enactment of the stations of the cross, as demonstrated in statements uttered by a number of anonymous, white-robed, and heavily made-up actors, two male and two female:

> First Station. Jesus is condemned to die.
>
> This just man must die.
>
> Why?
>
> Because he is just and we are not.
>
> He will bear our murders
>
> Our thefts.
>
> Our adulteries! He falters under the weight of our sins.
>
> They chose the heaviest wood!
>
> The hardest wood!
>
> Our sins make His cross heavy.
>
> (All together): Our sins.

Finally a female actor approaches Jesus, staggering under his wooden cross, and cries out, "Innocent lamb! See how my pride crushes you."

14. Two other films in this genre include *The Master and Margarita* (1994), based on the novel by Mikhail Bulgakov, and *He Who Must Die* (*Celui qui doit mourir*, 1957). Both are excellent, but the latter is particularly interesting in that it never reveals the passion play itself to the viewer.

The fact that Daniel does not appropriate this theme for his own version indicates that he repudiates this theology along with the overwrought tone and content of the original passion play. Yet it would be a mistake to suggest that theology is absent from this very secular presentation of the Jesus story. The passion play (set in the time of Jesus) and the frame narrative (set in Montreal after the so-called Quiet Revolution that disarmed the power of the Catholic church in Quebec) converge in a powerful sequence that culminates, as it must, in the death on the cross of both Jesus and the actor who plays him. In the passion play, Jesus' death is attributed to the callousness of Pilate and the machinations of Caiaphas, though it is clear that Caiaphas here stands in not for the Jewish people but for the Catholic establishment in Quebec, the corrupt nature of which is a major theme in Arcand's film. In the frame narrative, the death of the actor who plays Jesus emphatically negates the principle of causality, for it is caused not by greed, not by politics, and not by Satan or by God, but rather by sheer accident and human carelessness. The framing scene takes place during the troupe's final performance of the passion play. The priest had ordered an end to the performance of the play, out of fear that his superiors will punish him by reassigning him to an old-age home in Winnipeg. The players defy the order, and the priest calls in the police to stop the performance. But by the time they arrive Daniel, as Jesus, is already affixed to the cross; and the crowd objects to the fact that they cannot watch the play to the end. One irate and very strong spectator picks up the security guard and carries him off the scene. He does not pay attention, however, and runs straight into the cross on which Daniel is fastened. The cross topples, crushing Daniel's head. He does not die on the spot, but it is clear that the passion play is over. And soon Daniel's life will be as well.

What does one make of this death? In contrast to the Jesus of the Gospels, there is no one who wished the death of Daniel Coulombe, the Jesus of Montreal, and no one whose political or theological purposes are served by it. It is a senseless death, unburdened by theological meaning. The Jesus of the framing narrative is not resurrected, though some of his organs—the "gift of life"—live on in the two bodies into which they are transplanted.

If the death of this Jesus does not in any way remove sin or provide redemption, however, his life has. Despite its fictional nature and its highly critical stance toward the Catholic Church in Quebec, Arcand's film is more successful than any other Jesus movie in expressing Jesus' active transformation of the lives of those who followed him. In offering his four fellow actors an opportunity to work with him on the passion play, Daniel redeems their art, and, more subtly, their own self-esteem and human dignity. The people who flock to St. Joseph's Oratory to see the passion play are similarly moved. Daniel brings the person and story of Jesus alive for them for the first time—despite the fact that his version of the story debunks traditional Catholic narrative and theology in a way that angers the priest who commissioned them in the first place, resulting in the cancellation of the show and ultimately to Daniel's own demise. In the larger societal sense, Daniel and his group attempted to buck the forces of crass commercialism by presenting a passion play that emphasized love and compassion, while also holding themselves to high artistic standards. Even so, the film is hardly optimistic, suggesting that Daniel, like Jesus before him, did not succeed in transforming his society in any profound way.

Conclusion

What should we make of the fact that the biographical films that stay close to the Gospels are far less successful at conveying the spiritual message of Jesus' passion than those that do not claim to be faithful either to Scripture or to history? As I have tried to show, the narrative conventions of the biopic genre tend to push biographical Jesus movies to posit a primarily human chain of causality, and to attribute Jesus' death to the machinations of Roman and Jewish powers or to the individual failings and sins—pride, greed, naiveté—of the major personalities involved, namely, Caiaphas, Pilate, and Judas. When Satan appears it's in a human form with an unclear or ambiguous role in the drama. Only on the basis of faith and/or prior knowledge of the Gospels (or of theological interpretations of them), can viewers find God's salvific plan in the biopics' treatment of the passion. Further, even if we know intellectually that, according to the Gospels, God required the death of his Son on the cross, the biopics do not guide us into a transformative or spiritually powerful experience, even when they enact all or some of the stations of the cross, as many of them do.

Fictional films, on the other hand, can explore areas the biopics cannot. Scorsese can take us into the psyche of a man who is disturbed by visions and impulses, whose origins are opaque to him—does he hear the voice of God or the voice of the devil? The director further helps us to see the ways in which those around Jesus simultaneously were attracted to Jesus and misunderstood him, until the final moments when they recognize, just as Jesus does, the terrible truth of God's plan. Arcand allows us to be part of the audience that views Jesus' passion as enacted by Daniel and his troupe, but also to experience how Daniel has affected the lives of those around him. In both cases, the impact is not dependent on the resurrection, but inheres in the crucifixion itself, and the path that leads inexorably toward that event.

The pattern that I have sketched out derives from the role of films in our lives and experience, more than from the narrative and theology of the Gospel accounts themselves. Its principal message, however, may be to the next filmmaker who wishes to bring Jesus' passion to the silver screen. If the aim is simply to recreate a historical narrative that adheres closely to the Gospel accounts and seeks to help the audience envisage Jesus' own era and the political struggles that shaped it, then a biographical film, based, one hopes, on the latest research and archaeological evidence, might be an appropriate vehicle. But if the goal is to move viewers spiritually, that is, to help them (us) understand and feel the power of the gospel message, if only for the moment, then it is necessary to venture from the relative security of the biographical, Gospel-based cinematic conventions and to create a fictional, yet spiritually real viewing experience. All the Roman legions and all the blood in the world will not do as well as films such as Scorsese's *Last Temptation* and Arcand's *Jesus of Montreal* in helping us both to understand and to feel what Jesus might have meant to those who lived in his own time, or the transformative potential that his presence might have had, even if it was not fulfilled, in his time or in our own.

PART V

Other Traditions

The passion narrative is manifestly Christian. But other religious traditions have had to respond to it, both because of its intrinsic importance for inter-religious dialogue and because of the ways Christians have drawn on it in their relations with other religions—especially Judaism and Islam. In the best of times, interactions between Christians and Jews and between Christians and Muslims involve dialogue over the theological interpretations of the passion. In other times—and there have been many—the interactions have been violent. Indeed, the most violent times have seen the most frequent and belligerent references to the passion. Engaging the passion demands that we consider this part of our history.

In his essay "On *Pesach* and *Pascha*: Jews, Christians, and the Passion," Jeremy Cohen raises two poignant issues related to the passion—early Christian attempts to assert the supremacy of Easter (*Pascha*) over Passover (*Pesach*) and Jewish attempts to find meaning in the passion story. His reflections on both issues demonstrate how difficult engaging the passion can be—and how necessary it is. With regard to the first issue, Cohen focuses on the early Christian poem *On the Pascha* (On Easter). Usually attributed to Melito of Sardis (who died in the late-second century), the poem gives voice to the kind of vitriolic attacks Christians sometimes mounted against their Jewish neighbors at the very time both congregations were celebrating their most holy festivals. With regard to the second issue, Cohen draws on stories of Jewish martyrs through the ages, midrash, medieval and modern poetry, and art to illustrate the range of Jewish responses to the passion narrative. His conclusion challenges us to acknowledge and reckon with the myth of the Christ-killers—"with creativity, sensitivity, and above all, courage." This essay and Cohen's book *Christ Killers: The Jews and the Passion from the Bible to the Big Screen* is a good place to start.

Suleiman A. Mourad's essay "The Death of Jesus in Islam" surveys Qur'anic references to the crucifixion and to early, medieval, and modern interpretations of them. Along the way, Mourad introduces readers to the challenges of reading the Qur'an and to the historical and social context of the interpreters. He begins with a brief treatment of the references to Jesus' conception and birth, miracles, and mission—all of which point to his unique status as a prophet. He then looks at the ways Qur'anic references to the passion narrative treat various components of the story: the cross, the hours of darkness, perceptions of the witnesses, ways to understand *death*, and resurrection. Mourad shows that the Qur'an and its interpreters were aware of the stories of the canonical Gospels, some of the apocryphal Gospels, and varying Christian theological interpretations. Two themes run through Muslim treatments of the passion: a concern to defend the belief that God is one and to defend the claim that God always takes care of his prophets.

18

On *Pesach* and *Pascha*

Jews, Christians, and the Passion

Jeremy Cohen

Amidst this anthology of reflections on the passion,[1] reflections that repeatedly lead the reader from the scholarly and analytical to the personal and emotive, my own task concerns a darker side of the long history of engagement with the story of Jesus' trial and crucifixion: the nefarious role that Christian tradition has assigned to the Jews in this, the "greatest story ever told."[2] In *Christ Killers: The Jews and the Passion from the Bible to the Big Screen* (2007), I recently considered

1. Professor Cohen submitted this essay in 2008 for inclusion in this volume as originally planned. I am grateful to him for allowing me to use it in this significantly expanded volume, since it treats the passion from such an important perspective. Except for minor editorial changes, the content and references have not been updated. ED.
2. This essay derives from various studies that I have undertaken in the past: most directly from *Christ Killers: The Jews and the Passion from the Bible to the Big Screen* (New York: Oxford University Press, 2007), especially chapters 2, 3, and 7; secondarily from *Sanctifying the Name of God: Jewish Martyrs and Jewish Memories of the First Crusade* (Philadelphia: University of Pennsylvania Press, 2004); and more indirectly from *Living Letters of the Law: Ideas of the Jew in*

the history of the *myth* of the deicidal Jew, and this essay seeks neither to review nor to summarize the results of that endeavor. Rather, I wish briefly to raise and in a somewhat ruminative manner reflect on questions and issues arising from that study that bear on our present conversation.

As the controversy surrounding Mel Gibson's *The Passion of the Christ* made clear, age-old sensitivities concerning allegations of Jewish responsibility for Jesus' death remain pronounced on both sides of the Jewish-Christian divide. We can surely debate the extent to which Christians still view "the Jews" as deicides. Yet the liberality of educated Christians in the Western world today ought not to obscure the resilience of traditional beliefs in other parts of the world and among other segments of the population. For many Jews, the seemingly groundless hatred toward Jesus that the Gibson movie attributes to them speaks for itself. For many Christians, however, whose religious worldview has taken shape in the context of the post-Holocaust theology and Vatican II, the Jewish Christ killer is a Christian stereotype of the past, and the hypersensitivity and inability of Jews to put that past behind them painfully revitalizes inter-religious animosity and prejudice that otherwise might be bygones. In a word, the complexities of majority-minority relations, past and present, render our subject a particularly loaded one. Any fruitful academic discussion must strive considerately to disentangle itself from this entangling web of preconceptions and misconceptions, while recognizing full well that they lie deep at the heart of who we are and constitute an integral part of our story.

Indeed, the very word *myth*, emphasized in the opening paragraph above, may already have triggered some of those sensitivities among readers of these pages, and it demands several words of explanation.

Medieval Christianity (Berkeley: University of California Press 1999). Readers seeking additional bibliography on the topics considered in this essay can consult these longer studies.

For Christians, the passion comprises not only the greatest story ever told but also the greatest miracle ever to occur throughout all of terrestrial history. And yet, as I find myself explaining repeatedly to my students, historians do not deal in miracles as historical data. Limited by our understanding of the general nature of things, we have neither the tools nor the discursive categories to prove or disprove miracles and to classify them as fact or fiction in our reconstructions of the past. Can we definitively establish the facts of Jesus' last days? Can we prove who really engineered his death? Not with the sources available to us at present. Nonetheless, we are well equipped to deal with *beliefs in* and *stories of* miracles as historical data and events, documentation of the memories and beliefs that formed the very foundations of communities and cultures. Historians of religion label stories of foundationally important miracles "myths" not because they are false or fictional—the common, colloquial usage of *myth* or *mythic*—but expressly because they embody sacred, exemplary, and significant truths for those who tell them, truths that supply models for human behavior and in so doing afford meaning and value to human life. In this respect, the truth-value of myths might well exceed that of historical fact, even if myths defy scientific verification. In the case of the crucifixion, I question how much newly discovered historical information, were there ever to be any, would alter the significance of the myth of the passion for believing Christians.

Communities typically develop processes for ritualizing and reenacting the myths that play a central role in their self-definition, thus allowing for the reassertion of their collective identities on the part of individuals in any generation; and it is precisely through such means for ritualization and reenactment that we find the passion inspiring Jews and Christians to engage one another—and their respective cultures—in an interesting fashion. Here we shall look briefly at two instructive instances of this phenomenon: in a patristic attempt to assert the supremacy of the Christian Pascha/Easter over the Jewish Pesach/Passover; and in Jews' attempts to find meaning in the passion story for themselves. Elaine Pagels has argued persuasively that the anti-Jewish currents in the Gospel narratives of Jesus' life and death derive from intense intimacy of conflict *within* the first-century Jewish community,[3] and so too shall we see that formative moments in the history of the Christ-killer myth frequently derived from the proximity—physical as well as cultural—of Jews, Christians, and their respective religious traditions.

Whether the events that they commemorate occurred when (and how) we imagine, the early weeks of spring offer a singularly fitting time for the holy days of Passover and Easter. Spring bespeaks rebirth and renewal, as do Passover and Easter for Jews and Christians, signifying the momentous occasions that endowed them with their distinctive identities. Passover commemorates the exodus, the miraculous deliverance of the Israelites from their bondage in Egypt, the experience of redemption that molded their national destiny and served as the basis for their covenant with God. The Bible recounts that the ritual sacrifice of the paschal lamb, the Pesach, expedited the liberation and salvation of Pharaoh's Israelite slaves inasmuch as God, when he saw the lamb's blood smeared on the doorways of Israelite homes, passed over (*pasach*) and spared his people while smiting the firstborn sons of Egypt during the last, and most horrendous, of the ten plagues. Not by happenstance does Easter usually fall during the week of Passover; originally they coincided more exactly. Although Easter now commemorates the resurrection of Jesus, it originally

3. Elaine Pagels, "The Social History of Satan, Part II: Satan in the New Testament Gospels," *Journal of the American Academy of Religion* 62 (1994): 17–58; and, more generally, her *The Origin of Satan: The New Testament Origins of Christianity's Demonization of Jews, Pagans and Heretics* (New York: Random House, 1995).

marked the day of his crucifixion, which reportedly occurred either on the first day of the Passover itself (that is, on the fifteenth day of the Hebrew month of Nisan, as in Matthew, Mark, and Luke) or on the previous day ("of preparation of the Passover" sacrifice, as in John 19:14, namely on the fourteenth of Nisan). Easter was *Pascha*, since Jesus was the ultimate *pesach* or paschal lamb of God, whose suffering (*páschein*, as some church fathers who linked the term to *pathein* pointed out)[4] and the sacrifice of whose blood on the cross—its very beams recalled the poles on which the Jews roasted their paschal lamb—offered salvation, new life, and rebirth to those affirming that it freed them from enslavement to sin. Perhaps more than many other sacred times, Passover and Easter assume mythic meaning for Jews and Christians, charting direction, aspirations, and both behavioral and theological norms for a life of communion with God. No wonder that imperatives for ritualization and reenactment lie at the heart of the celebrations of each. Of all the "positive" (that is, the prescriptive "thou shalt") commandments in the Torah, only for two does Scripture ordain a specific punishment (in each case, excision from the community, traditionally understood to mean untimely death) for those who fail to observe them. One of these is the Passover sacrifice and the other circumcision—both of them rituals whose efficacy depends on the drawing of blood.

In the absence of the temple cult, Jews gather annually for a Passover seder, a festive banquet whose menu, rituals, and liturgy recreate the drama of the exodus for those assembled round the table. It does not suffice simply to tell the story and remember, but the participants must internalize and personalize the experience of salvation for themselves. The Passover Haggadah or seder liturgy

4. See C. Mohrmann, "Pascha, Passio, Transitus," *Ephemerides liturgicae* 66 (1952): 37–52, and B. Botte, "Pascha," *L'Orient syrien* 8 (1963): esp. 216ff.—both cited in Melito of Sardis, *On Pascha and Fragments*, ed. Stuart G. Hall (Oxford, UK: Oxford University Press, 1979), 23n.

reaches a climax with the talmudic instruction that "in every generation a person must see himself as if he personally left Egypt." In remarkably Passover-specific imagery—recalling both paschal sacrifice and the unleavened bread (matzah) eaten along with it—the apostle Paul echoed and reformulated the urgency of internalizing the vivifying miracle of the Pascha. Preaching to his flock of new Christian believers on the power of the cross (1 Cor. 5:7), he wrote, "Cleanse out the old leaven that you may be a new lump, as you really are unleavened. For Christ, our paschal lamb [*pascha*] has been sacrificed." Albeit metaphorically, Paul likewise emphasized how salvation in Christ demanded not mere recollection but participation in the experience of the passion:

> For I through the law died to the law, that I might live to God. I have been crucified with Christ; it is no longer I who live, but Christ who lives in me; and the life I now live in the flesh I live by faith in the Son of God, who loved me and gave himself for me. (Gal. 2:19-20)

Set against this background, a critical development in the emerging Christian idea of the Jew as Christ killer finds expression in *On the Pascha*, a work of liturgical poetry for Easter, by the second-century church father Melito. Most scholars have identified Melito as bishop of Sardis, a bustling Lydian city in western Asia Minor where pagans and Jews had lived side by side for several centuries, and where a noteworthy Christian community had recently begun to flourish. (See, for example, Rev. 3:1-6.) We read in a document preserved by Eusebius that Bishop Melito numbered among the Quartodeciman Christians, who, following the tradition of the Gospel of John, celebrated Easter on the fourteenth day of the Hebrew month of Nisan. The Bible had prescribed the late afternoon of this day for sacrificing the paschal lamb, and Jews still convene for the Passover seder early in the ensuing evening (which, in the Jewish liturgical calendar, already marks the beginning of the fifteenth of Nisan and the commencement of the Passover festival). When Melito and his congregation, who would not have reckoned that evening the start of the next day, assembled for their nocturnal Easter vigil, they therefore celebrated their Pascha at the very moment when the Jews of Sardis gathered for their Seder Pesach. And, if one attributes Melito's *On the Pascha* to the bishop of Sardis, one can best appreciate it as composed for precisely this intersection of Jewish and Christian sacred times.

Celebrating the moment of Jesus' passion, *On the Pascha* begins with a retelling of Israel's divinely wrought salvation from Egypt, facilitated by the blood of the paschal sacrifice. But then Melito asks rhetorically: Can one truly suppose that the blood of a sacrificial lamb could serve as the catalyst for so wondrous a miracle? Surely when the angel of the Lord who spared Israel from the smiting of the firstborn saw the slaughtered sheep and their blood, he understood that they signified something far greater: the salvific suffering and self-sacrifice of Jesus on the cross.

> O strange and inexpressible mystery!
>   The slaughter of the sheep was found to be Israel's salvation,
>   and the death of the sheep became the people's life,
>   and the blood won the angel's respect.
>   Tell me angel, what did you respect?
>   The slaughter of the sheep or the life of the Lord?
>   The death of the sheep or the model [*typos*] of the Lord?
>   The blood of the sheep or the Spirit of the Lord?
>   It is clear that your respect was won
>   when you saw the mystery of the Lord occurring in the sheep,
>   the life of the Lord in the slaughter of the lamb,
>   the model [*typos*] of the Lord in the death of the sheep. (31–33)[5]

5. This and all ensuing quotations draw from the edition of Melito cited above; numbers in parentheses refer to stanzas in Melito's poem.

Melito viewed Pesach/Passover as a prefigurative model, a *typos*, of Pascha/Easter. But once Jesus' passion commemorated by the Pascha took place, it rendered Pesach, its antique forerunner, void of all value.

> Once, the slaying of the sheep was precious,
> but it is worthless now because of the life of the Lord;
> the death of the sheep was precious,
> but it is worthless now because of the salvation of the Lord;
> the blood of the sheep was precious,
> but it is worthless now because of the Spirit of the Lord. (44)

The Jews, however, trapped by the limitations of their literalist hermeneutic, failed to understand as God's angel did. When God sent his divine lamb to redeem them, they did not recognize him but slaughtered him instead, just as the Egyptians sought to destroy God's "firstborn son Israel" (as in Exod. 4:22) many centuries earlier.

> It is he that has been murdered.
>
> And where has he been murdered? In the middle of Jerusalem.
>
> By whom? By Israel. (72)

Israel has killed Christ. Melito's liturgical commemoration of the passion makes no mention whatsoever of the Romans. The Jewish people bear collective responsibility for the crucifixion. Invoking a common etymology for the name Israel (*Yisra'el* = *yashur 'El* = he [that] sees God), Melito concluded that it has forfeited its status as God's chosen.

> But you did not turn out to be "Israel";
> you did not "see God,"
> you did not recognize the Lord. (82)

By perpetrating the murder of God, not only did the Jews bring about their own downfall, but they also unwittingly brought God's plan for the salvation of all humankind to fruition. In the passion, Pascha triumphed over Pesach, rendering it null, valueless, void.

Melito of Sardis may well have been the first poet of deicide, as some have suggested,[6] but what motivated him? Surely the close quarters in which Jews and Christians of Sardis lived together contributed to the hatred with which *On the Pascha* denounces the Jews, their treachery, their horrific crime, and their ignominious lot. Paul, the evangelists, and the church fathers who followed in their wake declared that the passion had rendered the law of Moses obsolete; they typically defined their own identity as Christians in contrast to that of a negatively constructed Jewish "other." Still, as Christianity spread throughout the Hellenistic world of the first centuries, many non-Jews took interest in the new religion precisely because it struck them as a Judaism tailor-made for gentiles. For those neither Jewish nor Christian, the similarities between Judaism and Christianity must have vastly outweighed the differences. Both proclaimed faith in the same God, both sanctified the same Scripture, and both looked forward to essentially the same messianic redemption. The former best suited the Jew, the latter, inasmuch as it did not require observance of biblical law, the non-Jew. That said, one can hardly wonder, especially at times of festivals—characterized by participatory ritual that struck many as meaningful, fun, and remindful of Jesus' own life—if many Christians gravitated toward the celebrations in Jewish synagogues and homes. In late-fourth-century Antioch, even after Christianity had become the official religion of the empire, John Chrysostom still preached vehemently

6. Eric Werner, "Melito of Sardis, First Poet of Deicide," *Hebrew Union College Annual* 37 (1966): 191–210.

against the mentality that led Christians, especially at holiday time, to relate to the Jews as if they and their rites were "the real thing."

> Where Christ killers gather, the cross is ridiculed, God blasphemed, the Father unacknowledged, the Son insulted, the grace of the Spirit rejected. . . . In a word, if you admire the Jewish way of life, what do you have in common with us? If the Jewish rites are holy and venerable, our way of life must be false. But if our way is true, as indeed it is, theirs is fraudulent.[7]

A Christian bishop of second-century Sardis could not but have perceived a similar danger. Conversions to Christianity notwithstanding, Sardis's Jewry was itself on the rise during this period, and by the middle of the next century had erected one of the largest, most lavishly built synagogues of the Greco-Roman world. The traditional seder liturgy opens with a declaration of hospitality for all who are hungry to come and participate in this ritual feast. How could Christian laypersons refuse? After all, did not Jesus do precisely this on the eve of his own passion? What better a way to commemorate the Pascha than by celebrating the Pesach? Yet for Melito—as for John Chrysostom two hundred years later—this threatened Christianity at its foundations. Passover and Easter were not compatible but mutually exclusive, binary opposites; as Melito put it, "a speechless lamb was [formerly] precious, but it is worthless now because of the spotless Son." For Melito, charging the Jews with deicide thus entailed considerably more than a matter of historical record. In maintaining the Pesach in face of the Pascha, the Jews of Sardis continued to function as killers of Christ; they subverted the meaning of the passion and rendered the crucifixion of the Christian savior valueless. Melito's typological understanding of the passion

7. John Chrysostom, *Sermons against the Jews* 1.6, trans. (with slight modification) in Wayne A. Meeks and Robert L. Wilken, *Jews and Christians in Antioch in the First Four Centuries of the Common Era* (Missoula, MT: Scholars Press, 1978), 97.

moved not only from Pharaoh's Egypt to Roman Jerusalem, but from Calvary to Sardis. And thus he inveighed against Sardis's Jews:

> And you were making merry
> while he was starving;
> you had wine to drink and bread to eat,
> he had vinegar and gall;
> your face was bright,
> his was downcast;
> you were triumphant,
> he was afflicted;
> you were making music,
> he was being judged;
> you were giving the beat,
> he was being nailed up;
> you were dancing,
> he was being buried;
> you were reclining on a soft couch,
> he in grave and coffin. (80)

Melito's characterizations of how the Jews who killed Jesus behaved—the first lines of the eight verses we have quoted—have no grounding in the Gospels. Yet they do attest to the developing rites of the Passover seder *that Jews were celebrating in very close proximity just as Melito read his inflammatory poem in church*: music, dance, ritualized merriment, eating bread and drinking wine, even "reclining on a soft couch." Pesach threatened Pascha, and Melito's reply was clear. Every time Jews rejoiced at their seder table, they denied the most basic of Christian truths that the observance of Easter witnessed. For Melito, that amounted to nothing less than crucifying Christ, time after time, year after year.

Some investigators have challenged the attribution of *On the Pascha* to a Quartodeciman bishop of second-century Sardis; the evidence, they argue, cannot justify identifying the work with any specific individual, place, or temporal context. Nevertheless, we can still read

On the Pascha as attesting to a need for differentiating Christianity from Judaism, even as the church claimed to have inherited the divine covenant and election from the Jews. For the work espouses what eventually became the normative, orthodox Christian stance on the relationship between Old Testament and New. On the one hand, opposing those Christians eventually remembered as heretics, Melito defies a dualistic (Marcionite) reading of salvation history and the sacred Scripture that records it. There were not, as heretical groups argued, two antagonistic cosmic powers: the creator of the material world and the spiritual God of heaven, who ordained Old and New Testaments, respectively. The one (and only) God of creation ordained both the Law of Moses and the new Christian covenant of grace. Hebrew Scripture elaborates the same prophetic, christological promise of salvation as the Gospel; one must simply interpret it in proper typological fashion. Thus construed, Pesach and Pascha are essentially identical; though grounded in different actual events, the miracles of the exodus and the passion give typological expression to the same understanding of salvation history. On the other hand, Melito needed to defend the integrity, the independence, and the superiority of Christianity relative to Judaism. He needed to demonstrate how the gospel had fulfilled the promise of the law, surpassing it with a truth that rendered its literal significance obsolete and lacking in contemporary relevance. The New Testament realized what the Old Testament had foreshadowed. Just as Melito explained elsewhere[8] how the passion had fulfilled and yet exceeded the promise of the Akedah (the binding of Isaac related in Gen. 22) as the father's ultimate salvific offering of his beloved son—whereas Abraham never in fact sacrificed his son—so too did the salvation of the Pascha

8. Melito, *On Pascha*, 74–75.

achieve and surpass, on a loftier spiritual level, the physical deliverance once offered by the Pesach.

This reading of Melito helps to explain much in *On the Pascha*. From repeated references to the *afikomenos* ("he that comes" to redeem, recalling the slice of matzah that Jews dubbed *afikoman*, designating the flesh of the paschal lamb in the seder liturgy), to a string of synonyms extolling the miracle of deliverance from slavery to freedom, to a list of the miracles that God the redeemer has performed for his people (remarkably similar to that of the poem "Dayenu" still sung by most Jews at their seder), language and contents of *On the Pascha* have led some scholars to consider it a Christian liturgical counterpart to the Passover Haggadah: a celebration of salvation. And yet, Melito's poem at the same time needed to explain why Easter had replaced the Passover, why the rituals of Passover had lost their validity and effect. He answered, in a word, because the Israel of the Pesach no longer saw God. It had thus ceased to be Israel, precisely as it continued to celebrate the rites of the model, even as its sacrificial murder of the Christian savior testified to his true character as the ultimate lamb of God. Robert Wilken has suggested[9] that Melito nowhere concerns himself with historical Jews, only the exemplary faithless people of Israel. Establishing its actions and character as deicidal allowed Melito to portray it as disinherited by the Pascha, just as the Pesach precipitated the downfall of the Egyptians. Those unmarked with the blood of the true lamb of God ceded their elect status, the biblical covenant between God and Israel, to those who affirmed its redemptive power. Christianity had now replaced Judaism in the drama of salvation history. Stereotyping the Jew as the murderer of Christ, *On the*

9. Robert L. Wilken, "Something Greater than the Temple," in William Farmer, ed., *Anti-Judaism and the Gospels* (Harrisburg, PA: Trinity Press International, 1999), 176–202.

Pascha defended the church's Old Testament legacy even as it sought conclusively to divorce itself from the synagogue.

Compared with the ultimate importance of the passion narrative for Christians, what significance has the Christ-killer myth had for Jews? As I noted at the outset, Jews of the past and present have proven quite sensitive—in the eyes of some, hypersensitive—to the suggestion that they bear responsibility for the crucifixion of Jesus. In the first modern Jewish biography of Jesus, Joseph Klausner compared the collective indictment of the Jews for plotting the death of Jesus to a condemnation of all Greeks for the murder of Socrates.

> The Jews, *as a nation*, were far less guilty of the death of Jesus than the Greeks, as a nation, were guilty of the death of Socrates; but who now would think of avenging the blood of Socrates the Greek upon his countrymen, the present Greek race? Yet these nineteen hundred years past the world has gone on avenging the blood of Jesus the Jew upon his countrymen, the Jews, who have already paid the penalty, and still go on paying the penalty in rivers and torrents of blood.[10]

An array of Jewish leaders and organizations has campaigned against the passion play at Oberammergau, with but slight success. And Abraham Foxman, director of the Anti-Defamation League of B'nai B'rith, expressed genuine fear as the release of Mel Gibson's *The Passion* approached: "We are deeply concerned that the film, if released in its present form, could fuel the hatred, bigotry and anti-Semitism that many churches have worked hard to repudiate."[11]

In the face of the accusation of deicide and the concerns that it generated, Jewish scholars over the course of time developed various

10. Joseph Klausner, *Jesus of Nazareth: His Life, Times, and Teaching*, trans. Herbert Danby (New York: MacMillan, 1925), 348.

11. "ADL Concerned Mel Gibson's 'Passion' Could Fuel Anti-Semitism if Released in Present Form," *Anti-Defamation League*, August 11, 2003, www.adl.org/PresRele/ASUS_12/4291_12.htm.

alternative strategies for defending themselves. They argued that, in presenting himself as messiah and son of God, Jesus transgressed against Jewish law and deserved the punishment that he received. They claimed that if Jesus' death constituted the "good news" of the salvation of humankind, as Christianity proclaims, then the Jews deserve thanks, not condemnation, for causing it. Indeed, did not Christian doctrine teach that God willed the sacrifice of his son on the cross? Some cited Jesus' prayer to God to forgive his crucifiers, "for they know not what they do" (Luke 23:34); did God not heed that prayer and forgive them? The same passage suggested that the Jews did not intend to kill their savior and should therefore not be judged responsible for having done so. Others flatly denied a key role in the crucifixion, claiming that the Romans, not the Jews, did the deed.

Curiously, one conceivable claim has rarely, if ever, appeared in this arsenal of defensive arguments: that the events of Jesus' arrest, trial, and crucifixion never occurred. Jews of late antiquity, the Middle Ages, and modern times have rarely discredited the essential plotline of the Gospels' passion narrative, even as they have rejected the Christian understanding and interpretation of that narrative. On the contrary, the passion narrative has repeatedly evoked ambivalent responses on the part of Jews through the ages: defensiveness on the one hand, engagement with the power of the myth and its symbols on the other. Beyond those moved by the Gospel narrative to convert to Christianity, Jews have sought to appropriate the power of the cross for themselves, reformulating its message to suit their contemporary circumstances and needs. Much as the frequently intimate proximity between Jews and Christians—or that between Jewish and Christian traditions—moved Melito to claim proprietary rights to the Pascha and the deliverance that it brought, so have Jews periodically reclaimed Jesus and the edifying messages of his passion. Two examples must suffice.

When bands of armed warriors attacked the Jewish communities of the Rhineland as the First Crusade got under way in the spring of 1096, many Jews opted to die a martyr's death rather than submit to forced conversion to Christianity; some, in fact, killed themselves and their loved ones before they fell into the hands of their attackers. Those who survived the pogroms understandably construed those martyrs as having emerged victorious in their confrontation with the Christian enemy: they did not abandon God or their faith. They proved themselves the true martyrs of God, martyrs whose awesome self-sacrifice facilitated their immediate entry to paradise and accrued merit for the entire community—objectives very similar to those of the crusaders, who strove to avenge and to emulate what their Martyr par excellence had suffered at the hands of the infidel. Simply put, the Jewish martyrologists remembered their slain heroes as having outmatched the crusaders at their own game. Consider the tale they told of one mother who slaughtered her four children minutes before the crusaders could apprehend them.[12]

> Who ever witnessed the like of this? Who ever heard of something like the deed of this righteous, pious woman, the young Mistress Rachel, daughter of Rabbi Isaac ben Rabbi Asher, wife of Rabbi Judah. She said to her companions, "I have four children. Even on them have no mercy, lest these uncircumcised ones come and take them alive and they be maintained in their error. . . ." One of her companions came and took the knife to slay her son, and when the children's mother saw the knife she burst into wild and bitter sobbing, and she struck her face and her breast, saying, "O Lord, where is your steadfast love?" The woman took the lad, small and very pleasant as he was, and slaughtered him, and the mother stretched out her arms to receive their blood, and she received the blood in her sleeves instead of in the chalice of blood.[13]

12. I have dealt at length with this story and its interpretation in chapter 6 of my *Sanctifying the Name of God* (106–29).
13. A. M. Habermann, *Gezerot Ashkenaz ve-Tzarefat* (Jerusalem: Tarshish, 1945), 34.

The story continues, but this brief passage will prove sufficient for the moment. We read that one of Rachel's children was named Isaac, recalling the biblical story of the *Akedah*, the binding and unconsummated sacrifice of the patriarch Isaac by his father Abraham. Christians interpreted the *Akedah* as a prototype of the crucifixion, God the father's sacrifice of his son, a prototype that blatantly demonstrated the completeness of the New Testament as opposed to the Old, inasmuch as Jesus died a martyr's death while the bound Isaac of Genesis did not. No wonder that various rabbinic voices, expressed in midrash and in liturgical poetry (*piyyut*) of the Middle Ages, dared to suggest that the blood of Isaac had in fact been shed on the altar, thereby reclaiming the true sacrifice of the son by his father for the Jews. But our story of Mistress Rachel of Mainz in 1096 ventured further still, as evidenced in the curious notation that "the mother stretched out her arms to receive their blood, and she received the blood in her sleeves instead of in the chalice of blood." A goblet or bowl of blood (*mizrak dam*), much like the sacrificial knife (*ma'akhelet*) that the Bible describes Abraham as brandishing in order to slaughter Isaac, recalls the rituals of the temple in Jerusalem and thereby presents Rachel's offerings as truly efficacious sacrifices to God. But a woman (who could not officiate in the temple) raising her arms and sleeves to catch the blood in a makeshift goblet evokes images of the crucifixion at one and the same time, as shown in an ivory from the eleventh-century Rhineland (see image on p. 353), precisely the provenance of the pogroms of 1096. In this well-known motif, under the extremities of the crucified Jesus' outstretched arms stand two women: Synagoga, the embodiment of the old law, of Israel of the flesh, under Jesus' left arm; Ecclesia, Holy Mother Church, personifying the new covenant of grace, under his right arm. In many such representations, as in this one, Ecclesia raises her arms (and sleeves) to capture the blood of the crucified

Christ, for this blood will bring salvation to her faithful children. As depicted in the Hebrew text, Rachel does much the same. She resembles not Synagoga but Ecclesia, with raised arms, her sleeves a makeshift chalice to collect and offer the blood of her sacrificed children.

At the end of this horrific scene, after Rachel kills the last of her children, we read that "she then placed them on her lap in her two arms, two on one side and two on the other, and they were writhing on her until the enemy took the room, and they found her sitting and lamenting over them."[14] Another eleventh-century Christian work of ivory from the Rhine valley (see image on p. 354) depicts a seated woman, surrounded by her female companions, bewailing a slain child who lies in her lap; in the background looms a city in ancient Judea. This grieving mother is none other than Rachel herself, recalled early in the Gospel of Matthew, where King Herod, having heard of the birth of the king of the Jews, orders the slaughter of newly born Jewish boys in Bethlehem:

> Then Herod, when he saw that he had been tricked by the wise men, was in a furious rage, and he sent and killed all the male children in Bethlehem and in all that region who were two years old or under. . . . Then was fulfilled what was spoken by the prophet Jeremiah: "A voice was heard in Ramah, wailing and loud lamentation, Rachel weeping for her children; she refused to be consoled, because they were no more." (2:16–18)

14. Ibid.

The Crucifixion of Jesus: Synagoga and Ecclesia, mid-eleventh century, ivory.

The Slaughter of the Innocents: Rachel Weeping Over Her Children, eleventh century, ivory.

Christians viewed the Rachel of Jeremiah's prophecy as their own no less than medieval Jews did. Like the innocent children of Judea, she died—and was buried—in Bethlehem. Her voice fittingly lamented their deaths, which heralded the birth of the messiah in Bethlehem, his passion in Jerusalem, and the suffering and salvation in the history of the church that would follow. The Hebrew chronicle even depicts Rachel in terms reminiscent of the Virgin Mary, labeling her *bachurah*, a term for a young maiden that the Bible uses to suggest a virgin, and depicting her husband and her children's father as not much of a husband or father. Our story demonstrates how Jewish memory could revere and construct its martyrs of the Crusade in terms that virtually ritualized and reenacted Jesus' passion, appropriating it and its power for themselves, and thus denying its efficacy for their Christian enemies.

The Jewish reclamation of Jesus has gained momentum in more recent centuries, as Jews have sought to emphasize the affinities between themselves and the Christian culture around them in order to secure entry and legitimacy in a distinctly modern world. Even as they continued to deny responsibility for the crucifixion, writers and artists found meaning and inspiration in Jesus' passion for Jews confronting their modern predicament. The sculptor Mark Antokolsky, for instance, and the painter Marc Chagall not only portrayed Jesus as a Jew but also identified with him and his suffering on a personal level. "Like Christ," Chagall wrote retrospectively and introspectively decades after World War II, "I am crucified, fixed with nails to the easel."[15] Writers of short fiction such as Shalom Asch and Avigdor Hameiri transformed Jesus into a Jewish historical character, not merely in the first century but in later periods as well. The Jewish nationalist poet Uri Zvi Greenberg (1896–1981) also fixated on the image of the crucified Jesus, as he wrestled with the state of his fellow Jews during the decades that spanned the eastern European pogroms, the horrors of World War I, and Hitler's Final Solution. In 1923, one year before he left Europe for the land of Israel, Greenberg published his "Uri Zvi farn Tzeylem" ("Uri Zvi in Front of the Cross"), a Yiddish poem in the shape of a cross (see image on p. 356) topped by the capital letters from above the Christian crucifix, INRI—the Latin initials for "Jesus of Nazareth, King of the Jews." Like other Jewish writers, Greenberg claimed Jesus for the Jews. Yet in unusually distinctive fashion, he railed against Jesus' own betrayal of his Jewish heritage. Over centuries of Christian history Jesus has

15. Ziva Amishai-Meisels, "The Jewish Jesus," *Journal of Jewish Art* 9 (1982): 102–103.

forgotten his Jewish origins, and with them he has lost any sense of kinship with his tormented brothers and sisters.

אורי צבי
פארן צלם
I N R I

“Uri Zvi in Front of the Cross.” *Collected Yiddish Works* (Jerusalem: Magnes, 1975), 2:432.

The crucified Jesus has grown ever more aloof to the suffering of Jews at his feet: a pile of severed Jewish heads, tattered prayer shawls, stabbed parchments, bloodstained shrouds. Greenberg the Jew may well have identified with Jesus—"each morning I am nailed up anew on the burning red crucifix"—but Jesus heeds him not:

> You've become inanimate, brother Jesus. For two thousand years you've been tranquil on the cross. All around you the world expires. Damn it, you've forgotten everything. Your petrified brain can't grasp: a Star of David at your head, over the star, hands in priestly blessing; under them, olive groves and ethrog [citron] gardens.[16]

Olive groves and citron gardens bespeak idyllic longings for the Holy Land, for there and only there, the Zionist Greenberg hinted, can a Jew internalize the power of the passion as one should.

Other writers in this volume testify to the resolve with which believing Christians have reformulated the passion narrative so as to internalize it, reenact it, and situate their own place within it. Here I have suggested that this pattern of reenactment derives from the mythic nature of the passion narrative itself, and in the connection between Pascha and Pesach, Christian Easter and Jewish Passover, in particular. The redemption proffered in the stories of the exodus from Egypt and the crucifixion of Jesus depends on symbolic participation in the miraculous events they depict, and this dependency has resulted in the ritualization of both stories by Jews and Christians, a creative process that naturally continues as one society, generation, or local culture gives rise to the next.

The limited scope of this essay has allowed for but little consideration of the actual role attributed to the Jew in the passion narrative. Yet one may not forget that the stories of Pesach and Pascha have their villains and their heroes, and their efficacy as myths flows directly from the condemnation of the former and the resulting triumph of the latter. The narratives and rituals of Passover and Easter

16. Quoted in David G. Roskies, *Against the Apocalypse: Responses to Catastrophe in Modern Jewish Culture* (Cambridge, MA: Harvard University Press, 1984), 268.

have defined their constituencies in contrast to evil, demonic others; and, in the case of the passion, that evil, demonic other is the Jewish killer of Christ. Rather than ignore it, contemporary engagement with the passion must acknowledge and reckon with this fact: with creativity, sensitivity, and, above all, courage. The consequences of demonizing Jews as Christ-killers have proven cataclysmic, and the challenges that it poses just never seem to go away.

19

The Death of Jesus in Islam

Reality, Assumptions, and Implications

Suleiman A. Mourad

The Qur'an refers to Jesus in ways that leave no doubt he enjoyed a special status in the eyes of Muhammad and his direct followers. As one of God's prominent messengers[1]—a distinguished list that includes Abraham, Moses, Jesus, and Muhammad—the Qur'anic Jesus is a human (Qur'an 4:172; 5:75), although unique in many ways, even so among prophets (Qur'an 2:253). One example of this is the

1. The Islamic tradition classifies prophets into two types. The first type is *nabī* (prophet) and includes such names as Adam, Noah, Sarah, David, Solomon, John the Baptist, and Mary. The second type is *rasūl* (messenger), and it signifies a prophet who was entrusted with a scripture. Hence, messengers are above prophets in that their responsibilities were not restricted to delivering the usual signs or warnings and summoning people to God, but they were also charged with starting new religions. Hence, Moses, Jesus, and Muhammad are the messengers and their messages are the Torah/Judaism, the Gospel/Christianity, and the Qur'an/Islam, respectively. Abraham, too, belongs to this distinguished list on accounts of the covenant and his special presentation in the Qur'an as the "first" monotheist (*hanif*). On the prophets in the Qur'an, see Brannon Wheeler, *Prophets in the Quran: An Introduction to the Quran and Muslim Exegesis* (London: Continuum, 2002).

fact that the Qur'anic Jesus had no human father. In this respect, the Qur'an upholds the virgin birth of Jesus and furnishes three annunciation stories. The first annunciation story appears in Qur'an 19:16-35, where a "spirit" from God proclaims to Mary that she will conceive a son; this story parallels the one found in Luke 1:26-35. The second annunciation story appears in Qur'an 3:42-49, where an angel tells Mary that she will conceive of God's word (*kalima*); this second story parallels the one in the apocryphal *Protoevangelium of James* 11:1-3.[2] A very brief third annunciation story in Qur'an 21:91 states that God blew his spirit into Mary's womb, hence she conceived Jesus. These stories do not necessarily reflect confusion in the Qur'an regarding the circumstances of Jesus' conception and the way it was caused. Qur'anic language in this respect is in agreement with examples from the Bible and the Gospels.[3]

The three Qur'anic annunciation stories attest to something that is supernatural about Jesus and one can even say unique to him. This is especially the case if they are read along such descriptions of Jesus as a word (*kalima*) from God (Qur'an 3:45; 4:171), and a spirit (*ruh*) from God (Qur'an 4:171). In addition, God empowered Jesus with the Holy Spirit (*ruh al-qudus*), as in:

> And We bestowed clear wonders upon Jesus son of Mary, and strengthened him with the Holy Spirit. (Qur'an 2:253)[4]

The uniqueness of Jesus among prophets is further attested in the miracle stories listed in the Qur'an, such as him speaking while still

2. On the similarity between these two Qur'anic annunciation stories and the Christian texts noted above, see Suleiman A. Mourad, "On the Qur'anic Stories about Mary and Jesus," *Bulletin of the Royal Institute for Inter-Faith Studies* 1, no. 2 (1999): 13–24.
3. For instance, in the binding of Isaac story in Gen. 22, God and God's angel are used interchangeably to indicate the one who was conversing with Abraham. Also, the Gospels furnish variant annunciation/birth narratives for Jesus, as in Matt. 1–2, Luke 1–2, and John 1.
4. See also 2:87 and 2:253. All quotations from the Qur'an are based on *The Qur'an*, trans. Tarif Khalidi (New York: Penguin Books, 2009).

an infant in the cradle (Qur'an 3:46; 5:110), which appears in the apocryphal *Arabic Infancy Gospel* 1; creating birds from clay (Qur'an 3:49; 5:110), which appears in the apocryphal *Infancy Story of Thomas* 2:1-5; and raising people from the dead (Qur'an 3:49; 5:110), which is encountered in Gospel stories such as the raising of Jairus's daughter (Mark 5:21-43) and of Lazarus (John 11:1-44).

Despite the tremendous significance of such a presentation of Jesus in the Qur'an, it is misleading to understand it and the terms that are used as echoing Christian beliefs or Christian definitions. To a Christian audience, such a presentation and theologically loaded terms—especially Jesus as *Logos* (Word of God) and Holy Spirit—attest to or assume Jesus' divinity. But to a Muslim audience this is absolutely not the case. The Qur'an categorically rejects Jesus' divinity (e.g., Qur'an 2:116; 6:101; 10:68; 18:4; 112:3), and on more than one occasion, it warns against those who say that Jesus is God (Qur'an 5:17; 5:72), God's son (e.g., Qur'an 4:171; 9:30; 19:35), or ought to be worshipped alongside God (e.g. Qur'an 5:116; 9:31). Moreover, despite the fact that the Qur'anic Jesus is presented as having no father, it is clear that he is the son of Mary. He is called Jesus son of Mary (e.g., Qur'an 5:114; 61:6), the Messiah Jesus son of Mary (*al-Masih 'Isa ibn Maryam*) (e.g., Qur'an 3:45; 4:171), the Messiah son of Mary (*al-Masih ibn Maryam*) (e.g., Qur'an 5:17; 5:75), or simply the Messiah (*al-Masih*) (e.g., Qur'an 4:172). The Qur'anic Jesus is therefore human.

Now with respect to the mission of Jesus, the Qur'an defines it as furnishing the link between Judaism and Islam. On the one hand, Jesus was sent to the Jews to confirm to them the veracity and applicability of the Torah. On the other hand, he was delegated with the announcement of the advent of Muhammad:

> Remember when Jesus son of Mary said: "Children of Israel, I am the

> messenger of God to you, confirming what preceded me of the Torah, and I bring you glad tidings of a messenger to come after me called Ahmad." When he brought them wonders they said: "This is sorcery manifest." (Qur'an 61:6)

Some Muslim scholars have taken this Qur'anic pronouncement as a confirmation that Christianity was a temporary religion to bridge the period from the time of Jesus until the advent of Muhammad.[5]

There is one additional mission for Jesus that is indicated in the Qur'an, and which in my opinion accounts for the serious division between Islam and Christianity regarding the dispute over Jesus (i.e., human vs. divine). The Qur'an describes Jesus as the "portent of the Hour" (43:61), and this description has been understood to mean that Jesus will return before the Day of Resurrection to finish his two-part mission.[6] In this respect, the Muslims believe that the Qur'an is identifying an "Islamic" future role for Jesus, and the implication is that Jesus ceased to be a mere "Christian" figure. He is also an Islamic figure, which explains why Muslims feel obliged not only to claim him but also to challenge and correct the Christians' belief about his divinity.[7]

The Passion Narrative (Death on the Cross) in the Qur'an

Yet, of all the Qur'anic material related to Jesus, nothing is as perplexing and confusing as the passion narrative, particularly the

5. See for instance Sayyid Qutb, *Social Justice in Islam*, trans. John B. Hardie (Oneonta, NY: Islamic Publications International, 2000), 317.
6. The Day of Resurrection is the preferable Islamic term that is used to indicate the resurrection of all creation to face judgment at the End of Times. On the return of Jesus before the Day of Resurrection, see, for instance, Suleiman A. Mourad, "Jesus according to Ibn 'Asakir," in *Ibn 'Asakir and Early Islamic History*, ed. James E. Lindsay (Princeton, NJ: Darwin Press, 2001), 31–37.
7. I am not here ignoring the fact that the Qur'an and Islam claim that all the prophets of God were Muslims. But we need to understand that in the sense of the original meaning of the term *Muslim*, that is, one who submits himself/herself to God and follows God's commands and law.

issue of Jesus' death on the cross. What the Qur'an says about it has been examined in modern scholarship, mostly by scholars engaged in religious dialogue or polemics.[8] One reason for the interest is the popular conviction that the Qur'an denies the crucifixion and death of Jesus. The belief is that the Qur'an upholds not only that Jesus did not die on the cross, but that he never experienced death while in this world. Muslim polemicists take this as proof that Christians are wrong and have invented the crucifixion narrative and inserted it into their revealed Scripture, thus corrupting it. Christian polemicists, however, take it as proof that Islam is misinformed, and thus could not have been a true religion revealed by God.

This presumed Qur'anic denial is tied precisely to a pair of verses (Qur'an 4:157–58), and it places Islam's scripture in direct contrast with the foundational dogma of the Christian faith. The text of these two verses reads,

> And their saying: "It is we who killed the Christ Jesus son of Mary, the messenger of God"—they killed him not, nor did they crucify him, but so it was made to appear to them. Those who disputed concerning him are in doubt over the matter; they have no knowledge thereof but only follow conjecture. Assuredly, they killed him not, but God raised him up to Him, and God is Almighty.

This is the only place in the Qur'an where the issue of Jesus' crucifixion is raised. Examples from the Islamic tradition demonstrate that although Muslim scholars have overwhelmingly rejected the

8. See for example, E. E. Elder, "The Crucifixion in the Koran," *Muslim World* 13 (1923): 242–58; Henri Michaud, *Jésus selon le Coran* (Neuchâtel: Delachaux et Niestlé, 1960), 59–71; Geoffrey Parrinder, *Jesus in the Qur'an* (New York: Oxford University Press, 1977), 105–21; Mahmoud M. Ayoub, "Towards an Islamic Christology, 2: The Death of Jesus—Reality or Illusion?" *The Muslim World* 70 (1980): 91–121; Giuseppe Rizzardi, *Il problema della cristologia coranica* (Milan: Istituto Propaganda Libraria, 1982), 141–43; Nilo Geagea, *Mary in the Koran: A Meeting Point between Christianity and Islam*, trans. and ed. Lawrence T. Fares (New York: Philosophical Library, 1984), 107–8; and A. H. Mathias Zahniser, "The Forms of Tawaffa in the Qur'an: A Contribution to Christian-Muslim Dialogue," *Muslim World* 79, no. 1 (1989): 14–24.

crucifixion of Jesus, they are sharply divided regarding the reality of his death. The possibility that Jesus actually died and was raised from death, shortly after the crucifixion (not his though), was argued by a number of leading early Muslim exegetes and became an essential view within the Islamic tradition.[9] This shows that, on the one hand, the way the Qur'an addresses Jesus' death allows for conflicting interpretations, and, on the other hand, what is perceived as the popular position in Islam—namely that Jesus did not die—is essentially favored by some Muslim and non-Muslim circles because it is rooted in Christian-Muslim polemics aiming at legitimizing one's own religion and proving the other religion wrong.

In this paper, I will offer my personal reflections on the passion narrative in an attempt to show that the denial in the Qur'an is not made to the reality of the crucifixion and death of Jesus, but rather to their theological implications. In other words, the Qur'an is looking beyond the crucifixion. Jesus' end was not death on the cross, but rather resurrection from death to eternal life. Moreover, I will argue that the theological basis under which the Qur'an operates was not as developed as that of the Islamic tradition later. Hence, Muslim scholars reflected on the issues of Jesus' crucifixion and death under a set of assumptions and in ways that exceed what the Qur'anic text says; these assumptions include the conviction that the traditional Christian passion narrative and its saving significance, as believed by Christians, are false.

Did the Qur'anic Jesus die?

I start my examination of the death of Jesus in the Qur'an with verse 3:55, which reads,

9. See, for example, the discussion in Neal Robinson, *Christ in Islam and Christianity* (Albany: State University of New York Press, 1991), 117–26.

> Remember when God said: "O Jesus, I shall cause you to die [*mutawaffik*] and make you ascend to Me. I shall purify you from those who blasphemed, and I shall raise those who followed you above those who blasphemed until the Day of Resurrection. Then to Me is your return, and I shall judge between you concerning that in which you disputed."

What concerns us here is the first sentence, "O Jesus, I shall cause you to die [*mutawaffik*] and make you ascend to Me." As witnessed by the debate in Islamic scholarship,[10] it has been very challenging to interpret the expression *mutawaffik* (from the root-verb *t-w-f*, commonly understood to mean to die), especially as linked to what comes next, "make you ascend to Me." What does *mutawaffik* mean? Several explanations have been offered, which can be summed up as follows. Some exegetes argued that God caused sleep to overcome Jesus and then raised him up to himself; hence the meaning of *mutawaffik* in their opinion is to be overcome by sleep. Other exegetes argued that verse 3:55 indicates the removing of Jesus from this world to the next world without death; here *mutawaffik* means that Jesus' time on earth came to an end. A third view maintained that *mutawaffik* implies the future death of Jesus, and that the words in verse 3:55 and their implications should not be understood to follow the exact sequence in which they occur. Hence they propose the following order: God will first raise Jesus up to heaven, then he will bring him down to earth in the future, when he will die. Essentially, all three positions reject the belief that Jesus died in the past. A fourth view, however, acknowledged that *mutawaffik* means indeed the death of Jesus, and that the verse also indicates his subsequent raise from death by God that occurred in the past.[11]

10. See the survey of Muslim exegetical sources in Benjamin T. Lawson, "The Crucifixion of Jesus in the Qur'an and Qur'anic Commentary: A Historical Survey," *Bulletin of Henry Martyn Institute of Islamic Studies* 10, no. 2 (1991): 34–62 and 10, no. 3 (1991): 6–40.

The promoters of the first three positions articulated them in light of their belief that God would not have left his prophets unprotected, and could not have allowed Jesus to be killed by his enemies. This belief is anchored in one of Islam's foundational dogmas, namely the belief in God's prophets, in God's ability to guide and protect them, and in the linear progression of God's messages and messengers. Therefore, in their efforts to explain away any possibility that God did not come to the rescue of Jesus, some Muslim exegetes maintained that God indeed prevented Jesus' death by interfering and lifting him up to heaven. Someone else was crucified in his place. Moreover, the view that Jesus was removed from this world without physical death was justified on the basis of a prophetic hadith that speaks of the return of Jesus to kill the antichrist, after which he will die and be buried by the Muslims in a grave next to Muhammad.[12] This hadith speaks of the future death of Jesus. Thus, there could not have been a past death, for no human can die twice since God creates humans, causes them to die, then resurrects them. Jesus can die once, and his death must be in the future.

But one notices straightaway that the hadith in question belongs to anti-Christian polemical literature; it was purportedly uttered by Muhammad when a Christian delegation from Najran (a region in western Arabia, south of Mecca) came to him and had an argument with him over the crucifixion of Jesus.[13] The prophet refuted them by pointing to the future return of Jesus. But the alleged circumstances of this hadith do not fit with the language of verses 4:157-58. To

11. For these views and their promoters, see for example al-Tabari (d. 310/922), *Jami' al-bayan fi ta'wil al-Qur'an* (Beirut: Dar al-Kutub al-'Ilmiyya, 1992), 3:288–90; al-Jishumi (d. 494/1101), *al-Tahdhib fi fafsir al-Qur'an* (Milan: Ms. Ambrosiana Library, F184 n.d.), f. 40a; and al-Razi (d. 606/1210), *al-tafsir al-kabir* (Beirut: Dar al-Kutub al-'Ilmiyya, 1992), 8:59–63.

12. See Mourad, "Jesus according to Ibn 'Asakir," 38.

13. See for example al-Tabari, *Jami' al-bayan*, 3:290.

assume so would imply that there were Christians who asserted in public that they killed Jesus, which is absurd, to say the least.

Moreover, the direct context of verses 4:157-58 clearly blames the Jews for crucifying and killing Jesus—such an accusation reflects Christian polemics against the Jews rather than an actual Jewish group living at the time of Muhammad or that of Jesus.[14] Qur'an 4:155 denounces the Jews for breaking their covenant with God and for killing God's prophets. The only example that the Qur'an lists following the accusation that the Jews killed God's prophets is the case of Jesus. So from the outset, one has to operate in the context that the Qur'an is listing the death of Jesus as evidence that the Jews killed him. Otherwise, if the Jews did not kill Jesus, then the Qur'anic charge that they killed God's prophets is baseless, to say the least.

As for the adherents of the fourth view, they also upheld that God came to the rescue of Jesus only from crucifixion. Jesus' death in this world occurred and was not prevented, though it was not caused by crucifixion. They articulated their position in light of the common meaning of the expression *mutawaffik*, namely that God caused Jesus to die, and that the raising to heaven, which refers to Jesus' resurrection, could only occur if preceded by his death. Yet they disagreed as to the nature of that resurrection: whether only in spirit or both in spirit and body.

Let's now turn to the issue of the crucifixion in verse 4:157. Unlike the disagreement among Muslim scholars regarding Jesus' death as seen above, they were in complete agreement in denying his crucifixion, although they offered differing explanations of what actually happened. The most popular explanation is that God rescued Jesus from crucifixion by making someone else look like him, and it

14. See, for instance, Jerome's words "after they killed the servants of God, and finally his Son": Yoram Tsafrir, "70-638: The Temple-less Mountain," in *Where Heaven and Earth Meet: Jerusalem's Sacred Esplanade*, ed. Oleg Grabar and Benjamin Z. Kedar (Jerusalem: Yad Ben-Zvi, and Austin: University of Texas Press, 2009), 86.

was that person who ended up crucified (again there is disagreement on the identity of that person). Another less popular explanation argues that one of Jesus' disciples volunteered to be crucified in his place.[15] But even the most popular view had its share of problems, as its theological implications could not be, according to some exegetes, sustainable. For instance, the philosopher al-Razi (d. 606/1210),[16] in his exegesis of the Qur'an, rejects the possibility that God could have made someone else look like Jesus, for that would inevitably lead to doubting the certainty of everything, including faith.[17] In other words, al-Razi's conundrum is: how can one be certain of anything if its reality is different from its apparent manifestation?

To put the debate in Qur'anic exegesis aside and return to verses 4:157-58, one notices that the emphasis throughout is on denying the death of Jesus, much more so than his crucifixion. Indeed, verse 4:157 starts with the claim that "the Jews" say they killed Jesus, and the retort to them at the end of verse 4:158 asserts that Jesus is not dead because God raised him from death to himself.

Let's examine further the entire parts of verses 4:157-58, as this can explain to us the Qur'anic language and the logic of the argument that the Qur'an is making. Again, the text of the two verses reads,

> And their saying: "It is we who killed the Christ Jesus son of Mary, the messenger of God"—they killed him not, nor did they crucify him, but so it was made to appear to them. Those who disputed concerning him are in doubt over the matter; they have no knowledge thereof but only follow conjecture. Assuredly, they killed him not, but God raised him up to Him, and God is Almighty.

15. For a range of these views, see al-Tabari, *Jami' al-bayan*, 4:351–55; and al-Razi, *al-Tafsir al-kabir*, 11:79–81.
16. When two dates appear in this essay, the first refers to the Islamic (Hijri) calendar; the second refers to the Western (Gregorian) calendar. The Islamic calendar begins in 622 C.E. of the Western calendar, the year of Muhammad's journey from Mecca to Medina. ED.
17. See al-Razi, *al-Tafsir al-kabir*, 11:79.

Clearly, the claim that "'It is we who killed the Christ Jesus son of Mary, the messenger of God'" is followed by the denial of both the killing and the crucifying of Jesus: "they killed him not, nor did they crucify him." The pair "kill"/"crucify" (*qatl/salb*) occurs twice in the Qur'an: the first instance is here in verse 4:157 and the second in verse 5:33, which prescribes the punishment in this world for those who fight Muhammad—be killed or crucified, have their limbs cut, or homelessness. My argument is that Qur'anic crucifixion (*salb*) means not only the act itself, but its consequence, and ought to be rendered as "death by crucifixion." Consequently, I suggest that one needs to read that part of verse 4:157 in the following way: *they did not kill him by crucifixion.*

Following the denial that Jesus was killed we find the explanation "but so it was made to appear to them" (*shubbiha lahum*). This expression means that something was made to appear to those who thought Jesus died on the cross, which is not true. It does not mean that someone was made to look like someone else. The Qur'an uses derivatives of the same root *sh-b-h* to indicate confusion and ambiguity, like in verse 3:7:

> It is He who sent down the Book upon you. In it are verses precise in meaning; these are the very heart of the Book. Others are ambiguous [*mutashabihat*]. Those in whose heart is waywardness pursue what is ambiguous therein [*ma tashabaha minhu*], seeking discord and seeking to unravel its interpretation. But none knows its interpretation save God, while those deeply rooted in knowledge say: "We believe in it. All is from our Lord." Yet none remembers save those possessed of minds.

It is clear given Qur'anic usage that *shubbiha lahum* signifies that something taken at face value as true leads to confusion and error. So, the expression *shubbiha lahum* in verse 4:157 can—and in my opinion does—only make sense if it contests the claim that Jesus' crucifixion led to his death. It is absurd to assume that the expression indicates someone else who was made to look like Jesus and was crucified, for it clearly refers to something that was mentioned earlier in the text. But prior to that expression only the crucifixion and death of Jesus were mentioned. It is equally absurd to argue that Jesus was made to look like someone else. This essentially leaves us with the possibility that the expression either denies the actuality of the crucifixion or asserts that Jesus is not dead as a result of his crucifixion.

Then verse 4:157 goes on to say, "Those who disputed *fihi* are in doubt *minhu*; they have no knowledge thereof but only follow conjecture." The terms *fihi* and *minhu* cannot be references to a person who was crucified in lieu of Jesus, for then this part of the verse would actually make the Qur'an deny that someone else was crucified in place of Jesus. Moreover, they could not be references to Jesus. Both refer to the same thing. If we accept that they refer to Jesus, then this part argues, *Those who disputed about Jesus are in doubt about Jesus*, which makes no sense. We only have a logical meaning if we read it as a reference to the crucifixion and understand this part of verse 4:157 as an added emphasis that what appeared to them (those who believed they killed Jesus by crucifixion) is a matter of false perception. In other words, *Those who disputed about the crucifixion are in doubt about the crucifixion.* This is especially the case given what comes next: "Assuredly, they killed him not, but God raised him up to Him." The Qur'an therefore is questioning the certainty (*yaqin*) of Jesus' death; note that there is no denial of the act of crucifixion in verse 4:158. And why is Jesus not dead in certainty? Because "God raised him up to Him." In other words, the verse is saying that one might think Jesus was killed by crucifixion, but he was not, because he was raised from death, and he is alive with God. Hence, those who asserted that he died on the cross, on the basis of what they saw, are wrong.

So I suggest the following translation for verses 4:157–58:

> They allege: "We have killed the Messiah Jesus son of Mary, the messenger of God." Nay, they did not kill him by crucifying him. They thought they did, and those who affirm that are confused; they have no knowledge about it except by speculation. In certainty they did not kill him because God raised him from death up to Himself.

In support of this interpretation is the fact that the contrasting of perception and certainty regarding one being dead or alive is addressed elsewhere in the Qur'an, as in verse 3:169:

> Do not imagine those killed in the path of God to be dead. Rather, they are alive with their Lord, enjoying His bounty.

There is no way here to argue that the Qur'an is saying that those who were killed fighting in the path of God did not die. They died indeed. But once they were raised from death, it is not proper anymore to refer to them as being dead. Clearly then, the Qur'an cautions against judging on the basis of apparent perceptions, which can be completely misleading; the misleading perception in this case is to say that someone is dead when he or she is alive in heaven.

It is evident, therefore, that the Qur'an in verses 4:157–58 is refuting issues of apparent perception that are in reality false: those who think that Jesus was killed by crucifixion are dead wrong because he was raised from death and is alive with God. In other words, the death of Jesus on the cross was annulled by his resurrection.

Nonetheless, the complexity of the Qur'anic language allowed for conflicting interpretations about Jesus' death. Examples from the Islamic tradition show that although Muslim scholars have overwhelmingly rejected the crucifixion of Jesus, they are divided regarding the reality of his death. The possibility that Jesus actually died and was raised from death was argued by a number of leading early Muslim exegetes and became an essential view within the Islamic tradition.[18]

Worth noting here is that the Qur'anic expression *shubbiha lahum* in relation to the crucifixion of Jesus is not and cannot be a reference to the docetic theology, as argued by some scholars,[19] for the latter revolves around the belief that Jesus was made to appear to his followers in a human form but that in reality he was God appearing in a shadow. But the Qur'anic Jesus is human in every form, which means that making any association with docetic theology is absurd. That we find references in later Qur'anic exegesis to explanations identifying the person who was crucified in place of Jesus, and which draw on some gnostic sources, is nothing more than later attempts by Muslim scholars to explain verse 4:157 by drawing on Christian sources that were known to them. It does not apply to the Qur'an, nor does it reflect a Muslim adoption of docetic or other gnostic theology regarding the nature of Jesus.

Interestingly, the issue of Jesus' death is actually raised in two other verses in the Qur'an:

> Peace be upon me the day I was born, the day I die, and the day I am resurrected alive. (19:33)
>
> I was a witness to them while I lived among them, but when You caused me to die [*tawaffaytani*], it was You Who kept watch over them. You are a witness over all things. (5:117)

These verses do not catch the attention of Muslim exegetes like verses 3:55 and 4:157–58, even though they, too, raise the issue of Jesus' death; most exegetes did not even make the connection between "the day I die" in 19:33 and the future coming of Jesus, although they

18. See, for example, the discussion in Robinson, *Christ in Islam and Christianity*, 117–26.
19. See, for example, Michaud, *Jésus selon le Coran*, 68–71; Rizzardi, *Il problema della cristologia coranica*, 143; and Claus Schedl, *Muhammad und Jesus: die christologisch relevanten Texte des Korans* (Vienna: Herder, 1978), 435–36. See also the discussion in Parrinder, *Jesus in the Qur'an*, 118–19.

tend to discuss the latter issue at length in connection with verse 3:55.[20] But according to the early Muslim authority on monotheistic traditions Wahb b. Munabbih (d. ca. 110/728), the Qur'an in 19:33 is quoting Jesus informing his disciples that he is about to die and be resurrected.[21] Moreover, if one were to accept that the reference to Jesus' death is intended as a reference to its future occurrence, then this should similarly apply to the case of John the Baptist about whom the Qur'an similarly says in verse 19:15:

> Peace be upon him the day he was born, the day he dies and the day he is resurrected, alive.

Both verses 19:15 and 19:33 use the imperfect tense with respect to the issue of death (*yamut/amut*); in the case of John the third person singular is used, and in the case of Jesus the first person singular is used. If in the case of Jesus, it means his future death, then John, too, did not die and is waiting to die sometime in the future. But this is absurd. If John died in the past, then the imperfect tense does not refer to a future death (this is one of the distinctive characteristics of Qur'anic language).

If one were, therefore, to read verses 4:157-58 in light of verses 3:55, 19:33, and 5:117, which say that Jesus did actually die, the conclusion can be drawn that verses 4:157-58 affirm the death of Jesus, which was followed or offset by God raising him from death.

Indeed, stories about and references to Jesus' physical death that occurred in the past are encountered in Islamic scholarship, even in works by authors who affirmed otherwise. For instance, the historian and exegete al-Tabari (d. 310/922) relates in his *History* that a group of people from Medina say that Jesus' grave is located on top of al-Jamma' mountain, south of Medina; actually this story dates Jesus'

20. See, for example, al-Tabari, *Jami' al-bayan*, 8:340.
21. Ibid.

time on earth to the period when the Persians ruled western Arabia (fourth century B.C.E.) since, as the story indicates, Jesus' tomb inscriptions were in old Persian.[22] The interesting thing about this report, regardless of its apparent ahistorical nature, is that 1) al-Tabari clearly believes that Jesus did not die, as attested in his exegesis of the Qur'an,[23] and 2) the report is not related on the authority of Christians or converts from Christianity, but rather on the authority of a Muslim—a certain Ibn Sulaym al-Ansari al-Zuraqi—who must have lived in Medina in the seventh century after the time of Muhammad. In another case, the Syrian mystic al-Nabulusi (d. 1143/1731), contrasting *al-mawt al-ikhtiyari* (voluntarily giving oneself to death) and *al-mawt al-idtirari* (being taken by death), uses the example of Jesus as someone who readily gave himself to death.[24]

The Christian Passion Narrative in the Islamic Tradition

Now what about the Christian passion narrative? Do we find any mention of it in the Islamic tradition? There is no doubt that the various Christian narratives about it were known to Muslim scholars. The historian al-Ya'qubi (d. 284/897), for instance, provides us with short synopses from the different Gospels regarding the passion story and contests them by simply stating the words of verse 3:55.[25] Al-Tabari, too, relates, on the authority of Wahb b. Munabbih, an interesting passion narrative that essentially takes its elements from the Gospels but leaves aside the issue of the crucifixion. According to this Islamized passion narrative, Jesus was grieved and terrified of

22. The tomb inscriptions read: "This is the grave of Jesus son of Mary, the messenger of God to the people of this land." See al-Tabari, *Ta'rikh al-rusul wa-l-muluk*, ed. M. J. De Goeje et al. (Leiden: Brill, 1879–1901), 1:738–39; and al-Tabari, *The History of al-Tabari*, ed. Moshe Perlmann (Albany: State University of New York Press, 1987), 4:123–24.
23. Al-Tabari, *Jami' al-bayan*, 3:289.
24. Al-Nabulusi, *Risalat al-Tawhid*, ed. Muhammad Shikhani (Damascus: Dar Qutayba, 1999), 111.
25. Al-Ya'qubi, *Ta'rikh al-Ya'qubi* (Beirut: Dar Ṣadir, 1960), 1:77–79.

death when he was told by God that he was to depart this world. He called upon his disciples for the Last Supper, waited on them, washed their feet, and asked them to pray to God to delay his death. Then Jesus was arrested and made to carry his cross to the place of his crucifixion, all the way being tortured and ridiculed. But when they reached the spot, God lifted him up to himself, and the one who was made to look like him was crucified in his stead. Mary and Mary Magdalene came to lament at the foot of the cross, but Jesus appeared to them and told them that God saved him and that nothing but good happened to him. He also asked them to rally the disciples to a place that he described, where he met them and gave them his final will. According to Wahb, Jesus died that day, and after three hours God resurrected him.[26]

One has to emphasize here that coming across references to the passion narrative in the scholarship of the Islamic tradition does not mean at all that the Muslims accepted its theological implications. Actually, the aspects of the theological implication that Muslim scholars could not tolerate were Jesus' divinity and his principal role in human salvation. They did accept another aspect of the passion narrative: God's intervening to save Jesus, and how all of that was an essential prelude for the advent of a new message and in preparation for the second mission of Jesus at the end of days. Indeed, this aspect, as noted earlier, is tied to a fundamental tenant of the Islamic dogma, without which one's faith is incomplete: the belief in God's prophets, in God's ability to guide and protect them, and in the linear progression of God's messages and messengers.

26. Al-Tabari, *Ta'rikh al-umam wa-l-muluk* (Beirut: Dar al-Kutub al-'Ilmiyya, 1991), 1:353–54; al-Tabari, *Jami' al-bayan*, 4:351–52.

Modern Reflections on the Passion Narrative

The debate regarding the proper way to understand Jesus' death and crucifixion and the issues they invoke is by no means restricted to medieval Islam. The twentieth century ushered in a new era when certain fundamental issues have been revisited by Muslim thinkers. With respect to the rejection of the theological implications of Jesus' passion as maintained by Christianity, we can still see it done with the same intensity as in the pre-modern times, although with sharper theological clarity. The Islamic reformist Rashid Rida (d. 1935), for instance, argues that if God allowed Jesus to suffer and be crucified, he has then demonstrated his injustice, since Jesus committed no sin to deserve suffering and crucifixion. For whatever degree of mercy and salvation that God intended to show or extend through Jesus' passion would be negated by God's gravely compromising his justice, and this is rationally absurd.[27] What we see here in the case of Rida is not only a denial of the crucifixion, but also an unreserved rejection of the fundamental role the passion narrative plays in Christian teaching regarding human salvation.

Another modern case takes an interesting twist with respect to the crucifixion and its meanings and theological symbolisms. The Egyptian scholar M. Kamel Hussein (d. 1977) wrote a novel entitled *Qarya zalima* (translated into English as *City of Wrong*),[28] in which he discusses the implications of the attempt to crucify Jesus. "The village of injustice," as the Arabic title is properly translated, means Jerusalem, and the book discusses the events of one day: Good Friday. Hussein sets the entire novel in the following context,

> The day was Friday.

27. Rashid Rida, *Tafsir al-manar* (Cairo: Dar al-Manar, 1948), 6:26–27.
28. *Qarya zalima* was first published in 1954 in Cairo by Matba't Misr. The English translation, done by Kenneth Cragg, appeared as *City of Wrong: A Friday in Jerusalem* (Amsterdam: Djambatan, 1959).

> But it was like no other day.
>
> It was a day when people went deeply into error, so deep in fact that they reached extreme sinfulness. Evil overpowered them and they became blinded from the truth even though it was brighter than daybreak light. . . . When they resolved to crucify him, their resolve was intended to kill the human conscience and extinguish its light.[29]

Hussein goes on to add that,

> He [Jesus] was the light of God on earth. When the people of Jerusalem insisted on extinguishing it, the world around them was darkened. This darkness is a sign from God to show that God has forbidden them the light of faith and the guidance of conscience.[30]

Hussein clearly rejects the reality of the crucifixion; in his interpretation, a complete darkness encased Jerusalem for three hours, during which Jesus was saved and lifted up to heaven. But he maintains that once the intention to crucify Jesus was set it acquired immense implication, regardless of the fact that Jesus was actually not crucified. In other words, if it were not for God's saving Jesus, they would have carried on with the crucifixion. And their intention meant their rejection of God and all that he symbolizes, hence its immense implications, which Hussein addresses in the following words:

> In the events of that Friday all the features of error and sinfulness were present. In each day of life the tragedy of that day is repeated. Let people, therefore, take cognizance of these features and eschew them. For only then they will find a wide capacity for doing good that truly gratifies them. Then, they will gain a pleasant and delightful life.[31]

29. Hussein, *Qarya zalima*, 1–2 (*City of Wrong*, 3–4). My translation attempts to reflect a language very close to the original Arabic, thus it varies a little from that by Kenneth Cragg.
30. Ibid., 230 (183).
31. Ibid., 264 (210).

Clearly, then, it is the lesson of that day that people need to eternally heed, as if salvation is dependent on that. Although what we see in the case of Hussein is yet another attempt to redefine the implication of the passion narrative by shifting the emphasis away from the person of Jesus and toward the ramification of human behavior and the lessons to be learned, yet, the passion narrative becomes a fundamental stage toward human salvation.

Conclusion

Examining the way the Qur'an presents the passion narrative necessitates a few words about the context in which the story operates in each of the two monotheistic traditions. Whereas Christianity considers the passion narrative—the arrest, trial, crucifixion, death, and resurrection of Jesus—as definitional for the Christian faith, Islam looks at it from a completely different standpoint. Christian theologians, except for a few, have affirmed throughout the centuries that God's sacrifice of his son, Jesus of Nazareth, was made for the salvation of humanity. Hence believing in the passion narrative is a fundamental component of the Christian faith. The Qur'an and the Islamic tradition, however, operate under a different set of assumptions, most importantly a strict monotheism that does not tolerate any perception of division within the divine entity.[32] Hence, from an Islamic point of view, speaking of the son of God, however hyperbolically, is a blasphemy. Even if one were to put aside the issue of Jesus' divinity, the Islamic tradition asserts that God protected his prophets, always came to their rescue, and never deserted them when they were persecuted by their enemies. Under this conviction, Muslim scholars have rejected outright that Jesus was made to suffer

32. Certainly some Muslim sects, past and present, introduced beliefs that, in the opinion of what is commonly referred to as mainstream orthodox Islam, violate this strict monotheism. Examples include a number of Shi'ite sects and the Baha'is.

and was crucified at the hands of his enemies, who went on to boast that they killed the prophet of God, for that implies that God could not or did not protect him. When one, therefore, examines the issues of the crucifixion, death, and resurrection of Jesus in the scholarship of the Islamic tradition, as compared to the Qur'an, one has to keep in mind the Muslim understanding of God as well as these assumptions regarding God's commitment to protect His prophets. It is under these assumptions that all Muslim scholars, past and present, have operated in their attempts to explain and comment on the Qur'anic verses addressing the issues of the crucifixion and death of Jesus.

The other important point that one needs to raise is that the Qur'an is a very complicated text in terms of its language, a fact attested in the state of Qur'anic exegesis and the disagreement among exegetes as to the proper interpretation of almost every verse. Sometimes, the ambiguity of the language left the exegete utterly helpless, as one can notice from the words of the famous Egyptian Islamic fundamentalist Sayyid Qutb (d. 1966) describing the death and resurrection of Jesus:

> As for how his death occurred and how he was raised to heaven, they are incomprehensible issues; they pertain to the category of the ambiguous verses [of the Qur'an] whose proper meaning is known only to God. There is no benefit from pursuing them, neither for dogmatic nor for legal purposes. Those who pursue them and turn them into a controversy end up in hypocrisy, confusion and complication, without ever getting to the absolute truth or satisfaction about something that should after all be deferred to God's knowledge.[33]

In another instance, Qutb adds that "the Qur'an does not offer details regarding the raising up [of Jesus]: Was he raised both in body and soul while still alive, or only in soul after his death?"[34]

33. Sayyid Qutb, *Fi zilal al-Qur'an* (Cairo: Dar al-Shuruq, 1992), 1:403.
34. Ibid., 2:802.

These comments are made by Qutb in connection with verses 3:55 and 4:157–58. It is clear that the complexity of the Qur'anic language and syntax as well as the theological implications of taking sides in this debate, given the diversity of Muslim opinions on the issues raised in these verses, persuaded him to caution the Muslims against making any speculations about the death of Jesus.

It is not my intention to prove that Muslim exegetes were wrong or that they could not have figured out the meaning of verses 4:157–58. Nor do I want to suggest that the text is simple. But a person does read and derive meanings that are shaped by the assumptions he or she brings to a text. It was inevitable, then, in my opinion, that the assumptions Muslim scholars brought to the Qur'an would prevent them from grasping its meaning. The Qur'an is offering a simple challenge to something the Muhammad movement could not tolerate, namely, that by killing Jesus his enemies defeated God. In other words, the movement could not accept, as a matter of basic belief, that Jesus' career ended on the cross, with God unable to intervene. For what would that mean about God's commitment to protecting them? They had to show that God was the ultimate victor because he could do something those who killed Jesus could not: he could raise Jesus from death, thus annulling it. But the issue was too complicated and was thus set aside without further consideration. It was Muslim exegetes who developed the theology of God's obligation to protect his prophets, a theology that left no way to accept Jesus' dying on the cross. God must have intervened to rescue him prior to that. Exegetical stories illustrating how God intervened and who was made to be crucified in Jesus' place attempt to explain a challenging issue, but these stories neither reflect a clear understanding of the issue by the Muhammad movement nor reflect factual history. Rather, they are theological speculations that employ known and conflicting narratives within the Christian tradition that deny the crucifixion of Jesus. (Muslims were not the only or first group to question the theological implications of the crucifixion: mainstream Christianity may accept it as foundational, but some early Christian groups [e.g., gnostics] rejected its reality out of hand as one of the conditions of their faith.)

Another important point that reveals how Muslim scholars could only understand verses 4:157-58 as they did relates to the use of these two verses in anti-Christian polemics. Once these verses were situated in polemics, their function became essentially to point out the error of Christianity regarding the saving significance of Jesus's crucifixion. In other words, by denying the reality of the crucifixion, the Muslim exegetes/theologians were undermining the foundation of the Christian belief system (of those against whom polemics was employed). Hence, the Muslim exegete became restrained within the parameters of polemical contextualization and exploitation of these verses, unable to come to a different reading.

PART VI

Ethics and Theology

The focus of this last section, theology and ethics, is by no means an afterthought to what has gone before. In fact, both approaches to the passion have been running themes in all of the other sections—sometimes implied, sometimes explicit. We saw concern with theology and ethics quite explicitly in the first essay, when Jouette Bassler identified the many ways Paul made them central to his understanding of the passion. The Christ-hymn in Phil. 2:6-11 illustrates this well, since it is a foundationally theological interpretation of Jesus' death on a cross that Paul uses to shape the life of the Philippian community. Not all liturgy, music, literature, and art is so explicit in theological and ethical matters; nor are other traditions necessarily concerned to make theological or ethical statements. But Christians have commonly given expression to their deepest beliefs in their music and liturgy; representations of the passion in paintings and sculpture adorn many churches and cathedrals; and literature—at all levels—is used to explore theology and ethics. Still, addressing these issues directly and systematically is a fitting way to engage the passion in this concluding section.

Katherine Sonderegger, an Episcopal priest who teaches theology at Virginia Theological Seminary, writes the first of the two essays—"Theological Themes in the Passion." After examining ways Christians have read Scripture in the service of theology, she works from Lam. 1:12 ("'Is it nothing to you, all ye that pass by?'") and other prophetic texts to expose what she calls "the structure of abandonment" that characterizes human "rebellion against God." In exploring the passion narratives, she finds this rebellion not only (or even primarily) in those directly responsible for the death of Jesus but in "all who pass by" and demonstrate "willingness to ignore the suffering of others in order to avoid inconvenience or disruption in [their] own lives." Sonderegger then argues that it is for just such people—in essence all of us—that Christ died. In engaging the question of how and why Jesus *had* to die, she uses both Scripture and the writings of a wide range of theologians past and present. In a voice that echoes the prophets, Sonderegger extends her theological reflections to ethics by addressing political and social conditions of our own times, drawing on journalists, artists, and poets to make the point.

In the second essay, William Werpehowski, a lay professor of Catholic theology at Georgetown University who focuses on Christian theological ethics, Catholic social thought, and the ethics of war and peace, offers "An Approach to Catholic Moral Life and Christ's Passion" under the rubric of "Self-giving, Nonviolence, Peacemaking"—three themes he sees as central to recent Catholic social teaching and in keeping with the love of Christ manifested in "the way of the cross." Werpehowski is in conversation with three prominent figures of the twentieth century whose "writings and deeds" exemplify the foolish yet realistic love Jesus demonstrated and demanded of his disciples: Dorothy Day, Thomas Merton, and Daniel Berrigan. The writings of the last three popes—John Paul II, Benedict XVI, and Francis—and the documents of Vatican II also inform Werpehowski's reflections. Like Sonderegger, Werpehowski explores Christian interpretations of the meaning of Jesus' death for a lost world and speaks in a prophetic voice about social forces that isolate, exclude, and kill—whether in war or through the unjust treatment of the poor and defenseless. He concludes with a series of pointed questions to those—both outside and within the church—who find the love of Christ too idealistic and therefore unsuited to real life to engage the passion.

20

Theological Themes in the Passion

Katherine Sonderegger

"'Is it nothing to you, all ye who pass by?'"
—Lamentations 1:12

These words from the prophet Jeremiah capture the heart of theological reflection on the passion of Jesus Christ and how Christians tie them to the brutal death of Jesus of Nazareth at the hands of the Roman procurator Pontius Pilate. But we cannot plunge into these doctrinal themes that grow out of them without paying a moment's attention to the biblical sources that spark Christian dogmatic work. The verse that I have cited as the sum of theological reflection is drawn from Lamentations, a book Christians read from their Old Testament. The passion of Jesus Christ, the suffering and death of a first-century Galilean Jew, is therefore illuminated and explained, remarkably enough, by texts written long before the event and addressed to a city (ancient Jerusalem) and not a solitary prophet and messiah of the people Israel.

Reading the Scriptures

Now, in one sense, we might consider this use of texts familiar and unremarkable. Anyone who has reached for lines from Shakespeare or George Eliot to illustrate a contemporary figure knows the power of literature to capture, illuminate, and grace events far outside its own historical setting. There would be no intertextuality without this literary ocean that ebbs and flows across many barriers. At times, theologians use the Old Testament in this way to explore the Christian universe. It is, in essence, a form of *illustration*, and any Christian who knows the Bible well draws on the riches of the Hebrew Scriptures to deepen, enlarge, and vivify a doctrinal theme. But properly speaking, Christians do not use the Old Testament in this way. It is not, in fact, a book of illustrations for Christians to mine for doctrinal or homiletical tasks. Such "prooftexting"—the citation of verses freed from their context—is not the proper Christian use of the Bible. Rather, the Old Testament, for Christians, is most truly and properly the *foundation* of theological work.

The books of the Christian Old Testament are the "scripture" referred to in the New Testament itself, in the Nicene Creed, and most significantly, in the words of Jesus, his disciples, opponents, and of the crowds Jesus came to teach. Thus, these books of instruction—Torah, broadly conceived—are known as the "Old" Testament to Christians in the same sense that the United States Constitution is normative and basic to present-day law. These books are "old" in the sense that any foundation is older than the finished building on which it stands. Thus, they lay Christianity's foundation, mark its borders, and maintain its integrity. They are primal.

Consequently, when Christians refer to Lamentations, or, more often, to Isaiah, in constructing the doctrine of Christ's passion, they make use of this foundational way of reading Jewish Scriptures. Indeed, the very formation of Israel's Scriptures follows this same pattern: Deuteronomy is grounded in Exodus; the later books of the Pentateuch—the "Five Books of Moses"—grounded in Genesis; and Genesis, as a whole, is grounded in the "primal history," the first four chapters of the Bible. This biblical pattern is further displayed in familiar interpretive methods: typology or figural readings; prophecy and fulfillment; foreshadowing and recollection; mimesis and anamnesis. But these methods are not themselves the biblical pattern. The pattern itself, the grounding of Sacred Books or "canon" and the grounding of Christian use in theology, is the primal conviction that these writings are Words of God, *Dei verba*, and are in this sense, unified, consistent, and comprehensive.

Many Christians, today and in times past, have argued that this foundational view of Scripture requires a doctrine of inspiration involving the inerrancy, infallibility, and uniformity of the Bible. They have taught that the Bible is *identical* to the speech of God, and thus reflects attributes of the divine nature: simplicity, impassibility, and perfection. But this is by no means the majority position of Christian theologians, nor, I believe, is it the proper one. Most fittingly, I believe, the Bible serves Christian theology as foundation, guide, and teacher—as torah—and see it as a collection of books that speak in their own earthly voices and out of their own human times, even while making known a single, divine reality and calling. Borrowing from the idiom of Swiss theologian Karl Barth, we could say that the biblical books are written by "witnesses"—not transcribers. They hear and report and answer the divine calling in their own words and confession; and we overhear their testimony. For Christians, in sum, there is only one "Word of God," one *Dei verbum* who is identical to the speech of God—the Word of God Incarnate, Jesus Christ. Because this is so, Christians take these "secondary" words of God, the Bible of both Old and New Testament, to refer properly, fully, and finally to the one Word of God, Jesus Christ, to ground our reflection on his life and teachings, and even more, on his passion, death, and rising to life again.

Abandonment

As human witness, the book of Lamentations guides and grounds the Christian doctrinal reflection on the passion of Jesus Christ. Consider the verse again: "'Is it nothing to you, all ye pass by?'" (NKJV)

These words echo, and for Christians reinforce, the christological themes sounded by the prophet Isaiah, who sets out, in a collection of poems or psalms, a lament for the enigmatic figure known as the "suffering servant." At times, this servant figure appears to represent the people of Israel, a whole nation elected to suffer in witness to the God of the covenant (Isa. 49:3). In this way, Isaiah mirrors Jeremiah, for the lamentations of Jeremiah are raised over the whole city of Jerusalem, besieged, destroyed, and humiliated. But the servant Israel is not always a collective—a people or a city. At times, in fact, the servant figure seems to be a single Israelite, a representative or substitute before the Lord God, who "bears the iniquity" of the people and whose visible wounds heal the healthy whose sickness lies deep within.[1] These themes of representation and substitution, of collectivity and individuality, figure prominently in Christian reflection on the passion; little wonder that these "Suffering Servant psalms" captured the theological imagination of the early church. Yet

1. See, for example, Isa. 52:13—53:12.

perhaps more significant still are the structural elements captured by the verse in Lamentations—"'Is it nothing to you, all ye who pass by?'"

Central to this verse is the structure of what we might call, "abandonment," referring to the way suffering affects those who "pass by" it. In Lamentations, there are two parties to the abandonment—the sufferer and the passers-by. Both Old and New Testament texts afford us ample room to discuss those who do more than walk by on the other side, who inflict the suffering. But Lamentations provides a central ingredient to any full consideration of the passion: it is an event in which others look on, or even more, move past with cruel or mindless indifference. There *are* "voyeurs" to the passion, and they have their place in the doctrine of Christ's passion. But those who are *indifferent* to the spectacle taking place before them are crucial to the Christian view of this event. In a particular and prominent way, they are the very ones on whose behalf this death takes place.

To consider this humiliating and despoiling death to be "nothing" is to constitute oneself, according to Christian doctrine, as the crowd, the people for whom Christ died. The structure of abandonment, then, dictates that the passion and death of Jesus Christ, which stands at the heart of Christian theology, is not simply a reflection upon a single death—though of course it is that as well—but also a reflection upon the groups, that day and always, that pass by the "place of the skull," the Roman wasteland set aside for crucifixion. Theology has given this more general structure a particular name when applied to the crucifixion: it is a "dereliction." In doctrinal terms, Christians would say that the dereliction of Christ is both objective and subjective: the passion of Jesus Christ concerns not only Jesus himself—the "object" of the passion—but also all humankind, the "subjects" of the passion.

The high art tradition provides many examples of the passion depicted as "abandonment" or "dereliction." These are not the familiar triptychs of medieval cathedral art or manuscript illumination. Rather, modern European painting gives us the Lament structure of crucifixion against indifferent passers-by. Consider the Gauguin crucifixions. In one of these paintings, Gauguin places the Crucified One as an elongated and distorted yellow body in the foreground of the canvas, while in the background, utterly detached from and unaffected by the oddly serene Christ, he depicts an ordinary scene of Bretan peasant life with the intense freshness celebrated in all his work. More striking still is the self-portrait Gauguin painted not long afterward. Here the artist stares into the viewer's space with complete disregard to the suffering "Yellow Christ" hanging behind him. Marc Chagall's crucifixion series echoes this same "dereliction structure," surrounding the cross with figures of modern life swirling around the dying Christ.[2] At times, as in the powerful *White Crucifixion*, the swirling figures are also sufferers, enduring pogrom and abandonment by the indifferent who look on coldly—perhaps even aesthetically—as we, their viewers, do. Even Rembrandt, the great Protestant painter and engraver, does not treat the trial and crucifixion in a traditional, churchly rendition. Instead, he shows the people in the crowd standing alone or riding on horseback, or talking among themselves in small groups or scattered pairs. They carry on life as if completely self-absorbed, indifferent to the three crosses pitted against the dark sky. "Life goes on," these paintings say, and violence is a ruthless and silent companion to the everyday.

We do not need the high art tradition to teach us this structure of abandonment, however, for we have seen, for instance, the

2. See Margaret Steinfels's essay on Chagall's crucifixion artwork elsewhere in this volume—ED.

photographs of prisoner abuse in Abu Ghraib: the prisoners stripped and shackled together; the dogs snarling, baring their teeth; the leering guards jauntily posing as if with big-game trophies; the humiliated bodies, eroticized in their misery and fear. One iconic image, however, especially haunts the conscience of anyone who studies the passion of Jesus Christ, since it depicts in silent eloquence the biblical theme of abandonment: a prisoner, hooded and covered in a shapeless tunic, stands on a box, wires dangling from his outstretched arms.[3] The photograph has become a spectacle: a public display of cruelty and power seen in every corner of the globe, an icon that shocks yet remains oddly powerless. Reporter Mark Danner refers to it as the "frozen scandal"[4]—an event fully exposed, universally condemned, yet locked in suspended animation. Viewers become inured to the flood of shocking images, everyone shakes their head, but nothing happens. "Life goes on."

The prisoner suffers amid indifference.

For Christians, those who wash their hands of guilt—from Pontius Pilate to the passers-by at Golgotha and from the generals and politicians to the silent citizens in our own land—all are exposed as guilty by the clear light shed from the tortured and condemned. Christians call this guilt "sin." It is most powerful when deeply concealed in indifference and self-absorption. It is principally for this sin that Jesus Christ dies, the righteous for the unrighteous. This is the central teaching of Christian theology of the passion.

It follows, then, that the structure of abandonment is expressed and exposed in every nation and age when suffering is met with callous isolation and blindness. This is what Christians mean when they say that Christ is crucified everywhere the poor and powerless

3. Compare the Banksy' "Christ with Shopping Bags" Emmie Donadio treats in her essay elsewhere in this volume—ED.

4. Mark Danner, "Frozen Scandal," *MarkDanner.com*, December 4, 2008, www.markdanner.com/articles/frozen-scandal.

are suffering and abandoned. This does not mean Christ dies in every age or that the poor and oppressed are themselves an *alter Christus* (a second Christ). Rather, Christian doctrine posits the underlying structure and force of sin—the "self curved in on itself," as Martin Luther put it—that is exposed and remedied in the unique passion of Christ. Because of the death of Jesus Christ, Christians say, the sin of abandonment is known for what it is: the willingness to ignore the suffering of others in order to avoid inconvenience or disruption in our own lives. This seemingly benign neglect is exposed as rebellion against God.

Jesus' "summary of the Law" addresses the neglect of those who suffer from another approach, though he anticipates his passion here also. In the Gospel according to Mark, Jesus answers the scribe's question about the first commandment with a commentary on the Shema, the ancient confession of God's uniqueness and sovereignty: "Jesus answered him, 'The first of all the commandments is, "Hear O Israel, the Lord our God is one Lord. And you shall love the Lord your God with all your heart, with all your soul, with all your mind, and with all your strength." This is the first commandment. And the second is like it: "you shall love your neighbor as yourself." There is no greater commandment than these'" (Mark 12:29-31). Note that the second part of the commandment—"love your neighbor"—concerns what we might call the "structure of compassion." Jesus teaches here that the intense preoccupation with our own lives, the single-minded pursuit of our own ends, the blithe defense of our own worldview—this "love of self"—is to be redirected to our neighbor; the structure of self-will is to be equated and extended to another. The lively interest in another expresses and confirms the proper worship of the One Sovereign God. The structure of abandonment is the violation of this greatest commandment.

Because this structure of sin opposes the greatest commandment of the law, indifference to cruelty is the hinge on which the passion of Christ turns. This may be surprising, since Christians over the centuries have mistakenly focused on the *agents* of the arrest, conviction, and crucifixion of Jesus. Tragically (and sinfully), Christians have identified these agents as the Jews of Jesus' day or, more terrible still, as all Jews, in every age—in the face of plain evidence, known in medieval as well as modern times, that crucifixion was a Roman punishment. The Gospels plainly record that fact, whether one considers the treatment of Pilate to be exonerating or, as I do, damning. To be sure, the agents of the passion must be incorporated in any *full* theological treatment of the death of Christ, so it is not surprising that Christians, and most secularists have come to fasten on the crowds, the soldiers, and the ruling elites of both the Jewish people and the Roman Empire as the guilty parties to this brutal death. Indeed, even in the traditional iconography of the church, depictions of the passion of Christ—the scourging and mocking, the examination and condemnation, the melancholy road to Calvary, the *via dolorosa*—are depictions of the cruelty, malevolence, and violence of the imperial forces who grasped, whipped, denounced, crowned, and nailed Jesus to a cross. His death, to be sure, is *for them* and in a special way, *by them.* The doctrine of the passion, however, is not, primarily at any rate, concerned with them. We might even say their actions confirm the structure of dereliction, finally allowing us to see that the passers-by—the multitude for whom this death is nothing at all—are the real concern of the doctrine of the passion. To this motley collection of ordinary folk, we now turn our theological attention.

A Just Crucifixion

If Christian theology is at all persuasive in its reflection on the death of Jesus Christ, we must conclude that those in the crowd of passers-by believe that their judgment about the rightness of their lives and about Jesus' death is correct. This is a far-reaching point, one that in the nature of the case threatens to reduce our own knowledge and judgment to silence. We might consider this doctrine akin to our attempt to conceive an idea apart from language or to grasp fully—to "execute"—the concept of a positive infinity. The ontological proof for the existence of God, especially in its Cartesian form, derives its force from just such reflections on the limit of thought. Conceptual anomalies of this sort may belong to that enigmatic group Wittgenstein believed could only "show themselves" as they could not "be said"; in his words, at the end of the *Tractatus*: "Of that which cannot be said, we should remain silent." Or, in a more literary setting, we might defer to Flannery O'Connor, who claimed that as the gospel remained utterly foreign to ordinary life and because of its supernatural grace it could only be depicted through the grotesque.[5] All these conceptual puzzles spring from the attempt to express within natural idiom a reality that transcends it. Such is the self-deceit of the great multitude of humanity certain of its own righteousness.

Christian theology, therefore, should by its own logic seek to discover how the judgment against Jesus Christ was found by his contemporaries and by ours to be correct, just, and fitting. The Bible points to this task in its own idiom when it repeatedly numbers Jesus among the transgressors, when, for example, it describes him in language drawn from the "Suffering Servant psalms" or, more daringly, when it refers to his "becoming sin" or "accursed" and

5. See, for example, Flannery O'Connor, "Some Aspects of the Grotesque in Southern Fiction," in *Mystery and Manners: Occasional Prose*, ed. Sally and Robert Fitzgerald (New York: Farrar, Straus & Giroux, 1969), 36–50.

"stricken."[6] The apostle Paul as well as the Gospel evangelists are at pains to say that Jesus was found guilty, that he was condemned by secular and religious courts, that he threatened the temple, mocked King Herod, desecrated the Sabbath, flouted purity laws, rode into the capital city on royal animals, was acclaimed king, stirred up rebellious crowds, and died—a royal claimant, "King of the Jews" written on the cross-beam by Pilate himself.

The New Testament does not attempt the self-deceptive stratagem adopted by many Christians in the postbiblical era. It does not suggest that this Jesus was a thoroughly pleasant, likeable, and inoffensive man who was condemned and killed for no earthly reason at all. It will not allow its readers to imagine, as Christians frequently do, that latter-day disciples of Jesus would naturally be faithful rather than treacherous, would obey rather than flee from danger, would recognize his radical and royal claim rather than find it offensive and scandalous, and would put themselves outside the city walls and outside cultic and imperial right to stand with him in the wrong. When Christians do this, or when filmmakers indulge in the sport of flattering their viewers by trivializing and demeaning Jesus' contemporaries, they undermine the very doctrine they seek to honor.

Just as we find terrorists threatening and offensive; just as we expect effective nation-states to protect their citizens; just as we find absolutes dangerous in a dangerous world; and just as we find it all-consuming to find our way in this world, day by day, without considering the foundation of our laws and practice: just so did most Romans and Jews authorities of the first century find the teaching, practice, and claims of Jesus of Nazareth offensive, dangerous, wrong, and beyond their ken. As for the passers-by, their rightness in the face of Jesus' suffering is expressed and summed up in their determination

6. See Isa. 53:12; 2 Cor. 5:21; Heb. 2:17; Gal. 3:13; and Isa. 53:4-8.

to "carry on," to "live their own life," and "cultivate their own backyard." It goes without saying that if Christian doctrine is correct, we will follow just these slogans in pursuing our own lives amid corrosive poverty, suffering, and torment. The self-numbing required to live a private life in the presence of misery is the state of inevitable wrongness that Christians believe requires a redeemer. This is the very structure, Christians teach, that cannot be seen apart from revelation and cannot be righted apart from Jesus' suffering. Those for whom Jesus' death is "nothing" must be awakened, theology says, made alert and alive to the torment they could once pass by without a glance or sigh. This is the work of the cross for the indifferent abandoners of this and every age. But what of those who did in fact take note of the cross of Christ? What does Christian theology say about those who brought Jesus to his brutal end?

Those who acted as the "agents" of the crucifixion—the praetorian guards who mocked and beat and crowned their prisoner with thorns; the imperial officer, Pilate, who could not bear to be troubled by this peasant one hour more; the Sanhedrin officials, who considered it fitting that "one die for the nation"; the passers-by who taunted and ridiculed and looked on a dying man as so much sport on a spring afternoon; the disciples who hid and betrayed and returned to fishing when the whole turmoil was over—all these architects of the passion of Christ found themselves convinced that this man had to die. Like the indifferent, the agents of the passion of Christ found themselves in the right against Jesus; like the callous and unmoved, the architects of the passion believed that a strong empire, a tolerable military career, an observant faith, and a prudent, efficient colonial administration could be realized only by a steely determination to execute transgressors.

In this, Christian theology generally has agreed. It is hard, in fact, to find another theme that is more prominent in the Gospels than this decree: that Jesus of Nazareth came into the world to die. Nineteenth-century biblical scholar Martin Kähler called the Gospels "passion narratives with extended introductions."[7] In every Gospel, Jesus predicts his own death. To his closest circle he discloses three times that "it is necessary that the Son of Man suffer many things, be rejected by the elders, chief priests, and scribes, and be put to death" (Luke 9:22). Traditionally, Christian theologians have taken as their point of departure the conviction that these agents of the passion, from Judas to Pilate, have done what God wills for the redemption of the world.

Some modern theologians have protested at just this point. For them, the passion is neither directly God's will nor a necessary decree for the world's deliverance. Rather, Jesus goes to the cross, these theologians say, as does every principled, courageous, and defiant leader: he does not will his own death, yet he knows that one who sets his sight on the "Beloved Community," the society of justice and peace, will make enemies; and these enemies may cost him his life. Jesus' death is *contingent*, not necessary—a tragic martyrdom that is the out-working of a moral and revolutionary life. But these are minor voices in the theological tradition. The great weight of the Christian past has taken up directly the Gospel claim that Jesus of Nazareth must die; and that that necessary death brings about a deliverance for others, and not for himself.

Jesus died, the tradition says, for his enemies and betrayers, for all those who considered themselves in the right against him, for all those who ignored and abandoned him—especially for them—and for those few disciples, a few women and Pharisees, who stood by his cross and took his broken body into their own care. He died, that is, for the whole human race, for all people, living and dead, in all

7. See *The So-called Historical Jesus and the Historic Biblical Christ*, trans. Carl E. Braaten (Philadelphia: Fortress Press, 1964), 80 n. 11.

nations and places, and for all creatures—for the cosmos as a whole. Only a universal scope of this sort corresponds to the Christian claim that the entire cosmos was created by God for a life of unimaginable closeness to deity, a participation in God that the Bible speaks of as "adoption as children."[8] That this closeness should be enacted through the brutal death of an innocent man is the difficult, enigmatic, and offensive teaching the Christian tradition has called the Doctrine of the Atonement.

Objective and Subjective Atonement

The Doctrine of the Atonement takes many forms in Christian teaching, but common to them all is the daring claim that the structure of dereliction is taken up into the very being of God: Christian theology claims that the true nature of deity itself is disclosed in the death of the one transgressor who dies for the nation. The character and identity of God are revealed in the divine act of entering into the structure of abandonment not as victor and judge, but as a tormented and abandoned human being. This is the teaching Christians term "the Incarnation." God becomes human, fully human, by taking on—to the bitter end—the misery, indifference, cruelty, and torment of human life, assuming without defense, without advocate, and without helper. God walks this "lonesome highway," the spiritual says, a way cut so deep into the ways of the world that it is not seen or noticed or mourned but by a few friends—a death too ordinary, shabby, and obscure to merit comment in the Roman annals. This, Christians say, is who God is; this passion the way God acts and saves.

We might put the Christian Doctrine of Atonement in another, less churchly way. God works, we might say, in little things. Always

8. See Rom. 8:15, 23; 9:4; Gal. 4:5; and Eph. 1:5.

in the small, obscure, discarded things God is present and at work, lifting up and overturning the world. The Bible speaks of these minor sites of God's agency as the "light things," the "least" or "last." Israel is the smallest nation of the peoples and empires of the earth; and from there springs the light of law and prophet. Benjamin is the least of the tribes of Israel; and from there is anointed the first Israelite king, the tragic Saul, and the first missionary to gentiles, Paul of Tarsus. Bethlehem is called "small among the tribes of Judah" by the prophet Micah; yet it is David's city. The sparrow is the tiny winged thing under the dome of the heaven, kept under God's providential care; the widow's mite the least coin in the treasury, yet more treasured than the gifts of the great; a "little cup of water" the minor gesture of kindness that defines discipleship. The poor and meek are the "little ones" of the kingdom, the little child is the weakest member of the family, and Galilee is the obscure and suspect region farthest from the center of cult and rule. These are the moments of God's own revolution. And the forgettable execution of a Jew from the provinces: this, Christians say, is the "light thing" that remakes the world.

God's remaking of the world is "objective" in Christian terms because it redeems the cosmos through a divine act alone, a suffering death that is effective just because it is without "subjective" accompaniment, because it is "nothing to all who pass by." The passion of Christ, Christians say, is saving quite apart from the world's attitude toward it. Faith does not make the cross saving; indeed, nothing can do this but God's own willingness to be abandoned as a criminal, a worthless rebel in a sober-eyed empire. This death makes peace—atones—by bringing God, the luminous ocean of life, into the relentless machinery of abuse and decay, so that divine life might illumine and inhabit it, healing it from within its very corruption and death. This is the pattern Christians call "substitution" or, in the words of the early church, the "gracious exchange." Christ, the anthem goes, "puts death to death." This is the "objective theory of the atonement," favored by early church theologians such as Athanasius and Origen, and famously by the medieval scholastic, Anselm of Canterbury.

The natural complement to such objective doctrines is the "subjective theory of the atonement," favored by Anselm's contemporary Abelard and developed in such modern theologians as the nineteenth-century German Protestant Friedrich Schleiermacher or the former Anglican archbishop Rowan Williams. Here, Christians say that the passion of Christ saves by making new persons out of old, by awakening love and compassion and justice in the cruel and indifferent hearts of humanity. The structure of abandonment is shattered by Christ's entering into dereliction, shattered and replaced by the structure of compassion, so that eyes now see what they once ignored, minds can accept what they once dismissed, and hearts can suffer what they once shunned, preferring to their own cold and inward-looking occupations a life lived for others. Christ's cross is no longer "nothing to all who pass by"; it is rather the "tree of life," the death that makes all others alive, and, as the last book of the New Testament puts it, a Tree whose "leaves are for the healing of the nations."[9] A "subjective theory" does not teach that sinners save themselves, however. Rather, Christ's own dereliction is the breaking of the prison that humanity makes for itself, a liberation that works inwardly as well as outwardly, freeing cruel and indifferent lives for tenderness, compassion, and hope. What Christ does alone, he does "for us," so that atonement is not perfected "without us," but rather within us. Humanity now participates in the movement outward, which is life "for" another.

9. Rev. 22:2.

This striking pattern of exchange and reversal is captured best, I think, in that enigmatic maxim of Søren Kierkegaard: the greatest Christian joy, he wrote, is to be found in the wrong against God. Here Kierkegaard touches on the theme that unites both subjective and objective accounts of the atonement, the theme of "judgment." Judgment is the dominant note of the passion in the Gospel according to John. After Jesus entered Jerusalem for the last time, John reports, he told the crowds gathered for the Passover feast: "Now is the judgment of this world; now the ruler of this world will be cast out. And I, when I am lifted up from the earth, will draw all people to myself."[10] The death of Christ is the world's judgment because it exposes and determines our right to be the wrong. This crucifixion, looked upon as something absent, as "nothing," is now suddenly disclosed as the gathering of all peoples to God. The rightness of *our* ways—our own "justification" or "righteousness," in biblical idiom—is now revealed as the structure of abandonment and cruelty, as "sin." Just as the world as a whole is drawn in nearness to God in Jesus' death, so the world as a whole—not its parts or individuals or nations, but the entire cosmos—is convicted of lawlessness. We neither see this nor discover it in our own inwardness; the structure of the world is entirely naturalized to us. That Jesus of Nazareth is found guilty, then and now, and executed by Roman authority is in fact the conviction, sentencing, and executing of this, our naturalized world. We are the guilty, those in the wrong before God. And as the wrong, Christians teach, we are put in the right by the passion and cross of Christ.

It may be that only the poetic vision can express the vertigo set off by the passion as it judges and inverts the ways of this world. W. H. Auden says it best, and we conclude with his words:

10. John 12:31-32 NKJV.

About suffering they were never wrong,
The Old Masters: how well they understood
Its human position; how it takes place
While someone else is eating or opening a window or just
walking dully along;
How, when the aged are reverently, passionately waiting
For the miraculous birth, there always must be
Children who did not specially want it to happen, skating
On a pond at the edge of the wood:
They never forgot
That even the dreadful martyrdom must run its course
Anyhow in a corner, some untidy spot
Where the dogs go on with their doggy
life and the torturer's horse
Scratches its innocent behind on a tree.

In Brueghel's *Icarus*, for instance: how everything turns away
Quite leisurely from the disaster; the ploughman may
Have heard the splash, the forsaken cry,
But for him it was not an important failure; the sun shone
As it had to on the white legs disappearing into the green
Water; and the expensive delicate ship that must have seen
Something amazing, a boy falling out of the sky,
Had somewhere to get to and sailed calmly on.[11]

11. W. H. Auden, "Musée des Beaux Arts," in *Selected Poems* (New York: Vintage, 1989), 79–80.

21

Self-Giving, Nonviolence, Peacemaking

An Approach to Catholic Moral Life and Christ's Passion

William Werpehowski

> Peacemaking is hard
> Hard almost as war.
>
> The difference being one
> We can stake life upon
> And limb and thought and love.
> —Daniel Berrigan[1]

Over the last fifty to sixty years, Roman Catholic attention to the Christian moral life has increasingly emphasized three themes.[2] First, faithful discipleship invites and demands reaching out to serve and

1. Daniel Berrigan, *Essential Writings*, ed. John Dear (Maryknoll, NY: Orbis Books, 2009), 53.
2. I want to thank David Cullison, "the Ghost," for a number of helpful conversations spanning many years on the topic of this essay.

be in solidarity with the least among us, that is to say, the materially poor, as well as those persons who are otherwise marginalized from the goods of social existence. Followers of Jesus Christ are to exercise a "preferential option for the poor" in pursuit of justice for them and for all. Second, Christian living is nonviolent. While official Catholic teaching affirms in principle that a national government has a right to defend its people from grave and unjust threat through policing and even "just war," the church has moved more and more in a direction that suspects violence of any sort, that asserts a fundamental moral presumption against war, and that aspires to nonviolence of spirit in everyday life. Third, Catholic teaching and theology draw a close and perhaps inseparable connection between the suffering of the poor and waging war. We discover stinging observations about the way inordinate military expenditures amount to a covert war against those most in need, and that insist that people in poverty suffer most, and thus most scandalously and unjustly, during and following wartime.

In this essay I present an account of these themes as they may be seen to emerge from Roman Catholic interpretations of the passion, death, and resurrection of Jesus Christ. The account ranges over a number of considerations regarding the character of Christian love, the meaning of human suffering, the significance of "voluntary poverty," the nature of the state, and the inevitably countercultural resistance to social forces that isolate, exclude, and kill. The passion story becomes a locus for identifying and then working out these particular perspectives and standpoints.

The Catholic sources I employ amount to a rather eclectic mix, but it will become clear soon enough that the writings and deeds of Dorothy Day, Thomas Merton, and Daniel Berrigan especially inspire and direct my inquiry. These three hardly form a unified front among themselves, let alone with the official teachings of their church. Day and Berrigan, for example, are absolute pacifists who categorically reject all war, whereas a case can be made that Merton was not. And of course, we need only add that the magisterium of the Catholic Church countenances in principle what Day and Berrigan reject in principle—waging a "just war." Still, the insights I explicate and extend from the three help to create a remarkable and timely moral vision.

Catholic Social Teaching

Before mining such insights, however, let's look more closely at the themes I identified above in the light of current Catholic social teaching.

The "preferential option for the poor" has become a major focus. Its justification begins with the notion that all human persons possess an ineradicable dignity owing to their status as beloved creatures of God with a destiny in promise to fellowship with him. Dignity is realized and perfected in the host of social relations we share with one another. *Social justice* has to do crucially with persons' ability actively to *participate* with others in such relations—as members of families, fellow workers, citizens, and the like. Thus injustice is present when our fellow human creatures are marginalized or excluded from the circle of empowered and empowering participation. In the extreme, but sadly too frequent, case, exclusion brings with it invisibility, the absence of any social recognition altogether. In light of its consideration of justice and injustice, Catholic ethics holds that the poor, the marginalized, and the invisible are owed a special, concerted effort, in virtue of their equality with all human beings under God, to bring them with their fellows into the circle of social participation. Solidarity with the poor for this purpose also includes attempting to see the world from their point of view rather than from vaulted vantages of privilege, exclusionary comfort, or domination.

Pope Francis has decisively endorsed this "option," which rose to prominence in the last century via the influence of Latin American liberation theology.[3] He writes that the "clear and direct" message of the gospel is to show "brotherly love" and offer "humble and generous service" in "justice and mercy" toward the poor, the lost, "those whom society discards." In union with God who hears the cry of the poor, Christians should, too. "We may not always be able to reflect adequately the beauty of the Gospel, but there is one sign which we should never lack: the option for those who are least."[4] The practical program that Francis lays out includes attacking the structural causes of inequality, promoting the full human development of the poor for taking part in social life, and performing "small daily acts of solidarity in meeting the real needs which we encounter."[5]

The grave and growing commitment to nonviolence in Catholic teaching emerged alongside and in conversation with traditional just war theory. Since the end of World War II, papal statements from Pius XII forward expressed concern over the damage and harm wrought by war, as well as over convenient and quick suppositions that war is and can be in reality an instrument of justice. A signature moment in the conversation was the US Bishops' 1983 proposal that there is a "presumption against war" that holds alongside the "presumption against injustice" that would warrant in certain cases violent resistance in defense of the innocent. The Bishops straightforwardly acknowledge the "paradox" that nonviolent

3. On the preferential option in Catholic social teaching, see, for example, Donal Dorr, *Option for the Poor and for the Earth* (Maryknoll, NY: Orbis Books, 2012). In his writings and in his actions, Pope Francis has addressed what he has called both an economy and a culture of exclusion. See his apostolic exhortation, "The Joy of the Gospel," http://w2.vatican.va/content/francesco/en/apost_exhortations/documents/papa-francesco_esortazione-ap_20131124_evangelii-gaudium.html, par. 53, 59, 212.
4. "The Joy of the Gospel," par. 194–95.
5. Ibid., par. 188.

opposition to injustice best reflects the call of Jesus to love and justice, but that violent response may yet be in our world a tragic moral necessity.[6] A decade later the bishops made the moral preference for nonviolence in international relations clearer and stronger, and offered an analysis of "peaceable virtues" such as courage, compassion, kindness, humility, hope, and patience to encompass the entirety of Christian life.[7]

Generally during the pontificate of John Paul II, hard questions were raised—many by the pope himself—about how just war theory functions ideologically as a rationalization for war, and how it is that war is *always*, whatever "good" it may do or promise to do, a "failure for humanity."[8] More recently and on the subject of nonviolence, Benedict XVI's comments on Jesus' injunction to love your enemies (Luke 6:27) are stirring:

> This Gospel passage is rightly considered the *magna carta* of Christian non-violence. It does not consist in succumbing to evil . . . but in responding to evil with good . . . and thereby breaking the chain of injustice. One then understands that for Christians, non-violence is not merely tactical behavior but a person's way of being, the attitude of one who *is so convinced of God's love and power* that he is not afraid to tackle evil with the weapons of love and truth alone. Love of one's enemy constitutes the nucleus of the "Christian revolution," a revolution not based on strategies of economic, political, or media power.[9]

6. National Conference of Catholic Bishops, *The Challenge of Peace* (Washington, DC: United States Catholic Conference, 1983), par. 78–82. Also William Werpehowski, "A Tale of Two Presumptions: The Development of Roman Catholic Just War Theory," in *Applied Ethics in a World Church*, ed. Linda Hogan (Maryknoll, NY: Orbis Books, 2008), 119–25.
7. National Conference of Catholic Bishops, "The Harvest of Justice Is Sown in Peace," November 17, 1993, www.usccb.org/beliefs-and-teachings/what-we-believe/catholic-social-teaching/the-harvest-of-justice-is-sown-in-peace.cfm.
8. "Address of His Holiness John Paul II to the Diplomatic Corps," January 13, 2003, www.vatican.va/holy_father/john_paul_ii/speeches/2003/january/documents/hf_jp-ii_spe_20030113_diplomatic-corps_en.html.
9. Benedict XVI, "Angelus," February 18, 2007, www.vatican.va/holy_father/benedict_xvi/angelus/2007/documents/hf_ben-xvi_ang_20070218_en.html.

The third, connecting theme—the inseparable link between the suffering of the poor and waging war—may be less overtly developed in official Catholic teaching than the other two, but its presence is unmistakable. As the Pastoral Constitution "Gaudium et spes" makes clear, the arms race is a "treacherous trap for humanity" because with it the needs of the lost are abandoned or ignored.[10] "It is an act of aggression, which amounts to a crime, for *even when they are not used,* by their cost alone, *armaments kill the poor by causing them to starve.*"[11] When armaments *are* used, "it is always the poor or the weak who pay for war, whether they wear a military uniform or belong to the civilian population."[12]

The Way of Life

For Dorothy Day (1897–1980), cofounder of the Catholic Worker movement, the stances endorsed above may be embodied and transformed in a Christian life marked by "voluntary poverty" for the love of God and neighbor. Here relinquishment and self-giving for the sake of the beloved coincide. Relinquishment, releasing our (death?) grip on bourgeois comforts and our attachments to them, is necessary because "we cannot even see our brothers in need without stripping ourselves."[13] This is also a feature of the love of God, the devotion that brings with it "indifference," or the readiness to forego whatever is a barrier to friendship with him.[14] Day is not sanguine about the difficulty of doing this:

10. Vatican II, "Gaudium et spes," December 7, 1965, www.vatican.va/archive/hist_councils/ii_vatican_council/documents/vat-ii_const_19651207_gaudium-et-spes_en.html.
11. Quoted from "Vatican Statement on Disarmament" (1975), in John Dear, *The God of Peace* (Maryknoll, NY: Orbis Books, 1994), 6–7.
12. *La Civilta Cattolica*, "Christian Conscience and Modern Warfare," July 6, 1991, quoted in Dear, *God of Peace*.
13. Dorothy Day, *Selected Writings*, ed. Robert Ellsberg (Maryknoll, NY: Orbis Books, 1992), 109.
14. For a classic theological statement, see Saint Ignatius of Loyola, *Personal Writings* (New York: Penguin Books, 2004), 289.

> But daily, hourly, to give up our possessions and especially to subordinate our own impulses and wishes to others—these are hard, hard things; and I don't think they ever get any easier.
>
> You can strip yourself, you can be stripped, but still you will reach out like an octopus to seek your own comfort, your untroubled time, your ease, your refreshment. It may mean books or music . . . or it may mean food and drink, coffee and cigarettes. The one kind of giving up is not easier than the other.[15]

So we "pray for an increase in the love of poverty, which goes with love of our brothers and sisters."[16]

Freely dispossessed and thus more free to see and to serve our neighbors along the general lines proposed by Pope Francis above,[17] Christians may also live out and more deeply live into their love of Jesus Christ. Day's Catholic vision rests, on one side, on the manifesto of the Sermon on the Mount[18] and, on another, on the gift and task of performing the corporal and spiritual "works of mercy" inspired by Matthew 25:26-41.[19] This is more than a merely moral demand. The hungry, thirsty, naked, homeless, and the rest are to be welcomed and relieved not because they *might be Christ* or *remind us of Christ* "but because they *are* Christ, asking us to find room for Him, exactly as

15. Day, *Selected Writings*, 110.
16. Ibid., 112.
17. While I do not focus here on Day's commitment to the structural reform of unjust political and economic institutions—which is part of Francis's call to action, as that itself is rooted in Catholic social teaching—it is clear that some such commitment, consistent with a stress on assuming personal responsibility, was important. "What we would like to do is change the world—make it a little simpler for people to feed, clothe, and shelter themselves as God intended them to do. And to a certain extent, by fighting for better conditions, by crying out unceasingly for the rights of workers, for the poor, of the destitute—the rights of the worthy and unworthy poor, in other words . . ." (ibid., 98).
18. Ibid., 262.
19. "The Spiritual Works of Mercy are: to admonish the sinner, to instruct the ignorant, to counsel the doubtful, to comfort the sorrowful, to bear wrongs patiently, to forgive all injuries, and to pray for the living and the dead. The Corporal Works of Mercy are to feed the hungry, to give drink to the thirsty, to clothe the naked, to ransom the captive, to harbor the harborless, to visit the sick and to bury the dead" (ibid., 98). The Matthean story of Jesus' end time separation of the blessed from those judged unworthy deals, of course, with "corporal" works.

He did at the first Christmas."[20] "Truly, I tell you, just as you did it to one of the least of these who are members of my family, you did it to me" (Matt. 25:40).

Dorothy Day's unrelenting realism in the identification of the poor and needy with Christ suggests some compelling claims. To serve the poor is to serve Christ and his cause of serving the Father and the reconciliation of the world to him. To see Christ in the poor is to see them not only in union with oneself, who also would live in Christ as a needy sinner who is yet mercifully embraced,[21] but also in the "hope that we can awaken these same acts in their hearts, too, with the help of God."[22] With all of this, to love the poor *is* to love Christ. Indeed, it is the only way of knowing and believing in our love. "The mystery of the poor is this: That they are Jesus, and what you do for them you do for Him. . . . The mystery of poverty is that by sharing in it, making ourselves poor in giving to others, we increase our knowledge and belief in love."[23]

The last sentence is telling. Love of the poor includes sharing freely in poverty, "making ourselves poor in giving to others." Just so we may come better to know and believe in the love who is Christ, the gift who and in whom we love. Implicit in this condensed theology of Christian life is the belief that disciples may be empowered to love, and to love the needy, in and from and through their living and resting in their own needs—including the need for divine mercy as

20. Ibid., 97.

21. Cf. Pope Francis's reply during an August 2013 interview to the opening question "Who is Jorge Mario Bergoglio?" He answered, "I am a sinner whom the Lord has looked upon." "Pope Francis: The Interview," *America: The National Catholic Review*, September 30, 2013, http://americamagazine.org/pope-francis-interview.

22. Day, *Selected Writings*, 329–30. The final phrase, "with the help of God," is significant in the description of the "hope," for Day is interested most of all in the sharing of Christ-like love itself, whatever the immediate "prospects" or "consequences." Love is not bound to such "in order to's." Hence she can write in another context: "And why must we see results? Our work is to sow. Another generation will be reaping the harvest" (92).

23. Ibid., 330.

the broken creatures they are, ever dependent upon God for their very being, rescue, and fulfillment.[24]

Disciples are to live in Christ and to love as Christ loved. But hatred and fear of others are contrary to love. The enemy, too, must be loved. Warfare and other levels of violence that systematically and interpersonally violate and degrade human persons are forbidden to those whose "manifesto," again, is the Sermon on the Mount. This "means that we will try to be peacemakers" nonviolently.[25]

Briskly but vividly enough, Daniel Berrigan (b. 1921) builds on the preceding and inches us forward:

> The ethic of Jesus is set down in some detail and embarrassing clarity in the fifth chapter of Matthew's Gospel. "Blessed are you makers of peace." And immediately, since we are to know that such a title is not cheaply conferred or claimed: "Blessed are those persecuted for the sake of righteousness."
>
> The "good works" that follow the ethic are indicated in the twenty-fifth chapter. Summoned to love the (former, transformed) enemy—and thereby transformed, reborn, ourselves—we are to undertake the works of justice and peace.[26]

Allegiance to God transforms the enemy into a former enemy and a present sister or brother. The alternative? "I was the enemy of my enemy. A sound definition of hell."[27] Hatred and fear give way to seeking justice, making peace, and the prospect of suffering and persecution.

24. See Arthur McGill, *Suffering: A Test of Theological Method* (Eugene, OR: Wipf & Stock, 2006). Sallie McFague appeals to McGill in her recent book *Blessed are the Consumers* (Minneapolis: Fortress Press, 2013), 163–67.
25. Day, *Selected Writings*, 262.
26. Berrigan, *Essential Writings*, 273.
27. Ibid., 272.

As Pope Benedict noted, nonviolent love is thus active, not passive, and resisting, not caving into or ignoring injustice. Nonviolent actions presuppose the unity of humanity established in creation and promised with the coming kingdom of God, which is "realized," Thomas Merton (1915–68) writes,

> in proportion as Christians themselves live the life of the Kingdom in the circumstances of their own place and time. The saving grace of God in the Lord Jesus is proclaimed to man existentially in the love, the openness, the simplicity, the humanity, and the self-sacrifice of Christians. By their example . . . Christians manifest the love of Christ for men (John 13:35, 17:21), and by that fact make him visibly present in the world.[28]

While we live in a time of "eschatological struggle," nevertheless,

> [t]his combat is already decided by the victory of Christ over death and over sin. The Christian can renounce the protection of violence and risk being humble, therefore *vulnerable*, not because he trusts in the presupposed efficacy of a gentle and persuasive tactic that will disarm hatred and tame cruelty, but because he believes that the hidden power of the Gospel is demanding to be manifested in and through his poor person.[29]

Thus, according to Merton, Christian nonviolent action for justice and peace will have these qualities:

1. It is distinct from not only moral passivity but also the "moral aggression" "designed . . . to bring out the evil we hope to find in the adversary, and thus to justify ourselves in our own eyes and in the eyes of 'decent people.'"
2. It is a struggle "for the truth, common to [oneself] and to the adversary, *the* right which is objective and universal." The nonviolent disciple is "fighting for *everybody*."[30]

28. Thomas Merton, *Passion for Peace* (New York: Crossroad, 2006), 90–91.
29. Ibid., 94. Compare Benedict XVI's remark about loving your enemies above, p. 407.

3. Means and ends are indivisible. "The manner in which the conflict in truth is waged will itself manifest or obscure the truth."[31]
4. The virtues of hope and humility are also indivisible; "the meekness and humility which Christ extolled in the Sermon on the Mount are inseparable from an eschatological Christian hope which is completely open to the presence of God in the world and therefore in the presence of the brother who is always seen, no matter who he may be, in the perspective of the Kingdom."[32]
5. Suffering for the truth is presumed to be the price of doing business. That is not to say one welcomes it as such. But whether it is yoked to voluntary poverty, civil disobedience, persecution, or being in one way or another counted as a traitor by everybody, suffering as a work of nonviolent love is accepted with the hope that there may be something "redemptive" about it—that is, it will contribute to liberating persons and communities from imprisoning distortions of human identity such as apathy, moral blindness, contempt, hatred, and other forms of prideful or slothful exclusion.

An important accompaniment to this particular ethic of nonviolence is a sharp skepticism about the state and its inevitable tendency to require of its citizens, in a host of ways, an idolatrous loyalty. Its putatively legitimate monopoly on the use of force and violent power for "good" permits time and again its claim to be the final judge of who lives and who dies. Dorothy Day and her fellows at the Catholic Worker were sensitively attuned to government practices, such as citywide "air raid drills" in the 1950s during the Cold War, that instilled fear and loathing for our Soviet enemies and therefore

30. Ibid., 89–90.
31. Ibid., 100.
32. Ibid., 104.

made easier a path to and even acceptance of nuclear war.[33] Draft card burning in America during the Vietnam War arguably began with Catholic Workers perceiving conscription and the rituals and symbols associated with it to take on a perverse sacramental status fueling worship of the United States of America. Berrigan makes the general point:

> Ideologies of "the nations," political or economic arrangements, however enlightened or democratic, can never be equated with the Realm of God. Indeed the Word of God addressed to the nations, as well as to revolutions of right or left, is always and everywhere the same: "Not yet. Not yet the Realm of God." And especially and always and irrevocably, the community of faith grants no compatibility, none, between the Gospel and the sanctified slaughter known as war.[34]

Reflecting on his years as part of the Catholic Worker community in New York City, Robert Ellsberg writes that "the Works of Mercy could not be separated from the Works of Peace. We were told to feed the hungry, while war destroyed crops and caused starvation. We were told to comfort the afflicted, while war brought misery and ruin."[35] With Ellsberg, then, linking the suffering of the poor with war and rumors of war comes fully into view. Voluntary poverty, he continues, "meant reducing the area given to self-interest, learning to locate the ultimate source of security elsewhere than in material values."[36] It meant being *both* more alive to human need, freed from the deadening weight of our "possessions," *and* unwilling to kill for their sake and the "way of life" they piece by piece embody. For Day it also meant "non-participation in those comforts and luxuries which have been manufactured by the exploitation of others."[37] As

33. See Robert Ellsberg, preface to Day, *Selected Writings*, xxxiii–xxxiv.
34. See Daniel Berrigan and John Dear, Testimony: The Word Made Flesh (Maryknoll, NY: Orbis, 2004), p. 221.
35. Ellsberg, preface to Day *Selected Writings*, xxxii.
36. Ibid., xxxv.

war is predominantly exploitative and destructive of the innocent and among them the poor, it follows that this Roman Catholic vision moves more or less in step with the counsel of the Quaker John Woolman: "May we look upon our treasures and the furniture of our houses and the garments in which we array ourselves and try whether the seeds of war have any nourishment in these our possessions or not."[38]

The Passion

Among our highlighted Catholic authors we find no formal "theology" of the passion stories. They are surely taken, however, to establish Jesus' identity as the incarnate Son of God and to set forth a way, the "Way of the Cross," as normative for discipleship. In this section, therefore, I offer an interpretation of his identity and his way that is necessarily more indirect and piecemeal than systematic.

The ethic presented above follows from belief and trust in the identity of Jesus Christ, fully manifested in his suffering, crucifixion, and resurrection. It holds that

1. Jesus' self-giving, suffering, and seemingly foolish love stands in communion and solidarity with his needy sisters and brothers for their own sake, and for the kingdom that his Father has prepared for them.
2. Jesus' love does not answer violence with violence, but is nonviolent and extends to enemies and persecutors.
3. It is a prophetic love that unmasks and unseats unjust, violent power, especially that of the imperial state.

37. Dorothy Day, "Poverty and Pacifism," *The Catholic Worker*, December 1944, www.catholicworker.org/dorothyday/daytext.cfm?TextID=223.
38. Phillips P. Moulton, ed., *The Journal and Major Essays of John Woolman* (New York: Oxford University Press, 1971), 255.

I attend to these three aspects in turn.

The beginning and end of Christian life is a particular and unique sort of love. "This is my commandment, that you love one another as I have loved you. No one has greater love than this, to lay down one's life for one's friends" (John 15:12-13). Regarding which, Berrigan remarks, "The instruction could make sense only here. It is a farewell, a legacy . . . the last night of the mortal life of Jesus."[39] Dorothy Day goes even further, concluding that by all appearances, Jesus' particular and unique love is foolish:

> He said we should forgive seventy times seven. He said to love your enemies. He told that foolish tale of the prodigal son, which . . . is madness and folly on the part of the old man who showed such a lack of appreciation for the sturdy qualities of the older son and contributed to the delinquency of the younger. . . . No doubt the youth fell again and again, and did the seventy times seven business work here? The folly of the Cross! The failure of the Cross![40]

In the lives of Christians, Day writes, such silly "love," or "mercy," or "self-sacrifice," or "martyrdom" "is small, hidden, misunderstood. . . . Oh, the loneliness of all of us in these days, in all the great moments of our lives, the dying which we do, by little and by little, over a short space of time or over the years"; for in our dying "we proclaim our faith. Christ has died for us . . . Christ continues to die in His martyrs all over the world, in His Mystical Body, and it is this dying, not the killing in wars, which will save the world. . . . Christ offered his death for the sins of the world. So we offer our own voluntary and involuntary pain and sufferings for the sins of the world, my own and others."[41]

39. Daniel Berrigan, *Testimony: The Word Made Fresh* (Maryknoll, NY: Orbis Books, 2004), 165.
40. Dorothy Day, "Have You Ever Been to Jail?" *The Catholic Worker*, April 1950, www.catholicworker.org /dorothyday /daytext.cfm?TextID=231&SearchTerm=war. Day references Matt. 18:21 and Luke 15:11-32.
41. Day, *Selected Writings*, 105.

We find in this patterning of the love of disciples after the love of Christ completed in his suffering and death a pattern of exchange. For our sake God "made him to be sin who knew no sin, so that in him we might become the righteousness of God" (2 Cor. 5:21). The "lost" are "found" in God in virtue of Jesus' self-giving Sonship, that is, his "being in union with the Father" expressed and manifested in his being made, out of love for them, one with the lost.

The narratives of the passion and death of Jesus can be seen to reveal the full dimensions of sin, of the loss of and estrangement from God. From one perspective, Jesus takes to himself the entire consequence of the human sinful condition, and "it is in the God-forsakenness of the Crucified One that we come to see what we have been redeemed and saved from: the definitive loss of God."[42] From another perspective, however, the world's rejection of the love of God in Jesus Christ is a point of departure. "The cross . . . unmasks or reveals the sin of the world," which is "the rejection of the love that casts out fear, the fear of the love that casts out fear, the fear that without the backing of terror . . . human society and human life cannot exist."[43] By bringing these two perspectives together, we can say that a life lived within a fearful and loveless death would *kill* by handing over or passing on its own abandonment. Nevertheless, in Christ there is also unveiled God's mercy, "the sign that the Father unconditionally accepts us, even though we are sinners"; for we in our sinful humanity may be in Christ who bears our lot, and are taken up into the Father's acceptance of Christ, raised from the dead.[44] We are taken up into that acceptance and hence into becoming a new being, *accepted in our need and despite our sin.* Christian love of neighbor in self-giving, voluntary poverty, dying to oneself, and so

42. Hans Urs von Balthasar, *Love Alone is Credible* (San Francisco: Ignatius, 2004), 93.

43. Herbert McCabe, *God Matters* (London: Continuum, 1987), 97.

44. Ibid., 99.

forth may point to, correspond to, and communicate this divine love. And neighbor love or *agape* corresponds to, reflects, and expresses a pattern of exchange in two ways that fit our ethic.

In the first place, the Christian who lives as one accepted by God sees Christ *in* the neighbor whom he or she is to love as oneself. This means that he or she views the neighbor, including the offending neighbor, as "he looks in the eyes of my Father in heaven." So loving encounters "can be resolved in faith only by seeing human sin where it truly belongs, in the Son of Man . . . and thus by seeing Christ's righteousness in this man himself, as the truth that has been given to him and toward which his existence is ordered. . . . Thus the Cross eliminates guilt by transforming it, through love, into love."[45] Sin or estrangement from God is taken into the love of Christ and exchanged with the lost's promised destiny in hope.

Second, the Christian who lives accepted by God in Christ is a Christ *to* the neighbor whom he or she is to love as Christ loves. Having received, resting in her need, the gifts that now constitute new life, she attends to the good of the neighbor in his or her real need and for his or her own sake through self-giving regard. One conducts oneself, as Luther put it, "as if his neighbor's weakness, sin, and foolishness were his very own."[46] In connection with the way of love embodied by Day, the idea is that one receives and in a sense bears the other's poverty for the sake of bearing it away, rather than ignoring it or making it a basis for selfish privilege or exclusion.

Similarly, in the case of work for justice, if violence is done to you, you resist nonviolently, bearing the violence in the hope of redemptively bearing it away, rather than returning it or passing

45. Ibid., 114.

46. Martin Luther, "Two Kinds of Righteousness," in *Martin Luther: Selections from His Writings*, ed. John Dillenberger (Garden City, NY: Anchor Books, 1961), 91. That Luther is a founder of the Protestant Reformation has not escaped this author. His comment on exchange is fully in keeping with the preceding—that is, the shoe fits.

it on lovelessly. As I elaborate below, Jesus' nonviolent cross and the exchange it effects and inspires would carry forward moral and spiritual empowerment for mutual recognition, human unity, and peace.

James W. Douglass offers a deft summary of Christ's living presence in the world in the terms of the position we have been exploring:

> What a genuinely "universal Catholicism" means . . . in regard to the presence of Christ in the world is that such a presence must be defined in a living way, as Christ himself defined it passively in terms of those in suffering need (Matt. 25:34-40) and as his own life and death unfolded his presence actively in terms of suffering love. In seeking out the presence of Christ in the world, Christians must therefore become less and less interested in themselves . . . and focus instead on the living reality of Christ . . . as the invitation of suffering need and as the graceful response of suffering love.[47]

Thus Christian faith should "center on suffering love as the redemptive reality and active presence of Christ in the world."[48] Nonviolent resistance displays "the inner dynamic of redemption" in that it aims to move "oppressors to perceive as human beings those whom they are oppressing"[49] in virtue of its commitment to human unity in justice, the refusal to contribute to an ever more divisive spiral of hatred and retaliation, and the willingness in neighbor love to suffer for the sake of reconciliation and peace. See it as a practice that reverses the things we do to make it easier to exploit, exclude, and kill by way of making our fellow humans more and more unrecognizable, other, inhuman, and ugly. Prior to, during, and

47. James W. Douglass, *The Non-Violent Cross* (London: Geoffrey Chapman, 1968), 53. Douglass, a Catholic Worker colleague of Dorothy Day, was with her and others influential and finally successful at the Second Vatican Council in their call for the absolute condemnation of acts of wars aimed directly at civilian populations. Douglass discusses this matter on pp. 100–36.
48. Ibid., 54.
49. Ibid., 71–72.

after "disfiguring" persons through violence, we will "distort the image" in which they were created through stereotype, caricature, demonization, and scapegoating. We will also find a way to degrade their environment by enclosing, polluting, or otherwise laying it to waste.[50] Embodied nonviolence may liberate us from such corrupt, enslaving visions and actions by holding a mirror to them and to their terrible and damaging consequences and reflecting it all back—to the unjust, to those "neutral," to the uninformed. In this manner we may correct our vision to see what we are doing or what is being done to human beings who are in their aspirations and suffering both bone of our bone and flesh of our flesh. Above all, the "goal of human recognition is sought through the power of voluntary suffering, by which the victim becomes no longer a victim but instead an active opponent to the man who has refused to recognize him as a man."[51] What is key is that the redeeming, liberating possibility emerges precisely in active, embodied, suffering encounter with and regard for the other *as a human being, as "one of (all of) us,"* which means an encounter and regard that does *not* return violence with violence.

Many sources in current Catholic theology and ethics underscore Jesus' rejection of violence against others throughout his passion. Benedict XVI, for example, said this during a television interview on Good Friday in 2011, with regard to warfare prevailing in the Ivory Coast:

> Above all we want to make the voice of Jesus heard. He was always a man of peace. It could be expected that, when God came to earth, he would be a man of great power, destroying the opposing forces. That he would be a man of powerful violence as an instrument of peace. Not at all. He came in weakness. He came with only the strength of love, totally without violence, even to the point of going to the Cross. This

50. I draw here from Patrick McCormick's remarkable analysis in *God's Beauty: A Call to Justice* (Collegeville, MN: Liturgical Press, 2012), 77–112.
51. Douglass, *Non-Violent Cross*, 71.

> is what shows us the true face of God, that violence never comes from God, never helps bring anything good, but is a destructive means and not the path to escape difficulties. He is thus a strong voice against every type of violence. He strongly invites all sides to renounce violence, even if they feel they are right. . . . This is Jesus' true message: seek peace with the means of peace and leave violence aside.[52]

Pope Benedict's commentary on "Holy Week" makes a related claim. "The Cross is and remains the sign of 'the Son of Man': ultimately, in the battle against lies and violence, truth and love have no other weapon than the witness of suffering."[53] The American Catholic Bishops also stress that "in all of his suffering, as in all of his life and ministry, Jesus refused to defend himself with force or with violence. He endured violence and cruelty so that God's love might be fully manifest and the world might be reconciled to the One from whom it had become estranged. Even at his death, Jesus cried out for forgiveness for those who were his executioners: 'Father, forgive them . . .' (Lk. 23:24)."[54] James Douglass gives pride of place to the same plea for forgiveness and with a fully universal reference. Analogous to nonviolent resistance's goal of eliciting a sense of common humanity, the purpose of the cross is to establish and move to recognition all humanity's union in Christ. Jesus' suffering love unto death embraces all human beings, "victims and executioners alike (for with respect to one another and to Christ, all men are both, and Jesus spoke of all): 'Father, forgive them for they know not what they do.'"

> In inflicting violence on one another, men know not what they do, for they know not the sacredness of their brothers' and their own humanity,

52. "Interview with His Holiness Benedict XVI," April 22, 2011, http://www.vatican.va/holy_father/benedict_xvi/speeches/2011/april/documents/hf_ben-xvi_spe_20110422_intervista_en.html.
53. Pope Benedict XVI, *Jesus of Nazareth: From the Entrance into Jerusalem to the Resurrection* (San Francisco: Ignatius, 2011), 49.
54. National Conference of Catholic Bishops, *The Challenge of Peace*, par. 49.

> which at its innermost core is one with the humanity of Christ. The violence of men at any place or time in history is the violence of Golgotha. . . . To pass over to the suffering servanthood of the man Jesus is to see, through his forgiveness, his redeeming presence in all men, oppressed and oppressors alike, and to see therefore the possibility of redeeming mediation through suffering love of any human conflict.[55]

Douglass's appeal to the "suffering servanthood" of Jesus is not accidental. His theology relies on the proposition that "to profess a true faith in Jesus Christ is to profess a faith in Jesus the Suffering Servant" of Yahweh, "a profoundly Jewish concept rooted in the Servant poems of Isaiah and exemplified in the living history of Judaism." The primary meaning of this concept in Isaiah "is that the Servant of God through his innocent suffering and death takes the place of the many who should suffer instead of him. The truth revealed . . . is therefore that salvation comes from suffering."[56] "But he was wounded for our transgressions, crushed for our iniquities; upon him was the punishment that made us whole, and by his bruises we are healed . . . through him the will of the Lord shall prosper. Out of his anguish he shall see light; he shall find satisfaction through his knowledge. The righteous one, my servant, shall make many righteous, and he shall bear their iniquities" (Isa. 53:5, 10–11). Berrigan also lends this concept—and these and adjoining biblical passages—considerable importance, but he does so in keeping with a set of strong convictions about the biblical prophets' twofold aim of challenging the idolatries of kingly, royal power that tempt us all and work to our ruin, and bringing light "to our unenlightened human tribe, to speak the truth, unwelcome as it is, of who we are, who we are called to become: friends, sisters, brothers of one another."[57] There is both a calling to account, a judgment, and a

55. Douglass, *Non-Violent Cross*, 72–73.

56. Ibid., 61. Douglass draws extensively from Oscar Cullman, "Jesus the Suffering Servant of God," in *The Christology of the New Testament* (Philadelphia: Westminster, 1959), 51–82.

promise of a people's renewal in justice and peace. The promise carries with it accountability as well. The peace that is promised is also a verb. "You make the peace. . . . Which is to say, you pay up. Peace must be paid for, as war is paid for."[58] With respect to the Suffering Servant passages in Isa. 53, Berrigan is wary of, shall we say, a royal court theology that puts a cosmic doctrine of expiatory sacrifice into the service of absolving the unjust from responsibility. The biblical report of the Suffering Servant's travails in Isaiah, *if it is given by the guilty*, looks and sounds like sanctimoniously "passing the buck." "We, authorities and people, were the more or less horrified witnesses of events. We were helpless to intervene. For God decreed all this, or at least allowed it to happen, in order to bring good out of manifest evil."[59] While Berrigan does not deny the Servant's expiation outright, he prefers to stress that when "God speaks up" in 53:11-12, "there is a notable modesty in the words. . . . The inspiration and example of the servant are praised." The Servant "invites the unjustified to the justice of God, that is to say, to holiness, to the all but unimaginable possibility of love." What is more, "power now flows from the once powerless one." Berrigan points out that verse 12, "Therefore I will allot him a portion with the great . . . because he poured out himself to death," "calls to mind the 'great hinge' of Paul's letter to the Philippians: 'He humbled himself and became obedient to the point of death—even death on a cross. Therefore God also highly exalted him and gave him the name that is above every name.'"[60]

57. Berrigan, *Essential Writings*, 245. For a very helpful statement, see Robert A. Ludwig, "Daniel Berrigan's Theology: Retrieving the Prophetic and Proclaiming the Resurrection," in *Faith, Resistance, and the Future: Daniel Berrigan's Challenge to Catholic Social Thought*, ed. James L. Marsh and Anna J. Brown (New York: Fordham University Press, 2012), 30–40. As Ludwig mentions, Berrigan has written book-length commentaries on the Minor Prophets, Isaiah, Ezekiel, Jeremiah, and Daniel.

58. Berrigan, *Testimony*, 96.

59. Daniel Berrigan, *Isaiah: Spirit of Courage, Gift of Tears* (Minneapolis: Fortress Press, 1996), 150.

Jesus is best comprehended and followed as standing in the tradition of Jewish prophecy, and against prophecy's "backdrop . . . where the Word of God is assaulted in the name of national ego and public expediency, and where idolatry is preferred to the demands of faith and hope, of love and justice."[61] In his final days he stands fast against "the imperial state, the ape of God. It presents itself in history as omnipotent, eternal, all wise, the one to which all must pay fealty. In its blindness to its own crimes, its tenacious violence, it must be named for what it is: the foremost agent and provocateur of death in world."[62] Jesus stands as the source of life. "I am the vine, you are the branches" (John 15:5). It matters to Berrigan that this last of Jesus' I-am statements (which refer to him as bread of life, light of the world, the good shepherd, the way, etc.) "is placed by John at the opening of holy week, the supper of Holy Thursday. Which is to say, the image is to be verified, tried, and convicted (and to that point proven truthful) in a Fallen world."[63] Such an image! For the fruit of the living vine is the cup, and the cup is "the cup of my blood, given for you."

> As the Vine included us, the branches, so the cup of "My blood" includes us, by fervent implication. The cup contains blood, the blood is "given, for you." The giving of one's blood supersedes the letting of blood. Violence yields to nonviolence. . . . Say it again and again, in a world dissolved in a welter of bloodletting: "The cup of My blood, given for you."[64]

It matters that the gift of life confronts the agent of death and exposes it, places it in judgment as the gift is itself judged, found in the wrong, and sentenced to die. This trial, this drama, is Jesus' prophetic

60. Ibid., 152–53.
61. Ludwig, "Daniel Berrigan's Theology," 34.
62. Berrigan, *Testimony*, 175–76.
63. Ibid., 52.
64. Ibid.

witness to the truth, calling out imperial violence and "death as a social method." In this light Christ Crucified is for Berrigan "God in trouble for being Godly, God under capital sentence, God sentenced to death, executed for being God, for being human. The crime: such acts, miracles, healings, stories, refusals, as serve to vindicate, honor, and celebrate human life."[65]

For Christians the upshot, if you will—the prophetic promise—is present in Jesus' being raised from the dead. It is an "ethic of resurrection," the gift of the God "who beat death at its own game." And so "the death game is not our game. We are called to undergo death, rather than inflict death. And in so acting, to cherish life."[66] Christians' acts of "solace and rescue," their works of mercy and prophetic witness, are all forms of nonviolent peacemaking that, however hard, remains what disciples may stake their life on, following the one who died on a stake, the gift of life, the prince of peace.

Conclusion

I have tried to present this (now to use shorthand) "ethic of resurrection" fairly and sympathetically. I have not defended or advocated it in the face of theological and ethical criticisms. Of course, such criticisms are legion. Pacifism is "sentimental," "unrealistic" about its moral and political effectiveness, and consequently irresponsible in passively permitting injustice to flourish among those who lack such fine scruples about violence and killing. Performing the works of mercy? That's merely the Band-Aid of "charity," diverting moral energies from pursuing "justice" through broader, lasting structural social and political change. Furthermore, the demands made of Christians are excessive, that is,

65. Ibid., 222.
66. Ibid., 220.

"unrealistic," too. The "voluntary poverty" that aims at solidarity with the poor and the refusal to clothe, house, and feed ourselves with goods that issue from exploitation and violence requires too much of us who are called to honorable ways of life before God, however "professional" or "bourgeois." Our responsibilities to work and family fairly require some compromise with or adaptation of these Christ-like ideals. This is all the more true with respect to our being "peacemakers" in a "prophetic" mode. We can't all be like Daniel Berrigan and his comrades with their civil disobedience, "beating swords into plowshares" at nuclear missile plants and so forth.[67]

The criticisms are reasonable and should be answered. There are resources in the ethic for such answers. Some of them begin with or presuppose a question about the terms of the debate. What, after all, *does it mean to be "realistic"* and live within the gospel of Jesus Christ, crucified and risen? Is it realistic to believe that there are such things today as "just wars"? Are we "keeping it real" when we don't face, as Pope Francis asks, the face of the poor concretely, in our daily lives, taking personal responsibility for their succor? May it not be pure fantasy to deny or dismiss a nexus linking war, preparation for war, injustice, exploitation, and the scourge of poverty afflicting our sisters and brothers? Can we avoid the seeming "reality" that governments spark devotion by courting fear and suggesting it treasonous to say "No" to the wars, any wars, fought in the name of "the people"? Is it realistic, or rather just *faithless*, to act in the world as if Christ is not risen, and hence as if God's triumphant power of self-giving, nonviolent love is not present and at work here and now? Can Christians think anything other than that the way to justice and

67. On September 9, 1980, Daniel Berrigan, his brother Phillip, and the rest of the "Plowshares Eight" took hammers to unarmed Mark 12A nuclear nose cones at the General Electric plant in King of Prussia, Pennsylvania. For this "disarmament action," they at first faced three to ten years in prison. After many appeals, they were sentenced in 1990 to time served.

peace in a fallen world will consist in bearing crosses, testing hope to the limit, and yet believing in the promise of truly human life? "No matter, the prophets say: In God's time that will come to pass which we are helpless to bring to pass."[68] No doubt the critics have responses to these questions, and so the conversation would proceed, one wishes, toward deeper understanding and movement toward the truth—which is to say, movement into the real world.

Regarding the demands this ethic of resurrection makes upon Catholic Christians, any conversation must aim, too, at fuller, mutual understanding for the sake of the truth all share. I can imagine that living that ethic certainly involves "a change of heart, for a beginning. A wrenching conversion of heart, a new understanding of peacemaking . . . as simply the life Christ summons us to."[69] One would try patiently to endure the hardship and suffering of self-giving better to love the poor in Christ. One would perhaps come to a taste of (a taste for?) what voluntary poverty intends, the "freedom that comes when there is nothing one fears to lose."[70] We might meet responsibilities at work and at home accordingly, becoming more intentional about what we do and what we consume, reflecting and trying to remove the violence in our midst and in our hearts, decrying the carnage of war, being more ready to empty ourselves for others, making a space for the needy, near and far, in our thoughts, prayers, and deeds. Practitioners might, on the one hand, struggle and thrive within what Day, following Therese of Liseux, called "the little way" where, relying on God's gifts of love and hope, our simple, everyday works of tenderness, mercy, and sacrifice may be trusted by grace simply to add to the balance of love in the world—"to make God loved, to make Love loved."[71] On the other hand, they

68. Berrigan, *Testimony*, 177.
69. Ibid., 96.
70. Ellsberg, introduction to Day, *Selected Writings*, xxxv.
71. Day, quoting Therese, in *Selected Writings*, 202.

might be steeled, even if at first begrudgingly, by Berrigan's reminder that peacemaking implies resistance against a political, economic, and cultural system "that makes us drudges and cowards and war tax-paying chattels, that adroitly adjusts our will and conscience, like the sinister clockwork of a time bomb—adjusts us to a world of injustice and cruelty and death."[72] In conscience, those who resist will consider that which they can, cannot, and "cannot not do."[73] Finally, living the demands of an ethic of resurrection seems to demand a life of worship, prayer, study, and contemplation. I fear this last word comes across as a throwaway "needless to say," and if it does I take the blame. But how much more, then, should it be emphasized! Day's work was "making room for Christ" in a fashion that included steady prayer, reflection, and daily mass. Berrigan's witness has been born of biblical reflection, spiritual discernment, and Ignatian practices of "entering" the biblical story—"be present to it, find your place there, live within it"[74]—including, I suggest, the story of Christ's passion. Both Catholics realized what Pope Francis recently observed and what Thomas Merton stressed throughout his life: that Christians need to nurture an "attentiveness which considers the other in a certain sense at one with ourselves."[75] True love has a "contemplative" character that permits us to serve another "not out of necessity or vanity, but rather because he or she is beautiful above and beyond mere appearances."[76]

72. Berrigan, *Testimony*, 97.
73. Berrigan, *Essential Writings*, 187–92.
74. Ibid., 92.
75. See especially Thomas Merton, *Conjectures of a Guilty Bystander* (New York: Doubleday, 1989), 156–58.
76. Pope Francis, "The Joy of the Gospel," par. 199.

Index of Scripture References